*V O L U M E   I*

# A
# New
# History of
# Philosophy

## ANCIENT & MEDIEVAL

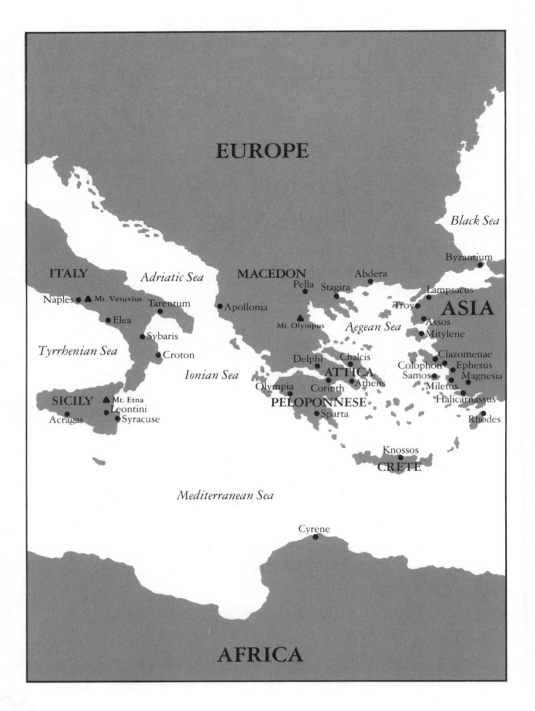

EUROPE

*Black Sea*

Byzantium

ITALY          *Adriatic Sea*          MACEDON          Abdera
                                                                              Lampsacus
Naples ● ▲ Mt. Vesuvius   Tarentum         Pella  Stagira                              ASIA
                            ● Apollonia                               Troy ●
    ● Elea                                                                       Assos
                                           ▲                     *Aegean Sea*  Mitylene
*Tyrrhenian Sea*        ● Sybaris       Mt. Olympus
                         ● Croton                                                Clazomenae
                                                          Delphi   Chalcis     Colophon ● Ephesus
                    *Ionian Sea*                                ATTICA    Samos ●   Magnesia
                                                       Olympia   Corinth  Athens   Miletus
    SICILY     ▲ Mt. Etna                                                  Halicarnassus
             Leontini                           PELOPONNESE
  Acragas ●   ● Syracuse                            ● Sparta                       Rhodes

                                                        Knossos
                                                        ● CRETE

           *Mediterranean Sea*

                              Cyrene ●

AFRICA

*The Greek World*

# VOLUME I

# A New History of Philosophy

## ANCIENT & MEDIEVAL

## Wallace I. Matson

*University of California, Berkeley*

Under the general editorship of
### Robert J. Fogelin
*Dartmouth College*

*HARCOURT BRACE JOVANOVICH, PUBLISHERS*

San Diego   New York   Chicago   Austin

London   Sydney   Tokyo   Toronto

Photo Credits: Page xviii: TAP Service, Athens; 146: © Leonard von Matt/Rapho, Photo Researchers; 180: Alinari/Art Resource, New York; 250: Giraudon/Art Resource, New York; 259: Smithsonian Institution/Courtesy AIP, Niels Bohr Library; 400: The Bettmann Archive/BBC Hulton; 427, 441: The Bettmann Archive; 446: UPI/Bettmann Newsphotos; 449: Brown Brothers; 473: © Archiv für Kunst und Geschichte, Berlin.

ISBN: 0–15–565728–3

Library of Congress Catalog Card Number: 85–82624

Printed in the United States of America

Copyrights and Acknowledgments

The author is grateful to the following publishers and copyright holders for permission to reprint material in this book:

ALLEN & UNWIN PUBLISHERS LTD.   For excerpts from *Plotinus* by A. H. Armstrong. Reprinted by permission of the publisher.

CLARENDON PRESS   For excerpts from *The Oxford Translation of Aristotle*, edited by W. David Ross. Reprinted by permission of the publisher.

W. HEFFNER & SONS, LTD.   For excerpts from *The Clouds* by Aristophanes, translated by H. J. and P. E. Easterling. Copyright the translators, 1961. Reprinted by permission of the publisher: W. Heffner & Sons Ltd, Cambridge, England.

OXFORD UNIVERSITY PRESS   For excerpts from *The Republic* by Plato, translated by F.M. Cornford (1945). Reprinted by permission of the publisher.

PENGUIN BOOKS LTD.   For excerpts from *The Nature of the Universe* by Lucretius, translated by R. E. Latham (Penguin Classics, 1951), copyright © R. E. Latham, 1951. For excerpts from "The Apology" in *The Last Days of Socrates* by Plato, translated by Hugh Tredennick (Penguin Classics, 1954; revised edition, 1959), copyright © Hugh Tredennick, 1954, 1959. Both reproduced by permission of Penguin Books Ltd.

RUTGERS UNIVERSITY PRESS   For excerpts from *On the Nature of Things* by Lucretius, translated by W. Hannaford Brown. Copyright 1950 by the Trustees of Rutgers College in New Jersey. Reprinted by permission of the publisher.

**To Karl Aschenbrenner**

„Das ist m e i n Kunderbaß, und
ik spiel drauf was ik will!"

# Preface

Philosophy, the most important subject in the college curriculum, is unlike any other and must be taught differently.

What is to be studied is a series of discourses concerning the nature of human reason, how it can lead (if it can) to knowledge of how things are, and what it prescribes (if it prescribes anything) about satisfactory living. This is an interconnected literature—a discussion that has been going on for twenty-five centuries. A particular philosophy is a conscious response to its predecessors and cannot be understood apart from them: Aristotle is incomprehensible without Plato, Kant without Hume.

Students of the sciences begin by learning the elements and then proceed in logical progression to the state of knowledge so far attained. The budding astronomer can ignore the epicycles of Ptolemy, the chemist need know nothing of phlogiston. Not so in philosophy. There are no 'elements of philosophy'. And instead of one philosophy triumphing over its rivals and forcing them out, we find that a few conceptions of reason and the good life have stood the test of time, continually reappear modified to fit altered circumstances of life, and seem in no danger of being permanently discredited—however much their relative popularities may wax and wane.

Since for these reasons the possibility does not exist of studying philosophy apart from its history, the most orderly and efficient way is to begin at the beginning, with Thales' pronouncement that all is water, and to recapitulate the process of criticism and reformulation that led to the atomism of Democritus and beyond to the present day. For this study *there is no acceptable substitute for original documents*—the writings of Plato and his predecessors and successors. This book is offered only as an aid to reading in the primary sources. The earliest documents are fragmentary; and the later, though complete, are often puzzling if tackled with no explanation of the context in which they appeared. It is hoped that this book will serve as a preliminary survey map of the territory to be explored.

Why explore it?—Because somewhere in it you will find yourself.

I am grateful to James Clark, Robert Cornett, William Hayes, Richard Haynes, Max Hocutt, Meredith Moraine, George Sessions, Stephen Voss, and most especially to Robert Fogelin, for their friendly help and encouragement. I thank also Professors William E. Mann of the University of Vermont, Walter O'Briant of the University of Georgia, and William Bernard Peach of Duke University, who reviewed the manuscript.

Wallace I. Matson

# CONTENTS

# I

## The Rise
## of Science
## and Philosophy

Charioteer, *from the Sanctuary of Apollo at Delphi, c. 470* B.C. *Bronze. Museum, Delphi.*

# 1

## What Went Before

WHAT IS THE NATURE of things? What are their causes and effects? How did they begin, and how did they get to be as they are?

Every culture has its answers to these questions. Science is the way of trying to discover their answers solely by the use of human observation and reason. Philosophy is rational reflection on the nature of reason.

The first beginnings of science were in the Greek city of Miletus early in the sixth century B.C. Philosophy arose soon afterwards. Wherever they exist, science and philosophy are built on the foundations laid there and then.

Thales of Miletus (625?–?547 B.C.; see Chapter 2), called the first "investigator of nature," said that water is the stuff from which all things come. To understand why the making of this remark counts as the most stupendous intellectual revolution in recorded history, let us survey a thousand years of previous thought.

### The Babylonian Creation Story

The Near Eastern peoples who were neighbors of the Milesians had traditional accounts of creation which depicted the world as arising (literally) out of a watery chaos. The oldest version that has survived is the Babylonian epic poem *Enuma elish* ("When above," its first words), written around 1500 B.C. but telling a story at least a thousand years older. It begins

> When a sky above had not yet even been mentioned
> And the name of firm ground below had not yet even been
>     thought of;
> When only primeval Apsu, their begetter,
> And Mummu and Tiamat - she who gave birth to them all -
> Were mingling their waters in one;
> When no bog had formed and no island could be found;
> When no god whosoever had appeared,
> Had been named by name, had been determined as to his
>     lot,
> Then were gods formed within them.[1]

The picture is of Apsu (fresh water), Tiamat (salt water), and Mummu (clouds and mist) mingled together. This is the beginning of things. Apsu is male, Tiamat female. Of their union two gods are born, Lahmu and Lahamu, who represent the silt that forms at river mouths. From them spring gods of earth, sky, and horizon, earth and sky being conceived as discs bounded by two horizon circles which at first are in contact but later are forced apart by wind.

After many more gods have come into existence, they have a battle. The old gods of chaos, led by Tiamat and Kingu (her second husband), fight against the younger generation who advocate order and authority. The leader of the progressive faction is Marduk, youngest of all, later to become chief god of Babylon. Marduk slays Tiamat and takes Kingu prisoner. The victors fix the war guilt on Kingu and put him to death. From his blood the god Ea makes the first human beings.

> They bound him, held him before Ea,
> Condemned him, severed his arteries.
> And from his blood they formed mankind.
> Ea then imposed toil on man, and set gods free.[2]

That is to say, humanity was created in order to relieve the gods from burdensome labor.

## How Myths Explain

This myth is not a mere flight of fancy. The Fertile Crescent was in fact formed from silt deposited by the rivers Tigris and Euphrates where they flow into the Persian Gulf. The begetting of Lahmu and Lahamu by Apsu from Tiamat is clearly a symbol of this continuing process. In a way, then, the mythmaker was the forerunner of the geologist. Myths as well as scientific theories may be based on observations, and both try to explain the unknown. So it is tempting to suppose that the one is simply the primitive poetical version of the other.

This thought, though not devoid of truth, can be misleading. Let us note some characteristics of *Enuma elish* that are typical of myths but not typical of scientific accounts.

In the first place, although the myth does explain how things come to be as they are, it does so only incidentally. The point of the story, the reason for telling it, lies in its moral: it is intended to answer the question "Why must we work so hard?" It tells us how the world came to be—not to inform us but to reconcile us to our laborious existence.

Second, the myth is anthropomorphic; that is to say, all actions are ascribed to beings who though not human act in the human way: they do *this* because they are aware that it is the means to get *that*, which is what they *want*. We should not suppose that some prehistoric Mesopotamian, impressed by his observation of the phenomenon of silting, decided to dress up his poetical description by personifying the forces involved. On the contrary, having no conception of an impersonal force, he could not talk about silting in any other terms. To explain is to remove puzzlement. Ultimately the only way to do it is to show how the puzzling thing is really just something familiar in disguise, or at least is like something we already know about. In a prescientific culture only the actions of human beings can serve as the model. If things are to be explained at all they must be conceived as being 'the same thing as' human activity.

The Babylonian saw that silt was deposited at the river mouth: a puzzling fact. Why should solid come from two liquids? Let him think of it as two parents begetting offspring, and it is 'understood'; that is, it fits into his system of familiar concepts. Justification works the same way. Why must we labor? Well, it is justice to condemn evildoers to hard labor, and if we are all made from the blood of the traitor god Kingu, there is no longer a problem. Not, at any rate, in a society where as a matter of course the sins of the fathers are visited upon the sons.

The human action model, from which mythological conceptions are derived, has within it three strains, three types of cause-effect relationships. One is that of *sexual generation*. Let us call the other two the *manipulative* and the *coercive*. There are two ways to get something done: the first is to do it yourself, to expend the energy of your own muscles in manipulating materials into the desired structure. The second is to use your power, authority, or wiles to coerce, order, or persuade someone else to perform the actual labor. The latter is the preferred method, the one appropriate to high dignitaries, hence to gods.

Nevertheless we find gods working both ways in *Enuma elish*. Marduk wields with his own hands the bow mace and net with which he kills Tiamat. Not that there is anything degrading about this kind of activity: in a primitive or 'heroic' society the king is expected to possess extraordinary personal strength and agility, and their exercise is not thought of as labor. But not only does Marduk use the weapons, we are told that he made them with his own hands. And later, as we have seen, the gods literally make the first human beings. However, the mythologist does not go into the details of other divine productions.

> Marduk bade the moon come forth; entrusted night to her;
> Made her a creature of the dark, to measure time;
> And every month, unfailingly, adorned her with a crown.[3]

Other passages display the ultimate refinement of the coercive strain, the *magical*: production by mere command without any physical exertion at all. Possession of this capacity is indeed made the test of godhood.

> The gods placed a garment in their midst
> And said to Marduk their firstborn:
> 'O Lord, thy lot is truly highest among gods.
> Command annihilation and existence, and may both come true.
> May thy spoken word destroy the garment,
> Then speak again and may it be intact.'
> He spoke - and at his word the garment was destroyed.
> He spoke again, the garment reappeared.
> The gods, his fathers, seeing the power of his word,
> Rejoiced, paid homage: 'Marduk is king.'[4]

Inasmuch as human beings do not in fact possess magical power, how can its ascription to the gods be based on the human activity model? By abstraction: the authoritative person's orders directly set in motion ministers and servants, who in their roles as mere executants are dehumanized and even spoken of as 'tools'—so that it is a short leap of imagination to the notion of commanding nonhuman and even inanimate nature. It is normal, so psychologists tell us, for children to pass through a state of believing in 'the omnipotence of thought', the capacity to make things happen merely by willing them. The human model is what it is believed to be, not necessarily what the human being is in fact.

## The Hebrew Account of Creation

Now let us turn to the story of creation at the beginning of the *Book of Genesis*. As in *Enuma elish*, the starting point is watery chaos:

> And the earth was without form, and void; and darkness was upon the face of the deep. And the Spirit of God moved upon the face of the waters.

After light is summoned into existence and day separated from night—acts not explicitly paralleled in the Babylonian epic—creation proceeds to separation of sea from sky and first appearance of dry land. In due course Yahweh creates everything else, man and woman last.

Numerous parallels and our knowledge of Jewish history make it certain that this story of creation descended from the family of Near Eastern myths of which *Enuma elish* is a representative member. But what a transformation in less than a thousand years! Instead of fecund gods spawning more gods, choosing up sides and massacring each other, creating the world and humanity almost as an afterthought, we are presented with a solitary God who majestically and methodically brings the world and all its populations into being and in appropriate order. Instead of gods identified with the principal divisions of nature, the one God is entirely distinct from His creation. And Yahweh's power is purely magical: he does not fashion anything, he does nothing but issue commands. (The account in *Genesis* Chapter 2 according to which He "formed man of the dust of the ground" and later made woman out of a rib, is an older less sophisticated version.) Only the moral of the story remains much the same as with the Babylonians: we must labor as just punishment for ancestral misbehavior.

This account of the beginning of things is the ultimate refinement of the coercive strain in the human action model. There is no possibility of improving on its severe simplicity, elegance, and majesty: it explains everything and it cuts off all demands for further explanation. It can be accepted or rejected, but neither expanded upon nor abridged nor amended. Any world view in which cause and effect are conceived on the model of command and obedience must come to this one in the end.

## Hesiod

We have noted that human agency affords a second and alternative model for cause and effect: push and movement. The development of mythology in Greece did not go in the direction of eliminating this strain. That is one reason why science began in Greece and not in Palestine.

The earliest Greek written literature, the poems of Homer (ninth–eighth? century B.C.) and Hesiod (*ca* 800 B.C.), are singularly free of magic. Of course Homer's gods have superhuman powers: they control the great forces of nature, but by manipulation—hurling the thunderbolt, shaking the earth, heating the furnace in the volcano. They can change their shapes and even make themselves invisible. But by and large, with allowance for these exceptions, when Homer describes an action we must refer to the subject of the sentence to discern whether the agent is divine or human. And the thousand verses of Hesiod's creation story, the *Theogony*, contain not a single instance of magic. Homer and Hesiod explain only in terms of personal agency. To be sure, Homer was telling a war story, not theorizing about the universe; yet Hesiod, who was theorizing, operated within the same conceptual framework. The early Greek writers never depicted the gods as bringing anything about by mere fiat, though often enough the divine *modus operandi* is unspecified. Both Greeks and Hebrews rendered the old myths more consistent with each other, 'rationalized' them, but in opposite ways: the former by eliminating the magic, the latter by eliminating everything but the magic.

Hesiod begins the world this way.

> Verily first Chaos came into being, but then
> Broad-breasted Gaia [Earth], of all things the seat
>     secure forever,
> And misty Tartarus in the depth of the broad-laned
>     earth,
> And Eros, who, most beautiful among the deathless gods,
> The limb-loosener, of all gods and of all men
> Overpowers the mind in their breasts and their
>     thoughtful counsel.
> From Chaos, Erebus and black Night came into being;
> But again from Night, Aither and Day were born,
> Whom she bore having been impregnated by Erebus,
>     uniting in love.
> But Gaia first bore, equal to herself,
> Starry Ouranos [Heaven], to cover her all over,
> In order to be for the blessed gods a seat secure
>     forever.
> She bore high Hills, graceful haunts of goddesses,
> The Nymphs who dwell among the woody hills.
> She also bore the barren sea, foaming in swell,
> Pontus, without delightful love. But afterwards
> Having bedded with Ouranos she gave birth to
>     deep-swirling Okeanos,
> And Koios and Krios and Hyperion and Iapetos
> And Theia and Rheia and Themis and Mnemosyne
> And golden-crowned Phoebe and lovely Tethys.
> After them the youngest was born, Kronos the crafty,
> Most terrible of the children. He hated his sturdy
>     sire.[5]

The poem goes on chronicling births and battles of gods, like *Enuma elish*. We need not pause to puzzle over what "Chaos" represents—not, it seems, chaos— or why Ocean (Okeanos) appears so late on the scene. What first impresses us is how alike the poem is to myths antedating it by a thousand years or more and how unlike the poem is to the science that succeeded it in its own land barely a century or two later. But something else besides the absence of magic links it to what followed. One man, a private citizen, in no way a priest or holy man, produced it. As far as we know he was motivated by curiosity and by the desire to get things straight. At the outset the Muses speak.

> We know how to say many false things like true ones,
> But we know how to utter truths when we want to.[6]

Greece was invaded repeatedly by peoples bringing exotic myths with them. Because the victors did not always destroy the vanquished, the old myths persisted beside the new, and sometimes they supplemented each other. The Olympian gods—Zeus, Poseidon, and the rest—were warriors not conceived to have created the earth nor to care for it like the fertility gods of the peasant living in Greece before the invasions from the north. Hesiod found the confused and conflicting myths in need of sorting out; hence his poem. Its tiresome (to modern taste) cataloguing marks the scientific attitude in embryonic form.

# 2

# The Milesians

HESIOD'S CONNECTION WITH THE beginnings of science is tenuous and indirect. He was a poor peasant of Boeotia, a backward region of mainland Greece that in his time was not yet out of the four-centuries-long Greek Dark Ages following the Dorian invasions.

On the other hand Miletus around the beginning of the sixth century B.C. was the commercial metropolis of all Greece, the most populous and powerful city of Ionia—located on the eastern coast of the Aegean Sea—a region renowned for luxury, sophistication, and frivolity. She was the mother city of some 70 colonies spread from Egypt to the northern coast of the Black Sea.

Hesiod's poem was known in Ionia, yet it could hardly have raised more than a breeze there where winds blew from Babylon, Egypt, Lydia, and Phoenicia, as well as from all the rest of the Greek world. Such scraps of poetry as we have from the time—none from Miletus itself—are the antithesis of Hesiod. Short lyric forms were preferred, intensely personal, treating in formal perfection of love, wine, and political skulduggery.

## Thales

Thales (625?–547 B.C.) was to the Greeks the most famous Milesian for much the same reasons as Benjamin Franklin is to us the most famous Philadelphian. He was renowned as statesman, engineer, geometer, and astronomer. His name was a synonym for ingenuity, and appeared in all the otherwise differing lists of Seven Sages. When King Croesus of Lydia menaced the independence of the twelve cities of Ionia, Thales gave them the sound advice, which they did not take, to establish a federal government with common citizenship. Of numerous stories illustrating his wisdom both theoretical and practical, many are spurious or at best preserve in garbled form some record of his activities. But none would exist had he not been a notably shrewd man.

We know with reasonable assurance the gist of four things he said: water is the stuff from which all things come; the earth is a disc floating on water; the stone of Magnesia is alive, because it can move iron; and all things are full of gods. Presumably these—at least the first two—derive from some general account that he gave of the world. But he wrote no book.

We do not know why Thales said that water is the primal stuff, nor what precisely he meant. Aristotle (384–322 B.C.; see Chapter 15) guessed that he got this idea "because he saw that the nourishment of all things is moist, and that warmth itself is generated from moisture and persists in it . . . ; and . . . also from the fact that the seeds of all beings are of a moist nature, while water is the first principle of the nature of what is moist."[1] Aristotle was also aware of the antiquity of this notion in myths. Others have speculated that Thales was impressed by water's being the only common stuff that ordinary observation shows to exist as solid liquid and vapor.

Undoubtedly Thales found the notion of a watery beginning in some of the myths we have discussed, and it is plausible to suppose he corroborated it from the difficulty the Milesians always faced in keeping their four city harbors from silting up. (Centuries later the silt won and Miletus was no more.) *Water* meant to him not $H_2O$ but the stuff of rain, springs, rivers, and the sea—a stuff patently of a nature to bring forth many things, the imaginative step to *all things* being a unifying generalization typical of scientific hypothesis formation.

Our ignorance of Thales' specific reasoning does not keep us from appreciating his achievement. The important thing is that he did have reasons: in some fashion he drew his conclusion from pondering on his observations of the way things are. But so also, in a way, did the prehistoric originator of the *Enuma elish* saga. What made Thales the first scientific thinker was his ability to state his conclusion literally and impersonally, to satisfy his understanding with a simple recital of the facts as he saw them and without translation into the model of coercive personal agency. He "left Marduk out."[2]

We may reach the same conclusion about Thales' mode of reasoning from his statement that the earth is a disc floating on water. He explained earthquakes this way: they happen when the underlying water is agitated, as with boats in a harbor when a storm comes up. The ordinary Greek explanation of an earthquake was that it was the sea god Poseidon shaking the earth with his trident. Again Thales does not depart far from the mechanism, but he "leaves Poseidon out." And his hypothesis has great power to unify: with some plausibility (in his context) he exhibits such disparate phenomena as silting, earthquakes, and the moisture of seeds as consequences of the same underlying fact.

The other two pronouncements ascribed to Thales, that the stone of Magnesia (i.e. magnetic iron ore) has a soul because it moves iron and that all things are full of gods, further confirm the scientific cast of Thales' thought even though they may on their face look like primitive animism. We have to translate his word *psyche* as *soul*, but we must not read modern religious connotations into it. For the Greeks of Thales' time it meant the vital principle: that which is in a living body and not a dead one and accounts for the power of self-movement that living things have. To say then that something so lumpish as a rock may yet have a *psyche* is not to personalize the rock but to depersonalize the *soul* by pointing out that the power of beginning a motion is not restricted to bodies with conscious wills. So also "All things are full of gods" appears to be the pouring of new wine into an old linguistic bottle. If the saying were religious it would be too extravagant. Thales was observing that in order to explain the workings of things it is not necessary to have recourse to person-like beings, gods, operating from outside. The forces are contained in the things themselves, or to speak more precisely matter is inherently capable of movement.

# Anaximander

Thales' pupil and successor was Anaximander (610–*ca* 547 B.C.). Like Thales he was a prominent citizen of Miletus, and commanded the expedition that founded the colony of Apollonia on the Black Sea coast. Unlike Thales, he wrote a book, the first prose treatise in European literature. Only one sentence has survived, but ancient references and summaries make possible a fairly clear conception of what it contained.

Anaximander is said to have been the first to draw a map of the known world. Perhaps his book was a companion piece to the map: it was a universal history, an account of cosmic evolution explaining how the world had come into being and what its structure was, and tracing geological and biological development. In agreement with Thales and all other early Greek thinkers he seems to have adopted from his mythologist predecessors the assumption that there *was* a development, that the world had not been the same for all past time. But while Thales had agreed further with the mythmakers in identifying the primal stuff as water, Anaximander had a different opinion: that things arose out of "the Boundless." This was not any one of the four great obvious divisions of nature—earth, air, fire, and water—that later came to be called 'elements', but "something intermediate," neutral, and indefinite in its properties yet capable of giving rise to the definite things. Anaximander argued that the elements "are in opposition to one another—air is cold, water moist, fire hot—and, therefore, if any one of them were infinite, the rest would have ceased to be by this time."[3] He reasoned that whatever is the origin of everything cannot be any one of those things in particular, hence not water. We are not told, in surviving summaries, how we should conceive the Boundless. Perhaps Anaximander thought of it as damp (neither wet nor dry) and tepid (neither hot nor cold). But he might have reasoned that it would be imperceptible since everything we can see or otherwise sense must have some definite nature. *Apeiron*, his word, can mean *infinite* or *indefinite* as well as *boundless*.

The Boundless is endless in extent and "ageless and deathless"; that is, it did not come into being and will not pass away. Because it is thus immortal, Anaximander called it "divine." This adjective, however, carried little, if any, connotation of personality.

The world we live in is only one of innumerable worlds that arise out of the Boundless at different times as well as (perhaps) at the same times in different places. This is the way a world comes into being. The Boundless is in "eternal motion." This motion, or at any rate the part of it that is to form a world, is whirling. Whirls bring about separation: in a vortex or whirlpool, the Greeks observed, heavy objects are brought together at the bottom while lighter ones are moved outwards. In consequence, "something capable of begetting hot and cold out of the eternal gets separated off." The *hot* and the *cold* are conceived as stuffs: the hot is fire; the cold contains earth, air, and water. The hot encircles the cold "like the bark around a tree." Subsequently the cold elements separate so that there is a core of earth surrounded by concentric rings of water, air, and fire, the whole system being in rotation.

Now a cosmic explosion occurs, presumably because of pressures built up by the fire heating the air and water. Earth and water remain where they were; fire and air are thrown outward, the air wrapping the fire in gigantic tubes encircling the earth. These are the major steps in world formation; and the process continues today, chiefly in the evaporation of the seas, which will one day dry up altogether. "The sea is what is left of the original moisture. The fire has dried up most of it and turned the rest salt by scorching it."

This is Anaximander's model of the world. At the center the earth, a drum three times as wide as it is deep, stays motionless—although not supported by anything—"on account of its equal distance" from everything else. Eighteen earth radii from the center is a gigantic hoop of air-covered fire encircling the earth. On the inner side of this tube there is a single round "breathing hole," "like the nozzle of a bellows," through which the enclosed fire shines out. This hole is what we see and call the moon. Twenty-seven earth radii out is an even greater hoop; the breathing hole in it is the sun, its diameter equal to earth's. Eclipses and moon phases occur when the holes are stopped up, completely or partially (we are not told by what). The planets and stars are also explained as holes in hoops, but the details are lost.

The notion of air wrapping up fire and rendering it invisible except at "breathing holes" may strike us as strange. However, Anaximander's word here translated air means primarily vapor, mist, fog. And fog obscures light—even bright light.

Evidently Anaximander attempted to fashion a unified theory to account for all heavenly fires. This is his explanation of lightning.

> He said that lightning is due to wind; for when it is surrounded and pressed together by a thick cloud and so driven out by reason of its lightness and rarefaction, then the breaking makes a noise, while the separation makes a rift of brightness in the darkness of the cloud.[4]

That is to say, the lightning cannot just appear out of nothing; fire must have been there all along, but wrapped up inside the cloud until the cloud breaks and reveals it for an instant. If this does not seem to us to be a satisfactory account of lightning and thunder, we must remember that no one had a better one before Benjamin Franklin.

To the question why Anaximander insisted on the existence of unseen hoops, there is no hint of an answer in the ancient sources. Why was he not content to follow common sense like all his predecessors and like his successor Anaximenes (sixth century B.C.), and regard the sun and moon simply as circular fiery bodies in the sky? The following conjecture is based on two features of his thought: his daringly original idea that the earth, though not falling, has no supports and his intuitive grasp of the principle that explanation should be comprehensive—should unify many seemingly diverse phenomena.

Thales taught that the earth floats on, is supported by, water. It must have occurred to Anaximander that this kind of explanation for the earth's stability would not do, for whatever might be postulated to hold it up must itself be provided with *its* supports, ad infinitum. So he said that the earth stays in place "because of its equidistance." Equidistance from what? And how would this count as an explanation?

The "equidistance" could only be from the other great masses in the universe, those we see in the sky: sun and moon principally. And being equidistant from them would explain lack of motion toward any of them because the system would be balanced, as it were: no more reason to move in any one direction than any other, hence no motion at all. If Anaximander reasoned this way, he was making use of a negative form of reasoning that was much later baptized the Principle of Sufficient Reason: if there can be no reason why a thing should happen in one way rather than another, then it will not happen at all. Moreover, the argument implies that if the earth were closer to one great mass than to another, it would move in the direction of the former—which is, astonishingly, an anticipation of the idea of gravitation.

However, appearances presented Anaximander with a grave problem: sun, moon, and earth certainly do not *look* as if they are always arranged symmetrically. The visible sun and moon are often seen together in the sky. Should not the earth, then, move toward them?

The hoops provide the escape from this quandary. Despite appearances, sun and moon are actually only the visible portions of otherwise invisible bodies that encircle the earth concentrically, hence with unchanging symmetry. Earth is always at the same distance from them.

If Anaximander's reasoning was something like this—and it does not seem possible to assign any other motive for the hoop idea—then at the very beginning of Greek science the essential nature of theoretical explanation was understood: a law, a natural regularity, holding universally and accounting for observations (the fall of bodies), and assumption of unobserved entities (hoops in this case), rendering other phenomena consistent with the law. Even if his reasoning was different, Anaximander's claim to recognition as a scientific thinker is unassailable. For the hoops must have figured in some general theory; there was no traditional or mythological precedent for them.

Anaximander's account of the world included a theory of human evolution. Here also he made a complete break with mythology, which always conceives of human beings as having appeared suddenly on the scene, either as growths out of the earth or as fashioned by gods in the form they now have. Anaximander, however, sought to incorporate human history into his generally evolutionary conception. He observed that "while other animals quickly find food by themselves, man alone requires a lengthy period of suckling. Hence, had he been originally as he is now, he would never have survived."[5] The young of the human species are helpless for long periods during which they survive thanks only to the resources of organized societies—which must themselves have evolved. Hence our kind must have developed gradually from some other form of life not so ill fitted to the world. Furthermore the theory that in the beginning there had been no dry land suggested that all life originated in the sea or along the seashore. "Living creatures arose from the moist element as it was evaporated by the sun." Sea creatures adapted to life on land: "The first animals were produced in the moisture, each enclosed in a prickly bark. As they advanced in age, they came out upon the drier part. When the bark broke off, they survived for a short time."[6] Human beings were "like other animals, namely fish, in the beginning. At first human beings arose in the inside of fishes, and after having been reared like sharks, and become capable of protecting themselves, they were finally cast ashore and took to land."[7] The mention of sharks is not fanciful but based on observation of certain sharks of the eastern Mediterranean that hatch their eggs inside their bodies, hence appear to be viviparous like mammals.

As noted earlier, only one sentence from Anaximander's book has survived in direct quotation.

> From what sources things arise, into them also is their destruction, as is ordained; for they give satisfaction and pay reparation to one another for their injustice according to the ordering of time.

The *justice* that figures in this sentence is a notion pervading Greek thought, akin to *balance of nature*. There is an impersonal and inexorable force—so the Greeks held—stronger even than the gods, that operates to keep anybody or anything from getting more than its *allotted portion*. 'Injustice', encroachment beyond bounds, is followed automatically by restorative retribution. This idea lies at the roots both of Greek moral conceptions and of their notion of a *law of nature* in the scientific sense. In the fragment from Anaximander's book we see it being developed in the latter direction.

## Anaximenes

The third of the great Milesians, pupil and associate of Anaximander, lacked his master's speculative daring. His world picture was more like that of Thales: the earth a flat disc, kept from falling by floating—but on air, not water. The sky is a vault; sun, moon, and stars are flat fiery bodies, "like leaves," that stick to it. This vault turns around the polar axis "like the cap on your head." Sun and moon do not go under the earth but behind high mountains.

Despite this regression to what must have passed as common sense in his day, Anaximenes (sixth century B.C.) is credited by historians of science with one important new conception, that of explaining qualitative change in quantitative terms. He held the basic stuff to be neither water nor the Boundless but air (or mist). The other elements, he taught, are nothing but air rarefied or condensed. When air is 'relaxed' it becomes fire; when compacted, 'felted', it becomes wind. Further condensation makes clouds of it, then water, and finally in its most condensed state it becomes earth. The rarer air is the hotter it becomes; the denser, the colder. The first recorded scientific experiment, and not the last to be misinterpreted by the experimenter, was performed by Anaximenes in demonstration of this doctrine. Blow hard on your hand, through compressed lips: the 'thick' air feels cold. Now open your mouth wide and blow gently: the 'thin' air is warm.

But if Anaximenes was an experimenter or even a careful observer of nature, why did he fail to notice that water expands—takes up more space—when it freezes, apparently contrary to his theory? Perhaps his theory has been misinterpreted by historians. The words translated rarefaction and condensation—quantitative terms since they involve the notion of amount of stuff packed into a given volume—can just as well be rendered as thickening and thinning, which do not necessarily refer to quantities. For there are thickenings and thinnings that do not depend on squeezing or stretching out, for instance thickening of puddings and jellies. It is not unlikely that this kind of process, along with 'felting' and 'slackening', furnished Anaximenes his model of how air is transformed into the other elements. If so, his status as first quantitative thinker is placed in jeopardy.

One sentence remains from Anaximenes' book.

Just as our soul, being air, keeps us together in order, so also wind [or breath] and air encompasses the whole cosmos.

This is the earliest surviving expression of the *macrocosm/microcosm* idea that the human animal, including the soul, is a tiny model of the universe; substances and relations found in us have their counterparts on the cosmic scale, so that one can reason from human nature to the nature of the whole world and vice versa.

## The Milesian Achievement

The first nonmythical account of the nature of things was bound to be a remarkable event, a mutation of a magnitude never seen before or since. It is staggering to find that this first naturalistic world view presents us with a picture of an evolving universe in which an earth without material supports becomes the habitat of life that itself evolves from fish to philosopher. It even began with a big bang!

Yet the content of Anaximander's brilliant speculation is of less significance than the form of Milesian thought. For all we know, some prehistoric tribe that has perished leaving no records may have had a myth of beginnings according to which the earth developed out of a Boundless, life arose first in the sea and then progressed to dry land, and so on. It would be just one myth among all the others, however, if nothing certified it but tradition and authority.

The core of the Milesian achievement is their invention of *critical* or *dialectical* thought about the world. Dialectic is a word with a bewilderingly large number of more or less technical uses, ancient and modern. Its original sense, however, is simply *conversational* or *argumentative*. People have always conversed about all manner of things. The great Milesian discovery was the possibility of conversing, arguing, about the origin and nature of things.

Myths are not conversations. Their format is that of the speaker addressing the silently listening audience. The listener may accept the myth or reject it, but not argue about it with the preacher. This is because there is no common regulative standard that preacher and congregation both recognize and to which both claim to have equal access. The preacher may be recounting traditional material. The auditor may object that the preacher has got the tradition wrong, that he is not telling the story as it should be told. And the objection may be supported, but only by appeal to an allegedly more authoritative reciter or document. If the listener admits the correctness of the recital but denies that things really happened as described, the only appeal in support must be to a rival tradition. That, however, would not be arguing but only expressing a preference; for all traditions as such are equal.

Or suppose the preacher claims to be communicating a new revelation. Then there may be argument to the extent that reasons can be produced for or against the belief that the person in question has the credentials necessary to establish status as a bearer of revelations; but that again would not be argument about the content of the alleged revelation, which must be accepted or rejected as a whole. A lay person has no basis for saying to a prophet that the message is true in its general outlines but needs to be corrected in this or that detail. To say it would be to set oneself up as a rival prophet and recipient of another revelation.

But *Anaximander criticized Thales*. The fundamental stuff could not be any one of the four 'elements', he declared, because "if one of these were infinite, the rest would be at once destroyed." His thought was this: the four elements have definite natures that oppose one another. Water, for example, puts out fire; fire dries up water. They can coexist—and observation shows that they do coexist—only if they maintain a balance of sorts. If one of them, say water, were infinite, it would have had the upper hand and already would have put out all the fire. Since this has not happened, no one of them can be infinite. But Thales' theory in effect makes water infinite. Therefore it cannot be correct as it stands.

Whether this is a good or a bad argument is of little importance; the point is that it *is* an *argument*. It is an individual person's private reasoning power being used together with the results of his observations to modify another individual's account of the most general features of the world.

Anaximenes likewise criticized Anaximander. No report of their conversation has come down to us, but we can imagine what it must have been like. Anaximenes evidently thought of air as a stuff whose nature is indefinite enough to escape Anaximander's objection to water, but still, unlike the Boundless, something found in experience—one might say closer to the facts. The process of thickening and thinning suggested itself to him as a way in which a stuff with a certain character might be transformed into something different, even opposite, while retaining its fundamental identity.

## Some Causes of the Mutation in Thought

Why the Ionian Greeks of this age, uniquely among the peoples of the world, took the step of emancipating themselves—some of them—from myth is a question to which through hindsight we can give a partial answer. Some of the important factors that we can recognize were commercialism, cultural cross-fertilization, absence of a priestly caste, and individualism.

All the cities of Ionia existed primarily through manufacture and commerce rather than agriculture. One of the few safe historical generalizations is that commerce is the chief incubator of intellectual innovation. For trading is more competitive than farming and demands more shrewdness, the ability to improvise responses to unfamiliar situations. And social mobility is fostered. For a trader with exceptional talent, industry, and luck can parlay a shoestring into a fortune; conversely, one without such gifts will eventually reach bottom. It is relatively harder to get ahead, or fall behind, where what matters most is land. A bumper harvest or a crop failure will be shared by all farmers alike, so that the social pattern tends to remain stable.

Farmers stay at home, merchants travel. Ionia was a major crossroad of the ancient world, where even stay-at-homes were used to exotic visitors with outlandish customs. But few Ionians stayed at home; their colonies and trading posts ranged from the Black Sea to Marseilles. Traveling all over the known world to trade not to conquer, they were obliged to deal with other peoples on equal terms, to learn their customs, and to exhibit at least the appearance of sympathetic toleration. In such circumstances rigid adherence to traditional folkways was difficult.

Nor did folkways lie heavy on the Ionians. The Greeks were one of the very few peoples who never developed a priestly caste and never recognized priesthood as a profession. Every city had its cults and temples, but for the most part the temple officials were ordinary citizens whose priestly duties and privileges neither occupied their entire efforts nor served to set them apart as a special group. In consequence, there did not exist in Greece an organized profession whose prestige and livelihood depended on belief in myths. The importance of this peculiarity of Greece can hardly be overestimated.

Furthermore, the contents of the Greek myths were predestined to be supplanted by science. The official Olympian gods made admirable characters for epic poems and dramas because of their intense humanness, but those same traits made it hard to take them seriously and literally as the august forces of the universe. Moreover they were not credited with having made the world; Greek creation myths had to do with the grandparents of the Olympians, obscure deities never worshipped. What there was of profundity in Greek religion centered on the awful and mysterious figures Allotted Portion (*Moira*), Justice, and the Fates, who were thought of as impersonal forces to which even Zeus was subject. These deities, seldom personified and then only in conscious metaphors, were easily transformed into Laws of Nature. We have already seen this process in Anaximander's remark about the manner in which world elements preserve themselves in balance: ". . . they give satisfaction and pay reparation to one another for their injustice . . ." We shall soon come upon further examples.

Last in this incomplete list we mention Greek individualism. Dialectic demands disputants who have their own opinions and enough confidence to broadcast them, to claim that they are right and everybody else hitherto has been wrong. Such a personality type is rather rare even today and was hardly heard of in most ancient civilizations, where society was everything and the individual nothing (unless happening to be a Pharaoh or high priest or other dignitary). Such innovators as there were commonly presented their views anonymously in the guise of newly discovered sayings of the men of old. Not so in Greece, where literature was anything but anonymous. It is no coincidence that the beginnings of science in Ionia are associated with the flourishing of the short lyric poem, the most personal of literary genres.

All this may help to understand how it came about that the Ionian Greeks developed the scientific world view. At best, though, we have begun to answer one question by raising several others. Why was Greek religion so different from other kinds in the neighborhood, and different in just the right ways? Why were the Greeks individualists, and the Ionians most individual of all? Even if we knew the answers, they would not be enough. The Greek miracle, as with reason it has been called, happened—and we still must perforce stand and gape at it.

# 3

# Pythagoras and Xenophanes

TWO MEN, BORN ABOUT the same time in cities near Miletus, carried Ionian philosophy westward to the Greeks of Sicily and southern Italy. Pythagoras (*ca* 570–*ca* 500 B.C.) and Xenophanes (*ca* 570–*ca* 478 B.C.) differed greatly in temperament and outlook, from each other as well as from their Milesian teachers. Xenophanes was closer in spirit to Miletus: the most enlightened man of his age, the founder of anthropology and (perhaps) of paleontology, and a ridiculer of superstition. On the other hand and despite his genius, Pythagoras was almost as much witch-doctor as scientist. We have a fair amount of information about Xenophanes the man (he wrote of himself), but very little about Pythagoras (he wrote nothing). Xenophanes had hardly any effect on subsequent thought; Pythagoras has with reason been called the most influential philosopher who ever lived.

## Life of Pythagoras

As far as we can judge, the Milesians pursued the investigation of nature for its own sake—"out of wonder," Aristotle tells us. This scientific detachment, however, was not shared by all the early Greek thinkers. Pythagoras was an organizer as well as a philosopher. He founded a brotherhood that was both a research institute and a church, or at any rate a lodge.

He was a native of Samos, an island barely separated from the Ionian coast. About 532 B.C., when already middle-aged, he left Samos—out of disgust, we are told, with the regime of the tyrant Polycrates—and went to Croton in the toe of the Italian boot. There he resided for some 20 years during which he attracted about 300 followers. For a time these Pythagoreans had control of the government of Croton, but were overthrown and massacred. Pythagoras fled to the neighboring city of Metapontion where he died. In his lifetime he had a reputation as a sage and scientific investigator.

## Taboos

A fundamental Pythagorean belief was in the kinship of all things that "have soul in them": not only all human beings but animals also and even, it seems, some kinds of plants. Pythagoras taught that when the body dies the soul neither perishes nor descends to the underworld but migrates into another body. The earliest reference we have to Pythagoras is a satirical story of his having called on a man to stop beating a dog, because he recognized in the yelps the voice of a departed friend.

Meat eating, therefore, was cannibalism and prohibited. Beans and laurel leaves were also to be shunned. Pythagoreans were enjoined to put on the right shoe before the left (but to wash the left foot first), to spit upon hair and fingernail trimmings, and so on. The purpose of these rituals was to purify the soul in the hope it would escape the wheel of rebirth and not be reincarnated after the next death into yet another bodily prison. It is not clear from the reports whether the liberated soul was supposed to go as an individual to some sort of heaven or whether extinction was taken to be its own reward.

Where these superstitions came from is not known. Although similar notions appeared in India about the same time, it seems more likely that both came from a common source somewhere north of the Black Sea than that India influenced Greece or vice versa. In any case Pythagoras lived in the era when Greece was being invaded by all sorts of 'mysteries'—religions distinguished from the official or Olympian cults by initiations—that is, symbolic rebirths; the promise of heavenly immortality for the initiated; and, usually, orgiastic rites designed to induce ecstasy (= standing outside oneself) and enthusiasm (= having god inside). Their appeal was greatest among people toward the lower end of the social hierarchy. The main and crucial difference between Pythagoreanism and commoner mysteries lay in the method for attaining ecstasy and enthusiasm: Pythagoras prescribed not drinks, drugs, or dances but the study of mathematics and natural science. That was the Ionian in him.

## Philosophy

Purification of the soul, Pythagoras taught, was achieved through *philosophy* (= love of wisdom), the intellectual activity consisting in *theory* (= looking at, contemplation) of the *cosmos* (= order—the world regarded as a structure). The Pythagoreans gave to all the italicized words in the preceding sentence the special senses they have borne ever since.

Pythagoras said there are three kinds of lives: the acquisitive, the competitive, and the contemplative—as for instance the three kinds of people who go to the Olympic games: those who buy and sell, those who compete, and those who observe. The third class is best. In putting it this way Pythagoras must have shocked the Greeks, who glorified sports heroes just as extravagantly as we do. But his point was that awareness is liberation: to understand the world—look at it with the penetrating eye of the intellect—is to rise in some measure above it.

## Mathematics and Harmony

The unwritten teachings of Pythagoras were secrets for the initiated only, and he was held in such reverence that his disciples and successors could obtain authority for their own discoveries only by attributing them to the Master. Thus there are insuperable difficulties in trying to ascertain what Pythagoras himself discovered. The following account summarizes doctrines held within the brotherhood in its first half century or so and which therefore *may* have originated with the Master.

Thales is reputed to have proved theorems in geometry, and Anaximander gave numerical values for the distances of sun and moon from earth. Pythagoras was the first, however, to make mathematics central in thought. Indeed he made the extreme and puzzling claim that "things are numbers." In order to get at the meaning and basis of this pronouncement let us begin, as perhaps Pythagoras himself did, with his great discovery of the harmonic relationships.

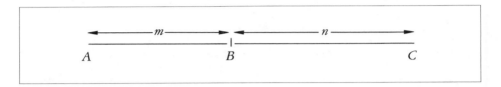

Suppose a string is stretched between the fixed points *A* and *C*—on a guitar, say—and *B* is a finger stopping the string on a fingerboard. Now if the distance *m* is half the distance *n* and each separate segment of the string is plucked, the shorter segment will sound an octave higher than the longer segment and together they will sound this *harmonious*—the word means agreeing—interval. If *m* is two thirds as long as *n*, that is, if *m/n* = 2/3, the harmony will be the fifth. If *m/n* = 3/4, the interval is the fourth. These are all harmonies, expressible thus by simple numerical ratios. As the ratios grow more complicated, the harmonies become discords.

Pythagoras is said to have discovered this fact about stringed instruments, yet it seems hardly possible that no musician had ever noticed it before. Players and instrument makers had to work with these figures. No matter; the genius of Pythagoras lay in noting the *significance* of the fact.

He saw that something with apparently nothing at all in common with numbers—what could be more remote from one another than an account book and a tune?—nevertheless could be understood through numbers, partook of the nature of numbers, and in sum *was* numbers. Today we still say that the interval of the fifth *is* 2:3, or that *A is* 440. "440 what?" we may be asked, and we reply "Vibrations per second." But to the further question "Vibrations of what?" we answer that it does not matter: string, air, skin—the essential thing is the 440. In thinking this way we approximate the Pythagorean attitude: the pattern, the structure, is what counts; and the pattern is always a number.

Number, pattern, is the same as limit; more exactly, it is what puts a limit, a bound, on what before was unlimited. Number imposes definiteness, therefore intelligibility, on an originally undefined, chaotic, and unintelligible continuum. When the stretched string is stopped and plucked at random, only random noises emerge. Harmonious, 'intelligible', sounds are the result of introducing number. In this spirit we can interpret the Pythagorean account of how the world came to be.

First the Unit came into being, they said, and immediately began to breathe-in the surrounding Unlimited or void. Like the Milesians, Pythagoras assumed an initial chaos which then became orderly—a Cosmos. The Unit "breathing-in the surrounding void" made that chaos, or a part of it, into something definite. Then the Unit produced Two, the first number (the Greeks thought of the Unit, One, as the producer of numbers but not itself a number), and so on until the entire number series, which *is* the cosmos, was generated.

This account may seem scarcely intelligible; the difficulty lies in Pythagoras' struggle to express his mathematical picture of the world in a language as yet lacking a suitable vocabulary. Pythagoras did not even have convenient numerals at his disposal. Pythagoreans represented numbers by dots, as we still do on dominoes and dice. This circumstance helps to explain how they could say that "things are numbers": the pattern of the dots was at the same time the pattern in the cosmos.

## Influence

There is little likelihood of ever resolving the riddles presented by our meager knowledge of Pythagoras and his followers. Why did Pythagoras deem science—mathematics especially—the key to salvation? The connection is not obvious. Nor, it seems, was it clear to all the Pythagoreans: in the course of time they split into two sects, one religious the other scientific. But why did the original religio-scientific organization attain political power more than once, in more than one city, and what was it like to be under its rule? What induced the common people to revolt and burn the Pythagoreans in their meeting house?

This we do know: Pythagoras' influence on science and philosophy has been enormous, perhaps unsurpassed. No doubt it would have been great even if he had been a relatively solitary thinker, like Anaximander before him or Heraclitus (*ca* 540–*ca* 480 B.C.; see Chapter 4) afterwards. But Pythagoras was the first man we know of to make an institution of science. And institutions have lives of their own. The Brotherhood went on for generations, centuries even, after the demise of the Master. Its institutional structure ensured the survival, albeit sometimes in debased form, of the 'theory of the cosmos'. In fact the subsequent history of Greek philosophy—emphatically including Plato (427–347 B.C.; see Chapter 11), the greatest Pythagorean of them all—is largely the story of further developments in Pythagoreanism and reactions against it.

Despite Pythagoras' Ionian background and the incorporation of Milesian theories and interests into his system, the general tenor of his thought is un-Ionian, is on the mystical rather than the rational side, and is but the first of many attempts to produce a synthesis of scientific water and religious oil. The mixture proved congenial to the Greeks of the luxurious cities of southern Italy, who were not Ionians but Dorians, a distinct strain speaking a different dialect of the Greek language. A more typically rationalist and therefore less influential immigrant to southern Italy was the poet-philosopher Xenophanes.

## Life of Xenophanes

Xenophanes was born in Colophon, a city some 40 miles north of Miletus. He is said to have "heard" Anaximander, who was 40 years older. When he was 25 the Persians conquered Ionia. Among thousands of other refugees, Xenophanes fled to Italy. There and in Sicily he lived past the age of 92. He did not settle in one place but moved about making his living as a composer-to-order, reciter of poetry, and master of ceremonies in aristocratic houses. But he was no mere hanger-on, as is shown by his vigorous denunciation of the adulation paid to heroes of sport and his pressing of the intellectuals' claim to preferment. The Greeks rewarded Olympic victors with "a conspicuous front seat at the festivals, board at public expense, and a gift as a souvenir. But," he protested, the athlete "is not as worthy as I am. For better than strength of men and horses is my wisdom. It is frivolous and wrong to set strength above wisdom." If some citizen happens to be a record holder, "not on that account will the city be better governed"; nor do Olympic victories "fatten the treasury."[1] The fragment from which these lines are taken unfortunately does not include an account of how Xenophanes' wisdom would accomplish these ends.

## On Religion

It was Xenophanes who ridiculed Pythagoras for having recognized a deceased friend's voice in the yelps of a beaten cur. Not only did Xenophanes think transmigration absurd, he even attacked the official Olympian religion. He condemned Homer and Hesiod on moral grounds, saying that they "ascribed to the gods all things that are a shame and disgrace among mortals, stealings and adulteries and deceivings of one another." An even more fundamental criticism of religion is his observation that man makes gods in his own image.

> The Ethiopians make their gods black and snub-nosed; the Thracians say theirs have blue eyes and red hair. Yes, and if oxen and horses or lions had hands, and could paint with their hands, and produce works of art as men do, horses would paint the forms of the gods like horses, and oxen like oxen, and make their bodies in the image of their several kinds.

In place of these discredited and disreputable deities, Xenophanes recommended recognition of

> One god, the greatest among gods and men, neither in form like mortals nor in thought. All of him sees, all of him thinks, all of him hears. He stays forever in the same place, moving not at all; nor is it fitting for him to go about, now here, now there. But without labor he shakes all things by his intelligent willpower.

This "one god" seems to have been identical with the world; that is to say, Xenophanes was a pantheist. This view is not different from that of the Milesians, all of whom regarded the world as a whole, or—what comes to the same thing— the basic stuff of the world as 'divine', implying that it enjoyed eternal life. The *modus operandi* of Xenophanes' "one god," however, represents a new and perhaps backward step. He accomplishes everything "by intelligent willpower," without himself moving. Xenophanes may have been saying no more than that nature is a cosmos, exhibiting an intelligible order—a point made by Anaximander when he said that the Boundless "steers all things." It looks, however, as though Xenophanes wanted to introduce or reintroduce animism into the scientific world picture, even if it was a purified and sophisticated mono-animism.

# The World

Some verses by Xenophanes have been preserved that bear on the nature of the world. They show that he continued Anaximenes' 'common-sense' reaction to the speculations of Anaximander, which were too advanced for general acceptance. The earth needs no support, Xenophanes averred, because it "goes on down indefinitely." Its surface, on which we live, is flat. The sun moves in a straight line; at so-called sunset it moves out of our visual range. (Xenophanes seems not to have been interested in geometry.) There is a new and different sun every day.

Xenophanes like Anaximander appreciated the significance of fossils as indications of geological history. Anaximander had reasoned that since fossil shells of marine animals are found inland, even on hilltops, the earth must be drying up. On the other hand, Xenophanes inferred that there is a cosmic cycle from wet to dry and back again: things are presently getting wetter, and the world will eventually dissolve into mud. This will in time dry up and deposit another fossil record. This theory is an advance over Anaximander's in taking account of dryland fossils (bay leaves).

Xenophanes made explicit the conception of intellectual progress that is the essence of scientific thought and is implicit in the Milesian practice of criticism.

> The gods indeed did not reveal everything to mortals from the beginning; but men search, and in time they find out better.

# 4

# Heraclitus

HERACLITUS WAS BORN IN Ephesus of a noble family. Despite differences that arose between him and his fellow citizens, he remained there all his lifetime of some 60 years.

He wrote a book *On Nature*, the world and humanity, from which approximately 125 fragments, 1,500 words, have survived in quotations by later authors. The book itself was probably not very long.

Heraclitus was an isolated figure, not much interested in details of Milesian natural science and scornful of Pythagorean mathematical mysticism. His intense concern was with the overall pattern of things, with how nature as a whole hangs together.

## The Logos

Heraclitus with inordinate pride claimed to have recognized the Logos of the cosmos, which despite its obviousness escaped the notice of everyone else. (Logos means 'word' in Greek, but also nearly everything connected with words: account, argument, reputation, pattern, proportion, ratio, reason, rationale, the hang of things.) His book began

> With this Logos, which is eternally valid, men keep on being out of contact, both before they have heard it and when they first hear it. For although everything happens in accordance with this *Logos*, men are like novices when they are put to the test of such words and deeds as I present when I define each thing according to nature and tell what it is. But as for other men, such things as they do when they are awake escape their notice, just as when they go to sleep they forget what they are doing.[1]

The Logos being "common to all" and "that with which people have the most intimate contact," failure to grasp it must be due to willful blindness. So Heraclitus did not concern himself with making his teachings easy to comprehend and was, therefore, called The Dark. But some of his sayings are not at all obscure.

> The Ephesians would do well to hang themselves, every grown man of them, and leave the city to beardless boys. For they have thrown out Hermodorus, the best man among them, saying, "We do not want anyone to be better than the rest of us. If there is anyone like that, let him go somewhere else and be better than other people."

(Hermodorus in fact went to Rome and wrote a legal code for the Romans.)

> Vast learning does not teach people to be intelligent. If it did it would have taught Hesiod and Pythagoras as well as Xenophanes and Hecataeus.

> Pythagoras son of Mnesarchus did more research than any other man, and working up these notes, he made his own personal wisdom—vast learning, bamboozlement.

Heraclitus' scorn for democratic equalitarianism was not unconnected with his contempt for Pythagoras and other eminent intellectuals. Democrats think political wisdom can be made by adding up ten thousand individual foolishnesses; Pythagoras tried to fashion a world view by putting together ten thousand separate items of information. To Heraclitus the absurdity was the same. The Ephesians failed to recognize that "law consists in following the advice of one man"; Pythagoras and Xenophanes failed to perceive how "listening not to me but to the Logos it is wise to agree that all things are one."

But did not Pythagoras conclude that all things are numbers and did not Xenophanes declare that the all is one god? Yes. And the Milesians had held that the world had arisen out of just one kind of stuff, water or 'boundless' or air. Their error, in Heraclitus' judgment, consisted in supposing that while all things had indeed come *from* one stuff, the things *now* existed as individuals on their own that could be understood each one by itself. But the unity of all things is not a condition that existed only in the past, like the one lump of clay from which many pots have been made, nor yet the mere resultant, like a mosaic picture, of putting together things each of which is a thing in its own right. There is not and cannot be any individual thing (short of the whole cosmos) that exists on its own and can be understood all alone.

Pythagoras had drawn up a table of Opposites.

left - right
unlimited - limit
even - odd
many - one
female - male
moving - resting
crooked - straight
darkness - light
bad - good
oblong - square

Everything on the right is good, everything on the left is bad. These opposites form the basic constituents of things; understanding consists in analyzing down to them. The world is the battleground of the *goods* and the *bads*.

On this Heraclitus commented: "They do not grasp how what disagrees agrees with itself. There is an adjustment of opposite tensions, as in the bow and the lyre." Here we have a stretched string again, but illustrating a different point. The bow and the lyre "disagree with themselves"—the frames want to go one way, the strings another—and just that disagreement makes effective unities of them: "they agree with themselves." To understand the bow and lyre is to understand the universe.

Opposites, Heraclitus declared, are "the same." Some oppositions are merely subjective: "the way up and the way down are one and the same"—it depends only on whether you are at the top of the hill or the bottom. Sea water is pure or nasty depending on whether you are a fish or a human being. "Doctors who cut and burn complain that they are not paid enough for doing these things"—in the context of lifesaving surgery even excruciating pain is a good and should be paid for. Other opposites—day and night, hot and cold—are "the same" in forming unities by regular succession. Still other pairs are such that one member would have no meaning without the other: if there were no injustices, "men would not have known the name of justice." Even in what common sense sees as one simple thing, a river for example, closer scrutiny reveals oppositions: "over those who step into the same rivers, different and again different waters flow."

## War

Although opposites cannot exist apart from each other, they really are opposed. This opposition, *war,* is the world force. "Homer should have been dishonorably discharged and flogged," Heraclitus said in another remark designed to shock the Greeks, "and Archilochus too." The crime of these poets was pacifism: both had prayed that war might cease from among gods and men. But if it did, that would be the collapse of everything. "You should know that war is universal and justice is strife and everything happens by strife and necessity." No doubt the tension of opposites at the basis of things is only metaphorical war, but Heraclitus seems to have held that literal war is a good thing too as a selective process.

> War is everybody's father and everybody's king, and some he shows to be gods and others men; some he makes slaves, others free.

Heraclitus' discovery of the Logos was not merely the insight that tension lies at the bottom of things. Universal war is an incomplete metaphor if we think of war as confusion with a chancy outcome. The strife that is the cosmic process is measured, patterned, and orderly.

> The sun will not overstep measures. If he does, the Furies, guardians of Justice, will find him out.

Thus the Logos is the Law of Nature.

> One thing is wise: to discern the rule whereby all things are piloted through all.

> Those who speak with common sense must strengthen themselves with what is common to all, just as a city with its law, and much more strongly. For all human laws get sustenance from the one divine law.

It is confusing to call both the pattern of natural events and the commands of legislators laws. But to Heraclitus both are expressions of the inherent and fitting balance of things. Neither the one nor the other is thought of as a command. Divinity does not ordain the behavior of nature; rather,

> God is day, night, winter, summer, war, peace, fullness, hunger; his changing is as
> when oil, being mixed with aromatics, is named after the scent of each.

God *is* nature—an intelligible whole, not a separate directing intelligence.
Heraclitus shared Xenophanes' contempt for popular religion.

> In vain they purify themselves with blood from blood pollution—as if a man who
> stepped into mud washed it off with mud . . . And they pray to these statues, like
> people talking to houses—not at all recognizing what gods and heroes are.

## Fire

Furthermore, nature is basically fire. This identification seems to have been
meant both literally and figuratively. Fire was the universal stuff for Heraclitus as
air was for Anaximenes and water for Thales: everything either is fire or can be
converted into it or made from it.

> All things are exchanged for fire and fire for all things, just as for gold merchandise
> and for merchandise gold.

Heraclitus would have to admit that all things likewise are exchangeable for water
or air or earth: there is a cycle of 'turnings' from fire to earth and back again. The
primacy of fire stems from its vivid immediate presentation of the tension and
activity, the 'life', without which all things would pass away. Heraclitus solemnly
summed up his world view thus:

> This cosmos did none of gods or men make, but it was always and is and will be ever-
> living fire, kindling in measures and going out in measures.

Here Heraclitus explicitly rejects an idea common to all his predecessors: that the
complexity of the world has evolved from an original simplicity. He had to deny
evolution. The Milesian story was of a time when opposites did not exist and of
development from that state into a condition where many different things persist,
including opposites which are independent of each other: there are hot things and
cold things, and if all the cold things were destroyed the hot things would still be
left. Both the beginning and end of the evolutionary process thus are irreconcilable with the Heraclitean Logos, which demands a 'steady-state' universe. Every
particular thing is a balance of tensions, in unstable equilibrium, like the opposed
forearms of Indian wrestlers. Hence sooner or later every particular thing must
change, but "in measures." Every change must be balanced by an opposite change;
and God, the cosmos, the all-embracing ever-living fire, cannot change—*it* has no
opposite.

## The Soul

In the Ionian tradition of explaining the human animal as a *microcosmos*—'little
world', a summation in miniature of the elements and forces of the universe—
Heraclitus declared the soul to be fire. The doctrine accords with the clammy

coldness of corpses (about which he made what every right-thinking tomb-tending Greek must have deemed his most outrageous remark: they are "more fit to be thrown away than turds"). Hence "it is death for souls to become water" and "a dry soul is wisest and best." Drunkenness is deplorable, for "a man when he is drunk is led by a beardless boy, stumbling, not noticing where he goes, having his soul wet." Alcohol wets the soul though plain water does not, it seems.

Heraclitus denounced many other varieties of wrongdoing, all of which are due in the end to human stupidity in not apprehending the Logos. This teaching, that vice ultimately is nothing but ignorance, is fundamental in Greek ethics.

# 5

---

# The Eleatics

ELEA (OR VELIA) WAS a city on the southern Italian coast founded about 535 B.C. by Greeks driven out of Corsica by the Carthaginians. Xenophanes lived there for a time; there is probably some connection between his "one god" and the emphasis on the unity of Being in the philosophy of the two most eminent Eleatics.

## Parmenides

Parmenides was born about 515 B.C. and lived until after the middle of the fifth century. He became a philosopher through the teaching of Ameinias, a Pythagorean who "though poor was a gentleman." (Nothing more is known about Ameinias.) While still a young man, however, Parmenides developed a philosophy of his own, severely critical of certain Pythagorean beliefs. Following the precedent set by Xenophanes, he set it out in Greek epic verses.

The poem is in three parts. The first is a prologue (preserved complete) relating in elaborate images how the poet is conveyed in a chariot drawn by "immortal and very intelligent mares" and guided by the Daughters of the Sun to the heavenly palace of "the goddess." This personage welcomes him graciously and outlines the instructions he is to receive:

1.  . . . It is proper for you to learn everything, both the unshaking heart of well-rounded truth and on the other hand mortal beliefs in which there is no true assurance.[1]

The second and third parts, called (by later editors) *On Truth* and *On Belief*, contain this instruction. Although only meager fragments of *On Belief* survive, we have *On Truth* almost intact. Nevertheless, it presents some of the most vexing problems of interpretation in all of philosophy. Many scholars would not accept the following account; see the end-of-chapter note.

## On Truth

The order in which the fragments of *On Truth* are here presented is probably though not certainly correct. The translation attempts to be literal, but it should be borne in mind that every translation—especially of an ancient document—is an interpretation.

2. Come, listen and carry the story away: I will tell you what the only ways of inquiry are for thinking. The one way, that it is, and it cannot not be—that is the path of persuasion, for truth attends it. The other way that it is not and there is a necessity for it not to be—that I tell you is a byway absolutely not to be looked into. For you could neither recognize Not-being—that is not possible—nor tell about it.

3. For to think and to be are the same.

4. See how absent things are nevertheless steadfastly present to thought. For you shall not cut off Being from cleaving to Being, neither scattering itself every which way through the cosmos, nor crowding together.

5. It is all one to me where I start out from; for I shall come back there again.

6. It is required to say and to think that Being exists. For it can be, but nothingness is not possible—these points I direct you to consider. For I prohibit you from going on that first way of inquiry. But then also avoid that one on which know-nothing mortals wander—two-headed, since incompetence guides the rambling awareness in their breasts. They are carried along blind and deaf, muddled undiscriminating types, who take it for granted that to be and not to be are the same and also not the same. The path of them all is backward-turning.

7. For this shall never be proved: Not-being is. You must keep your thought off this road of inquiry. By no means let habit, from much experience, force you to drive your unseeing eye and echoing ear and tongue down this road. But judge by reason (Logos) the very controversial argument that I present.

8. Just one account is left of the road that is. Along the road are indeed many signs that being ungenerated it is also imperishable. For it is whole of limb, unshaking, and without goal. It never *was*, nor *will* it be, since it *is, now*, whole, one, continuous. For what generation of it will you seek? How and from what did it start? I will in no way allow you to say or think "from Not-being." For it is neither sayable nor thinkable that it should not be. And what necessity would have driven it to grow, later or sooner, starting from nothingness? Thus it is necessary that either it completely is, or is not at all. Never will convincing force allow that from Not-being anything but itself can arise. On this account Justice has not relaxed the leg-irons and allowed for generation and destruction; she holds fast. Here is the decision about these matters: it is or it is not. But then it has been decided, as is necessary, to abandon the second alternative as unthinkable and unnameable, for it is no true way. The other, that it is, has been decided to be the real way. But how could what is, perish afterwards? How could it come into being? For if it came into being, it would not *be*, nor if it were going to exist sometime. Therefore coming-into-being is extinguished and perishing is not to be asked about.

Nor is it divisible, since it is all alike. Nor is there somewhat more of it in some place, which might keep it from holding together; nor is there somewhat less of it somewhere else. But the whole is full of Being. So it is all continuous: Being draws close to Being.

Motionless within the bonds of great chains it is beginningless, unstopping, since coming-into-being and perishing have been driven far away—true confidence expelled them. The same, staying in the same place, by itself, it lies, and thus it remains secure. For mighty Necessity keeps it in the chains of limit that confines it round about, because it is not fitting that Being should be incomplete. For it is not in need. If it were, it would need everything.

Thinking, and what thought is for, are the same. For you will not find thought without Being, inside which it is, once having been uttered. For nothing else exists or will exist outside Being, since Fate has put it in leg-irons to be whole and unmoving. Names for it will be all the following, such as mortals have postulated, persuaded that they are true: coming-into-being and perishing; being and not being; and changing place and exchange of bright color.

But since there is an outermost limit, it is complete from every direction, like the mass of a well-rounded ball equally balanced in every direction from the middle. For it is necessary that there be neither somewhat more nor somewhat less here or there. For neither is there Not-being that would put a stop to its meeting its like; nor is there Being of a sort that might be more here or less there than Being, since it is all safe from violence. For being equal from every direction, it lies uniformly within limits.

This concludes *On Truth*.

## On Belief

*On Belief* begins

At this point I stop confident speech and thought for you about truth. From here on learn mortal beliefs, listening to the deceitful arrangement of my words.

For they set their minds to name two forms, of which one form is not necessary—here they have gone astray. They distinguished the opposites in appearance and assigned signs separated from each other: to one, the ethereal fire of flame, being weak, very light, in every direction the same as itself, but not the same as the other. But that other also is in itself opposite, thick in appearance and heavy.

I am telling you this whole plausible world-view in order that no mortal mind may ever get ahead of you.

A dozen brief fragments indicate that the goddess taught Parmenides beliefs of mortals concerning embryology, physiology, and psychology of sex; the naming of things, the structure of the cosmos, and astronomy—including the first recorded mention of the discovery that the moon shines by reflected sunlight.

## Being

This poem is in form a report of a divine revelation—like the *Theogony* of Hesiod, supposedly written under the inspiration of the Muses. We must not be deceived by this literary convention. Real goddesses do not argue, but this one supports her pronouncements with a *very controversial argument* and lambastes those who think otherwise as "two-headed know-nothings" and so on. The dialectic that began with Anaximander's objections to Thales here rises to a new intensity. The goddess (again unlike real goddesses) explicitly appeals to Reason (Logos). Moreover, the doctrine that she wants to establish has nothing to do with the existence or action of divinities—Fate, Justice, and Necessity are conventional personifications, not persons—and indeed for the first time in Greek thinking about the cosmos the very notion of the divine is not invoked at all.

What does the goddess teach as the Truth? That Being or Reality is ungenerated, imperishable, one, continuous, indivisible, motionless, beginningless, unstopping, the same everywhere, complete from every direction, and the same as thought. And what is her very controversial argument? That Being could not be generated, for two reasons. First, since Being is all there is, it would have to be generated out of what there is not, which is absurd. Second, waiving the first point and supposing that Being could come from nothingness, there could be no reason why this event should occur at one time rather than any other—so it could not occur.

The principle underlying the second argument is just the same as what Anaximander used to show why the earth though unsupported does not move: there must be a reason why things happen as they do—the Principle of Sufficient Reason. So if there *cannot* be any reason why something should go one way rather than another, it *cannot* go at all. The first argument appeals to another form of Sufficient Reason, the Principle of Causality: every real thing must have a real cause. From this the goddess concludes that reality cannot just pop up out of nothing—nothingness by definition not being a real thing.

What then is Being? Leaving aside for the moment its sameness to thought, we note that the adjectives with which the goddess describes it indicate that it is an eternal and undifferentiated continuum. It was of course not a new thought to Parmenides that the fundamental basis of all things had to be of this sort. Thales' water, after all, was (at least to begin with) all the same kind, and Anaximander's Boundless even more so, we might say. Anaximenes with his thickening and thinning tried to introduce some internal differentiation; he is the obvious target of the goddess' pronouncement that there cannot be "more here and less there." Now it will be remembered that the Pythagoreans, while retaining much from Anaximenes, had tried to improve on his story by adding an explicit account of a beginning of things: it happened when "the Unit inhaled the Void." (The Unit brings in the mathematical nature of reality; the Void was probably conceived as a very refined Anaximenean *air*.) Void is Not-being, Nothingness—or so Parmenides' goddess deems it—a thought that spurs her to divine fury in denouncing those who believe that something can come from nothing, "that Being and Not-being are the same and not the same," as she sarcastically formulates it in a double self-contradiction.

Returning now to the sameness of Being with thought, this too is no novelty. All of Parmenides' predecessors had incorporated a rational element into the ground of things: Thales said that "All things are full of gods," Anaximander said the Boundless "steers all things," Anaximenes' air was the soul of the world, Heraclitus' Logos and Xenophanes' god functioned similarly to ensure that things form a cosmos not a chaos. Anaximenes indeed had explicitly identified the macrocosmic thinking of air with the microcosmic thinking of each human being, and this idea may be implicit in the others as well.

Parmenides was thus in these important respects a continuator of what was already an established tradition. What was his contribution?

First, he thought rigorously. If the world has an underlying unity, it must be a real unity, not concealing within itself any diversity at all. And if nothing can come from nothing, this fact must not be bypassed by calling nothingness by another name—Void or Air. And if the cosmos is rational, its rationality—which we know directly in our thinking—must be built into the most fundamental level of Being, not outside it, as in the myths of the gods, or half-in-half-out, as in Xenophanes' god and the Pythagorean Unit. So fundamental reality must be absolutely homogeneous, admitting no internal differentiation of any kind. And it must not be merely "steered" by thought, it must *be* thought.

Second, and more important for the subsequent history of science and philosophy, Parmenides reflected on knowledge itself—on the kinds of things we know and the ways we have of knowing them. While Pythagoras is said to have sacrificed a hundred oxen in celebration of discovering the Pythagorean Theorem, it remained for his Eleatic critic to apprehend its full significance: an eternal truth had become *known.* An eternal truth, for it was discovered, not invented, and had been true and would continue to be true forever—though there was a time when no human being knew it and there will be a time again when nobody any longer knows it. And now, after Pythagoras' proof, known *with certainty*—not merely used successfully as had the Egyptians and others. How was it grasped? By pure Logos, the mind's eye seeing it without owing anything to the eyes in the face, which could be deceived. Pythagoras sat down and thought deeply, but also he observed the sky, listened to plucked strings, and diagnosed diseases by tasting bodily fluids. In all these ways he swelled his "vast learning," without troubling to make systematic distinctions in ways of knowing. But the goddess commands Parmenides to reject his "unseeing eye and echoing ear and tongue" and instead "judge by Logos." That alone can yield certain knowledge.

Knowledge of what? What are the eternal truths, known by pure thought, *about?* Points, lines, circles, triangles . . . *geometry.* The word means earth measurement; but of course the study is not bound to particular plots of land, or land at all. It is, as *we* should say, the science of the metrics of space.

Now let us take another look at the list of the characteristics of Being: ungenerated, imperishable, one, continuous, motionless, beginningless, unstopping, equally balanced in every direction from the middle, and the same as thought. Except for the sameness to thought, what this list applies to, and the only thing it applies to, is *space. The Being of Parmenides is space that is the same as thought.*

This may seem a strange or even unintelligible conclusion, but it can be clarified.

If the goddess is talking about space, why doesn't she say so? one may ask. The reason is that the Greeks had words for room, place, extent, distance, emptiness, and so on—but no word that we would translate as *space* in the scientific sense. Parmenides grasped the concept but lacked a word. Since his notion is, as we have seen, a development continuous with his predecessors' thoughts about fundamental Being, he uses their word.

But how can anyone seriously maintain that all that is real is homogeneous, motionless, empty space? Obviously reality is full of diversity and frantic motion. First, let us expunge the word 'empty'. Parmenides thinks and writes of Being as *full.* Full of what? Of Being! Next let us remember that this Being is *fundamental* reality, which does not preclude the existence of derivative forms. Thales thought that fundamentally everything was—and is—water, but that did not prevent dust from being dry. Chariots, goddesses, and Parmenides himself are diverse, generated, and moving. This does not mean they are unreal; it does mean, however, that they are not real all by themselves. They are modifications of what *is* real all by itself, and that is space.

Now let us come to grips with what may seem the strangest feature of all, the identity of space and thought. Preliminarily it may help to note that at the present day certain Indian philosophers hold that space thinks.

It is likely that Parmenides based his teaching on another assumption embedded in Greek thought, which we shall see was stated explicitly in the philosophy of Empedocles (*ca* 490–430 B.C.; see Chapter 6), another Italian Greek, a few years later: that when somebody knows something, knower and object of knowledge must have something in common. Now what is known best of all is Being, which is space. That is to say, space is the most intelligible thing there is. Therefore, it must have something in common with thought. But nothing is like thinking except thinking itself. So space must think, in some sense. The conclusion is perhaps reinforced by the reflection that space, the matrix of all the particulars, sets them in order—the essential work of intelligence. (This reconstruction of Parmenides' reasoning is entirely speculative, but it acquires some corroboration from the fact that Plato and Aristotle, as we shall see, explicitly argued that what knows eternal truths must itself be eternal.)

Now what about particular things—heavenly bodies, boys and girls, goddesses, Parmenides—that come and go? They get no mention in *Truth* except by implication in the remark that "coming-into-being and perishing, being and not being, and changing place and exchange of bright color," which apply to them, are "names for it [Being] such as mortals have postulated, persuaded that they are true." If we are right, this is the goddess' way of declaring that the reality of particulars lies in their spatial-metrical properties—a view which, whether or not it began here, has a long history that is not yet over. As for their other characteristics—the bright colors, the coming-into-being and perishing that (so to speak) flesh them out—these can be recognized only by the "unseeing eye and ringing ear," which do not yield "true confidence" but only "mortal beliefs." While the goddess does not say that such beliefs are false, she does downgrade them to cognitive inferiority. No certainty can be reached about them. They constitute a realm of brute fact, not to be brought under the sway of the Principle of Sufficient Reason. In other words, there is not and cannot be any *science* of particulars. Since particulars are what make up nature, the alleged science of which is physics, Parmenides is declaring scientific physics—the quest of all his predecessors—to be forever impossible. Reality is indeed one and indivisible (*i.e.* there is only one Space, from which no part can be subtracted) and thoroughly intelligible. But as to its particular modifications, we can do no better than wager on the basis of past performance. The goddess, when she gets to them, "stops confident speech." This is the crisis that Parmenides bequeathed to his philosophical successors.

The genesis of the crisis lies in Parmenides' reflection on knowing. He was the first to make a clear distinction between knowledge on the one hand derived from pure reason, which yields certainty about how things *must* be, what they *necessarily* are; and on the other hand tentative 'beliefs' based on experience, which are never certain since further experience may force their revision or abandonment. This is the basic distinction in Theory of Knowledge or *epistemology*. Furthermore, according to Parmenides, the two ways of knowing have different objects: on the one hand *necessary being*, fundamental reality, *substance*; on the other hand derivative being—arrangements, modifications, or mere appearances of the fundamental reality. This is the fundamental distinction in Theory of Being or *ontology*. Since epistemology and ontology together constitute metaphysics, the core discipline of philosophy, Parmenides has a strong claim to be considered the founder of philosophy.

## Zeno

Not unexpectedly, the Pythagoreans made fun of Parmenides' very controversial proof. What they said we do not know, but we do know what was retorted. Parmenides, though he founded no institution, had as a disciple a man 25 years younger, Zeno of Elea (*ca* 495–*ca* 430 B.C.), who was endowed with incomparable critical sharpness.

Zeno wrote a book defending his master by showing that the Pythagorean account of things and of space as consisting of a 'many'—that is to say an aggregate of units or 'numbers'—led to the absurd consequence that nothing ever moves. The book is lost, but references in Aristotle's writings allow us to reconstruct four arguments.

If space is made up of units—if there is some fundamental thing the repetition of which is space—then some particular stretch of space, say a distance of a hundred yards, must consist of either a finite or an infinite quantity of those units laid out one after the other. If this quantity is infinite, motion cannot occur, as Zeno shows by two arguments:

*Achilles and the Tortoise*   If Achilles, the fleetest of all runners, races with a tortoise that has a head start, Achilles can never pass it nor even quite catch up. For Achilles must first reach the position the tortoise occupied at the start, by which time the tortoise will be some distance ahead. When Achilles completes that distance, the tortoise will again be a certain length ahead. And so ad infinitum, Achilles continually reaching places where the tortoise *was* but never where the tortoise *is*. Since by the hypothesis there are an infinite number of such places, Achilles can never get through all of them, as he must if he is to catch up with the tortoise. It is impossible to go step by step through an infinite series to the end, for by definition there is no end.

*The Stadium*   Moreover, motion can never even get started. Suppose you set out to run from one end of a stadium to the other. Before you can get to the opposite end, you must pass the halfway mark. But before then, the quarter mark. Before that, the one-eighth mark; and so ad infinitum. Before passing any mark you choose, however close to the starting point, you must first have passed, in succession, an infinite number of marks still nearer to the starting point—which means you can never start at all.

Therefore, if a finite space consists of an infinite number of units, motion is impossible. But of course motion is not impossible. Therefore, a finite space cannot consist of an infinite number of units.

Zeno had also a more straightforward argument against infinity of units: the units must have either no size or some size. If they have no size, then even an infinity of them cannot add up to a finite size: no amount of nothing equals something. But if the units have each a size, however small, an infinity of them will make an infinite size.

Consequently, because these arguments have shown the impossibility of space consisting of an infinity of unit spaces, the hypothesis that space is a 'many' reduces to this: space consists of units of finite size, 'grains' we might call them. Zeno next showed that this hypothesis also lead to the impossibility of motion.

*The Arrow*   "The flying arrow is at rest." Let A–E be a (much magnified) representation of part of the path of a flying arrow. AB, BC, and so forth are the grains of which it consists, according to the hypothesis. Each has a left edge, a right edge, and a midpoint; this follows from the supposition that each *has* some extension, tiny though it be.

The tip of the flying arrow is at the grain BC. If it is to reach the end of the path it must successively be at the grains CD and then DE. But how is it to move from BC to CD? Since these are grains, spatial minima, there can be no movement

*within* either one. That is, the arrow cannot move from the middle of BC to the right edge of BC—which is also the left edge of CD—and onward to the middle of CD, and so on. It must 'jerk' from BC to CD *in no time at all*—for if it takes time to make this transition, it will be moving *within* a grain. Nevertheless, the arrow *does* fly from A to E, and it takes time to do so. How is this time consumed? Since the jerks take no time, the time must be spent by the arrow *resting* first at AB and then after an instantaneous jerk resting again at BC, and so on. *There is never a time, no matter how short, when the arrow is not resting.*

Strictly speaking, this argument does not show that if there is a many made of finite elements, then motion is impossible—only that every motion is made up of a sum of nonmotions. That, however, is almost as great an affront to common sense.

Consideration of Zeno's fourth argument, *The Racecourse*, is omitted, as its reconstruction from Aristotle's brief and ambiguous description is difficult and controversial. It is fairly clear that it aimed to show an actual contradiction in the notion of a grainy many.

Thus did Zeno "pay back with interest" the jeers of Parmenides' detractors by "showing that their own views led to even more ridiculous conclusions."[2] His form of argument, *reduction to absurdity*—which shows that there must be something wrong with opponents' views because when reasoning from them logically one can deduce a contradiction or other obviously false conclusion—is a potent weapon. The so-called paradoxes, which are valid arguments of this form, to this day are (or ought to be) embarrassments to those who assume a many, such as mathematicians who conceive of lines as ordered sets of points (rather than as paths of moving points).

## Note

The account of Parmenides given here has an ancestry going back at least to Simplicius (sixth century A.D.), the philosopher who preserved most of *On Truth* for us. Nevertheless, it is radically at variance with the kind of interpretation that currently may be called standard, *i.e.* accepted by the majority of scholars. The following is a sketch of the standard interpretation.

The difference between *On Truth* and *On Belief* is absolute. Everything in the former is put forth by Parmenides as the truth; everything in the latter is certified to be false—indeed, a journey down the Path of Not-being that the goddess at the outset forbade Parmenides to set foot on. (Accounts differ as to what Parmenides' point was in writing the lengthy and detailed *On Belief* if it contained nothing but falsehoods.) What *On Truth* tells us about reality is that it is ungenerated, indestructible, unchanging, homogeneous, and spherical. The only real world, therefore, consists of a homogeneous undifferentiated sphere. (Whether this sphere is material, or is in some sense ideal, is not agreed.) All differentiation and change, including all forms of motion, are nothing but illusion. (Thus neither the goddess nor Parmenides himself can really exist.)

These conclusions are reached (we are told) as results of rigorous logical argumentation: Parmenides was the father of logic and held that we must in every case prefer its conclusions over beliefs taught by the (illusory) senses. Accounts of what the actual argument was differ from interpreter to interpreter; the following is typical.

Such remarks as "you could neither recognize Not-being . . . nor tell about it" and "nothingness is not possible" indicate that Parmenides held a thesis about language to the effect that negative judgments are meaningless. That is, if I say that A is not B, I am trying to say something like "A, with respect to B, is Not-being"; but as there cannot be any Not-being, the statement fails to make sense. (In the document supposedly devoted to expounding this view there are almost as many negative as positive judgments.) Moreover, if I say that A is B, I can mean nothing other than that A is identical with B; for instance, "Thales is wise" must mean "Thales is identical with wisdom."

From these suppositions it follows, first, that there can be only one thing; for if there were two, A and B, then it would be true that A is not B—but that, Parmenides is supposed to have held, is not even meaningful. Secondly, whatever properties the one thing has, it has (or rather, is) forever and changelessly.

In the standard interpretation, the goddess sums up the conclusion of this reasoning with "Mere names therefore will be all the following: . . . coming-into-being and perishing, being and not being, and changing place and exchange of bright color." (In text we render this passage as "Names for it will be all the following: . . ." Either translation is possible, since the same Greek word means both "therefore" and "for it"; however, there is nothing in the Greek corresponding to "mere," which the carefuller standard interpreters therefore write as "(mere)".)

With regard to Zeno, the standard interpretation holds that his 'paradoxes' are straightforward attempts to show that pure reason can prove the impossibility of motion, which is therefore mere illusion.

Readers interested in pursuing the subject further should consult Volume I of Sir W. K. C. Guthrie's monumental *History of Greek Philosophy* for the standard interpretation. The view taken here is presented more fully and defended in two papers by the author, "Parmenides Unbound" and "Eleatic Motions," in the journal *Philosophical Inquiry*, 1980 and 1984 respectively. A more accessible account, the basis of this interpretation, is in Chapter 5 of Giorgio di Santillana's *The Origins of Scientific Thought*.

# 6

# Empedocles

EMPEDOCLES OF ACRAGAS (now Agrigento), a city on the southern coast of Sicily, was of the next generation after Parmenides; 490–430 B.C. is a reasonable guess at his dates.

He wrote two poems: one *On Nature*, the other called *Purifications*. The latter begins with a charming address to the poet's fellow citizens.

> Friends, who dwell in golden Acragas, down below in the great city and upon the heights, dedicated to good works, cordial hosts to strangers, unacquainted with meanness, hail.[1]

Empedocles then introduces himself.

> I, an immortal god, no longer subject to death, walk around among you all, honored fittingly with garland crowns and flowery leis. Whenever I enter the prosperous towns with these men and women, I am held in reverence: they follow me, countless numbers, asking me what is the shortcut to riches; some demand prophecies, others seek to hear the word that heals all kinds of diseases, for long indeed have they been stabbed by pains hard to bear. . . .
>
> But why should I take any notice of such things, as if I were doing something great just because I surpass mortal men who perish in many ways?

If this sounds smug to modern taste, the remaining autobiographical fragments convey an opposite impression equally excessive perhaps in self-pity.

> There is an utterance of Necessity, an ancient decree of the gods, eternal, sealed with broad oaths: whenever one of them—the demigods who are allotted eon-long life—defiles his dear limbs sinfully with murder, or swearing a false oath follows Strife, thirty thousand seasons must he wander apart from the blessed, through this time being born in all the forms of mortal beings and exchanging the wearisome paths of life. For the power of air pursues him into the sea, but the sea spits him out on to dry land, earth then into the rays of the blazing sun, which throws him into the tornadoes of the air. Of these I too now am one, a fugitive from the gods and a wanderer, who trusted insane Strife.
>
> For already once I was a boy and a girl and a bush and a bird and a dumb salt-water fish. . . .
>
> I cried and wailed when I saw the unfamiliar place.
>
> Alas that the pitiless day did not destroy me sooner, before I conceived of the wretched business of devouring flesh through my lips!

The two violently contrasting tones are not inconsistent, for Empedocles is near the end of his 10,000-year stretch of punishment ( = 30,000 seasons: the Greek year was divided into spring, summer, and winter), and

> toward the end they go among earthly men as prophets and song-writers and doctors and princes; from there they ascend as gods exalted with honors, sharing fireplace and table with the other immortals, exempt from human aches, untiring.

Empedocles was, as we might have expected, a prophet, song-writer, doctor, and prince.

This tale of the soul's wanderings through the cycle of rebirths, the appointed punishment for the sin of cannibalism (for all living things are akin), is orthodox Pythagoreanism, down to the impassioned exclamation

> Wretches, utter wretches, keep your hands off beans!

Indeed, it is the earliest surviving detailed account of these beliefs.


## On Nature

Empedocles' importance in the history of thought, however, comes not from his Pythagorean raptures but from the account of the cosmic cycle in his other poem, *On Nature*. Here the influence of Parmenides is decisive. In almost the very words of the sage of Elea, Empedocles denounces believers in real generation and destruction.

> Children they are—for they do not carry their thoughts any distance—who hope that what before was not real can come into being, or that anything can die and perish altogether. For coming into being, out of what is in no way real, cannot happen, and the perishing of what is real is impossible and unheard of.

Both this and the like remarks of Parmenides were aimed at the Pythagorean vision of the world's originating when the Unit "inhaled the Void"—the only instance ever of Greeks denying the principle Nothing from nothing. Parmenides concluded that what is real, being the same as what can be known with certainty, must be the objects of mathematical truths, which do not come into being or pass away or move. But Empedocles, continuing the passage just cited, says

> For it will always be there, wherever anyone puts it.

Empedocles' reality, then, can be moved, although

> Of the whole, no part is either empty or too full

—that is, as with Parmenides the reality is coextensive with space and is not 'thickened and thinned'.

To learn more about reality, we are not to follow Parmenides and determine by reason ignoring the senses. On the contrary,

> Come on, consider with all your cunning, whichever way each thing is clear. Do not trust something more because you see it than because you hear it. Do not put loud

sound above the revelations of your tongue. Do not refuse trust to any other organ whereby there is an opening for intelligence, but get understanding of each thing in the way appropriate for making that thing clear.

Parmenides found Truth only in what pure reason grasps; about changing things moving in space we could do no better than make plausible guesses. But Empedocles, who as we have already seen was not temperamentally inclined to be skeptical, reaffirms the possibility of acquiring genuine knowledge of the world through eyes, ears, tongue, and other sense organs. The possibility of physics, science of nature, is reaffirmed.

## The Roots and The World Cycle

This is Empedocles' world picture in brief: there is not one basic stuff but four "roots of all things"—earth, air, fire, and water—of which all changing and perishing particulars are mixtures in various proportions. Besides the roots there are two forces: Affection, which mingles the roots, and Strife, which tends to separate them. The cosmic process recurs in cycles. At one time, the "reign of Affection," the world is a sphere consisting of all the roots thoroughly mixed together, only the force of Strife being outside. But Strife enters and begins the work of separation. At its completion, the "reign of Strife," the four roots exist in their pure states—apart from each other—forming a sphere now having earth at its core and covered by successive layers of water, air, and fire. Then Affection begins to take over once more to complete the circle of existence and initiate another turn. The present state of the world is one in which Strife is gaining over Affection.

This account marks an advance in clarity and definiteness of explanation. To understand why, let us reexamine what went before.

## A Brief Review

In myths, especially when the origins of things are pictured in sexual terms, anything may produce anything. In the serious scientific kind of account initiated by the Milesians, if B is said to originate from A it is up to the philosopher making the claim to show how A can produce B without violating the principle Nothing from nothing. In some sense, that is, B must already be in A, must indeed be a sort of A or part of A. The earliest scientific criticism, that of Thales by Anaximander, is a complaint that this condition has not been properly satisfied. If everything comes from water, then dust must come from water. But dust is essentially dry, while water is just wetness, by no means fitted to produce dryness.

Anaximander tried to make his own system immune to this kind of attack by conceiving the Boundless to be of no particular quality yet containing within it all the qualities, or at any rate something capable of producing them. If, however, it was thought of as simply a mixture of them all, it could hardly be said to explain anything: it is easy but uninformative to say of a thing that it originated by separating out of a mixture containing it. On the other hand, if the Boundless was not merely a mixture, what was it? To call it "capable of generating the opposites," without further specification of what made it capable, would be to offer only an empty verbal formula.

Anaximenes succeeded in providing a definite answer to the question how one stuff could be the origin of all things. Everything is air, he held, the different properties of things being due to the thickening or thinning of the air of which they are composed. This idea that one stuff can exist in several states corresponding to different observed characteristics is valid and at the base of scientific explanation as we understand it today. Indeed the views of Anaximenes persisted in more or less unchanged form for two centuries after his death. If they did not achieve permanent acceptance, the reason was not that their author failed to grasp the essentials of explanatory form but that his particular account was implausible in its details. There seem to be more differences between fire and air, wood and water, than differences in density or thickness can account for.

Viewed from this angle, Empedocles' four-roots theory appears as what results from denying the possibility of reducing all things to one basic stuff. Greek pre-scientific common sense took for granted four world masses, differing at least in appearance. Empedocles was then in a way fashioning common sense into scientific philosophy. But his pondering over the dialectic of Parmenides made him a more profound thinker than that description suggests.

Parmenides stimulated Empedocles to think about what precisely is involved in the conception of change. When Empedocles eats a loaf of bread, which thereupon becomes part of the bones and flesh that make up Empedocles, nothing can really have vanished and nothing can really have come into being. But the bread was brown, porous, moist, and hot; Empedocles' fingernail is yellowish-translucent, dense, and cool. What happened to the brown? Where did the yellow come from? *We* should begin our explanation by distinguishing between a thing and its qualities; so, we shall see, would some Greeks—later, however, than Empedocles. The Sicilian did not question the common-sense assumption that a thing simply is all its (what we should call) qualities: bread simply is the brown plus the porous plus the moist plus the hot, and so on. These are its constituents, which must be accounted for if change is not irrational.

## Mixtures and Evolution

Empedocles' solution was simple and elegant. He assumed that there are a limited number of fundamental quality-stuffs and that the vast variety of things in the world can be accounted for as mixtures of the fundamentals—as all the thousands of colors can be made from mixing a few pigments (but not from just *one* hue). Bright-dark, hot-cold, thick-thin, wet-dry—from these pairs of qualities, essential constituents of the four roots, all other kinds can be derived as combinations. For instance (Empedocles' own examples), bone is made of one part earth, one part water, and two parts fire. Flesh and blood contain all four in nearly equal proportion, the difference due to a slight excess or deficiency of earth.

No mixture endures. But mixture and separation go on in a patterned manner according to the stage of the world cycle. Animal forms, including the human, evolve in two ways. In the period when Affection is gaining over Strife, parts of animals are spontaneously generated in the earth.

> Many heads grew up neckless, and naked arms wandered around lacking shoulders, and eyes rambled destitute of foreheads.

Affection unites them, mostly into monsters.

> Many grew with faces and breasts on both sides; offspring of cattle had human faces, and again ox-headed human beings.

Only a few survived who happened to fit together so as to be able to nourish and reproduce themselves. In the transitional period from the reign of Affection to that of Strife (such as our age), however, "undifferentiated creatures" arise from the earth, "not yet displaying the lovely form of limbs, nor the voice and organ appropriate to men." These spherical bisexual beings are later split into individuals of the modern type by the further working of Strife.

These fantasies contain the germ idea of survival of the fittest but are inferior to the soberer evolutionary theory of Anaximander. Indeed not only in its details but in its leading concepts, Empedocles' thought is somewhat in the direction of a reversion to mythmaking. The cosmic force of Affection—which he often refers to as "Aphrodite" and which he explicitly equates to human sexual desire—leads us almost back to the "begat" type of world origins.

## The Human Animal

Empedocles was a doctor, and his immediate influence was more on medicine than on philosophy or science in general—although the distinctive feature of Empedoclean medicine was that it purported to be based on philosophical principles. Like other philosophers, Empedocles held that a human being is a microcosm, and thus composed of the four roots. Disease, he held, consists always in disproportion among the roots; therefore, treatment should aim at restoring balance. Feverish patients should consequently be plunged into cold baths. This kind of premature theorizing elicited an angry protest from the Ionian doctors who based their prescriptions on careful observations and long experience.

> All who, on attempting to speak or to write on medicine, have assumed for themselves a hypothesis as a basis for their discussion—heat, cold, moisture, dryness, or anything else that they may fancy—who narrow down the causal principle of diseases and of death among men, and make it the same in all cases, postulating one thing or two, all these obviously blunder. . . .[2]

But as in many parallel cases, the protest was probably more valid against disciples than against the master. Empedocles made scientific studies in physiology, especially in respiration, though he supposed wrongly that we breathe through the pores of the skin as well as through the nostrils. As far as we know, he was the first to recognize that perception requires an explanation: how is it that we gain information about the world outside us through our sense organs? His answer for vision is that

> By earth we see earth, by water water, by air bright air, by fire destructive fire; affection by affection, and strife by dreadful strife.

That is to say, sensation occurs when a portion of one root contacts another of the same. The pores of the eye are of a size to let fire, *i.e.* light, pass through to the light within while keeping out water.

The problem arises: how can *On Nature*, which insists that all mixtures are unstable and perishable, be reconciled with the *Purifications*, which teaches the transmigration and therefore the immortality of the soul? The only possible solution seems to be that the soul is not a mixture; and if it is not a mixture, by elimination we arrive at the conclusion that the soul is a piece of Affection—of which Empedocles sang

> Look upon her with your mind, do not sit with eyes in a daze: her we recognize as implanted in the parts of mortals. By her influence we think kind thoughts and work in concord, calling her by the names of Joy and Aphrodite.

# 7

# Anaxagoras

THE NAME OF ATHENS is synonymous with philosophy, yet philosophy arrived there late and encountered opposition that it met nowhere else in Greece.

Its arrival was possibly a by-product of the all-out attempt by Xerxes, Shah of Iran (Persia) to subjugate mainland Greece and especially Athens. At any rate Anaxagoras (*ca* 500–*ca* 428 B.C.), a young man of about 20, turned up in Athens around the time of Xerxes' defeat. He was a citizen of the Ionian city of Clazomenae, which as subject of the Iranian empire was obliged to draft soldiers for the army, from which naturally they deserted to the Athenians when they could.

## Miletus Comes to Athens

What Anaxagoras brought to Athens was the world view of the Milesians. The earth, he taught, is a flat disk at the center of the cosmic whirl—only one among a large, perhaps infinite number of such whirls—for

> . . . we must suppose that . . . men have been formed elsewhere too, and the other animals that have life, and that these men have inhabited cities and cultivated fields as with us; and that they have a sun and a moon and the rest as with us; and that their earth brings forth for them many things of all kinds of which they gather the best together into their dwellings, and use them.[1]

Our world and every other whirl is the result of separation by centrifugal force from an initially homogeneous mixture.

> But before they were separated, when all things were together, no color at all was clear; for the mixture of all things prevented it: of the wet and the dry, the hot and the cold, the bright and the dark; and because of much earth in it and seeds unlimited in multitude, no one like any other.

The picture suggested is of a dim, tepid, moist, brown, dirty vastness quietly suspended in space.

What, more precisely, are the "things" and "seeds" that go into this mixture? *We* may be puzzled by a list that includes "the wet" and "the bright" (qualities) and "earth" (substance) all on the same level, but neither Anaxagoras nor any of his predecessors made this kind of distinction. A stuff just *was* its characteristics: water *was* 'the wet and cold', fire *was* 'the hot and dry'. "All things . . . together" was a chaos of all possible characteristics. We must not suppose, however, that if we cut apart this chaos with a fine knife or studied it with a powerful microscope we would have seen 'the hot' or 'earth' all by itself. It is a distinctive feature of Anaxagoras' system that

> the things in the one cosmos are not separated from one another nor cut apart with an axe, neither the hot from the cold nor the cold from the hot.

But what then are the "seeds, no one like any other" if they are not simple single characteristics? Perhaps the answer is this: Anaxagoras was insisting that nothing is *just* hot, nothing is *merely* bright; everything—however small, however pure—is a complex of characteristics. He held in fact that everything is infinitely complex.

> Everything must be in everything; nor is it possible to be apart, but everything has a part of everything.

This applies not only to the initial chaos but to the present state of affairs as well. Nothing can come from nothing; with uncompromising rigor Anaxagoras interpreted this principle to mean that if bread eaten and digested becomes flesh, then flesh—all the characteristics of flesh—must have been present in the bread from the beginning.

> How can hair come from what is not hair, or flesh from what is not flesh?

Bread is brown and porous, and every crumb however fine is similar. The red of blood nevertheless is in the bread; though

> Our senses, being weak, are unable to discern the truth.

Our insides, not so weak, can extract the blood 'seeds' from the bread. This process, digestion, is not one of reducing the bread to its smallest particles some of which are blood—there are none. It is rather removing these blood characteristics from their fusion with all the others. Thus if there were a loaf of 'pure' bread—breadstuff in which nothing else were fused—we would be unable to tell it from ordinary bread by looking, feeling, or tasting; yet it would not nourish us.

## Mind

The one great exception to the doctrine of mixture, and the second distinctive feature of Anaxagoras' philosophy, concerns Mind.

> In every thing there is a portion of everything except Mind: but there are things with Mind in them also.

And further

> Other things contain a portion of everything, but Mind is boundless and self-ruled and mixed with nothing, but exists alone, itself by itself. For if it did not exist by itself, but were mixed with anything else, it would partake in all things. . . . And the things mixed with it would hinder it and then it would not rule over anything the way it does being one thing by itself. For it is the thinnest of all things and the purest, and it has all knowledge about everything, and the greatest strength. And whatever has life, both bigger and smaller, Mind rules it.

The word translated as Mind, *nous*, has the special connotation of intelligence that grasps the significance of pattern. Like the Affection and Strife of Empedocles, Anaxagoras is here making this intelligence into a cosmic force but more intellectual, as befits an Ionian Greek. Like Empedocles too he is taking his cosmic model from humanity: Mind in us 'knows' us and 'rules' us; so also in the world at large. Though like everything else it is a stuff, it is not 'mixed', fused with anything. If it were, it would "lose its power"—as the black that is in snow is imperceptible, 'powerless' because it is so diluted. Mind, then, is not mixed but "present," and present only in some things, those that have life—for it is the life principle too.

We return now to the initial stagnant mixture of "all things together."

> Mind ruled the revolution of the totality, so that it revolved in the beginning. And first it turned around in a small area, but it revolves over more now and will revolve over still more. And Mind knew all the things mixing and separating and splitting. And how things were going to be and how they were, that do not now exist, and what things now exist and how they will be; all these Mind arranged, including the present revolution of the stars and the sun and the moon and the air and the aether that are separating off. This very revolution produced the separation. And the thick is separated from the thin, the hot from the cold, the bright from the dark, and the dry from the damp.

## Significance of Anaxagoras

Most historians interpret Anaxagoras' philosophy as a further development of Empedocles', and both are considered replies to a supposed Parmenidean doctrine of the impossibility of diversity and motion. Since as we have seen Parmenides held no such views, we need not force the later thinkers into these molds. There is some reason to believe that Anaxagoras never met Parmenides; in any case the surviving fragments of Anaxagoras' book contain no clear indication that he was engaged in dialectic with Parmenides.

On the other hand, both Empedocles and Anaxagoras—but no one before them—explained sense perception, and Anaxagoras' theory is the opposite of Empedocles'. Anaxagoras held that perception is a stimulation of sense receptors by opposites of their composition. Thus the eyes, which are dark inside, can perceive light; the skin can perceive what is colder or hotter than itself, but not what is at the same temperature. That is to say, all perception is irritation. In this theory, which as a matter of fact is correct in principle, the scientific insight of Anaxagoras shows to its best.

In making the universe out of "seeds unlimited in multitude, no one like any other," Anaxagoras may have been consciously criticizing Empedocles' attempted reduction of all differences to a small number of basic oppositions. Be that as it may, there are sound reasons that derive from experience and common sense for preferring Anaxagoras. The world is just too full of a number of things; it is far from plausible to suppose the only ultimate differences are those between hot and cold, wet and dry. How could that account, for example, for the differences between color, or between sweet and sour? If you are going to hold, as all the thinkers before Anaxagoras did, that nothing comes from nothing and that the world is built up out of characteristically qualified stuffs—that the ingredients of things are a heat-stuff, a white-stuff, a sour-stuff, and so on—then if you think logically you must arrive in the end at the philosophy of Anaxagoras: every difference is a basic difference. "How can hair come from what is not hair?" It must have been there all along, but hidden from our perception—as whitewash, garlic, and perfume hide other colors, tastes, and odors.

Yet in achieving consistency, Anaxagoras exhibits at the same time the bankruptcy of this kind of thought. To explain how bread nourishes us by saying that it contains flesh, bone, and hair fused and hidden in it is too easy and really explains nothing. Our thirst for explanation is a demand to be told in some sense, though we may not be sure just what, that hair *does* come from what is not hair. An explanation is supposed to provide a unified view of the things explained. And this we do not achieve when the terms with which we explain the things are just as diverse, complex, and lacking in unity as the things we are trying to explain. Empedocles' explanatory instinct was thus in a way sounder than Anaxagoras'.

We have suggested that Empedocles' Affection and Strife were the reintroduction of mythical elements into the world picture. The same criticism can be leveled at Anaxagoras' Mind, though from another viewpoint this very feature was thought to be the glory of his philosophy. Aristotle praised him thus: "In saying that Mind is present in nature just as it is in animals, and that it is the cause of the cosmos and of every order, he seemed like a sober man beside his predecessors talking at random."[2] Socrates too was excited and struck by the nobility of the thought. Yet Socrates complained that when he read on in Anaxagoras' book he was let down completely by "the man's making no use at all of Mind as cause of the ordering of things, but ascribing as causes airs and aethers and waters and such-like nonsense."[3] And Aristotle reproached him thus: "Anaxagoras makes use of Mind as a gimmick for producing the world, and whenever he is in difficulty about what the cause is of why something must exist, he drags Mind in; but in other cases he makes everything rather than Mind the cause of what happens."[4]

But these complaints seem unfair. They accuse Anaxagoras of having failed to do what he had no intention of doing. Mind to him was just that force—mechanical, even material—that separated and arranged things, not in order to bring about some desirable pattern which it foresaw but because it was its nature to separate and articulate things. He called it Mind only because he saw an analogy or identity between this cosmic process and the faculty in us that recognizes and initiates processes. The likeness goes no further, as Mind for Anaxagoras is not a person, not a divinity in any sense. The very words god and divine—used by all his Ionian predecessors, though frequently in nonreligious ways—are entirely absent from those writings of his that survive, and probably did not occur in his book at all.

## Persecution of Anaxagoras

Anaxagoras lived for some 30 years in Athens. He was teacher, companion, and protégé of Pericles (*ca* 495–429 B.C.), whom he "freed from the superstitions of the multitude whom it was his task to guide."[5] Enemies of Pericles, and of the political and intellectual enlightenment that he introduced into Athens, initiated a prosecution against Anaxagoras about 450 B.C. on charges of 'impiety'—he had said that the sun was a red-hot stone and the moon was earth, rather than divinities—and, for good measure, pro-Iranian activities. He was convicted and sentenced to death, but Pericles had influence enough to connive successfully at his escape. He returned across the Aegean Sea to the city of Lampsacus at the western mouth of the Dardanelles, where he set up as a schoolteacher. For centuries after his death the Lampsacenes celebrated his anniversary as a school holiday.

# 8

# Leucippus and Democritus

NOTHING FROM NOTHING—THAT was a principle to be upheld come what might, for to abandon it or admit exceptions to it would be to give up the fundamental reasonableness of things and to let in all manner of magic and superstition. Empedocles and Anaxagoras explicitly stated the consequence that so-called generation and destruction could be only mixing and separating of things that already existed and did not themselves come into being or pass away or undergo change of their essential natures. The problem all the early thinkers set themselves was that of determining what the basic stuffs were and how the production of derivative things was to be understood.

## The Early Greeks and Experimentalism

In our age we have been brought up to regard all questions about how things are constituted as issues for settlement by the natural sciences. Recognizing Anaximander, Empedocles, and the rest as intellectual ancestors of today's physicists, chemists, biologists, and so on, we tend to evaluate their achievements according to whether they carried out their investigations in a manner akin to what we consider the proper scientific methods: observation and experiment. Our touchstone for a really scientific thinker, even in the fifth century B.C., comes down to whether he performed any experiments, or at least made some observations, relevant to confirming his theories.

In consequence historians who want to vindicate the scientific nature of early Greek thought make much ado over Anaximenes' blowing on his hands, Xenophanes' observations of fossils, Pythagoras' string plucking, and Empedocles' mention of the fact that if you put your thumb over one end of an open pipe and stick the other end into a tub of water, the pipe will not fill until you remove your thumb from the end of the pipe.

These four instances, however, constitute nearly the complete list of observations or 'experiments' conducted over a period of two centuries by the thinkers we have been discussing. Nor is it likely that they made more but failed to record them or did so in works that have been lost; for even in the later history of Greek science observation is almost entirely limited to astronomy and medicine, and experimentation is unknown. Thus historians of an opposite persuasion find it easy to show that the early Greeks were by this agreed test not scientific at all, but religiously inspired seers or even frivolous guessers who were sometimes lucky.

Noting also that the questions the Greeks first tried to answer were the grandest possible—What is the world made of? How did it come to be as it is? How does it work?—some commentators applaud Thales and his successors for their daring. Others, less romantic, remark that if they had limited themselves to more modest endeavors they might have enjoyed more success.

Both the favorable and the unfavorable assessments are questionable. We naturally tend to think of our predecessors as having wandered around striving for but not attaining the goals that we at last have achieved. We suppose that the inventors of rounders really wanted to play baseball but were not clever enough to invent it. Aristotle was the first but not the last to write the history of philosophy in this way: according to him the earlier accounts of the world were "lisping" partial anticipations of the doctrines that he was first to expound in perfect form.

However, the principle that nothing develops that does not have some use at every stage of its career is as true of intellectual as of biological evolution. "It is an adequate description of science to say that it is 'thinking about the world in the Greek way.'"[1] But we must avoid the hasty conclusion that present-day conceptions of how scientific investigations ought to proceed exhibit even in a general way what the earliest Greek thinkers were doing.

## Why Experimentalism Was Irrelevant

Let us consider again the experiment that Anaximenes is said to have performed: when you blow hard against your hand through tightly compressed lips your breath feels cool; when you blow gently against your hand through wide-open lips your breath feels warm. Therefore, Anaximenes inferred, hot = relaxed, cold = felted.

Modern physics teaches that Anaximenes' conclusion was dead wrong. Gases become hotter when compressed, cooler when rarefied. The correct explanation of the effect on the hand is that when breath is blown gently it remains at body temperature, which is usually higher than that of its surroundings, and is felt as warm. When blown sharply, however, the compressed and thereby heated air in the body expands on exiting. This expansion lowers the temperature because the breath molecules dissipate some of their energy in pushing aside the atmospheric molecules. If the experimenter is warm enough to sweat, evaporation effects must also be considered. When sweat evaporates, the skin is cooled because evaporation is the escape from the liquid to the gaseous state by the more energetic water molecules. If the layer of air in contact with the skin is still, however, it soon becomes saturated with water molecules, and further evaporation is stopped or slowed down. Blowing on the saturated layer replaces it with drier air and allows evaporation to speed up, permitting further cooling of the skin.

It is of course no discredit to Anaximenes that he did not know this explanation. He could not possibly have formulated it nor even understood it, for he did not and could not operate with such notions as molecules and energy. Not because he was unaware of certain facts that were discovered later and that he might have discovered himself; rather, the ground had not been prepared for the *theory* in terms of which the notions have meaning.

Moreover, *Anaximenes was right*, if he claimed no more than that the blowing test was a confirmation of his theory. He was entitled to say "If my theory of 'the thicker the colder' is correct, then a whistle ought to be colder than a yawn—and it is." It does not follow from this that his theory *was* correct, for the modern physicist is equally entitled to say "If the atomic theory and the principles of thermodynamics and of statistical mechanics are true, then a whistle ought to be colder than a yawn—and it is." The same fact may be a confirmation of two or twelve different theories. Confirmations of a theory are not of much interest unless at the same time they disconfirm some rival theory. Even in this kind of case, the so-called 'crucial experiment', the outcome is seldom clear-cut because of differing possible descriptions of the phenomenon. Anaximenes' experiment can illustrate this complication. His description of what occurred was in terms of relaxed air versus thick air. The modern physicist describes it as a matter of contrast between expanding and moving air on the one hand and stationary air on the other, also calling attention to the presence of sweat on the skin—something that Anaximenes may well have been aware of but did not think of putting into his description since its relevance would not have occurred to him. We see in this example, which is typical, that a description of the facts a theory must account for is itself by no means independent of the current theories.

We have raised vast questions to which we shall return time and again. At present the point to grasp is that there is nothing regrettable in the early thinkers' not having been experimentalists. The sorts of questions they were trying to answer were not such as to lend themselves to the experimental approach, and attempts to deal with them by laboratory methods could have led only to irrelevance and confusion.

## The Kinds of Reasons They Did Have

Someone may object that the history we have examined displays a maximum of irrelevance and confusion. The question "What is the world made of?" was absurdly too grand, and not surprisingly the different answers—water, the Boundless, air, numbers, fire, four roots, everything—were barely more than guesses. If these men were not mythmakers, neither were they scientists nor the forerunners of sober science.

Part of the reply to this kind of objection is contained in the story so far told. The men who are the subject of this chapter said that the world is made of atoms and void—which it is—and said this only about a century and a half after Thales ignored Marduk. It seems reasonable to suppose that the history of Greek thought about these matters does after all represent a progress. In reviewing the succession of thinkers I shall try to show both that they asked the right questions and that they went about answering them in the right way.

To the reproach that the questions they asked were too grand, these men might well have replied by asking what lesser questions they ought instead to have pondered. Ought they to have abandoned the search for the constituents of the world and turned to investigating what beeswax is made of? Or grass? Or why the petals of a rose are arranged neatly in a circle? Such inquiries would not have been easier ones, nor would any amount of clever manipulating of wax and roses have yielded answers. The principal reason was lack of a set of conceptions in terms of which an abstract analysis of cause and effect, and other essential ideas, could be expressed. The history of philosophy and of science is largely the history of the development of the conceptual framework without which observation is futile and experiment frivolous. The Greeks began this work in the right way.

The question these men set out to answer, and did answer, can be put in this form: what sorts of things can conservation laws apply to? More fully: if we are to hold fast to Nothing from nothing, what must the characteristics be of whatever can qualify as a thing? And how can the world be accounted for as made up of these things?

The things of our experience change, but they must be combinations of unchanging things if magic is to be avoided. But, now, what might an unchanging ingredient be like? The notion of an ingredient comes to us from our experience of putting things together—houses from stones and mortar, puddings from eggs and flour. These are the stuffs with which we start. But no one would suppose *they* are unchanging; they have their own ingredients. Mortar is composed of lime, sand, and water. The lime we make by heating limestone, but the sand and the water are just there. Perhaps those two, then, are basic ingredients? Just what is water, though? How do we tell whether something is water? By its wetness, transparency, liquidity. However, we can boil it into vapor or freeze it into ice, and these have quite different marks of identification. If what is changeless is that whose identifying marks remain the same, then water will not do. Shall we say, then, that it is just the marks themselves—heat, wetness, whiteness—that do not change but only come and go? In that case, where do they come from and where do they go?

Either there are basic unchanging constituents of all things or there are not. No Greek accepted the latter alternative. Very well, if there are basic constituents of things, there must be some means, at least in principle, of identifying them—there must be a way to tell the difference between what is a basic constituent and what is not. The identifying marks of these basic constituents must be either such as can be sensed—visible, audible, flavored, odorous, textured, or some combination of these—or not. The history of early Greek thought to this point in our discussion can be viewed as the exhaustive exploration of the former alternative: that the identifying marks of the fundamental ingredients of things are given to the senses—that they are such as heat or moisture.

## Things and Properties

The Greeks knew as well as we do how to distinguish between things and their properties. If they had not, they would never have been able to take inventories and itemize bills—the two activities, in fact, that gave rise to writing and mathematics. A dozen eggs and a pound of flour might figure as items in a Greek kitchen list, but never 12 yellows and 13 whites. In theorizing, however, it was difficult to maintain a distinction that is easier to recognize than to formulate. If there are unchanging ingredients of everything, what can their properties be? If you got hold of a piece of basic stuff, surely it would be a thing. And though it might be too small to see or feel or taste, it would have to have some color, some texture, some flavor, and would by definition have to have these properties eternally— which is as much as to say that it would *be* those properties.

So at any rate the thinkers we have dealt with so far all agreed. The question about basic stuffs was for them the same as the questions: how many basic properties are there and how can nonbasic properties be understood as complexes of the basic ones?

The early thinkers fall into two groups: those such as Anaxagoras and (probably) Anaximander who held that all the qualities we can discriminate are equally basic, and men like Anaximenes and Empedocles who taught that some qualities are basic and the rest are derivative. The primary difficulty with the derivative quality theory, as we have seen, is that it is arbitrary, vague, and implausible. How is one to justify pronouncements such as that fire is thinned air or bone is earth-water-fire in the ratio 2:2:4? Just what is meant by earth, and so forth, in this formula? If earth is 'the cold and dry', it is hard to see how the number of things that the world is full of could result from mixing it with 'the hot and damp', and so on. Bones, and indeed nearly everything, ought to be rather tepid and moist.

Reflections like these no doubt led Anaxagoras to maintain an infinity of basic stuffs. Yet besides the grave disadvantage already noted, that such a theory is incapable of explaining anything, it also suffers from implausibility. Everything has every quality, but the predominant ones mask the more diluted ones from our perception. It is difficult to believe, however, that the flavor of Limburger cheese is already present in a glass of sweet milk, hidden only by the bland flavor of the milk. Or that the foaming of sea water in the surf is the coming to the top of the hidden white parts of water. The theory must furthermore ignore many qualities, including all those of sound. The clanging of a bell can by no means be accounted for as the releasing of noises hitherto drowned out by silence.

Perhaps Anaxagoras did not sense a difficulty about sounds because already he regarded them as processes and not things. A sound is something that happens, not something that exists in the sense of 'standing there'. If it had occurred to Anaxagoras that being red might be more like being noisy than like being solid, he might have discovered the theory that solves his problems: the atomic theory. We do not know whether it was an insight of this kind that led Leucippus (fifth century B.C.) and Democritus (*ca* 460–*ca* 360 B.C.) to formulate their theory, but at any rate we can see in hindsight that their conclusions could have been reached by this route.

## Leucippus

"No thing just happens, but all things from a rationale (Logos) and by necessity." This single sentence is all that remains from the writings of Leucippus of Miletus, who worked out the conception of the atom and thereby completed the quest begun by his fellow citizens Thales and Anaximander a century earlier: how change can really occur without violating the principle Nothing from nothing. According to tradition Leucippus was an associate in the philosophy of Parmenides, but nothing is known about him as a person, not even approximate dates. His philosophy was taken up and developed by his pupil, the famous Democritus. It is possible to disentangle the contributions of each to some extent, but it seems better to grant blanket credit to Leucippus for the fundamental discovery of atomism and then to present the theory as worked out by Democritus.

## Democritus

Of Democritus somewhat more can be said. He was a native of Abdera in northern Greece, a city founded by the citizens of Teos who left their native Ionia en masse in 546 B.C., refugees from the Iranian conqueror. He lived, we are told, for more than a century. He devoted his life and extensive fortune to travel and scientific investigation, saying that he "would rather discover one causal explanation than gain the kingdom of the Iranians."[2]

Democritus was one of the most prolific authors of his century, writing some 60 books. Not one has survived. We have fewer than 300 fragments, none of more than a few lines; and nearly all these are moralizing reflections. Very little has been preserved of his natural science and nothing of his mathematics, although there is reason to think he was among the foremost ancient mathematicians. The work of no other major figure in intellectual history has perished so utterly.

## Atoms and Void

However, the Democritean theory is so simple and elegant that this loss obscures our knowledge of it very little. It can be stated in a few lines. The world, Democritus held, consists of the full and the empty, of atoms and void. An atom, that is to say an 'uncuttable', is what will be reached if a body is divided up as finely as possible. Division cannot go on to infinity, not because such a process is unimaginable but because in fact slicing a thing only detaches its constituent particles from each other, and those particles themselves are perfectly solid—absolutely hard. Nothing can penetrate them; they can suffer no sort of internal change. They have bulk and shape. And it is their nature to move and jostle one another, sometimes entangling and sometimes freeing themselves from entanglements. That is all. An atom by itself has no color (not even black or neutral gray), odor, flavor, noise, heat, cold, or dampness.

## Qualities and Processes

What then are color, flavor, and the rest? Democritus pronounced: "By custom color, by custom sweet, by custom bitter; in reality atoms and void." Those things are "by custom" that owe their being to agreed patterns of human activity. In saying that colors exist "by custom" Democritus meant to deny that they were 'out there' as constituents of the world, of reality, in the sense that they would continue to be just what they were apart from the activities of human beings. Democritus had an insight that we might express by saying that being red is more like being noisy than like being egg-shaped. This made possible the solution of the puzzlements about change that had led into the blind alley of Anaxagorean infinitism.

The theory of Anaxagoras claimed that there are as many "seeds" as there are possible sensory discriminations. Yet much that we discriminate was tacitly excluded, notably sounds. Anaxagoras asked "How can flesh come from what is not flesh? or hair from what is not hair?"—profound questions. It seems plausible, even inevitable, to answer that the flesh and the hair were there all along but hidden. But to ask "How can a bang come from what is not a bang? or a whistle from what is not a whistle? would be silly; to suggest that they were there all the time, but drowned out, would be insane. Yet sounds are just as much discriminable qualities as meatiness and hairiness.

Anaxagoras did not ask the 'silly' questions because he realized that sounds are not things or even parts of things, but processes. You pluck the string or strike the gong, setting it in motion—the motion can be seen and felt—and it produces its effect on the ear through the medium of the air. The hearing of the sound, the sensation we experience may or may not be a motion in us. But it is evident that what exists outside us is certain bodies in motion—the same things that were there before being struck or plucked, but now moving, or moving differently. Although in order to make a certain sound a string must have a certain length, diameter, and tension, the sound is the consequence of those qualities and not another thing or quality of the same order. Sounds can be reduced to motions, vibrations. Or as Democritus would have put it, the adjectives by which we discriminate between sounds—loud, high-pitched, musical—are "by custom"; they do not signify anything different from adjectives applicable to motions, such as rapid and energetic. Sound is motion, and to perceive (hear) sound is to be moved in a certain way: perceiving a sound is like perceiving an earthquake only faster.

The perception of colors, tastes, and odors does not seem to be like this. Colors come and go, but not so fleetingly as sounds; and although not everything makes a noise all the time, everything has some color. Hence colors were (and still are) thought of not as actions of bodies but possessions—'properties'—things in their own right, even if always dependent on some body or other. So also for tastes and smells. The basic constituents of the world, it was thought, would not be colors but bodies that had colors. For how could a body not have a color any more than it could fail to have a shape?

Plausible and sensible as these considerations may seem, Democritus saw that it was necessary to deny them if the principle Nothing from nothing was to be preserved while avoiding the Anaxagorean dead end. If colors and tastes are actions not things, conservation laws need not apply to them but only to what acts—the atoms moving eternally in the void.

Thus did Democritus solve the first great problem of early thought, the question of what the ultimate constituents of the world must be. It should be evident that although the solution could only have been achieved by a thinker of genius, yet also it was in a certain way inevitable. It could not have been reached before the proposals of Empedocles and Anaxagoras had been made and criticized; furthermore, atomism was bound to be the conception that succeeded them. It is hardly necessary to point out that experimentalism was irrelevant to the whole endeavor.

The history of thought is not everywhere neat and tidy. Thinkers like Heraclitus, Parmenides, and Pythagoras do not fit easily into the dialectic scheme leading from Anaximander to Democritus. All the same they had their part to play in the process. Relying on an ancient tradition that Leucippus was "an associate in the philosophy of Parmenides," most histories state the relation of atomism to Eleaticism this way: Parmenides showed that what was real could not have come into being, could not be destroyed, could not change. Identifying 'what is not' with empty space, he claimed further that nothing could move (for motion requires empty space to move *in*); in consequence, all appearance of diversity and motion is illusory. Leucippus and Democritus then reconciled the rigor of Parmenidean logic with the reality of change by making each atom a Parmenidean changeless world, which nevertheless was only one reality among many and which could enter into changing relations with other realities moving in the void—the existence of which these philosophers daringly affirmed in the face of the truism that Not-being does not exist.

However, if as we have contended Parmenides never denied the reality of motion, some other conception of how his teaching influenced atomism is needed. Perhaps the clue is to be found in a puzzling remark by Aristotle, ". . . in a sense these men [Leucippus and Democritus] too make all the real things to be numbers and products of numbers."[3] By their denial of nonconserved properties to their atoms they were able to reinstate an earlier, Pythagorean atomistic conception of the world in spite of the Eleatic criticism. In any case, the Democritean atom satisfies the demand of Parmenides that whatever is to be an object of rigorous science must be unchanging. The possibility of scientific physics is thus vindicated.

## Problems of Atomism

Democritus provided a satisfactory theoretical solution of the problem how basic stuff must be conceived, but this fact was not recognized by all the Greeks or even most of them in Democritus' day or later. It took more than 2,000 years for atomism to become received opinion. Some of the reluctance to adopt the atomic viewpoint was due to religious prejudice. But there were genuine difficulties in the way of acceptance. Atomism solved some problems only by creating others; or if it did not create problems, at any rate it brought them to the fore.

These troubles had mainly to do with perception, a topic which here for the first time becomes prominent in philosophy and has ever since been a major, at times an obsessive, preoccupation. The difficulties faced were of two kinds.

The first had to do with the mechanics of perception, especially of vision. If nothing really exists except atoms moving and colliding in the void, then to see a tomato or to hear a bell must be somehow to be involved in various atomic collisions. All interaction of one thing with another is impact. Therefore, when I see a tomato it must be in some way hitting me or at least hitting something else that is in turn hitting my eyes. To put it as the ancient critics did, atomism reduces all the senses to one, the sense of touch. But this is implausible. Seeing a tomato does not seem at all like being hit by a tomato, or like being hit by anything. Anyway, what could the missile be? Not the tomato, for it is still there on the vine.

To this question, which is essentially one for physics, the kind of answer required is that the tomato communicates motion through a medium to the sense organ. There is some reason to believe that Democritus developed a theory of the proper type; namely, one according to which the object "imprints" itself in the air, this imprint being propagated to the eye. However, the doctrine of vision that became official among the atomists was the different one of atomic images. Objects, it was held, continually throw off thin films from their surfaces, like the skins off snakes; these fly through the air and, entering our bodies through the eyes and moving the soul atoms (for the soul is composed of atoms too—fine, spherical, especially mobile ones), produce the perception.

This theory is as unsatisfactory as it sounds. It fails to explain how the film from the tomato is detached from the tomato which it surrounds without breaking or tearing and how in its flight through the air it shrinks to an appropriate size for entering the pupil. Nor does it account for failure to see things in the dark.

But its greatest embarrassment is not a mechanical but a conceptual difficulty. Even if the films could be plausibly shown to work as required, they would still not explain perception. We should have only some assumed mechanism whereby images of things get inside our skins. Very well then, what we call perceiving a tomato is really perceiving a tomato-film. That tells us what the *object* of our perception is. The question still remains, what is it to *perceive?*—whether what is perceived is a tomato or a tomato-film. Is perceiving just nothing but having an image inside oneself? Perhaps that conception has some superficial plausibility, but it cannot survive the least scrutiny. It is an example of a stratagem that we shall encounter all too frequently among philosophers, that of purporting to get rid of a difficulty by merely reproducing the difficulty at another level. If the relation that we call perception between a person and a tomato is puzzling, then just as puzzling—in the same ways and for the same reasons—must be the relation between the soul (whether atoms or whatever) and some internal simulacrum (however it got there) of the tomato.

This difficulty in turn generates another, of which Democritus himself was vividly aware. Democritus should have said (we proclaim in hindsight) that to see a tomato is to be affected by an illuminated tomato in a certain way that it is up to physics and physiology to explain. But instead, his theory implied that what we call 'seeing a tomato' is really seeing, or somehow dealing with, not the tomato but something else: the image in us. The tomato, being atoms moving in the void, has (for example) no color. But what we see is red. Therefore, what we see is not the tomato. (Here Democritus fell into a trap that not all philosophers even today know how to avoid.) What we see is something subjective, "by custom." It is not *really* a part of the world. (How it can be part of us, yet not part of the world, is hard to explain.) Yet whatever we know of the tomato clearly must be derived from what we call seeing, tasting, and so forth, the tomato. Indeed, all our knowledge of everything must come back at some stage to perception. So Democritus himself imagined the senses speaking to the mind thus.

> Miserable mind, taking from us those things in which you have confidence, yet you throw us down? The fall will be *your* downfall.

In despair, Democritus declared that

> In reality we know nothing. For the truth is down at the bottom.

In a more optimistic mood, however, Democritus distinguished between

> two kinds of knowledge, one legitimate, the other bastard. To the bastard belong all these: sight, hearing, smell, taste, touch. But the legitimate kind is distinguished from these. . . . When the bastard kind is no further able to see into smaller things, nor hear nor smell nor taste nor perceive by touch, and yet there has to be further investigation, then the legitimate kind takes over, having a finer instrument for knowing.

Here is illustrated another philosophical strategem, 'pounding the table'. Democritus, faced with an acknowledged difficulty (explaining how we can know there are only atoms while admitting that our knowledge is based on perception, which reveals no atoms), declares with vigorous emphasis that a solution exists.

It is probably unfair, however, to criticize Democritus thus. In the passage cited, he was calling attention to a distinction whose reality cannot be denied: that between what we know by looking and what we know by reasoning. Reason as a sort of supermicroscope is a naively pictorial model, likely to mislead if taken too seriously, but not otherwise objectionable.

## Mechanism

Mythical thought explained the things and events in the world as ultimately due to operations and intentions of cosmic persons, just as we ascribe human doings to human intentions. The earliest scientific and philosophical outlook discarded superhuman agents as explanations. Nevertheless the tendency to retain some kind of cosmic consciousness remained, more or less, in all the thinkers from Anaximander, whose Boundless steered all things, to Anaxagoras' Mind, which started the whirl in the primeval soup.

Atomism discarded this last remnant of animism. Previous thinkers supposed that motions of bodies must in the end be results of intention; Democritus held that, on the contrary, intention must be explained as a production of bodily motions. In Anaxagoras' philosophy, everything after the beginning of the rotation proceeded as a consequence of the motion thus originated. In Democritus, since there is no ultimate mind-like explanatory entity, there is no beginning of motion either. All the atoms have *always* been in motion.

Things happen, as Leucippus put it, "from a rational necessity." The necessity is mechanical—that is to say, it is the kind of necessity exhibited in a machine, where the turning of the second gear is a necessary consequence of the turning of the first. Various things may happen to atoms that collide. Two atoms may stick together if their shapes are right and they hit in the right way—if one, for instance, has a hook-like projection that happens to fit into an eyelet of the other. Or perhaps one atom will knock a second loose from its union with a third. Or after bumping the atoms may go their separate ways, but in other directions and at other speeds than before the collision. Yet given two particular atoms on a given collision course, there is only one possible outcome. What kind of result the collision will have (hooking or disconnecting or deflection) is determined already by the speeds and directions of their approaches. If you knew what their motion was before collision you could tell in advance what their motion would be after collision. The cause (the initial motion) determines the effect (the subsequent motion), and there is no leeway.

But why were the atoms moving in that particular way before they collided? Because of collisions in which they were involved previously. But why were those what they were? Because of still earlier collisions. And so, literally, ad infinitum. There never was a time when the atoms did not exist and there never was a time when they were not moving and colliding.

This does not banish intention from the world, for some atomic motions occur as a result of intention. For instance, you might smash a vase in anger. The intention was to smash the vase, and it did shatter. Anger was the motivation. Democritus' point is not that this kind of account is false but that it is not ultimate. Anger is a certain pattern of motion of the atoms that make up a soul. They are moving that way because of motions that have been imparted to them previously, for instance by images coming through the eyes and ears from persons making rude sounds and insulting gestures.

An ancient story illustrates the difference between the mechanistic Democritean type of explanation and the traditional purposive or intentional kind. The great poet Aeschylus (525–456 B.C.) had met an unusual fate: while he was strolling along a beach an eagle flew overhead and dropped from its talons a tortoise, which striking the poet on his head killed him. The explanation that satisfied most Greeks was supplied when someone recalled that an oracle had foretold that Aeschylus would die of "a bolt from Zeus." That had been taken as meaning he would be struck by lightning; but since the eagle was the bird sacred to Zeus, the oracle was after all fulfilled by this outcome.

Democritus, however, was not satisfied with this account. He went to the beach and observed the habits of eagles. He found they were fond of tortoise meat. To get at the meat, an eagle would fly into the air with the tortoise in its talons and let go of it above a rock, thus cracking the carapace. When this habit of eagles was joined to the fact that the deceased was bald, Democritus had his explanation.

Both accounts accomplished what explanations are meant to do: they relieved puzzlement. The death of the poet was odd; it did not fit into the ordinary expected pattern of happenings; it seemed capricious and in a sense unnatural. What explanation had to do was show that regardless of how contrary to first appearance, the event was in reality understandable, something to be expected if one knew enough beforehand. The oracular explanation did this by ascribing the event to a divine intention. This kind of explanation, as we have noted, is always available. To say that the death was the will of Zeus was to make the event like familiar ones, and to point out that a clever interpreter of oracles could have seen it coming somehow made it all the more understandable. It discouraged the raising of the question of why the will of Zeus was of just this sort. On the other hand, Democritus' explanation showed the unusual event to be after all just another item in a regular pattern of things, an incident that did not differ (except in tragedy and interest) from what goes on every day at the beach. Although the account does contain a reference to intention—namely the desires of eagles to eat turtle meat—the death itself is not ascribed to intention of eagles or gods or anyone. But neither is it random: "Nothing just happens, but everything from a rationale and by necessity."

This kind of explaining, reduction to a pattern of cause and effect without reference to intention, was criticized by Aristotle who complained that Democritus explained everything ultimately by the single formula "Thus it happened formerly also." To Aristotle, saying that did not relieve puzzlement but multiplied it. For if one event is strange, other events like it must be strange too. And to point out that the one is a member of a class containing a hundred instances is only to create the need for a hundred explanations.

Aristotle's criticism overlooks the circumstance that while not everything can be explained, there is no need to do so, for not everything is puzzling either. If anything is to be explained, some things must be taken for granted, must be regarded as routine and familiar. If indeed Democritus had accounted for the event by searching coroners' reports and discovering that a hundred other men had died by being hit on the head with turtles dropped by eagles, Aristotle's complaint would have been justified. However, that is not what Democritus did. He showed how the event in question was only in accidental aspects different from something in itself not startling—the cracking open of turtles by eagles.

One might ask, though, which explanation was the true one—the oracular or the Democritean? Evidently Democritus' cannot be discarded, cannot be just false; for eagles in fact do behave that way with turtles. If, then, someone who knew about it nevertheless wanted to uphold the oracle, he would have to say "Yes, but what happened really was that Zeus made use of the regular habits of eagles in order to fulfill his intention." When the mechanistic explanation is known, the intentional one cannot cancel it—it can only be superadded. And while the mechanistic explanation can stand by itself, the intentional one cannot. The mechanistic explanation does not disprove the intentional, but it does tend to exhibit the intention as an unnecessary addition. In many cases this has the same effect as disproof has. To calculate the orbits of comets is not to show that comets cannot be portents of disaster. Nevertheless, as a matter of psychology it is hard to believe that comets both foretell disasters and inevitably arrive on schedule. This is true even though there is always a sufficient supply of disasters so that no one need worry about being proven wrong after warning that when a comet appears, look out, something dreadful is going to happen.

## Democritus' Picture of the World

Though Democritus preferred discovering one causal explanation over becoming the Shah of Iran, except for the Aeschylus case he was not notably successful in this respect. We have seen how his attempt to explain visual perception failed. His account of taste was more plausible: vinegar tastes sour because it contains very sharp atoms that prick the skin of the tongue. Honey, on the other hand, is composed of large round atoms that roll caressingly over the tongue. But as ancient critics pointed out, not only does this kind of theory fail to account for the subjectivity of tastes, it also abandons the main principle of atomism; for in effect it makes the tastes of things properties of the individual atoms—even though it does reduce these properties to shapes. Moreover, how on this basis is Democritus to account for so common a phenomenon as the souring of wine or milk? The shapes of the atoms could not change. We might add that the theory seems to be an instance of something else common in philosophy, the failure to recognize a metaphor as such. A little reflection should convince us that when we say of aged cheddar cheese that it tastes sharp, we do not mean literally that the sensation we have when we eat it is indistinguishable from, confused with, or even closely akin to what we feel when our tongue is scratched.

Nevertheless, modern investigations have established correlations between tastes of things and the (literal) shapes of the molecules composing the substances tasted. The Democritean account was of the right *type*.

The following is an ancient summary of Democritus on thunder and lightning.

> Thunder is produced by an unstable mixture forcing the cloud enclosing it to move
> downward. Lightning is a clashing together of clouds by which the fire-producing

atoms rubbing against each other are assembled through the porous mass into one place and pass out. And the thunderbolt occurs when the motion is forced by the very pure, very fine, very uniform and "closely-packed" fire-producing atoms, as he himself calls them.

We see in this how Democritus is not giving, nor really even attempting to give, anything more than a description of how thunder and lightning *might* occur consistent with the atomic theory. It does not rule out other alternatives that might be equally consistent.

No more could be expected of atomism at this early stage. Atomism was a philosophical theory, a deduction of what properties could and could not be ascribed to the substantial constituents of the world. If in our day we look upon atomism as capable not merely in principle but in actual fact of providing the basis for detailed explanations of all sorts of phenomena, including lightning, that is because physicists now have the tools and methods that Democritus lacked. A mathematical science of motion is indispensable. Democritus, who was a mathematician, may have had some notion of this need and may have begun to try working it out. There are a few hints of these interests in the fragmentary remains.

Democritus' picture of the cosmos and of how it came to be was embarrassingly primitive. He supposed, like all the Ionians, that the mechanism of cosmic formation was a whirl, which separated the atoms out of the chaos into concentric rings of more or less similar kinds: fire (or rather the atoms that generate fire) outside, the massive atoms that make up earth in the middle, air and water in between. He held that the earth was a flat disc supported on air. These old-fashioned views were put forward long after the Pythagoreans had advanced excellent reasons for believing the earth to be a sphere.

## The Good Life

Like most sages, Democritus from time to time made pronouncements on human behavior in ethics, politics, and education. We happen to have more of his sayings on these topics than on any others. They show him to have been a man of good sense, shrewd ("If you cannot understand the compliments, you may be being flattered"), and an advocate and practitioner of the life of cheerfulness.

> He who would be cheerful must not busy himself with many things, either by himself or in company; and whatever he busies himself with, he should not choose what is beyond his own power and nature. But he should be so on guard that when a stroke of fortune tempts him to excess, he puts it aside, and does not grasp at what is beyond his powers. For being well filled is better than being stuffed.

Some of the ethical maxims, however, are of an elevation often supposed to be incompatible with a materialist philosophy.

> Refrain from wrongdoing not from fear but from duty.

> The doer of injustice is unhappier than the sufferer.

Goodness is not merely in refraining from being unjust but in not even wishing to be.

The cause of error is ignorance of the better.

Democritus enjoyed an extraordinarily long life. According to one account, when he was in his final illness his sister—who looked after him—was disappointed at the prospect of going into mourning, thus being prevented from taking part in the annual women's festival. Democritus told her to cheer up and to bring him loaves fresh from the oven every morning. For the three days of the festival he prolonged his life by sniffing the hot bread, and then cheerfully expired in his 109th year.

# II

## Socrates
## Plato
## Aristotle

# 9

---

# Intellectual Life in Athens

ATTICA IS A TRIANGULAR piece of land bounded on two sides by sea, on the third by mountains. It is about half as large as the state of Rhode Island, had in ancient times about half as many inhabitants as Rhode Island has today—four or five hundred thousand—and half lived in Athens, thus somewhat smaller than modern Providence. What occurred in Athens in the fifth and fourth centuries B.C. was of unsurpassed importance in shaping the culture and politics of Europe—and consequently of America—to this day.

By frustrating the design of Iran to impose Oriental despotism on all Greece, Athens first of all assured that there would be a Europe. In 490 B.C. the Athenians, almost single-handedly, defeated the Iranians under Shah Darius in the battle of Marathon. Ten years later the far greater invasion mounted by Xerxes extended all the way down the Balkan peninsula, capturing and burning Athens—but the Athenians had abandoned the city. Their navy, at the head of the combined Greek fleets, destroyed the invader's ships off the island of Salamis. In the following year Greek soldiers under Spartan leadership were able to crush the enormous Iranian army at Plataea on the northern border of Attica. The Athenian fleet then liberated the Ionian cities from their subjugation of 60 years.

## Athens at Her Highest Point

Athens, already before the wars the greatest of Greek cities, emerged as leader of an anti-Iranian confederation of naval powers. Each city was bound to contribute ships to the common fleet, but the practice grew of allowing money donations in lieu of ships. These assessments soon became in effect annual tributes paid to Athens, which now found herself—almost but not quite by accident—at the head of an empire. For half a century (479–430 B.C.) Athens was either at peace or engaged only in what one might call routine wars. The Athenian navy was put to the work of ridding the eastern Mediterranean of pirates. Commerce was able to flourish as never before. Money and talent were available for adornment of the city with splendid public buildings, chief of which was the Parthenon, great temple to Athena, goddess of intelligence and patroness of the city. This era is called the Periclean Age after the statesman who was the leader of the more democratic party in Athens and, roughly speaking, prime minister for the 30-year period after 461 B.C. Never before or since was there a period of such concentrated production of works of the highest quality in architecture, sculpture, and drama (invented only shortly before the Persian wars). Pericles himself described Athens as it was at its summit when he spoke in commemoration of the soldiers who died the first year of the great war between Athens and Sparta—the war that brought the Periclean Age to a tragic close.

Our constitution does not copy the laws of neighboring states; we are rather a pattern to others than imitators ourselves. Its administration favors the many instead of the few; this is why it is called a democracy. If we look to the laws, they afford equal justice to all in their private differences; if to social standing, advancement in public life falls to reputation for capacity, class considerations not being allowed to interfere with merit; nor again does poverty bar the way: if a man is able to serve the state, he is not hindered by the obscurity of his condition. The freedom which we enjoy in our government extends also to our ordinary life. There, far from exercising a jealous surveillance over each other, we do not feel called upon to be angry with our neighbor for doing what he likes, or even to indulge in those injurious looks which cannot fail to be offensive, although they inflict no positive penalty. But all this ease in our private relations does not make us lawless as citizens. Against this fear is our chief safeguard, teaching us to obey the magistrates and the laws, particularly such as regard the protection of the injured, whether they are actually on the statute book, or belong to that code which, although unwritten, yet cannot be broken without acknowledged disgrace.

Further, we provide plenty of means for the mind to refresh itself from business. We celebrate games and sacrifices all the year round, and the elegance of our private establishments forms a daily source of pleasure and helps to banish the spleen; while the magnitude of our city draws the produce of the world into our harbor, so that to the Athenian the fruits of other countries are as familiar a luxury as those of his own.

If we turn to our military policy, there also we differ from our antagonists. We throw open our city to the world, and never by alien acts exclude foreigners from any opportunity of learning or observing, although the eyes of an enemy may occasionally profit by our liberality; trusting less in system and policy than to the native spirit of our citizens; while in education, where our rivals from their very cradles by a painful discipline seek after manliness, at Athens we live exactly as we please, and yet are just as ready to encounter every legitimate danger. . . .

Nor are these the only points in which our city is worthy of admiration. We cultivate refinement without extravagance and philosophy without softness; wealth we employ more for use than for show, and place the real disgrace of poverty not in owning to the fact but in declining the struggle against it. Our public men have, besides politics, their private affairs to attend to, and our ordinary citizens, though occupied with the pursuits of industry, are still fair judges of public matters; for, unlike any other nation, regarding him who takes no part in these duties not as unambitious but as useless, we Athenians are able to judge at all events if we cannot originate, and instead of looking on discussion as a stumbling-block in the way of action, we think it an indispensable preliminary to any wise action at all. Again, in our enterprises we present the singular spectacle of daring and deliberation, each carried to its highest point, and both united in the same persons; although usually decision is the fruit of ignorance, hesitation of reflection. But the palm of courage will surely be adjudged most justly to those who best know the difference between hardship and pleasure and yet are never tempted to shrink from danger. In generosity we are equally singular, acquiring our friends by conferring not by receiving favors. . . .

In short, I say that as a city we are the school of Hellas; while I doubt if the world can produce a man, who where he has only himself to depend upon, is equal to so many emergencies, and graced by so happy a versatility as the Athenian. And that this is no mere boast thrown out for the occasion, but plain matter of fact, the power of the state acquired by these habits proves. . . . We have forced every sea and land to be the highway of our daring, and everywhere . . . have left imperishable monuments behind us. Such is the Athens for which these men, in the assertion of their resolve not to lose her, nobly fought and died; and well may every one of their survivors be ready to suffer in her cause.[1]

"Our constitution . . . favors the many instead of the few; this is why it is called a democracy." The rise of Athens as a military and commercial power was paralleled by an extension of political power to the whole body of citizens. Most Greek cities witnessed continual battles, often of frightful atrocity, between 'the few' rich and 'the many' poor. The struggle in Athens was conducted without much violence, although it was not lacking in bitterness. By the time of Pericles every citizen had a vote in the Assembly, the legislative and executive body of Athens; every citizen could sit on the huge juries—they numbered as many as 1,501 jurymen—that administered Athenian justice; and he might occupy various important civil and military positions, some through election, some through choice by lot. This was the famous Athenian direct democracy. However, because women, slaves, and resident aliens—a large class since naturalization was seldom granted—took no part in politics, the number of adult male citizens was relatively small, perhaps a tenth of the entire population. Practically every citizen knew every other citizen. In this situation, where there was no equivalent to newspapers or mass media of any sort, personal prestige was extraordinarily dependent on powers of verbal persuasion. In addition, the Athenians were notorious for their fondness for lawsuits, and in the law courts everyone had to speak his own piece—though someone else might coach him or write his speech. Hence public speaking came to be the most highly prized of skills, creating great demand for teachers of the art.

## The Sophists

The men who made a profession of satisfying this need were called sophists. The name, from *sophos* = wise or skilled—half of philo*sophy*—originally had no connotation of intellectual sharp practice. No doubt some sophists were no better than they should have been; yet there was nothing inherently objectionable in the profession, or indeed in the characters and particular teachings of the great sophists of whom we know.

The sophists were the first professional intellectuals of Greece—professors before there were universities. Unlike the architects, sculptors, and dramatists of Athens, they were almost all foreigners and did not dwell permanently in Athens. They were itinerants who gave courses of lectures in one city, then moved on to another. Their instruction was not limited to lessons in public speaking in the narrow sense of elocution, style, and arrangement of topics. They taught also whatever they deemed necessary for their pupils to know in order to speak impressively, and many sophists believed that nothing less than familiarity with all the latest discoveries in science, mathematics, and technology would do. Thus Hippias of Elis appeared at the Olympic games splendidly attired, boasting that he had himself made from scratch every article of adornment he wore, and that he was prepared to talk extemporaneously on any topic at any length.

## Protagoras

The first and greatest sophist was Protagoras of Abdera (*ca* 485–410 B.C.). He advertised that his pupils went away from him the first day better than when they came, the second day better than the first, and so on for the duration of the course. Specifically he claimed to teach "prudence about personal affairs, how to run your household the best way; and how to speak and act most efficiently about public concerns."[2] What his teaching methods were we do not know, but they must have been effective; for he practiced sophistry for 40 years and was able to charge enormous fees, the equivalent of several thousand dollars. However, students who did not think the instruction was worth that much had to pay only what they declared under oath to be the proper amount. He boasted that very few availed themselves of the loophole.

Protagoras' career in Athens was terminated about 440 B.C. when he read—some say in the house of Euripides the tragic poet—his book *On the Gods*, which began

> As for gods, I have no way of knowing whether or not there are any, or what they might be like. For many are the barriers to knowing: the obscurity of the matter, and the shortness of human life.

For this impiety the Athenians banished him and publicly burnt all the copies of his book they could collect. The tendency of Greek thought ever since Thales, as we have seen, was in the direction of an understanding of the world that was nonreligious or at least did not rest on belief in anthropoid divinities. Protagoras seems to have been first, however, to make an explicit declaration of agnosticism which his critics held to be not really different from atheism.

The teaching of Protagoras on which his lasting fame in philosophy rests was uttered at the beginning of his book *On Truth*.

> Man is the measure of all things, of things that are that they are, of things that are not that they are not.

According to Plato, Protagoras meant the individual man, not the human species, and the things of which he is the 'measure' are the objects of sense perception. Plato links the saying with another attributed to him, that "as a thing appears to a man, so it is for that man." If the air seems chilly to me, then it *is* chilly, as far as I am concerned, no matter how sultry others may find it. If things seem different to you, then they are different—different objects—to *you*. There is no sense to the question "Yes, but what are they *really*, apart from what you and I may think?" Every judgment is necessarily subjective; there is no objective vantage point from which we might see things as they are in themselves, unaffected by our perspective. (This is a major thesis running through the entire history of philosophy and perhaps more vigorous at the present time than ever before.)

Plato says further that Protagoras adopted this view because he agreed with Heraclitus that everything is in constant motion. It seems more likely, however, that the basis of the doctrine came from closer to home; namely, from his fellow townsman Democritus. The relations between Protagoras and Democritus are puzzling. There may have been some influence, but who got what from whom cannot be determined. However that may be, Democritus had maintained that the tomato is a set of atoms in motion—and so am I, including my eye, brain, and 'soul'. Seeing a tomato must be some interaction of these atoms, and it must differ in different persons. Not everyone's soul can be expected to be of just the same kind of atoms moving the same way. This led Democritus to despair of the validity of sense perception: "In truth we know nothing about anything, but opinion for each individual is the flow toward him" of the images from things. Evidently Protagoras adopted this view, rejecting the Democritean saving clause about another knowledge that is 'legitimate'.

Skepticism of the claims of science and religion to yield absolute truths was made by Protagoras the basis of a humane, tolerant outlook and teaching. We cannot know how things are, but we can know what opinions, when held and acted upon, further a tolerable existence. One opinion is not truer than another, but it may be better; a wise man is one who gets rid of opinions that lead to pain and acquires others that make for happiness. Education is adjustment. The wise man is civil, urbane, sophisticated; these are qualities that can be imparted for a fee.

## Nature versus Convention

Being professional traveling men, the sophists cultivated a detached attitude toward the differences of law and custom between one Greek city and another. Like modern anthropologists, they were aware of how much the ordinary Athenian or Corinthian took for unchangeable human nature was in fact the result of Athenian or Corinthian upbringing and did not exist elsewhere at all. The distinction between what was 'by nature', the same for all human beings, and what was 'by convention', a matter of agreed-on rules, was a principal topic of discussion throughout the century. It was a moral more than a sociological debate. Convention, custom, upbringing tended to be looked upon as *mere* convention, hampering artifice, to be discarded by the enlightened. No doubt the contention of Hippias that all Greeks were by nature friends and brothers was amiable enough. Antiphon (*ca* 479–411 B.C.), one of the few native Athenian sophists, went so far as to declare that even the distinction between Greek and barbarian was not according to nature, for "by nature all of us are created equal in all respects." But before the century was out the discussion took a sinister turn.

In 431 B.C. the Peloponnesian War began between Athens and her sea empire on one side, Sparta and her allies on the other. It lasted an entire generation—27 years—and ended in total defeat of Athens and exhaustion of all Greece. Most Greek cities including Athens were at war most of the time, but the Peloponnesian War was more intense than usual. It was a world war in the sense that almost no city of the Greek world was able to remain neutral throughout. It was a commercial war, for the main cause of it was the jealous hatred of Athens on the part of Corinth, the number two trading city of Greece. "All wars are made for the sake of getting money," Plato said, and while there may be exceptions, this one was not.

It was to a large extent a class war also, a vast number of concurrent civil wars. Athens was a democracy, Corinth a plutocracy, and Sparta a barracks state. But every city was, as Plato again noted, really two cities—one of the rich, another of the poor. Athens and Sparta/Corinth polarized the Greek world. Athens required the cities in her empire to have democratic constitutions. This meant that within each there was, as a matter of course, a standing conspiracy of the rich to revolt and call in the Spartans and Corinthians; and, of course, there was a democratic underground in every city allied with Sparta.

Methods of warfare and the conduct of winners toward losers—which in the earlier part of the century had tended to be relatively humane, or as we used to say 'civilized'—became atrocious. When at the end of the war Athens had to surrender unconditionally, the proposal of the Corinthians was to level the city to the ground, kill all the men, and sell the women and children into slavery. Sparta, to her everlasting credit, vetoed the plan. But if it had been carried out, it would have been doing to the Athenians only what they had earlier done to others—in at least one case to a tiny city whose only offense was refusal to abandon neutrality.

Athens should have won the war; she lost principally because of the disastrous outcome of the expedition against Sicily in 413 B.C. Alcibiades—who had grown up in the house of Pericles and was the cleverest, handsomest, and most arrogant young man of the times—proposed the capture of the great city of Syracuse. He was placed in charge, along with two other generals, of the greatest force the Athenians or any Greek city had ever assembled. Just before his departure, Alcibiades was accused of offenses against the state religion but allowed to proceed to Sicily anyway. Once he was there, however, a ship was sent to fetch him back to stand trial for his life. Naturally he took the opportunity, when it presented itself, to escape. He made his way to Sparta, where he advised the Spartan generals on effective strategies to use against Athens. Meanwhile, the Sicilian expedition was put under the command of Nicias—an upright, popular, stupid, and superstitious general—who bungled everything, and who in the end lost every ship in his fleet, every man in his army, and his own life. After that the outcome was hardly in doubt, although Athens managed to hold out for nine more years.

Intellectual and political life was progressively brutalized. Athenian aristocrats overthrew the democracy in 411 B.C., but were themselves soon ejected by a democratic counterrevolution. Both coups were bloody. The views of Thrasymachus, a sophist, and Callicles, an Athenian aristocrat, are typical of social thought at the time. Like Antiphon and earlier sophists, they made central the distinction between nature and convention. But far from saying that by nature all men are equal, they held the contrary: that men, like beasts, are naturally unequal, and what is natural is for every man to get what he can by any means. Law, morality, fair play—everything that the Greek summed up in the notion of 'justice'—is a conventional, artificial obstacle that a clever man will circumvent and be a better man, a more excellent, 'virtuous' man, for doing it. "Injustice is virtue."

Thrasymachus, who deserves to be called the first sociologist, derived this paradox in the following manner. In every city there exists some group of men, it may be small or large, that in fact controls the preponderance of power. This power elite dictates what the laws are to be and indoctrinates the citizenry in obedience to these laws, calling it 'justice', the pattern of life approved by every right-thinking man. But how is the content of the laws determined? Thrasymachus declared that in every case the laws command action that will be in the interest of the power elite. Obeying laws, justice, is therefore nothing but serving "the interest of the stronger party." Usually when you are looking out for someone else's interest you are neglecting your own, and if you are doing it voluntarily you are a fool. Justice, therefore, is stupidity, and natural excellence, 'virtue', is the same thing as injustice.

The question whether political obligation is absolute had been raised and answered negatively half a century earlier by Sophocles (*ca* 496–406 B.C.) in his play

*Antigone*. But Sophocles did not deny political obligation; he held only that there are duties to kinfolk that take precedence. Thrasymachus in contrast rejected the whole idea of obligation to the state. The only genuine 'natural' obligation anyone has is that of looking out for himself. Nor (he held further) has any man of intelligence ever thought otherwise; the clever ones have merely invented obligation as a most effective means for furthering their own ends.

Plato's great-uncle Critias, another Athenian of aristocratic lineage, wrote a play in which he set out a sociological theory of religion. Men, whose nature is always to serve themselves, lived a miserable anarchic life until some wise man devised laws to regulate their behavior and police to make them obey. Only then did civilized life become possible—but just barely, because these measures curbed misbehavior only in public. The system was perfected when another "man of wise counsel" invented the gods: superpowerful invisible personages who see everything and punish secret lawlessness. The wise man got people to believe in gods by linking them to the great forces of nature, lightning and other terrifying phenomena.

Critias saw that religion is mythology, but he believed myths to be socially indispensable. The wise inventor of religion "concealed the truth under untrue words"—people will truly be wretched if they are unjust, because when the rule is every man for himself, everyone takes the hindmost. What Critias forgot—or did he?—when he revealed the secret of religion to an audience of twenty-five thousand, was that once the word gets out that the myth is nothing but a myth, its effectiveness is drained away.

# 10

## Socrates

ON A WINTER MORNING in 423 B.C., during a truce in the Peloponnesian War, twenty-five thousand spectators gathered in the theater of Athens to witness the new farce by Aristophanes (*ca* 450–*ca* 388 B.C.). He was departing from his usual political themes to satirize science and sophistry.

### Aristophanes: *The Clouds*

An old man, hopelessly in debt because of his horse-fancying son's extravagance, resolves to learn from the sophists the cleverness that will enable him to cheat his creditors. For this purpose he enters the Thinkateria, a sleazy institute inhabited by hungry, dirty, pasty-faced disciples of the great Socrates, who makes his dramatic entrance in a basket suspended high in the air. Haughtily he explains: "I could never have found out the truth of celestial matters without suspending my judgment and subtly blending my intellect with its kindred air."[1] Then he begins to instruct the old man in the new atheistic science, which, as we would have expected after his entrance line, turns out to be the system of Anaximenes.

The Chorus of new deities, the Clouds, make a melodious entrance and then speak.

> Greetings, ancient one, seeker after the Muses' lore. And greetings to you, high priest of subtle twaddle; what is it you want? You're the only one we'd listen to, of all these smart modern professors—except for Prodicus; we like you both, him because he's so wise and clever, and you for the way you strut about the place looking down your nose at everyone, fancying yourself as a real ascetic and showing off because you're a friend of ours!

OLD MAN   My godfathers, what voices! How holy! How solemn and portentous they sound!

SOCRATES   Yes, they're the only divinities there are; the rest are all a lot of hogwash.

OLD MAN   But what about Olympian Zeus? Surely he's a god, isn't he?

SOCRATES   Zeus? Don't talk nonsense, there's no such person.

OLD MAN   What do you mean? Who sends the rain, then? Just tell me that for a start.

SOCRATES   The Clouds, of course. There's good evidence to prove it. Just think; have you ever seen it raining when there were no Clouds about? But if it's Zeus who sends the rain, you'd expect him to do it on clear days sometimes, while they're having a holiday.

OLD MAN  Well, I must admit that fits your theory very neatly. You know, I always used to think it was Zeus pissing through a sieve. But tell me where the thunder comes from; I do get so frightened by it.

SOCRATES  The Clouds make it, by rolling around.

OLD MAN  How do you mean? You do have some wild ideas!

SOCRATES  When they're forced together full of water, some force makes them hang down under the weight of moisture; and then being so heavy they crash into one another and burst with a frightful din.

OLD MAN  But who does all this forcing? Isn't it Zeus?

SOCRATES  Good God, no; it's the Heavenly Vortex.

OLD MAN  Vortex? Oh, of course, how silly of me, there isn't a Zeus; it's Vortex now who rules instead, is it? But you haven't explained about the noise of thunder yet.

Socrates explains that thunder is only the likeness in the sky of the rumblings that accompany indigestion from overeating. He goes on to explain lightning with more homely illustrations, pointing out incidentally that if Zeus means to hit perjurers with his bolts, he has missed some of the most notorious while managing to strike down innocent oak trees and even his own temples.

The old man, however, proves too stupid to learn the new science. So he goes home and persuades his son to enroll in the course on how to make the wrong side appear to be right. The instruction is all too successful. Requested by his father to sing a song, the son sneers at the old poets and launches into "a disgusting piece by Euripides about a man raping his own sister." Annoyed at his father's outrage, he not only physically abuses the old man but proves by sophistical rhetoric that he was right to do so.

SON  Please answer this question: did you ever hit me when I was small?

OLD MAN  Yes, but only for your own good and because I was fond of you.

SON  Well then, isn't it right for me to be equally fond of you, and therefore hit you, if as you say being fond of a person is the same as hitting him? If I used to get whacked such a lot it wouldn't be proper for you to go scot-free, would it? I'm a free man just as much as you are, you know . . . I expect you'll say that it's the custom only for children to be beaten; but my answer to that is that old men are in their second childhood and that they ought to be beaten more than the young because they have less excuse for being naughty.

OLD MAN  But all over the world it's against the law for a son to beat his father.

SON  But wasn't that law instituted by a man just like you or me? And didn't he have to win over our ancestors to get it adopted? Why shouldn't I be able to pass a new law, that in future sons should hit their fathers back? . . . Take roosters and other creatures like that—look at the punishing they give their fathers. And they're no different from us, are they? . . .

OLD MAN  Well, if you want to model yourself on a rooster, why don't you eat dirt or go and roost on a perch?

SON  Don't be absurd. That's got nothing to do with it; Socrates wouldn't think so, anyway.

When the son threatens to beat his mother as well, his father can stand it no longer. Gathering his cronies together he puts the Thinkateria to axe and torch, roasting staff and student body alive.

Socrates was butt of another farce produced at the same festival, and two years later he was again held up to ridicule. So in 423, in his middle forties, he was already well known in Athens as a prominent avant garde intellectual. Aristophanes—who we gather from the play was well informed about Ionian science and who according to Plato was personally on friendly terms with Socrates—presents him as one who makes fun of the official gods of the city, introduces in their stead 'new divinities', and corrupts the youth. Socrates at his trial denied that there was a word of truth in these accusations, but that was a quarter of a century later. And all that he specifically denied was that at the time of his trial he had any interest in "things in the sky and below the ground." But even according to Plato's account he had had such interests "when he was young."[2] Dangerous as it may be to infer realities from a caricature, we can probably conclude that Socrates in middle life was adept at natural science, had a reputation for cleverness at argument, and was the object of devotion on the part of a number of younger men. In the farce he accepts payment for his teaching (though he is not shown as demanding it) and he is the head of a regular school with a secret doctrine revealed only to the initiates. It is likely that Aristophanes misrepresented his victim in these respects, though the error is natural enough if (as there is some evidence from tradition) Socrates was once a member though not head of such a school—that of Archelaus, who carried on the science of Anaxagoras at Athens after the latter's departure.

Aristophanes, only about 20 years younger than Socrates, must have known about him from the time he first attracted public attention. On the other hand, Xenophon (*ca* 431–*ca* 352 B.C.) and Plato, our other two sources of information, were both born more than 40 years after him and could have associated with him only in the last decade of his life. This circumstance may explain in part why their picture of him is so different from the one drawn by the comic poet.

## Xenophon

Xenophon's book *Reminiscences of Socrates* was written expressly to refute the charges of irreligion and corrupting the youth. This it does so well that if it were the whole truth about Socrates his condemnation would be unintelligible. Xenophon describes a man who asked students of science whether they had solved their own problems of living so neatly that they could afford the time for investigating the heavens. This man concerned himself with upright living, reducing all the virtues to prudence, and was always ready to give sensible advice. For instance, to a man unable to support 14 genteel but indigent female relatives, he pointed out that they did know how to do something from which they could earn money, namely weaving. So the man set up looms in their mansion, and soon they prospered, whereupon they began to complain about the idleness of the master of the house. Socrates solved this problem too by drawing an analogy with the shepherd's dog who earns his keep not by giving wool but by protecting the wool producers. So all lived happily. Putting a man like Xenophon's Socrates to death would have been as inexplicable an injustice as electrocuting Ann Landers.

## Plato's Portrait of Socrates

The fullest and most accurate information about Socrates is of course found in the writings of Plato, who was a member of the Socratic circle for ten years or so. His elder brothers and other members had associated with Socrates for a generation before then.

Socrates (469–399 B.C.) was the son of a stonecutter and a midwife. Later tradition has it that he himself worked at the trade of stonecutting or sculpting, but this has no support from Plato, who indeed has nothing to say about how Socrates made his living. At his trial he attributed the poverty of his later years to neglect of his personal affairs made necessary by his divine mission. In the war he served as a heavy-armed infantryman; soldiers of this classification had to be able to afford rather expensive battle gear. From youth onward he associated on terms of equality with the highest Athenian society. He prided himself, moreover, on never taking fees for his teaching or conversing. The general impression is of a man of independent income, not large but enough for the satisfaction of his few wants.

Socrates was almost as famous for his self-sufficiency as for his talk: he went barefoot, wore the same cloak winter and summer, ate notably simple food, and drank water in preference to wine. When the occasion demanded, however—as when invited to a party celebrating a tragic poet's winning of the prize—he dressed himself in suitable finery and literally drank everyone else under the table.

Socrates is perhaps the first Greek, at any rate the first private citizen, of whom we possess a detailed description. He was short, stocky, muscular, potbellied, snub-nosed, pop-eyed, and bald.

Socrates was the most famous asker of questions who ever lived. Always a notable talker, in middle life he gave up all other pursuits to devote himself to the 'examination of life'. Just by asking questions Socrates on the one hand attracted to himself the unqualified devotion of numbers of first-rate men, including a world genius, Plato; on the other, he so infuriated so many of his fellow citizens that they condemned him to death. How this came about, what Socrates meant by examination of life, and why he did it, we are told by Plato in the *Apology*—which purports to be and beyond doubt in substance is the speech that Socrates made in his defense when on trial for irreligion and subversion.

A young man named Chaerephon, who admired Socrates extravagantly, asked the oracle at Delphi whether anyone was wiser than Socrates. The reply was negative. Socrates when told of this expressed puzzlement; he had abandoned his scientific pursuits out of a conviction that if truth about the nature of things was attainable at all, he at any rate had not enough talents in that direction to discover it. But since the oracle was the voice of the god Apollo, it could not lightly be dismissed. So Socrates set out to investigate the wisdom of the world. He questioned whomever he came across who was reputed by others or by himself to be the possessor of extraordinary wisdom. The politicians when asked about the rationale of their endeavors were quickly reduced to incoherence. Poets were found to be incapable of explaining their own poems. Craftsmen knew what they were talking about when on the subject of their specialties, but they would insist also on talking rubbish about affairs of state. These people, however, were none of them aware of their own ignorance until Socrates in his cross-examinations made it obvious. Socrates concluded that the oracle was right in the sense that to know that one is ignorant is to be wiser than one who knows not even that much.

These interrogations often went on before an audience of highly amused young men. It is hardly surprising that many victims were happy to get their revenge when three bigots hauled Socrates into court.

But the exposure of pretentiousness was only incidental to Socrates' mission, which was positive and of the utmost seriousness. In the *Apology*, Socrates says that in obedience to the god

> I shall never stop practising philosophy and exhorting you and elucidating the truth for everyone that I meet. I shall go on saying, in my usual way, "My very good friend, you are an Athenian and belong to a city which is the greatest and most famous in the world for its wisdom and strength. Are you not ashamed that you give your attention to acquiring as much money as possible, and similarly with reputation and honor, and give no attention or thought to truth and understanding and the perfection of your soul?" And if any of you disputes this and professes to care about these things, I shall not at once let him go or leave him; no, I shall question him and examine him and test him; and if it appears that in spite of his profession he has made no real progress towards goodness, I shall reprove him for neglecting what is of supreme importance, and giving his attention to trivialities . . . This, I do assure you, is what the god commands; and it is my belief that no greater good has ever befallen you in this city than my service to the god; for I spend all my time going about trying to persuade you, young and old, to make your first and chief concern not for your bodies nor for your possessions, but for the highest welfare of your souls, proclaiming as I go "Wealth does not bring goodness, but goodness brings wealth and every other blessing, both to the individual and to the State."[3]

When the jury voted to condemn him, Socrates refused to compromise on any penalty that would have required him to keep silent, for, he said, "the unexamined life is not fit for a man to live." Examining life meant, for Socrates, getting clear about what is worthwhile and why. The unexamined life pursued by most people consists in doing what is expected, out of fear or habit, and taking for granted the validity of the attitude current in the society. If the norm to which you conform is debased, your life will naturally be unsatisfactory. But even if the current standards happen to be impeccable, to follow them without examination is not a fit way to live—because what is uniquely human, reason, is not brought into play concerning matters of ultimate importance. Socrates thought that in the end questions of what ought to be done, what kind of life is the best, are capable of being answered by the intellect: virtue is knowledge. To care for the soul, then, or to examine life is to reason about the good and your relation to it. By no coincidence was KNOW THYSELF inscribed in the temple of Apollo at Delphi where the oracle pronounced Socrates the wisest of the Greeks.

It is plain too that Socrates did examine life in some systematic way and came to conclusions about how life ought to be led that went beyond mere recommendation of 'virtue'. Socrates had a philosophy. Otherwise there would be no explaining why Plato would have paid him the homage he did. What was that philosophy? Plato tells us in vivid terms and in detail.

## Does Plato Portray Socrates Accurately?

Plato said that in the Dialogues he presented Socrates "adorned and rejuvenated." Many scholars believe that much of the adornment consisted in making Socrates express doctrines that the historical gadfly never dreamed of but were in fact later inventions of Plato himself, so that—except in the *Apology* and perhaps a few other early writings—we cannot learn what Socrates' philosophy was by reading Plato. In particular (these scholars hold) the celebrated Theory of Ideas, that true reality consists of Triangularity—Beauty Itself, Justice, and other Beings apprehended by the mind's eye, of which visible triangles, beautiful boys, and just actions are half-real, imperfect copies—was Plato's invention. The principal support for this view is the brief remark by Aristotle that Socrates "did not separate the Ideas"; that is, did not theorize that Triangularity has a being of its own apart from and prior to any and all particular triangular things.

The main consideration in favor of Plato's having presented an essentially accurate report of Socrates' thought is that Plato certainly meant to honor the memory of Socrates, which would hardly be done by making him into a mouthpiece for doctrines he never thought of. This argument is most impressive as regards the *Phaedo*, which purports to describe the final day of Socrates' life. To take so sublime a frame and deceptively insert one's own portrait into it would be blasphemous. But if whatever is ascribed to Socrates in the *Phaedo* must be genuinely Socratic, then his philosophy included immortality, preexistence of the soul, and the Ideas.

## The Socratic Revolution

Plato wrote an intellectual biography of Socrates, *Phaedo* 96A–101E.

> When I was young, Cebes, I had an extraordinary passion for that branch of learning which is called natural science; I thought it would be marvellous to know the causes for which each thing comes and ceases and continues to be. I was constantly veering to and fro, puzzling primarily over this sort of question: Is it when heat and cold produce fermentation, as some have said, that living creatures are bred? Is it with the blood that we think, or with the air or the fire that is in us? . . . [But] at last I came to the conclusion that I was entirely unfitted for this form of inquiry. . . .
>
> Then I heard someone reading from a book by Anaxagoras, and asserting that it is Mind that produces order and is the cause of everything. This explanation pleased me. Somehow it seemed right that Mind should be the cause of everything; and I reflected that if this is so, Mind in producing order sets everything in order and arranges each individual thing in the way that is best for it. Therefore if anyone wished to discover the reason why any given thing came or ceased or continued to be, he must find out how it was best for that thing to be, or to act or be acted upon in any other way. On this view there was only one thing for a man to consider, with regard both to himself and to anything else, namely the best and highest good, although this would necessarily imply knowing what is less good, since both were covered by the same knowledge.
>
> These reflections made me suppose, to my delight, that in Anaxagoras I had found an authority on causation who was after my own heart. I assumed that he would begin by informing us whether the earth is flat or round, and would then proceed to explain in detail the reason and logical necessity for this by stating how and why it was better that it should be so. I thought that if he asserted that the earth was in the centre, he would explain in detail that it was better for it to be there; and if he made this clear, I was prepared to give up hankering after any other kind of cause. . . . It never entered my head that a man who asserted that the ordering of things is due to Mind would offer any other explanation for them than that it is best for them to be as they are. I thought that by assigning a cause to each phenomenon separately and to the

universe as a whole he would make perfectly clear what is best for each and what is the universal good. I would not have parted with my hopes for a great sum of money. I lost no time in procuring the books, and began to read them as quickly as I possibly could, so that I might know as soon as possible about the Best and the Less Good.

It was a wonderful hope, my friend, but it was quickly dashed. As I read on I discovered that the fellow made no use of Mind and assigned to it no causality for the order of the world, but adduced causes like air and ether and water and many other absurdities. It seemed to me that he was just about as inconsistent as if someone were to say "The cause of everything that Socrates does is Mind" and then, in trying to account for my several actions, said first that the reason why I am lying here now is that my body is composed of bones and sinews, and that the bones are rigid and separated at the joints, but the sinews are capable of contraction and relaxation, and form an envelope for the bones with the help of the flesh and skin, the latter holding all together; and since the bones move freely in their joints the sinews by relaxing and contracting enable me somehow to bend my limbs; and that is the cause of my sitting here in a bent position. Or again, if he tried to account in the same way for my conversing with you, adducing causes such as sound and air and hearing and a thousand others, and never troubled to mention the real reasons; which are that since Athens has thought it better to condemn me, therefore I for my part have thought it better to sit here, and more right to stay and submit to whatever penalty she orders— because, by the Dog! I fancy that these sinews and bones would have been in the neighborhood of Megara or Boeotia long ago (impelled by a conviction of what is best!) if I did not think that it was more right and honorable to submit to whatever penalty my country orders rather than take to my heels and run away. But to call things like that causes is too absurd. If it were said that without such bones and sinews and all the rest of them I should not be able to do what I think is right, it would be true; but to say that it is because of them that I do what I am doing, and not through choice of what is best—although my actions are controlled by Mind—would be a very lax and inaccurate form of expression. Fancy being unable to distinguish between the cause of a thing, and the condition without which it could not be a cause! It is this latter, as it seems to me, that most people, groping in the dark, call a cause— attaching to it a name to which it has no right. That is why one person surrounds the earth with a vortex, and so keeps it in place by means of the heavens; and another props it up on a pedestal of air, as though it were a wide platter. As for a power which keeps things disposed at any given moment in the best possible way, they neither look for it nor believe that it has any supernatural force; they imagine that they will some day find a more mighty and immortal and all-sustaining Atlas; and they do not think that anything is really bound and held together by goodness or moral obligation.[4]

Here we have before us the Socratic revolution, or counterrevolution, in philosophy. At first glance it may look as if Socrates was advocating a return to a pre-Milesian animistic view of the world. In a sense he was: the explanation of things in general was again to be based on the model of human decision. What he proposed was, however, more intellectual than a mere will-of-the-gods account. Socrates wished to bring to the fore not the element of command but that of deliberation. When we act deliberately, we are trying to bring about some state of affairs that we deem good. If subsequently called upon to justify—explain—why we did what we did, we describe the good that we aimed to produce. The offering of these justifications is the way we make our actions intelligible, the way we persuade ourselves and others of our reasonableness.

Socrates supposed that nothing can be understood finally unless we know what its reason is, in this deliberative or intentional sense. That is why all explanation—

even of the shape of the earth—must be given in terms of the Best. Socrates assumed that an explanation always existed to be found. As for the mechanistic explanation of the Democritean type, he incorporated it into his scheme but subordinated it, calling the pushes and pulls of material parts mere 'conditions' rather than causes.

Was this reintroduction of purpose into the world view a return to religion? In a way. But Socrates' reverence for the gods did not make him picture the world as a machine created or activated by a personal being outside or inside it. When we justify our actions we deem it sufficient to point out the good that we aimed to achieve. Usually we do not think it necessary or even possible to picture that good in personal terms. In our model of justification the good itself is sufficient reason for our activity. Just so, Socrates thought that the Good, though not a person or having any personal characteristics, was the real cause or sufficient reason of all things. Things, he believed, automatically aim at the good—and in his terminology that is the same as saying that the good is the supreme cause. This is the fundamental thought of almost all Greek philosophy from Socrates on: that value is the central notion in any reasoned account of things; how things are is to be understood in terms of how things ought to be.

Likewise the conception of how human beings are to be understood is revolutionized. The pre-Socratics tried to understand the human animal as an organism in interaction with the environment. The old Ionian conception is implied in the first lines of the *Iliad* where Homer, describing the destructive wrath of Achilles, sings that it "sent to Hades many mighty souls of heroes, but left *them* to be spoils for dogs and feasts for vultures." That is a literal translation, though instead of the italicized "them" all English versions use "their bodies." For the contrast that Homer takes for granted between the heroes *themselves*, left lifeless on the battlefield, and on the other hand their souls which like their breaths—or indeed *being* their breaths—have left them, is so strange to us as to be unintelligible without explanation. Compare the reply of Socrates to Crito who asks how they shall bury him.

> Any way you like—that is, if you can catch me and I don't slip through your fingers. (He laughed gently as he spoke, and turning to us went on:) I can't persuade Crito that I am this Socrates here who is talking to you now and marshalling all the arguments; he thinks that I am the one whom he will see presently lying dead; and he asks how he is to bury me! . . . You must assure him that when I am dead I shall not stay, but depart and be gone. That will help Crito to bear it more easily, and keep him from being distressed on my account when he sees my body being burned or buried, as if something dreadful were happening to me.[5]

Even those of us who do not believe that we possess immortal souls would agree that if we *did* have them, then our selves would be identified with them and not with our bodies. But this conception of the soul has a history. "It was Socrates who, so far as can be seen, created the conception of the *soul* . . . something which is the seat of [a human being's] normal waking intelligence and moral character."[6]

The contrast between body and soul—the former gross and corruptible, the latter subtle and undying—is of course not Socrates' invention. It is found in all sorts of non-Greek cultures, and in Greece is the basis of all forms of Orphic religion including the Pythagorean. Socrates' conception of the soul was a development of Pythagoreanism; as we shall see, so is most of his and Plato's philosophy.

But we encounter first in Socrates the conception of a soul that is not just a very thin and subtle kind of bodily stuff but rather not bodily at all. He was able to give some sense to the notion of a real, individual, active thing that was not a body because he already recognized in his philosophy the Ideas, which were just such objects; and the Ideas in their turn are descendants of Parmenides' Being, objects of thought that are the same (or nearly the same) as thought.

## The Crime of Socrates

If Socrates was indeed an adherent of the Pythagorean philosophy, some light may be cast on the otherwise vexing question of why he was charged with irreligion. No doubt the main motive, as is common in such accusations, was to inflame the greatest possible prejudice and to do so with the least expenditure of effort in providing proof. However, the exact words of the indictment are curious: "Socrates does not honor the gods that the city honors, but brings in new divinities." Both Xenophon and Plato point out indignantly that Socrates meticulously observed all the ritual requirements, and dismiss the latter part of the indictment as an obscure and frivolous reference to the interior "divine voice" that Socrates claimed to hear from time to time warning him not to do this or that. However, the word translated "divinities" may just as well be rendered as "conceptions of divinity," in which case the charge was that Socrates tried to make radical revisions in religious beliefs—a charge of more substance and more in line both with what we know of Socrates and with the claim of the prosecutor Meletus that Socrates was a complete atheist. What might the new "conceptions of divinity" have been? Pythagoreanism was, let us remember, a kind of religion, and one that provoked hostility throughout Greece.

The accusation that Socrates "corrupted the youth" was even vaguer than that of irreligion. Socrates pointed out in his defense that no attempt was made to produce witnesses to the fact. Xenophon attests that there was hatred of Socrates for his having been the teacher of Alcibiades and Critias. The former was believed to have committed monstrous sacrileges and certainly did commit a treason of such magnitude that it may have been *the* cause of losing the war. The latter, a religious skeptic, in the hour of defeat was installed under Spartan auspices as bloodthirsty chief of the Thirty Tyrants. Other members of the Socratic group were notorious for their contempt of democratic government and popular beliefs in general. Xenophon protests that Socrates tried to reform Alcibiades (Plato makes the same point more subtly), and gave up associating with him when his efforts met no success; and that Critias and others hung around Socrates only to learn cleverness. Plato, however, scorns to conceal Socrates' anti-democratic views. Socrates thought it absurd to leave to the experts decisions about relatively unimportant technical matters such as the design of ships, while letting every ignoramus and sot have his say and his vote on policy matters of the highest consequence.

Although resentment of these attitudes and a perhaps unjustified inference of guilt by association must have played their part in producing the verdict against Socrates, there is no strong reason to suppose that he was really condemned for something other than what he was charged with. The indictment remains the classic complaint against the intellectual innovator of every age and country: "He does not honor the gods that the city honors, but brings in new divinities. And he corrupts the youth."

If bigotry triumphed in the case of Socrates, it was a unique occasion in ancient Greece. There is no record of anyone else in Athens or elsewhere having been put to death simply for holding views deemed pernicious. When centuries later the Christians introduced the practice, it was on a wide scale, and the usual method of execution was not the administration of an alkaloid but burning alive.

## The Death of Socrates

In Athens condemned men were usually put to death immediately after the trial. However, for religious reasons this was impossible in the case of Socrates. So for a month afterward he was kept in a prison where every day he was allowed to converse with his friends. Crito, a rich man, arranged to bribe the guards and let him escape, but Socrates refused to go. In living all his life in Athens—although free to move elsewhere—he had consented to live by the laws, even if those laws were so administered as to result in his unjust condemnation.

Plato's account of how Socrates died is one of the most moving passages in European literature.

> When he had spoken these words, he arose and went into a chamber to bathe; Crito followed him and told us to wait. So we remained behind, talking and thinking of the subject of discourse, and also of the greatness of our sorrow; he was like a father of whom we were being bereaved, and we were about to pass the rest of our lives as orphans. When he had taken the bath his children were brought to him—(he had two young sons and an elder one); and the women of his family also came, and he talked to them and gave them a few directions in the presence of Crito; then he dismissed them and returned to us.
>
> Now the hour of sunset was near, for a good deal of time had passed while he was within. When he came out, he sat down with us again after his bath, but not much was said. Soon the jailer entered and stood by him, saying:—To you, Socrates, whom I know to be the noblest and gentlest and best of all who ever came to this place, I will not impute the angry feelings of other men, who rage and swear at me, when, in obedience to the authorities, I bid them drink the poison—indeed, I am sure that you will not be angry with me; for others, as you are aware, and not I, are to blame. And so fare you well, and try to bear lightly what must needs be—you know my errand. Then bursting into tears he turned away and went out.
>
> Socrates looked at him and said: I return your good wishes, and will do as you bid. Then turning to us, he said, How charming the man is: since I have been in prison he has always been coming to see me, and at times he would talk to me, and was as good to me as could be, and now see how generously he sorrows on my account. We must do as he says, Crito; and therefore let the cup be brought, if the poison is prepared: if not, let the attendant prepare some.
>
> Yet, said Crito, the sun is still upon the hill-tops, and I know that many a one has taken the draught late, and after the announcement has been made to him, he has eaten and drunk, and enjoyed the society of his beloved; do not hurry—there is time enough.
>
> Socrates said: Yes, Crito, and they of whom you speak are right in so acting, for they think that they will be gainers by the delay; but I am right in not following their example, for I do not think that I should gain anything by drinking the poison a little later; I should only be ridiculous in my own eyes for sparing and saving a life which is already forfeit. Please then to do as I say, and not to refuse me.
>
> Crito made a sign to the servant, who was standing by, and he went out, and having been absent for some time, returned with the jailer carrying the cup of poison. Socrates said: You, my good friend, who are experienced in these matters, shall give

me directions how I am to proceed. The man answered: You have only to walk about until your legs are heavy, and then to lie down, and the poison will act. At the same time he handed the cup to Socrates, who in the easiest and gentlest manner, without the least fear or change of color or feature, looking at the man with all his eyes, as his manner was, took the cup and said: What do you say about making a libation out of this cup to any god? May I, or not? The man answered: We only prepare, Socrates, just so much as we deem enough. I understand, he said: but I may and must ask the gods to prosper my journey from this to the other world—even so—and so be it according to my prayer. Then raising the cup to his lips, quite readily and cheerfully he drank off the poison. And hitherto most of us had been able to control our sorrow: but now when we saw him drinking, and saw too that he had finished the draught, we could no longer forbear, and in spite of myself my own tears were flowing fast; so that I covered my face and wept, not for him, but at the thought of my own calamity in having to part from such a friend. Nor was I the first; for Crito, when he found himself unable to restrain his tears, had got up, and I followed; and at that moment, Apollodorus, who had been weeping all the time, broke out in a loud and passionate cry which made cowards of us all. Socrates alone retained his calmness: What is this strange outcry? he said. I sent away the women mainly in order that they might not misbehave in this way, for I have been told that a man should die in peace. Be quiet then, and have patience. When we heard his words we were ashamed, and refrained our tears; and he walked about until, as he said, his legs began to fail, and then he lay on his back, according to the directions, and the man who gave him the poison now and then looked at his feet and legs; and after a while he pressed his foot hard, and asked him if he could feel; and he said, No; and then his leg, and so upwards and upwards, and showed us that he was cold and stiff. And he felt them himself, and said: When the poison reaches the heart, that will be the end. He was beginning to grow cold about the groin, when he uncovered his face, for he had covered himself up, and said—they were his last words—Crito, I owe a cock to Asclepius; will you remember to pay the debt? The debt shall be paid, said Crito; is there anything else? There was no answer to this question; but in a minute or two a movement was heard, and the attendants uncovered him; his eyes were set, and Crito closed his eyes and mouth.

Such was the end of our friend; concerning whom I may truly say, that of all the men of his time whom I have known, he was the wisest and justest and best.[7]

# 11

# The Life of Plato

FOURTEEN MEN ARE MENTIONED by name as having been with Socrates when he drank the hemlock. Several of them went on to expound philosophies of their own. A middle-aged Athenian named Antisthenes (*ca* 455–*ca* 365 B.C.) stressed Socrates' self-sufficiency, indifference to external goods, and insistence that moral virtue should in conduct be preferred to every other consideration. He was the founder of the Cynic school. Euclid (*ca* 450–368 B.C.), from the neighboring town of Megara, established there a school in which the art of dialectical discussion was cultivated. Aristippus (*ca* 435–366 B.C.), though not present in the prison, returned to his home city of Cyrene in North Africa to teach that pleasure—rational and cultivated pleasure, of course—is the sole end in life. This might have been a development of one strain in Socrates' philosophy, for as we have seen he was no ascetic. Xenophon, author of the Socratic memoirs, was off to the wars in Iran. Plato was ill.

Plato at the time was not quite 30 years of age, having been born in 428 or 427 B.C. into an aristocratic Athenian family. He counted descent on his mother's side from Solon the lawgiver and through his father from the god Poseidon. Although we know nothing of his childhood and youth, we can guess that they must have been full of disorder and early sorrow, since the disaster of the expedition to Syracuse occurred when he was 14 and surrender to Sparta took place when he was 23. Presumably he fought in the war.

Socrates was a friend of Plato's family, particularly of his elder brothers Glaucon and Adeimantus, from the time when Plato was a schoolboy. When Socrates, after his conviction, was persuaded to propose as an alternative penalty to death a fine of 30 minas (about $15,000), Plato and three other friends offered to guarantee payment.

We have Plato's own word that two catastrophes discouraged him from pursuing the political career he and his family had assumed he would follow. Athens, during the Spartan occupation of 404–403, was required to set up an authoritarian government under a group soon known as the Thirty Tyrants. Their leader was Critias the playwright, Plato's great-uncle, and his mother's brother Charmides also belonged. Plato was invited to join them and was inclined to accept—as he was thoroughly in sympathy with their intention to abolish the evils of democracy. However, they went too far for him, particularly in their arbitrary dealings with Socrates, whom they tried to gag and to involve in their terroristic policy. Plato was as relieved as the rest of the Athenians when this bloody clique was overthrown after eight months in power. He had hopes that the restored democracy would turn out to be a good thing; it made a promising start by declaring an amnesty for all political crimes. But then four years later one of the leading politicians accused Socrates of irreligion and succeeded in having him put to death. Plato turned to the long-range plan of teaching men how to be decent rulers.

## Involvement with Syracuse

Eleven years after the execution of Socrates, Plato traveled to Syracuse, the dominant Greek city of Sicily, in whose politics he was to be curiously involved for the rest of his life. Syracuse was ruled by the tyrant Dionysius, a man of great energy and few scruples, who was engaged in the defense of Greek Sicily against the (Semitic) Carthaginians. He did not like what he found: "I arrived and saw what they call there the 'dolce vita'—a life filled with Italian and Syracusan banquets, with men gorging themselves twice a day and never sleeping alone at night, and following all the other customs that go with this way of living."[1] Dionysius did not care for Plato either. The story is told that the tyrant had Plato kidnapped and sold into slavery; he was ransomed when a friend chanced to recognize him in the slave market on the island of Aegina near Athens. Plato does not mention the incident, and it is hard to believe that if he had ever actually been a slave he would have been uninterested in the abolition or reform of slavery, as his writings indicate he was. On this trip, however, he had taken the opportunity of meeting the leading Pythagoreans of the region, and had made the acquaintance of the tyrant's brother-in-law Dion who was, in Plato's view, all that a philosophical young man ought to be.

## The Academy

On returning to Athens Plato founded the Academy, so called from the grove sacred to the demigod Academus where it was located outside the city walls. This was an institution where men came together for higher education and research in mathematics, astronomy, and philosophy. It was perhaps not the first such establishment—the "Thinkateria" of *The Clouds* must have been a caricature of something actually existing—but it was the first recognizable university of which we have a record. Its unbroken life span of 915 years has not yet been exceeded.

## Second and Third Sicilian Visits

When he was 60 years old and had been guiding the Academy for 20 years, an opportunity presented itself that Plato could not let pass. He had written in his greatest work, the *Republic*, that only the union of philosophy with absolute power could put an end to the ills of the human condition. The prescription had become famous. He had indeed stated that there was just one possibility for effecting fundamental political reform.

> No one will argue that it could never happen that the offspring of kings and rulers would be natural-born philosophers. Who could say that if they were born this way, they would have to be corrupted? It would be hard to save them, that we admit; but who will argue that in the whole course of time not a one might be saved? But surely the occurrence of just one would be enough, if he had an obedient city, to bring about all those things that are unbelievable now.[2]

In 367 Dionysius died, bequeathing the tyranny to his son Dionysius Junior. The boy, not yet out of his teens, was said by his uncle Dion, Plato's admirer, to be of a philosophical disposition. The two joined in inviting Plato to come to Syracuse and take charge of his education—an offer that could not be refused.

Plato arrived only a little while before a falling out between the young tyrant and his uncle led to Dion's banishment. Dionysius liked to talk with Plato, but wanted flattery not philosophy. Plato returned to Athens without having accomplished anything. Nevertheless, four years later Dionysius invited Plato to return and sent a warship to fetch him. If Plato would come, he wrote, there might be a reconciliation with Dion. Otherwise not only would Dion remain in exile but his wealth was in danger of being confiscated.

This time on arriving at the Syracusan court Plato began by asking Dionysius certain questions. The answers convinced him that the tyrant was neither proficient nor interested in philosophy. From the start the two did not get on. Dion was not recalled, and his property was confiscated. Plato became virtually a prisoner, even in danger of his life. After two years he was allowed to depart as a result of pressure brought to bear by Archytas, the ruler of Tarentum, a Pythagorean and an old friend.

Shortly afterwards Dion led an expedition of Sicilian exiles against Dionysius; it was successful. But Dion, once installed in power, also behaved in a high-handed way. Before long he was assassinated by a close colleague, an Athenian at that. Such was the melancholy end of Plato's one great try at putting philosophy into practice.

By then Plato was 67 years old. He continued as president of the Academy until at the age of 80 he died suddenly and peacefully while attending a wedding.

## Writings

Uniquely among Greek writers of the classical period, Plato had the good fortune to have his complete works survive and in good texts. Partly this was due to his foresight in founding an institution with a library. Ancient and modern critics generally agree in ranking Plato as the foremost prose stylist of Greece, if not of all European literature.

Presumably he began writing soon after the death of Socrates and continued for the rest of his life, a period of more than half a century. Except for the *Apology*, all his works are in the form of dialogues, conversations, although some are very one-sided. Socrates is the main speaker in all but a few; he is represented as being present in all save one.

Twelve letters purportedly by Plato have also survived. The longest and most important, the Seventh, fortunately is the one whose genuineness is least open to doubt. It is Plato's own Apology for the part he played in Sicilian affairs.

Mainly by stylometry, a statistical technique based on variations in usage, scholars have arrived at agreement in classifying Plato's dialogues into three groups: early, middle, and late. Besides the *Apology*, the early group includes the short so-called dialogues of search, where typically a presumed expert in $X$ is asked by Socrates what $X$ is and is found unable to provide a satisfactory answer. Thus in the *Euthyphro*, a young man who professes special knowledge of religious matters is interrogated about holiness; in the *Laches* two prominent generals get into difficulties when trying to define courage. The questions asked are not formally answered, though in every case a good deal of doctrine is propounded. In the

*Euthyphro,* for instance, the important point is made that ethics cannot be a mere branch of theology since surely the gods approve of what is right because they recognize its rightness—which must therefore be a quality prior to divine approval. We get the impression that these dialogues give us the most faithful—they certainly give the most vivid—portrait of Socrates in action.

The longest and most important of these early writings are the *Protagoras,* scenically the most elaborate, often hilarious, and argumentatively a puzzle; the *Gorgias,* a somber attack on power politicians; and the *Meno,* concerned officially with the question of whether virtue can be taught but most interesting for the attempted proof that we learned geometry before we were born.

The middle dialogues—perhaps written between the founding of the Academy and the Sicilian affair—include the three great masterpieces *Republic, Phaedo,* and *Symposium.* The last is another scenically elaborate piece: Socrates at a banquet with the leading intellectuals of the day, all talking about love. *Phaedrus* treats of love, the soul, and oratory. The first half of *Parmenides* is an astoundingly penetrating criticism of the theory of Ideas put into the mouth of the aged Eleatic philosopher represented as conversing with Socrates, then around 20 years of age, who has just invented the theory. The other half is an exercise in abstract dialectical reasoning that continues to baffle interpretation. *Theaetetus* is a long dialogue about knowledge in which Plato attempts to demolish the views ascribed to Protagoras that knowledge is based on sense perception and is relative to the individual perceiver.

Of the late dialogues only one, *Philebus,* has Socrates as principal speaker. Its subject is the good life, and particularly the place of pleasure in relation to other kinds of good. *Sophist* and *Statesman,* despite their titles, are concerned mainly with questions of the logic of classification. A "Stranger from Elea" is the main speaker. *Timaeus* is practically an essay, put into the mouth of one Timaeus from Italy, on the nature and origin of the universe. The *Laws,* Plato's last and longest work, is a conversation between a Spartan, a Cretan, and an unnamed Athenian concerning the best constitution for the new city of Magnesia planned to be founded in Crete. Nearly all the talking is done by the Athenian, who is of course Plato.

# 12

---

# The Theory of Ideas

> Unless either philosophers assume the role of kings in the cities or those who are now called kings and potentates philosophize in earnest and sufficiently, and these two things converge into the same: political power and philosophy, while the various types who now pursue each separately from the other are excluded by compulsion, there can be no cessation of evils, dear Glaucon, for cities, nor, I believe, for the human race.[1]

This, perhaps the most famous sentence in Plato's writings, is a succinct expression of the leading idea that informs his whole activity. Plato was convinced that society had to be reformed—which meant to him, as it would to any Greek, giving the city new laws. How could it be done if the city was Athens? Solon, his mother's ancestor, had been entrusted by the whole people with that task and had done it very well. But that was long ago. The events of his youth convinced Plato that there could be no hope of real reform through democratic machinery. Plato tells us that one of two things is bound to happen to any high-minded person who ventures into politics: either he fails to compromise his principles, and then he will be at best ignored, at worst put to death; or he will compromise, and then he will be no better than the rest and probably worse. The conclusion, though, is not that nothing can be done; it is that reform must come from the top. "Kings and potentates" must become philosophers, or vice versa; the notion of a whole people in a democracy becoming philosophical is not to be thought about.

Plato's solution to his personal problem was the opening of a school for the training of philosophical kings and potentates. He proposed, that is, to train philosophers; if any of them should happen to become kings or potentates, then—but not until then—ills might cease for cities.

## Knowledge versus Belief

What should aspiring statesmen learn? The answer of the sophists, that they should learn public speaking, is out; Plato's statesmen are not to persuade but to command. They must learn what a city should really be like, what the real good of political organization is. That is what Plato set himself to teach—or rather, what he proposed to put a few talented young men into position to grasp for themselves.

This kind of proposal put Plato at once into diametrical opposition to sophists of the Protagorean sort: "Man is the measure of all things . . . What seems so to a man, is so for that man." Plato devotes much writing to establishing a firm distinction between knowledge and (mere) belief or opinion.

The distinction is an ordinary one that all of us would grant; our differences come when we ask how far we would be willing to let it be pressed. Certainly there is a difference between the physician who has knowledge of the cause and cure of rheumatic fever, and on the other hand the lay person who has only belief, gleaned perhaps from newspapers. But just what is the difference? Is it one of degree or of kind? Was there a certain day in medical school when the student stopped having belief and started knowing? Does not the physician, when it comes down to cases, only follow what the author of the medical textbook says? Perhaps we would be more likely to admit a sharp distinction between knowledge of a riot the eyewitness or participant has and belief formed by reports in the media. Here also, though, might we not be forced to admit that the person on the scene was so overwhelmed and had so narrow a view of so few incidents that someone else, perhaps the chief of police many miles away or even a private citizen in front of his television set, knew better what was going on?

These remarks are meant to suggest that you or I might find it hard to draw a sharp and general distinction between knowledge and belief. And we should probably take it for granted that there might be both knowledge and belief concerning the same subject matter—that Jones might have knowledge of recent English history or organic chemistry or the binomial theorem while Smith has only a few opinions. We may be surprised, then, to find that Plato's distinction is not only sharp but is such that the objects of knowledge are quite distinct from those of belief.

We shall be less surprised, however, if we recall the contrast Parmenides drew between that about which there is Truth and the realm of mere mortal guesswork. The object of true knowledge for Parmenides was mathematical, while all that the senses acquaint us with could be only surmised. That is the beginning of Plato's distinction.

This distinction is not implausible when applied to mathematics on the one hand and on the other what Plato's translators usually call "the sensible world." We all have had, or should have had, the experience of proving or at least comprehending the proof of a theorem in geometry. Before we prove that the sum of the interior angles of any triangle is two right angles, we may already suspect or believe it; nevertheless, when the line is drawn through the apex parallel to the base and we tick off the angles successively and find that they are equal to the sum of angles around a point on one side of a straight line, something happens. We have what has been called the "Aha!" experience; there is an interior "click" when we (to use Plato's expression) see with the mind's eye the necessity of its being so. In this moment we attain knowledge. It is quite different from being told, however authoritatively, and believing, however piously, that it is so.

> Education is not what it is said to be by some, who profess to put knowledge into a soul which does not possess it, as if they could put sight into blind eyes. On the contrary . . . the soul of every man does possess the power of learning the truth and the organ to see it with; and . . . just as one might have to turn the whole body round in order that the eye should see light instead of darkness, so the entire soul must be turned . . . until its eye can . . . contemplate reality.[2]

Knowledge is something you must find for yourself; a teacher may only show you where and how to look. Once you have it, though, it is yours and cannot be taken away. We can be persuaded out of our beliefs about politics or biology or religion or even mathematics—but not out of our knowledge. Once we know, have experienced the click, we are proof against propagandizing, brainwashing, and seduction. We do not defer to authority on those subjects—we *are* the authorities.

## The Different Objects of Knowledge and Opinion

But is it not obviously the case that there can be both knowledge and belief concerning the same object? Does not the budding geometrician first have a belief about the angle sums of triangles, and then by going through the proof acquire knowledge of the same truth about the same triangles? Plato said he does not. His belief, which is a changeable wavering affair, is about this or that visible triangle—now drawn here in the sand, later swept away. The theorem, on the other hand, is an eternal truth: not coming into being and not subject to change or destruction. This truth, which is the object of knowledge, is about something itself eternal and changeless.

That the truth and the knowledge of it cannot be about particular changing triangles is easily seen (so Plato argues) when we notice that (1) the theorem as a matter of fact is not exactly true of any actual drawn triangle and (2) the significance of the truth does not in any way depend on the actual existence of a triangular object. (If this is not clear, consider the theorem that the interior angles of the chiliagon—the plane figure of a thousand straight sides—sum to 1,996 right angles.) When we measure the angles of actual triangles very precisely and find that they do not sum precisely to two right angles, we do not on that account reject the theorem. On the contrary, we conclude that the figures we are dealing with are not exactly triangular. But the more carefully we draw them, with sharper pencils on smoother paper, the more they *participate in* the Idea of Triangle. The Idea is then not only the object of knowledge, it is at the same time the standard for judging. A triangle is a 'good' triangle just to the extent that it participates in the essential character of triangularity that is this Idea.

The Idea, then, is intelligible but not visible—it is seen with the mind's (or soul's) eye only. It is timeless, changeless, birthless, deathless. The particular visible triangles depend for their being on the Idea; if there were no Idea, there could be no particulars participating in it, that is, being triangular. But not conversely. For if all the particular triangles disappeared, the Idea would not be affected in the least. The Idea is the Being or Reality of the particular sensible triangles.

If this reasoning is admitted, then there is at least one Idea—and of course there are also Ideas of Circle and Line and other geometrical entities. These are fit to be objects of knowledge sharply distinguishable from belief. Therefore, there is such a thing as objective knowledge and Protagoras was wrong. With reason Plato inscribed over the entrance to the Academy NO ONE WITHOUT GEOMETRY MAY ENTER.

## The Generalization from Mathematics

If we have interpreted Parmenides correctly, he had already concluded that mathematics is knowledge and has an intelligible rather than visible object. So

Plato's originality does not lie in the preceding argument—which, furthermore, at most only requires the sophist to admit an exception to his general teaching. After saying "one opinion is as true as another," he must now add "except in mathematics." But Protagoras could do that without much embarrassment. Ethical and political relativism are untouched.

Plato made the argument into a potent antirelativist weapon by generalizing it. He held that there are Ideas wherever there is language; therefore, objects of knowledge exist in every field including ethics and politics, for we can at least talk meaningfully about them. The possibility of political knowledge thus exists. We are to get it by intuiting the relevant Ideas, as knowledge of triangles consists in grasping triangularity.

No argument for the existence of Ideas outside mathematics is to be found in Plato's writings. Typically, Ideas are introduced abruptly and without explanation, as at *Phaedo* 65D.

> Here are some more questions, Simmias. Do we recognize such a thing as absolute justice?—Indeed we do.—And absolute beauty and goodness too?—Of course.

But since antiquity commentators have held that Plato would have taken something like the following line of justification if challenged.

We cannot make any meaningful assertions without using some general terms. By 'general term' is meant a word that is not a proper name. A proper name designates one and only one individual: Plato, Socrates, the moon, the sun, Athens. Proper names are like labels to be pasted on particular objects; general or 'universal' terms (man, satellite, city, heat, color, red) refer indifferently to members past, present, or future, real or imaginary, of some class.

The meanings of proper names are (so Plato presumably held, whether consciously or not) the particulars that they label. The word "Socrates" means the individual man who drank the hemlock. Plato, if the occasion arose (perhaps with a foreign visitor), could explain what he meant when he used this word by pointing at the individual and saying "I mean *him*." On the other hand, the meanings of universal terms cannot be identified with definite particulars—they are not proper names—or indeed with any class of particulars. If they could, they would cease to have meaning when the members of the class ceased to exist; "dodo" would have no longer been a meaningful word after 1628, if that was the year of the demise of the last dodo. But the meaning of a meaningful word (so Plato would hold) must be something real. Therefore, there must be real things to be the meanings of "dodo" and "humanity" and "justice," just as we have shown that there are meanings of "triangle" and "odd." These objects are the Ideas: ungenerated, changeless, indestructible, intelligible, not visible objects of knowledge—just as Triangularity is, and for the same reasons.

When we say then that this or that action is just, we are asserting that the action participates in the Idea Justice. If you deny it, one of us must be wrong, just as one must be wrong if we disagree over some property of triangles. What exactly, though, is this participation? It is not that the Idea is physically contained in the object or event, or that part of it is—the Idea is not a body and is not divisible. To participate in an Idea is to copy or exemplify it. Though again, the word "copy" must be understood in a special sense. For if anything is a literal copy of anything else, the two are particulars; and if a copy occupies space, so does what it copies. But the Ideas are not occupiers of space, they do not have location, they are not particulars at all. The truth is that the Platonic relation of participation, said to hold between an Idea and a particular, is not explicable in terms of any other more familiar relation—it is unique. (Plato in effect admits this in the dialogue *Parmenides*.)

The Idea of Justice is that which gives meaning to statements about justice. It is also the standard for judging actions with respect to their justice. To say of somebody that he is just, or not so just, is to make a remark about the extent of participation in the Idea. If our judgments about justice are open to interminable debate, as our statements about triangles and circles are *not*, the reason is that our awareness of the Idea of Justice is dim. If we had no science of geometry, we would be confronted with similar uncertainties and controversies about triangles. It is not unlikely that Egyptian and Babylonian surveyors did quarrel on occasion. But the Ideas were already there. So their differences of belief could have been resolved, even if in fact they were not. It is the same, Plato thought, with justice. The object of knowledge is there. The thing to do is to work out a science that will be to justice as geometry is to triangles and circles.

## A Note on Terminology

Plato uses two common Greek words, *eidos* and *idea*, for the object of knowledge. Both words derive from the Indo-European root *(v)id-* "see" and both commonly mean shape, form, look, outward appearance, kind, sort. Plato also uses a variety of other expressions for the notion. Instead of "the idea of equality" he may write locutions translated as "the equal itself," "absolute equality," or simply "the equal"—relying on context to indicate the special sense.

The *English* word 'idea' was introduced of course from Greek, but it has a history of its own, the tracing of which will be a major concern of this book. In ordinary twentieth-century speech it is sometimes used in very much Plato's sense, as in such expressions as 'the idea of a university' and 'an ideal gas'. But more commonly it indicates something, a thought, in someone's mind. I have my idea of a good time and you have yours, and they may not be the same. And when my mind goes, the ideas are gone too. That is to say, 'idea' in modern English more often than not refers to something 'mental' or 'subjective'. Nothing of course could be farther from Plato's conception of Ideas as constituting the absolute reality, in no way dependent on our thinking, but being the standard for thinking right. For this reason many translators, including the author of this book, are reluctant to use the English word for the Platonic notion. Commonly the word 'form' is used instead, and Plato's Theory of Forms is discussed. In this book, however, the word 'Idea' will be retained, the reader cautioned to keep always in mind that when—Greek or English—it occurs in Plato's writings it has the sense we are here attempting to grasp, and no other.

A related complication: Again because of developments in philosophy centuries after Plato, today we tend to classify the possibilities for reality into just two kinds, the physical and the mental. Ideas, in the twentieth-century sense of the word, are clearly mental. Plato's Ideas, not being mind-dependent, are not mental. But they are not physical either. So what are they?

Sir Karl Popper (1902–) and some other present-day philosophers have questioned the sufficiency of two bins to contain all of reality. Two apples and two more apples are physical; the thought that two and two are four is mental; but what about the *truth* that two and two are four? Not physical, but not mind-dependent—it was discovered not invented—nor could the total destruction forever of all conscious life make two and two cease to be four. There is then (these philosophers hold) a "third world" besides the mental and the physical to which these realities belong. This doctrine is a return to Platonism. Platonic Ideas are denizens *par excellence* of the Third Realm.

## Dialectical Apprehension of Ideas

Plato uses the word 'dialectic'—'talking-through'—to name the process of attaining knowledge of Ideas. It is exhibited in the Dialogues as a method of successive approximations. Typically Socrates raises the question "What is $X$?" where $X$ may be virtue, knowledge, justice, figure, temperance, courage, holiness, color, or what have you. A respondent then offers an example of $X$ or a list of things that display $X$-ness. Whereupon Socrates complains that he wants to know not what things are $X$ but what the very nature of $X$ is, what makes $X$-ish things $X$-ish. To this urging the respondent produces a verbal formula that is supposed to describe this nature. Socrates then asks questions tending to lead to recognition of the inadequacy of the formula: it applies to things that are clearly not $X$ or, conversely, fails to apply to clear instances of $X$. The formula is then amended in light of the objections but is examined again and found to be vulnerable in some other respect. And so on until either the dialogue ends with the original question formally unanswered or—rarely—a satisfactory definition is discovered.

In the first book of *The Republic* the question "What is Justice?" is pursued through three stages. (1) Justice consists in telling the truth and paying your debts. This is rejected on the ground that it would not be just to tell the truth to a madman or to give him back a lethal weapon we had borrowed from him. (2) Justice is helping friends and harming enemies. This is modified by adding the qualifying clause that the friends must be really good and the enemies really bad. But even then it is still unacceptable to Socrates who declares that to harm someone is to make the victim worse; that the only way for a human being to be made worse is to be made morally corrupt, *i.e.* unjust; and that it could obviously never be the work of justice to create injustice. (3) Thrasymachus the sophist then introduces the sociological analysis that "Justice is the interest of the stronger party." This subversive doctrine is refuted, at least formally, but the book ends without a definition of justice having been reached.

The goal is attained only in Book Four, after the ideal city has been described. It is found to be (4) the disposition existing in that city of members of each class (rulers, civil servants, soldiers, and workers) to mind their proper business, and especially the disposition of those who are not rulers to refrain from meddling in politics. In the individual, (5) justice is the quality possessed by one whose reason, aided by the faculty of virtuous indignation, keeps the appetitive nature in check.

Someone who has read only the foregoing bare-boned summary will doubtless find (4) and (5) very strange as defining Justice, and open to hosts of objections. Moreover, it may be asked, if Plato thought that was what Justice is, why did he not come right out and say so? What is more (it might be added), the very first definition offered was clearly the best of all. Why was it thrown out on account of so outlandish a tale as that of giving a knife back to its owner who has suddenly become a homicidal maniac? All rules have their exceptions; surely paying debts *is* justice in all *normal* cases.

Let us consider the last objection first. Plato often employs the outlandish-exception stratagem. For example, in the dialogue *Charmides*—where the question is "What is temperance?"—when the suggestion is made that temperance is the same as modesty, Socrates quotes a line from Homer saying that it is not good for a beggar to be modest. And that is the end of that definition! But in both cases Plato was making a valid and important point. He spells it out in the *Charmides*. Temperance, whatever it is, is agreed to be a virtue. A virtue is a characteristic that it is good to have *in all circumstances*—or at any rate such was Socrates' and Plato's fundamental conviction. But modesty, and giving things back to their owners, are not good in all imaginable circumstances. Hence they cannot be *definitions* of virtues, even though there are few or even no actual cases in which they are not good things.

Another point of capital importance is made in these rejections: *Right conduct cannot be reduced to following rules*. Whether a certain action is an instance of repaying a debt is a fact ascertainable by checking off a list: Is article P the property of person A? Did A lend P to B? Did B promise to give it back? Is B now giving it back? If the answers to all these questions are affirmative, then the action is the repayment of a debt—no matter what the other circumstances of the transaction may be. But whether an action is the *right* thing to do always *is* dependent on its context, and no rules can specify all contexts in advance. Similarly the question "Is So-and-so behaving modestly?" can be given a definite answer in terms of objectively describable demeanor. Etiquette books list the rules. But there are no conceivable rules that can be enunciated in advance such that compliance with them will guarantee *right* behavior. You and I know this; for even if we do not (yet) possess the wisdom of Socrates, at least we have enough moral insight to *see* that it is not right to put mad persons in possession of knives or to be shy and retiring if we have to beg for a living.

The rejection of (3), "Justice is helping friends and harming enemies," is also more complex than it seems on the surface. (The informal, flowing, conversational style is deceptive; Plato expects his readers to *work*.) Certainly the sentiment was and is widespread, yet it cannot form part of a rational morality. In the first place it is relativistic and leads to paradox: B may be at the same time A's friend and C's enemy, so it would be right both for A to help B and for C to harm B, which is absurd. Further, since one may have (perhaps through ignorance of real character) friends who are bad people and enemies who are good, it could turn out to be right to harm the good—likewise absurd and morally intolerable.

These defects can be remedied by adding the proviso that the people in question must be really good and really bad, respectively—incidentally calling attention to the distinction between moral reality and appearance. The stage is now set for the main event: Socrates' contesting of the claim of popular morality that the doing of harm can sometimes be a requirement of justice. But if we expect him to argue that wrongdoers should never be punished—resist not evil, turn the other cheek—we shall be disappointed. Socrates in fact held that punishment is benefi-cial to the wrongdoer, so that a rational criminal will turn himself or herself over to the police just as he or she would go to a doctor voluntarily if stricken with disease. His contention is that the only way to harm people is to make them morally worse. (At his trial he told the Athenians that they could kill him but could not harm him. Now we understand what he meant.)

So much for popular morality. One who has followed the dialectic carefully to this point will have perceived the insufficiency and at least partial wrongness of "what everybody believes." This is the first stage of the progress to enlightenment. Puzzlement has replaced confident taking-for-granted. The respondent knows that he does not know.

One possibility is that there is really no such thing as justice, it is a sham or a trickery. Now Thrasymachus is brought in to advocate that viewpoint. Like all characters in the Platonic dialogues he was a real person. Plato writes his speech, but here as always he states the position that he detests with more force and eloquence than its advocates could muster—indeed in this case so well that many readers to this day judge Thrasymachus to have been the 'winner' in the ensuing debate with Socrates. However that may be, Thrasymachus is at last silenced— but still leaving up in the air the question of what justice is.

Thus at the end of *Republic* Book I, the reader has come to this position: Justice is not what it is commonly supposed to be; but there is such a thing. Now the positive part of the dialectical inquiry can begin.

All the 'dialogues of search' conclude at a stage like this. Plato repeatedly said that books can be no substitute for personal encounter in dialectic—for they are dumb things, unable to gauge the respondent or to help sort out the confusions that actually arise in an attempt to think things through. In the *Republic*, nevertheless, the constructive dialectic leading to comprehension of the Idea of Justice is sketched. It is long and convoluted, involving the intellectual construction of an Ideal (therefore Just) State and comparison of its constitution to the soul of the Just Man. (Macrocosm and Microcosm again.) It issues in the preceding pronouncements numbered (4) and (5), summed up in the platitude that Justice (or right conduct in a general sense) is Minding Your Own Business. But in the process of getting to this formula a profound understanding of what *is one's own business* has been inculcated, so that the person who has gone through the dialectical process now has an insight—"Aha!" "Click!"—that would have been entirely lacking if the dialectic had been skipped. One who was *merely* told that Justice is minding one's own business would be no better off than a student of geometry merely told that $a^2 + b^2 = c^2$.

Furthermore, the insight into the Idea of Justice shows how it comprises within itself the valid elements in the rejected definitions, which were not wrong but insufficient. The Just State—where everyone fulfills his or her proper function and does not interfere with others—is one where "the truth is spoken" and everyone receives what is "due"; where friends who are really good are helped (and those who are really bad are improved if possible); even indeed the State wherein the interest of the stronger party is the rule, for the stronger party is there the wiser, which is the stronger by nature and right.

Yet in an important sense one who understands all this still does not comprehend the essential nature of Justice. Understanding, like reform in the State, must come from the top down. The different Ideas are not individual, separate, intelligible objects such that knowledge consists in collecting them one after the other. They constitute a hierarchical system, and complete knowledge of any one demands knowledge of those higher up—ultimately knowledge of the highest of all, the Good Itself.

## The Good

Plato makes reference to the Idea of the Good only in the *Republic*, and there in a mysterious manner. As in the visible world the sun is both visible and the source of visibility of other things, so in the intelligible world of Ideas the Good is the source of intelligibility—of truth and being. The Good is, however, not truth and being but something higher still. We are told no more than this about the Good. "There is no writing of mine about these matters, nor will there ever be one," Plato wrote late in his life.[3] "For this knowledge is not something that can be put into words like other sciences; but after long-continued intercourse between teacher and pupil, in joint pursuit of the subject, suddenly, like light flashing forth when a fire is kindled, it is born in the soul and straightway nourishes itself." The education that Plato prescribes for philosophers is directed to preparing for this insight.

Education for human beings must start with experience of the sensible world, for there is nowhere else to start. It must, however, soon rise above the sensible. Plato describes succinctly in the *Symposium* how one is to achieve knowledge of Beauty Itself: One begins with love of one particular beautiful body. Then one realizes that "the beauty exhibited in all bodies is one and the same," so that one becomes a "lover of all physical beauty, and will relax the intensity of the passion for one particular person." At the next state, beauty of soul is perceived to be of more worth than that of the body. Onward and upward, one comes to appreciate the beauty of a well-devised code of laws, the beauty of the sciences, and at the climax one will see Beauty Itself—"absolute, existing alone with itself, unique, eternal, and all other beautiful things as partaking of it, yet in such a manner that, while they come into being and pass away, it neither undergoes any increase or diminution nor suffers any change."

After this we should not be surprised that the nature of Beauty Itself and of The Good cannot be put into words. The ascent to the Good, as to Beauty, is by way of generalization and abstraction. Plato prescribes ten years' training in mathematics followed by five in dialectic as preparation for the grand revelation of The Good.

In face of all this it may seem the supreme impertinence to venture a guess as to what The Good was supposed to be. But after all, Plato did tell us something about the Good—it is the source of intelligibility—and in the *Phaedo* and elsewhere he told us of what intelligibility consists. Putting these together, it seems to follow that The Good is the supreme principle of purposive explanation. The Good is not indeed a common goal that everything aims at, as if the good for each thing were something external to that thing; it is rather the unitary source of all the diverse values that are in the different things and that make those things part of the intelligible cosmic pattern.

If this is not clear perhaps an analogy with the sort of explanation advocated by Democritus will be of some help. In Democritean mechanism, explanation consists in specifying the motions of the thing to be explained and the causes of those motions. Specifying them means not only describing them in particular but in exhibiting them as instances of some general pattern—to anticipate the history of science, to show how they exemplify the *laws of motion*. Now in Platonic explanation the kind of generality aimed at is similar. Plato wants to be able to say of anything proposed for explanation that it exemplifies such-and-such a kind of goodness, which is subordinate to a higher (more general) good. For Democritus motion is not only the highest conception in the explanatory system but at the same time the most pervasive fact. For Plato the analogous place in the explanatory system is held by Good. The Democritean world would collapse if motion stopped; Plato's would be annihilated if things ceased to have value.

When applied to the 'sensible world', this explanatory scheme resulted in the arbitrary and fantastic story of creation in the dialogue *Timaeus*. The god, being good, wishing in consequence that the goodness of the Ideas might be increased, copied them in matter—that is to say, imposed form onto a preexisting chaos. Air, fire, and water are made of particles which are regular solids whose faces are resolvable into halves of equilateral triangles; these triangles are the ultimate building blocks (Platonic atoms), and that is why these three elements are convertible one into the other. Earth on the other hand is made of cubes, which in turn come from isosceles right triangles. The cosmos is a living being, but spherical and smooth; nothing outside it to perceive nor anywhere to go, hence no need for sense organs or limbs; nothing to eat, hence no mouth. Man, the microcosm, begins like the world-animal—that is to say the head is basically spherical, but on account of various needs the symmetry must be spoiled and this excellent sphere must be joined to a trunk and limbs. Plato does not claim certainty nor even high probability for this account—just as Parmenides who, when he came to the world of "mortal guesswork," "ceased trustworthy thought." Plato had little interest in the 'sensible world' as such; indeed he averred that it was at best half real because fundamentally contradictory. He arrived at this conclusion in the following manner.

> Now if there is something so constituted that it both *is* and *is not*, will it not lie between the purely real and the utterly unreal?
> It will. . . .
> Of all these many beautiful things is there one which will not appear ugly? Or of these many just or righteous actions, is there one that will not appear unjust or unrighteous?
> No, replied Glaucon, they must inevitably appear to be in some way both beautiful and ugly; and so with all the other terms your question refers to.
> And again the many things which are doubles are just as much halves as they are doubles. And the things we call large or heavy have just as much right to be called small or light. . . . Then, whatever any one of these many things may be said to be, can you say that it absolutely *is* that, any more than that it *is not* that? . . . Can you think of any better way of disposing of them than by placing them between reality and unreality?[4]

To point out that a double Martini is only half a quadruple Martini and to conclude from this that the world is only half real is dismissing the world in short order indeed. So strongly did Plato feel that relativism of any sort is incompatible with true Reality.

## The Soul

The Pythagorean antecedents of Plato's philosophy are nowhere more to the fore than in his theory of the soul. He held the soul to be immortal in both directions—existing before birth as well as after death of the body. We have seen how in Greek thought generally the soul was conceived as substantial, that is to say material, but made of very fine matter. Some Pythagoreans of Plato's time advanced the radical (and fruitful) notion that the soul was not substantial at all but rather an "attunement" of the body, that is to say, the functioning of the body rather than some gaseous internal organ with its own function. We know of this conception only through Plato's rejection of it. In the *Phaedo* it is held that the soul is immaterial but nonetheless substantial. Plato could say this, which to other Greeks would have seemed contradictory, because in the Ideas he had succeeded in conceiving a nonmaterial kind of substance; so at any rate had he convinced himself.

Such as they are, the arguments presented for immortality in the *Phaedo* are the best, it seems, that can be fashioned. At any rate, all those that have subsequently been proposed are variations on Plato's. The principal if not sole argument is that only that which is composite can suffer destruction; but the soul, not being material and therefore not being composite, cannot suffer destruction. If sound, this argument proves, as Plato noted, preexistence as well as survival.

# 13

## Plato's Politics

PLATO HAD A PASSION for static order. His love of mathematics; his theory of Ideas; his dislike of the moving, changing, "sensible" world; his ethics and politics all express it.

Most of what human beings do consists in arranging things in more or less orderly fashion (big exception: use of explosives, which of course the ancients did not have). Thinking itself is an ordering; understanding is the perception of order. Mathematics is the general science of ordering. Hence there is nothing remarkable in a philosopher's evincing a preference for order over disorder. However, there are different kinds and levels of order.

### Static and Dynamic Orders

One ordering distinction is between a motionless arrangement of things—the Parthenon, say—and an orderly process, such as a choral dance. A circle drawn in sand exhibits static order; the stars' endless revolving in lesser and greater circles around the pole displays dynamic ordering.

Both kinds of order play prominent roles in Greek thought. From the very beginning of the written record, dynamic order is recognized and stressed—for instance in the fragment of Anaximander: "They [the elements] give justice and recompense to each other for their injustice according to the order of time."

But ordinarily dynamic processes have static states as their goals (building for the sake of the house), so that there is a natural human tendency to prefer states over processes. This was all the stronger amongst the Greeks, inasmuch as they were not accustomed to thinking historically and had little notion of progress. It was more usual to suppose that cosmic and human affairs had degenerated. Hesiod said we are living in the wretched age of iron, following a silver age after a golden age. Empedocles fit the present era into the period when baneful Strife is gaining over blameless Affection. Plato may not have believed literally any of the myths of fall, though he composed some himself; yet certainly his view of human affairs was that most changes are for the worse. What he hoped to do in politics, the best he thought could possibly be done, was to create a decent political arrangement and then insulate it against all change.

It is difficult for us to appreciate how different the ancients' notion of time was from ours. We think of time as what clocks measure, but the Greeks had no clocks. (Or hardly any. They had water clocks, like hour glasses, to measure small intervals—for example the period allowed a litigant to make his speech in court.) Daylight was divided into an equal number of hours by the position of the sun, so that an hour in summer was twice as long as one in winter. Calendars were inaccurate, and every city had its own. Years were not numbered but referred to by the names of officeholders—as if we could say "In the third year of the Fillmore presidency" but could not say "in 1853," and had to remember somehow, when talking to a Canadian, that that would be the same as "14 years before the British North America Act."

Correlative with lack of precise time units was the absence of mathematical techniques for dealing with them if they had existed. Velocity was only a qualitative notion to the Greeks. Motions were fast or slow, but miles per hour were not thought of. Geometry—in Plato's day already developed almost to the stage familiar to us from Euclid's textbook—treated of the timeless and motionless relations between points, lines, areas, and volumes. Dynamic definitions of these notions were available—such as that of a circle as the path of a point moving at a fixed distance from a given point—but it was the path that was studied, not the process of making the path. Now Plato, as we have seen, was prone to identify reality with the object of knowledge in the strict sense. Hence if there was no knowledge of motion, in the strict geometrical sense, motion was not real, or at any rate not real enough to interest the philosopher.

These facts do not of themselves explain why, for instance, Plato disliked democracy. But they may help to understand why he was prone to argue in ways that seem odd to us: in democracies different individuals and groups have diverse aims, *therefore* democracy is bad; the laws of Sparta and Crete remained unaltered for centuries, *therefore* they were good; "those who keep watch over our commonwealth must take the greatest care not to overlook the least infraction of the rule against any innovation upon the established system of education either of the body or of the mind. . . . The introduction of novel fashions in music is a thing to beware of as endangering the whole fabric of society."[1] In the whole enormous body of Plato's works there is nowhere a reference to inventions and technological improvements, nor any indication of awareness that new ways of doing things— for instance new weapons and military tactics—might necessitate changes in the political structure or at least make them desirable.

## Plato's Opposition to Democracy

Pericles eulogized Athens for the brilliance and stimulation of its public life, for its libertarian political system free from professional politicians, and for the versatile, enterprising, and self-reliant citizenry encouraged by this constitution. It is not surprising that Plato, writing half a century after Pericles when Athens had suffered military disaster and had been through three violent revolutions, took a more critical attitude toward popular rule. He even attacked Pericles himself by name. In the dialogue *Gorgias* (519), Socrates says in reference to him and to Themistocles and Cimon as well:

> You praise the men who feasted the citizens and satisfied their desires, and people say that they have made the city great, not seeing that the swollen and ulcerated condition of the State is to be attributed to these elder statesmen; for they have filled the city full of harbors and docks and walls and revenues and all that, and have left no room for justice and temperance.

In his passion Plato went so far as to try to prove that these statesmen had not made the people better under their care, by pointing out that each of them at the end of his career had been turned upon and prosecuted by the populace—an ironical argument to put into the mouth of Socrates.

Plato's bitter attack on Athenian democracy in Book 8 of the *Republic* seems to have been conceived as a point-by-point reply to Pericles' praise. Plato complains that Athenian freedom is mere anarchy, the laws being contemptuously flouted. Instead of magnificence he sees frivolity and debilitating luxury; instead of versatility he sees dilettantism, leading in the case of the nonprofessional politicians to graft and incompetence. Almost by definition a democracy can have no agreed aim for policy; and the necessity to flatter the electorate is bound to put into office men of a popularity incompatible with possession of the knowledge indispensable for the most difficult of all arts, statesmanship. Plato thought it absurd that the Athenian assembly relied on the advice of professional naval architects when the question was how ships should be built, but never asked for the credentials of anyone with a ready tongue who chose to orate on how to sail the ship of state.

## Plato's Utopia

The greatest of Plato's dialogues, the *Republic*, addresses no less a question than what is the best kind of human life. It contains at least a reference to every important Platonic doctrine, and often the principal discussion. But it is most famous, as its more accurately translated title *On the Constitution* implies, for its sketch of an ideal body politic—the earliest Utopia.

In opposition to the Periclean ideal of versatility, Plato finds the reason for communal living in specialization of function. People living in isolation or very small groups would have to do so many different things that they would not develop much skill at any of them. Only if there are enough customers for shoes to support a full-time shoemaker will shoes be made expertly and efficiently. If others can spend all their time at carpentering, the carpenters will have better shoes and the shoemakers better houses. The ideal state, for Plato, is that community in which the principle of division of labor is carried to the ultimate, where every task is performed by an expert—in particular, and above all, the task of ruling. However, since it was not clear to the Greeks that ruling is a skill like shoemaking or doctoring that can be taught to suitably qualified persons, Plato had a job of persuading to do.

Socrates begins by describing the simple life of a rustic community in which all the necessities are provided. Nothing is said of any government. But the description of dinner served on leaves and with roasted garbanzo beans for dessert does not appeal to Glaucon (Plato's older brother and Socrates' foil in the dialogue), whose opinion it is that civilized persons should eat off crockery and have proper sauces for their food. With a show of reluctance, Socrates then declares that if such luxuries—and others that will come in their train—are to be provided, the state must become swollen with perfumers, caterers, and the like. To support the larger population the state must acquire more territory. That will need an army. In keeping with the principle of division of labor, the soldiers must be professionals not draftees. Socrates next describes the character desirable in these "guardians" and what kind of education is needed to develop it. Then "What do we have to decide next? Isn't it which of these shall be the rulers and which the ruled?" "Certainly," says Glaucon.

When the train of thought is put thus in skeleton outline, a reader may well be astonished. It is *not* obvious that the next question is which of the soldiers should rule the state. Greek cities were not always nor even usually ruled by professional military men—though Sparta, significantly, was. Worse, we have here—and only here—a blatant violation of Plato's one-person-one-job principle. Furthermore, we soon find that the state over whom the best of the soldiers are to rule is to be a puritan socialist community with stringent regulations against luxuries. Yet it is never suggested that the army, having been created only to make high living possible, has been deprived of its function and ought to wither away. Plato's great literary skill keeps us from raising these objections immediately.

Not everyone is fitted by hereditary nature to be a ruler; and as there is a great social division between the soldier-ruler class on the one hand and the civilian-worker-producer on the other, Plato expects that there will be grumbling at the assignments. He proposes to deal with it by the stratagem of the "noble lie"; the people are to be told that each individual has one of three metals in his soul: gold for rulers, silver for soldiers, brass for workers. Socrates thinks it may be hard to get people to believe this at first, but a generation or two of propaganda should accomplish it.

For the guardian class Plato proposed a mode of life shocking to everyone, even to the Spartans whose customs it most closely resembled. In the first place, Plato declared that women should not be debarred from being soldiers or even rulers if properly qualified—and he expected that some would be. He was consistent indeed in not shrinking from this consequence of the principle of the career open to the talents. Nowhere in Greece did women take part in politics, officially at any rate, and upper class Athenian ladies lived in almost complete seclusion. (Aristophanes tells us that they were susceptible to alcoholism.) However, the Pythagorean societies admitted women; this may have been the source of Plato's feminism.

Second, private property and families were to be abolished among the guardians, who were to live communally in state-owned barracks. Sexual intercourse would be allowed only during certain stated periods each year, and even then choice of partners (who might or might not be the same during different festivals) was to be determined at the highest policy level in accordance with two main considerations. First, just enough children should be produced to keep the number of guardians constant. Most children of guardians, Plato believed, would inherit the guardian qualifications; those who did not should be degraded to the worker class. Plato also made formal provision for promotion of exceptionally bright worker children to the guardian class, though it is not clear how this could be practically accomplished. Second, the superior guardians—the bravest warriors, mainly—should breed more offspring than the rest. Anticipating psychological difficulties in carrying out these proposals, Plato arranged for the sexual pairing to be determined by what looked like a lottery but was actually rigged by the senior guardians. (Telling the literal truth about facts was not a national virtue of the Greeks.)

Children are to be taken from their mothers as soon as possible after weaning and reared in state nurseries. Parents are not to know which are their natural children and vice versa. Besides improvement of the stock—Plato was the first advocate of applying scientific breeding principles to the human animal—the purpose of these measures is elimination of sources of division among the guardians, as well as production of the maximum esprit de corps. With no personal or family interest to further, the guardians are to devote all their energies to state service.

Plato also hoped that all guardians of about the same age would love one another as brothers and sisters, and honor those of the older generation with the respect due to parents, so that the class as a whole would be one big happy family. These hopes have been ridiculed by critics from Aristotle on. However, the principle of increasing efficiency and devotion to an institution by abolishing private life was adopted by the Catholic Church in the tenth century, with some success, limited mainly by the circumstance that monks and priests were still after all members of known families and interested in furthering the careers of their "nephews." The Turkish janissaries, the Sultan's guards who had all been kidnapped in infancy (from Christian families) and raised by the state, furnish an even closer parallel to the Platonic system. These soldiers are said to have been of unsurpassed zeal, though unhappily they tended to be more loyal to their own commander than to the Sultan. But in Plato's ideal city their commander would be the philosopher king, so this problem would not arise.

## Education

As befitted the first university president, Plato believed that education is all important. Much of the *Republic* is in consequence devoted to two treatises on the education suitable for guardians. The first deals with elementary education from childhood to age 18. Plato's primary interest here being moral training, he was content to leave the usual Greek curriculum ("music," *i.e.* everything presided over by the nine Muses: all the arts and sciences, and gymnastics) alone, except— and it is a big exception—that literature, especially Homer, must be censored. Gods must not be depicted as doing anything objectionable. Not only must they not tell lies (that Plato disapproves of) and swindle, they must not change their form—change of the best could only be toward the worse—or laugh. Heroes must not be depicted as weeping at the death of comrades; that would imply a wrong view of death as an evil. If Homer were expurgated according to Plato's directions only a few disjointed passages would remain, making up an unintelligible sequence. Plato had a sense of humor, of a sort.

Drama is forbidden altogether on the ground that whoever played the villain might not be able to shake off the part after leaving the stage. Neither would foreigners be allowed to present dramatic performances, for fear of the effect on the audience.

All exciting, softening, and sad music would have to go, presumably leaving only hymns and marches in the repertoire.

It would be wrong to suppose that Plato was hostile to art as such. On the contrary, he insisted that the guardians should be reared in beautiful surroundings. However, he was convinced, perhaps with reason, that certain forms of art excite unseemly, dangerous, and immoral emotional reactions. Such would have to go; art is not a sufficient excuse for itself.

Plato's hostility to poets was also that of a rival. He contended that poets profess knowledge that they do not have: they dress up a counterfeit of wisdom and foist it on to the gullible public. Both poets and demagogues are enemies to the philosopher who alone grasps the reality not the imitation.

For all his insistence on the distinction between knowledge and mere belief, the elementary education is designed to produce belief only. Children are to be taught dogmatically, though by gently persuasive methods, what is right and wrong, true and false. The aim is to produce guardians steadfast in their allegiance to the official wisdom of the state. To that end the students are subjected to continual tests of a practical sort: they are exposed to (simulated) dangers and temptations while examiners note their reactions. Those whose adjustments are nonoptimal are eliminated from the program. (It is natural to speak of Plato's proposals in the jargon of personnel management. Intelligence tests, personality inventories, aptitude tests, Rorschachs, bugs, one-way glass—all this apparatus would have been regarded by Plato as a godsend.) The survivors serve two years' military training from age 18 to 20.

Higher education, in conjunction with military service in the reserves, takes 15 years: 10 years of mathematics, including astronomy, then at last 5 years of dialectic. This education, presumably of the sort offered at the Academy, is supposed to produce knowledge not belief—indeed it is to culminate in the intellectual vision of the Form of the Good. In a famous allegory Plato compares humanity to prisoners chained in a Cave from birth, never allowed to see anything but shadows of puppets on the wall. These they take for reality. Dialectic is like being released from the bonds, being allowed to see first the puppets and the fire casting the shadows, then being led out of the cave into the sunlit world. The dazzling of the eyes would be painful and the changes in the ex-prisoner's conception of what the world was like would be confusing; but no one who experienced the transition could deny in the end that it was worthwhile. At last the sun itself could be glimpsed. If such a prisoner went back into the cave, Plato continues, he would not be able to make out the shadows so well as those who had remained there; he would be thought stupid, his stories of the outside world would be ridiculed, and he might himself suffer harm if the prisoners could get their hands on him. (The fate of the philosopher among the ignorant.) Nevertheless, the guardian who has received the state education and has become a philosopher must be forced to go back into the cave since—much as he would rather be philosophizing—he has an obligation to administer the affairs of the state, to help the unphilosophical people who do not know what is good by running their lives in the proper way. That is so in the ideal city. But Plato is emphatic that if a philosopher tried to meddle in the politics of a democracy, either he would compromise his ideals so that he ceased to be a philosopher or he would suffer the fate of Socrates.

## The Virtues of the Ideal City

The ideal city, being ideal, must embody the four traditional virtues or excellences recognized by the Greeks: wisdom, courage, temperance, and justice. Wisdom obviously is the particular virtue of the ruling class, as courage is of the soldiers. Temperance or self-control, Plato tells us, is discerned in the cheerful and enthusiastic acquiescence of the worker class in being ruled by the philosopher kings. Justice is the condition in the whole state of everybody minding his or her own business, doing what he or she is best fitted to do, and not getting in other people's way: most particularly and importantly, not meddling with the philosophical government.

## Practicality and Desirability

Putting the constitution of the ideal city into effect somewhere by popular vote was out of the question. Nor for that matter could any worthwhile reform be expected from the people; contrary to Pericles, Plato deemed the many just as incapable of judging a policy as they were of initiating it by decree. Leaving these obstacles aside, the city would have to start out with a population of children under the age of ten, their elders being hopelessly corrupt already.

But the practical impossibility of bringing the city into existence did not matter much. "Laid up in heaven" it still fulfilled the function of serving as an ideal standard by which to measure the shortcomings of actual societies and to indicate the directions that their improvements should take. Plato devoted his last and longest work, the *Laws*, to the detailed working out of a legal code for a second-best but (he thought) feasible city-state. The essential feature of the ideal city of the *Republic* was that its ideally philosophical rulers should not be hedged in by traditions or written rules but should be free to apply their wisdom to the direction of affairs. (We have seen why wisdom and going by rules are antithetical.) Plato never gave up his conviction that this was theoretically the best solution for the problem of politics. However, the longer he ran a school for statesmen the more pessimistic he grew about finding suitable young persons and making them into philosophers who could be trusted with such responsibility. In his dialogue *The Statesman*, he concluded that since these godlike beings were not to be found, the best practical arrangement was to go to the opposite extreme of minutely detailed legislation—by philosophers, of course—providing for all foreseeable contingencies so that discretionary powers in rulers could be as nearly as possible abolished: a government of laws not men. In the city depicted in the *Laws*, private property and family life are retained and officials are elected (by a complicated franchise) for stated periods. General supervision is to be exercised by the ominously named Nocturnal Council, composed principally of retired officials and a few persons who, having been granted security clearances, were allowed to travel abroad. Thus Plato conceded the conceivability of someone elsewhere having a good idea.

# 14

## Plato on the Human Good

A HUMAN BEING, ACCORDING to Plato, is a soul imprisoned temporarily in a body. The body is gross and corruptible matter; the soul, an immaterial but still particular thing. To Plato belongs the dubious distinction of being the first philosopher whom we know to have asserted the real existence of an immaterial thing. It is a difficult question how something that has no boundaries in space, nothing to mark it off from anything else including other souls, could be said to be imprisoned in a body or anywhere else—or to be free or to be, for that matter, a particular thing at all. These questions, however, Plato does not raise.

When we are told that the soul is distinct from the body and immaterial, we have not been told much. How is man divided between body and soul? The soul is, as for Socrates, the seat of consciousness and is that which is virtuous or wicked. Plato seems to make the division roughly this way: the soul is what can be active when the body is not moving. We can think, plan, perceive, and love or hate when we are quite motionless—hence thinking, willing, and emoting belong to the soul. We say "I think," "I intend," "I love"—not "My body thinks," "My body intends," "My body loves." However, we also say "I see, hear, smell" rather than "My body sees, hears, smells." Modern philosophers, if they assert a dualism of soul (or mind) and body, tend to put seeing and sensing in general on the side of the soul (or mind). On the other hand, Plato thinks of seeing as something the eyes do, hearing as an activity of the ears, and so on. And one sometimes does say "My eyes have seen the . . ." "My nose told me that . . ." Perhaps the most common expressions in this area are "I saw it with my own eyes" and "I heard him with my own ears." Such kinds of speech suggest a metaphor of the sense organs as tools— indeed 'organ' *is* the (Greek) word for tool—and this is the conception that Plato favors. Strictly speaking, he tells us in the dialogue *Theaetetus*, we should say that the soul sees through the eyes, hears through the ears. Sensing is therefore partly bodily, partly soulful. It follows that the soul when liberated from the body cannot see, hear, taste, smell, or feel; it will be as if you were deaf, dumb, blind, and so on. The prospect did not strike Plato as horrible, for the soul would still be able to contemplate the eternal Ideas.

Pains, the pleasurable sensations that we call (following Plato) the bodily pleasures, and some of the more impetuous emotions are obviously bound up with the body. Plato viewed most of these as contaminations of the soul by the body, the positive punishments as it were of imprisonment in the flesh. In the *Phaedo*, Socrates is depicted as welcoming the approach of death.

For the body is a source of endless trouble to us by reason of the mere requirement of food; and is liable also to diseases which overtake and impede us in the search after true being: it fills us full of loves, and lusts, and fears, and fancies of all kinds, and endless foolery, and in fact, as men say, takes away from us the power of thinking at all. Whence come wars, and fightings, and factions? Whence but from the body and the lusts of the body? Wars are occasioned by the love of money, and money has to be acquired for the sake and in the service of the body; and by reason of all these impediments we have no time to give to philosophy; and, last and worst of all, even if we are at leisure and betake ourselves to some speculation, the body is always breaking in upon us, causing turmoil and confusion in our enquiries, and so amazing us that we are prevented from seeing the truth.[1]

## The Three Parts of the Soul

In the *Republic*, Socrates draws a detailed comparison of the soul to the state—indeed the pretext for describing the ideal city is to make this comparison possible. Both people and cities can be just or unjust, we are told. The inquiry is after the nature of justice in people, but studying the justice of cities should be easier because there it is "writ large."

As the city has three classes—rulers, soldiers, and workers—so the soul has three parts: reason, corresponding to the philosopher kings; at the opposite end the animal drives, appetites, constitute a kind of spiritual proletariat like the workers; in between is the "spirited element," like the soldiery. Socrates tries to show that there must be this third part between reason (which of itself does not initiate action) and appetite by calling attention to the fact that you can be angry with yourself for yielding to a temptation. That part of (the real) you that is angry must be different from both appetite (which only wants) and reason (which only thinks).

Justice in the individual is that harmonious arrangement where reason, aided by the spirited element, rules the appetites, and the appetites in their turn are satisfied to be ruled. They are not suppressed; but as in the ideal city the workers may neither rule nor have an income exceeding a proper amount, so the appetites must be provided for with temperance. Plato's conception of justice and indeed of virtue in general has much in common with what nowadays is talked of as mental health. Out-of-balance souls are of various sorts: too much spirited element and we have the military man, the Spartan type; if the necessary appetites—the cravings for respectable possessions—dominate, the result is a plutocrat; the person who makes no discrimination between desires—putting them all on a par and following the whim of the moment—is, of course, the democrat; and lowest of all, the archvillain, is the monster ruled by unlawful lusts, the Tyrant. Socrates describes the tyrannical man as one who in his waking life is obsessed by those "desires, terrible in their untamed lawlessness, which reveal themselves in dreams" to even the most respectable of us.

When the gentler part of the soul slumbers and the control of reason is withdrawn, then the wild beast in us, full-fed with meat or drink, becomes rampant and shakes off sleep to go in quest of what will gratify its own instincts. As you know, it will cast away all shame and prudence at such moments and stick at nothing. In fantasy it will not shrink from intercourse with a mother or anyone else, man, god, or brute, or from forbidden food or any deed of blood.[2]

The anticipation of Freud in this passage is all the more striking for being perhaps the first treatment in literature of dreams as other than omens or super-natural messages.

## Happiness and Pleasure

If you read only the *Phaedo* and the *Gorgias*, you would come away with the notion that Plato was an extreme ascetic puritan, opposed to pleasure as such and on principle. There are long passages in other dialogues that confirm this opinion. Nevertheless, Plato's official doctrine concerning the end of life—that toward which a rational person's endeavors will be directed—is that it is happiness, and that happiness necessarily includes pleasures. Discrimination is demanded. The bodily pleasures of food, drink, and sex are not really pleasures (so Plato taught) but only seem to be; they are really transitions from a painful to a neutral state. But there are pleasures that do not depend on antecedent discomfort, for instance the smelling of flowers and the doing of philosophy. These are real. Moreover, the philosopher, who knows both of them, pronounces the pleasure of contem-plating logical necessity to be far superior to that of sex. If the sensual Tyrant disagrees, we need pay him no notice for he is acquainted with only one side of the comparison.

## Virtue and Knowledge

Socrates was famous for his pronouncements that virtue is knowledge and that no man does evil voluntarily. Plato's version or elaboration of these doctrines is somewhat complicated. In the *Protagoras*, Socrates shows with more or less suc-cess that not only are temperance and justice aspects of wisdom but courage is also—for courage comes to knowledge of a situation and the skill to operate effectively in it, coupled with a proper appreciation of what is really to be feared (disgrace) as opposed to what only seems dreadful (pain and death). A cowardly man running away from the battle is doing wrong involuntarily: like everyone at all times he is pursuing what seems to him the good, but he is mistaken about what it is. Thus virtue is knowledge of the good: the recognition of what is genuinely worthwhile, the insight not to be distracted by the nearness of present pleasures, and command of the means to attain the goal. Plato takes for granted that there is no point in recommending a line of conduct if it is not possible to show that the individual who pursues it will derive some personal advantage. However, the harmony of the soul that is virtue is so much more advantageous to the individual than any other good whatsoever, that a cool calculation of advantage to the self will result every time in preferring it to anything else—even, as Socrates showed, to life itself.

## Immortality

The division of the soul into three parts, as well as that of the city into three classes, was modeled on the Pythagorean conception of the three lives: contem-plative, honor-seeking, and mercantile. But in what sense are the parts of the soul parts? One would like to suppose that Plato meant aspects or functions or classes of functions. It is hard to see what else could be intended by the notion of parts of an immaterial thing. Unfortunately for this conception Plato twice stated, apparently in all seriousness, that these parts have different locations: reason in the head, spirited element in the chest, appetites in the belly and farther south. The head is separated from the trunk by the neck, we are told, to keep the reason as far away as possible from the lower parts. Now we might expect Plato to take advantage of this separability, gained at so great a cost in consistency, to declare that only reason survives death; and so he does, in one passage (*Timaeus*, 69). As we shall see, this is essentially the line that Aristotle was to take. However, elsewhere Plato, the good Pythagorean, insisted on personal immortality. The soul that survives cannot be just an abstract reason; it must be identifiably the soul of Socrates or Critias. In order for this to be so, Plato conceded, even when separated from the body the soul must retain the memories, desires, aversions, hopes, and fears of Socrates and Critias in the flesh: it must be the whole person. Hence even the lusts of the body must keep on existing in a disembodied life. It seems to follow, though Plato does not acknowledge the point, that Socrates' hope for a postmortem existence free from the distractions of the flesh was doomed to disappointment; the distractions would keep on existing, chemically pure as it were. Until, that is, the vicious propensities could be purged away by postmortem punishment. Plato held that punishment must aim at the reformation of the wrongdoer, else it is mere revenge unworthy of civilized people. He believed that this office could best be performed under the ideal conditions and long stretches of time between incarnations. Hence *Phaedo, Republic*, and *Gorgias* all conclude with stories—supposed to be "something like the truth"—of the judgment and punishment of souls. As is usual in such fantasies, hell (or more accurately, purgatory) is described at greater length and more vividly than heaven. They share with Christian doctrine a common descent from Orphic and Pythagorean teachings.

Plato is original in attempting to give rational proof of the soul's immortality instead of taking it on the authority of revelation or tradition. The *Phaedo* presents several arguments. The doctrine of recollection is appealed to, to show that since we know what equality is, but never observe any two things exactly equal in all respects, we must have picked up the notion before birth. Considerations of symmetry require that if the soul existed before birth it must exist also after death, otherwise all the souls would have perished by now. Furthermore, since destruction consists always in being broken up, separated into constituent parts, the soul being immaterial and simple cannot be destroyed. The soul is not an Idea, but it is akin to Ideas—being immaterial and intelligible—and therefore must share their independence of time. Finally, the climactic argument: since soul is life—is that which imparts its life to any living thing—the soul cannot die; the sentence "The life principle is dead" would be as contradictory as "The number three has turned even." Of these arguments, only the one based on the alleged simplicity of the soul has enjoyed much subsequent popularity. With few exceptions philosophers have not deemed it possible to prove that the soul is immortal, though some have sought to show the impossibility of disproof.

## Religion

Plato was also the first to attempt a rational proof of the existence of a god or gods. In the tenth book of the *Laws*, as a preliminary to a discussion of religious legislation, questions are raised concerning the rational foundations for belief in gods. Cleinias the Cretan says it is obvious from the order of the universe; this is the Argument from Design. The thought behind it is of course as old as humanity. We have the testimony of Xenophon that Socrates more than once held forth on this subject with spacious eloquence. But then the Athenian Stranger of the dialogue observes that atheism is on the increase, being fostered by the teachings of the Ionian materialist philosophers who purport to explain everything in terms of matter in motion. It is therefore desirable to turn their own weapons against them. So he then advances what later came to be called the First Cause or Cosmological Argument. The gist of it in Plato's version is that not everything that is in motion can be moved by something else; we must come at some stage to something capable of moving itself, and only soul has this property. Therefore the original cause of motion in the universe must be a world soul. Furthermore, every self-moved object now existing must have a soul. This includes not only human beings and other animals but the sun, moon, and stars, which are living beings of great rationality, as indicated by the elegance of their motions.

At this point he proceeds to draft the scheme for a religious inquisition—a set of laws that had to wait fifteen hundred years to be put into force. Irreligion is of three kinds: it is bad to deny the existence of gods; it is worse to admit their existence but deny their care for us; worst of all is to affirm that they can be bribed. All those professing atheistic views are to be put in solitary confinement for five years, during which time they are to be lectured to every night on the proofs for the existence of gods. Then they will be released but watched. If they relapse, they are to be put to death and their bodies thrown unburied outside the boundary of the state.

Considering his zeal for divinities and his enormous reputation as a religious philosopher, it is surprising to find that Plato's detailed views on the nature of the gods would hardly have satisfied most believers. If the Athenians of Plato's time had enforced conformity to the official religion by the methods recommended in *Laws*, there can be little question what Plato's fate would have been. He held toward the city cults the same blend of intellectual contempt and moral indignation expressed by Xenophanes and Heraclitus. What did he believe to be literally true of the gods? This question is extraordinarily difficult to answer.

The dialogue *Timaeus* is largely devoted to describing how a divine being, called simply The Craftsman, created the visible world by copying and multiplying the Ideas in that which was at his disposal, namely space. The Craftsman did it in order that the excellence of the Ideas might be as far as possible multiplied—as if someone were to make any number of plastic copies of the crown jewels. He made the visible world to be an exemplar of order. He created human beings, making their heads spherical because that is the most excellent shape. But then he had to compromise to give them eyes and ears and noses, and had to attach the ridiculous appendages of the trunk and limbs. His job was all like that.

Plato never suggested, however, that the Craftsman ought to be worshipped. In the first place, although he made the world (including the world soul and the lesser souls), we hear nothing of his remaining after the event. What is more, there is no way of telling whether Plato thought this account of creation to be the literal truth or whether he was engaged in illustrating logical relations in the form of a story. In any case the Craftsman did not create order as such—he only recognized it in the eternal Ideas. Nor (as we learn from the *Euthyphro*) could he or any other divinity be the source of moral values. What is right is inherently right, no more the creation of gods than the multiplication table is.

Plato's positive religious beliefs perhaps came to no more than this. There are divinities, that is, superhuman souls. Each star has one, and there is a soul of the whole cosmos. These souls are responsible for the excellent order of the world. It is fitting therefore to pay them reverence. They are not providential, however; there is no point in praying to them, asking them for help when in need. To do so would betray a crude, indeed irreligious, view of things. Plato was a Deist two thousand years before Deism.

# 15

# Life of Aristotle

NO ONE EVER FOUNDED and advanced so many fields of science and learning as Aristotle—"The Philosopher," as he was unambiguously referred to in the Middle Ages. He created formal logic from the beginning and left it so completed that no major renovation was made for more than 2,000 years. Darwin honored him as the greatest biologist of all time. He wrote the first systematic treatise on ethics, a book that holds its own with the latest contributions to the field today. His *Poetics* is a parallel contribution to literary criticism. Only now is the fundamental rightness of his conception of the mind coming to be properly recognized. His metaphysics, his scheme of conceptualization and explanation, was for centuries the skeleton of western thought; some of the bones are still in place and likely to remain. He wrote the first scientific study of comparative politics.

This awesome man was born in 384 B.C., 15 years after the death of Socrates, in the small city of Stagira on the north coast of the Aegean Sea at the base of the peninsula on which today stand the monasteries of Mount Athos. Like Abdera to the east, Stagira was largely Ionian in population and culture. Aristotle's father was an eminent doctor, physician to the king of Macedon, at whose court Aristotle may have spent some years of his childhood. He was orphaned at an early age.

In 366 B.C., when he was 17 or 18, he went to Athens to finish his education at Plato's Academy, then about 20 years established as the recognized center of higher learning. Plato was away at the time on his second visit to Syracuse. However, they soon met, and Aristotle's association with the Academy continued for the remaining 19 years of Plato's life, as student and then member of the faculty. Plato is said to have called him "the reader"—he was the first notable book collector—and "the Mind (*nous*) of the school." We are also told that shortly before Plato's death doctrinal disputes arose between the two, and according to Aristotle's account the teaching of Plato in his last years approached out and out number mysticism. Nevertheless, Aristotle movingly said of Plato that he was "a man whom it would be blasphemy for bad people even to praise."

Plato bequeathed the presidency of the Academy to his nephew Speusippus. Of this philosopher, also an enthusiast for numbers, it is enough to say that he spread the story that his uncle was not really the son of the man Ariston but of the god Apollo. So together with Xenocrates (396–314 B.C.), another eminent Platonist, Aristotle accepted an invitation to join Hermias, former fellow student at the Academy and now philosopher-king of the two cities of Atarneus and Assos on the coast of Asia Minor near the site of Troy. Marine biology was prominent among the researches Aristotle carried on in three years spent in the region. He married Pythias, the niece and adopted daughter of Hermias. The marriage was a happy one but brief; Pythias died less than ten years later. Afterwards Aristotle married Herpyllis, a lady from Stagira. In his will he provided handsomely for her and for their son Nicomachus, but he directed that he was to be buried in the same tomb with Pythias.

In 343 B.C., Aristotle was summoned to Pella, capital city of Macedon, to be tutor to the crown prince Alexander, then 13 years of age. Aristotle's personal acquaintance with King Philip, dating from childhood, no doubt had something to do with the appointment—but he probably also owed something to the influence of Hermias, who was an ally of Macedon. (And who came to a horrible end on that account. In violation of safe-conduct, he was seized by agents of the Shah of Iran to whom he was nominally subordinate. Accused of treason, he was tortured to gain information but revealed nothing. Finally he was crucified. His last words were "Tell my friends that I have done nothing to be ashamed of or unworthy of philosophy.")

## The Macedonian Conquest

When Aristotle was still a boy the kingdom of Macedon absorbed his home town along with a number of other cities in northern Greece. The lifetime of Aristotle coincided with the expansion of that kingdom over all of Greece and Asia Minor into India. Macedon was the central force of the fourth century and Aristotle stood near the center of power.

The Greeks drew a sharp line between themselves and barbarians (*i.e.* people who, not speaking Greek, could utter only "bar-bar-bar"); nevertheless, Macedon was a borderline case. It was vast in area by Greek standards; it was a monarchy, a form of government that had not existed in Greece proper for centuries; and its language, though akin to Greek, was not easily intelligible. On the other hand the Macedonians worshipped the same gods, consulted the oracle at Delphi, and competed in the Olympic games. The relation of Macedon to Greece was somewhat like that of Czarist Russia to Europe.

The royal family of Macedon was rather wild, its members given to assassinating one another. King Philip was no model of temperance, but he was steeped in the culture of Greece, and was extraordinarily intelligent and energetic. He developed the finest army the world had ever seen, drilled in enormously effective new tactics, and he had the best intelligence service. Personally he was fearless. His enemy Demosthenes (384–322 B.C.), the Athenian orator, said of him: "To gain empire and power he had an eye knocked out, his collarbone broken, his arm and his leg maimed; he abandoned to fortune any part of his body she cared to take, so that honor and glory might be the portion of the rest." With these resources he conquered the kingdom of Thrace (between Macedon and the entrance to the Black Sea) in 342–41 B.C. and then turned his attention to Greece.

Philip was no vulgar bandit out for booty. He sincerely desired to make Greece strong by imposing unity. All the Greeks loved freedom and prided themselves on being free men. This meant many things to them. In general, however, there was a feeling that freedom was incompatible with having to take orders from a ruler remote and secluded and of another people. Hence the Greeks always resisted being incorporated into political units of more than a few thousand citizens. This made for admirable diversity between states and public spirit within each state. But the disadvantage was incessant warfare of Greek against Greek and consequent vulnerability to external attack.

Much of Greece had achieved a temporary unity in the face of the threat from Iran a century and a half earlier. But the attempt of Athens to give the anti-Iranian alliance some permanence had raised fears of imperialism that resulted in counterpressures culminating in the ruinous Peloponnesian War. Always there were Greek statesmen and intellectuals, notable among them the sophists Hippias and Isocrates, who pleaded for pan-Hellenism—but always jealousy frustrated them. One city after another was dominant but the balance-of-power policy ensured that none was able to maintain a superior position long enough to accomplish anything great. Constant warfare impoverished the people, carried on in this century mainly by mercenary troops often more dangerous to their employers than to the enemy.

In consequence, there were patriotic statesmen in the Greek cities including Athens who welcomed Macedonian suzerainty. Yet generally the sentiment was violently against it.

Aristotle tutored Alexander for three years. Then in 340 B.C. Philip went off to the wars against those Greek cities that dared oppose him. He made his 16-year-old son Regent of Macedon in his absence, putting an end to the tutorial sessions. We would like to know what Aristotle taught Alexander. The partial answer is that he went through Homer's *Iliad* with him. Further than that we know nothing more than that relations seem to have been cordial.

Armed opposition to Philip ceased after the decisive battle of Chaeronea in 338 B.C. However, the king pursued a conciliatory policy, especially toward Athens, which retained independence, as did many other cities. The result was that even Philip did not put an end to Greek intercity bickering. But the country was pacified, and Philip was ready to embark on the grand project dreamed of by apostles of Greek unity: the conquest of Iran. He was ready to set out in 336 B.C. when he was murdered at the instigation of his divorced first wife, Alexander's mother.

## The Lyceum

The expedition to Asia was delayed two years while Alexander, ascending the throne at age 20, put down some attempts at rebellion in Greece and assembled his army. In the midst of these preparations in 335 B.C., Aristotle was in Athens again. Speusippus had died and the presidency of the Academy was vacant once more. It went not to Aristotle but to his old traveling companion Xenocrates. Aristotle thereupon rented some buildings near the temple and gymnasium named for Apollo Lyceus ( = Lycian god? god of light? wolf god?) and inaugurated the second of the schools of Athens, the Lyceum. It is said that Alexander contributed generously to the foundation. There was on the grounds a covered walk or colonnade, in Greek a *peripatos*, where classes were held when the weather was suitable; from this the Aristotelian philosophy got the alternative name Peripatetic.

The Lyceum reflected its founder's philosophy and interests. That meant emphasis on the natural sciences, especially biology, and history. There was an extensive library, collections of plants and animals both live and preserved, and curious objects of all sorts. In these respects the Lyceum supplemented the Academy. In later antiquity, Alexandria in Egypt became under royal patronage the great center of scientific research, eclipsing the Lyceum. But in fact the original faculty of the Museum of Alexandria were nearly all graduates of the Lyceum, so that one might almost regard that institution as Aristotle's school relocated.

For twelve years Aristotle conducted the Lyceum without any recorded unto-ward events. This was the period during which Alexander conquered Egypt, Phoenicia, and the vast Iranian empire all the way to Afghanistan, and began his experiment of fusing Greek and Oriental cultures. Aristotle went on teaching: graduate seminars in the morning, more popular lectures in the afternoons and evenings. Then in 323 B.C. Alexander died. In Athens, as elsewhere in Greece, there were anti-Macedonian riots and attacks on the army of occupation. Aristotle escaped lynching, but his Macedonian connections exposed him to grave danger. With notable lack of originality, the Athenians trumped up a charge of impiety against him. He was accused of having paid divine honors to his murdered friend Hermias in an elegy composed to his memory—in other words, he had "brought in new gods"! At these developments Aristotle sensibly departed from Athens "in order" he said "to prevent the Athenians from sinning a second time against philosophy." He went to Chalcis on the island of Euboea, the mother city of Stagira. *In absentia* the Athenians stripped him of all the honors he had been granted. When he heard of this he declared that he was sorry, but not too sorry.

He did not live long in Chalcis. A chronic stomach complaint proved fatal a year later, in 322 B.C., when he was 62 years old.

## Characteristics

Many books on Aristotle have as frontispiece a photograph of a portrait bust in the Art History Museum, Vienna. It is of noble appearance, exactly what the Philosopher should have looked like. Unfortunately, the ascription to Aristotle is almost certainly spurious. The only physical description we have of him makes him thin-shanked, bald, with small eyes set close together. He had a speech impediment.

In the *Nichomachean Ethics*, Aristotle described the proud man, more literally the great-souled man, who is concerned with honor on the grand scale. This cannot be taken in its entirety as a self-portrait since such a man is evidently conceived as being a great statesman or general. But most of what is said about his deportment is obviously Aristotle's conception of how any man of some importance should behave. Since it is hardly conceivable that Aristotle should have had an ideal of behavior that he did not live up to, we may take this much as autobiography.

> It is a mark of the proud man to ask for nothing or scarcely anything, but to give help readily, and to be dignified towards people who enjoy high position and good for-tune, but unassuming towards those of the middle class; for it is a difficult and lofty thing to be superior to the former, but easy to be so to the latter, and a lofty bearing over the former is no mark of ill-breeding, but among humble people it is as vulgar as a display of strength against the weak. . . . He must also be open in his hate and in his love (for to conceal one's feelings, i.e. to care less for truth than for what people will think, is a coward's part), and must speak and act openly; for he is free of speech because he is contemptuous, and he is given to telling the truth, except when he speaks in irony to the vulgar. He must be unable to make his life revolve around

another, unless it be a friend; for this is slavish, and for this reason all flatterers are servile and people lacking in self-respect are flatterers. Nor is he given to admiration; for nothing to him is great. Nor is he mindful of wrongs; for it is not the part of a proud man to have a long memory, especially for wrongs, but rather to overlook them. Nor is he a gossip; for he will speak neither about himself nor about another, since he cares not to be praised nor for others to be blamed; nor again is he given to praise; and for the same reason he is not an evil-speaker, even about his enemies, except from haughtiness. With regard to necessary or small matters he is least of all men given to lamentation or the asking of favors; for it is the part of one who takes such matters seriously to behave so with respect to them. He is one who will possess beautiful and profitless things rather than profitable and useful ones; for this is more proper to a character that suffices to itself. Further, a slow step is thought proper to the proud man, a deep voice, and a level utterance; for the man who takes few things seriously is not likely to be hurried, nor the man who thinks nothing great to be excited, while a shrill voice and a rapid gait are the results of hurry and excitement. Such, then, is the proud man.[1]

## Writings

In his youth Aristotle wrote dialogues in the Platonic manner, which were also Platonic in their ideas. They are said to have been elegant literary productions; but none has survived. What we have of Aristotle's writings—a great deal: 1,462 pages in the standard text, nearly as many words as in the Holy Bible—all dates presumably from after his departure from the Academy, and most of it from his period of tenure as head of the Lyceum.

These works are treatises on particular subjects, like modern scholarly books and monographs; indeed, except for the medical literature, they are the earliest surviving scientific papers. Some clearly were intended for use as lecture notes, though rather fully written out. There is great variation in the polish and organization.

Not all this is Aristotle's fault even apart from the fact that not all the treatises were meant for publication. The manuscripts did not remain in the Lyceum library but were shipped to Asia Minor, where for more than a century they were hidden in a damp cellar. The Roman general Sulla, when conquering the region in the first century B.C., liberated them and sent them back to Rome. An intelligent Greek editor, Andronicus of Rhodes, was employed to arrange them. He did the best he could. However, as there was no way to determine dates of composition, some of the subject-matter divisions into which Andronicus put these works resulted in collections of pieces put one after the other that had been composed years apart. Since Aristotle constantly revised his opinions, the resulting 'works' often contain passages difficult to reconcile with one another. This is true in greatest degree of the longest and philosophically the most important of all, the *Metaphysics*—so entitled, indeed, for no other reason than that Andronicus, knowing of no inclusive title for the more or less related but separate monographs making up this collection, referred to them as "the books after (*meta*) the *Physics*."

Modern scholars have had some success in working out a more coherent order on the basis of the assumption that the development of Aristotle's thought was away from Platonism in the direction of a more materialistic and Ionian view of things. Therefore, of two opinions on the same subject the more Platonic must be the earlier. But this assumption still leaves many problems unsolved. Stylometry—so successful for establishing the order of the Platonic works—is of hardly any use here for many reasons, the chief being that we cannot be sure which Aristotelian works were earliest and which latest, and therefore have no basis for comparisons. In any case, the difference is only about 20 years as compared to the 50 of Plato.

## Style

Complaint is often made of the dryness, awkwardness, and obscurity of Aristotle's style. Certainly his prose does not flow with the grace of Plato's either in the original or in translations. But then it was not intended to. Aristotle tried to express his thought with precision. To that end he did not shrink from inventing a technical vocabulary and from deliberate repetition of words rather than substitution of near-synonyms. Plato usually had some emotional attitude toward what he was discussing, and he had great power to evoke that attitude in his readers. Aristotle, on the other hand, strove for scientific detachment. The distinction between serious science and mere attitudinizing largely reduces to this difference: it is hardly an exaggeration to say that the beginning of scientific medicine among the Greeks can be dated from the appearance of diagnoses set out in exact matter-of-fact sentences. Despite the brilliance and nobility of their presentation, Plato's arguments are sometimes so abbreviated that they fail to convince. As befits the inventor of formal logic, Aristotle argues with thoroughness and (usually) logical validity, though this often makes for a certain tedium.

Paradoxically, translations of Aristotle sometimes are obscure or misleading just because the original is precise and terse. For example, the seventh book of the *Metaphysics* begins with a famous sentence only four words long: *To on legetai pollachôs*. These are common Greek words. And although Aristotle is using the third in a slightly technical way, one who had read a few pages of his logical writing would have no difficulty with the notion, that of predication. The verb *legetai* would mean in ordinary Greek 'is said'; here it means 'is predicated'. *To* is the definite article and may be omitted here. *Pollachôs* means 'variously' or 'in many ways'. So the sentence might be put 'Being is predicated in many ways'. But some translators seem to think this too cryptic. Here is a sample of their work.

> The word 'being' has a variety of senses.

> 'Being' has many meanings.

> There are several senses in which a thing may be said
>     to 'be'.

All these are interpretations. They claim, perhaps rightly, that Aristotle is talking about a word and not what the word stands for. They assume that to say it is "predicated in many ways" comes to the same thing as saying that it has many 'meanings' or 'senses', though that is not obvious or even true (in general). The third translation (by Sir David Ross) uses thirteen words for Aristotle's four and at least gives the impression that Aristotle means the same tomato may be said to 'be' in several senses, whereas he may have meant instead that the way in which tomatoes 'are' is not the same as the way in which recipes for tomato soup 'are'—or he may have meant both at once.

Of course difficulties of this sort bedevil every translation of every author, but somehow they seem to be more exasperating in the case of Aristotle's writings than they are for almost anyone else.

It is perhaps best to say on the whole that Aristotle belongs with those philosophers such as Spinoza and Kant whose works are difficult at first but reward patient study.

# 16

# Aristotle's Philosophy of Nature

NUMBERS ARE DISCOVERED NOT invented, are independent of any-body's beliefs, are objects of real knowledge, are eternal and unchanging, are invisible but intelligible, and they confer order on whatever they are applied to. Whatever Ideas are, they are like numbers in all these respects. The concept of Number then is that on which reality is modeled in the Platonic philosophy.

Analogously there is a central concept in Aristotle's philosophy, but it is very different from Number. It is Organism. A plant or an animal or a person is an individual thing, made of a certain kind of matter, having a certain form or structure determined by and determining its particular function or capability. It developed in a regular way out of relatively unformed diverse matter (its food) according to a pattern built into the seed from which it sprang. It will in turn produce seeds, which if all goes well will develop into other mature individuals, and so on. Understanding the organism consists in being able to give a detailed account of it along these lines. Understanding anything else—the city, the history of philosophy, the cosmos—is fundamentally similar. Biology, not mathematics, is the key science.

## The Four Causes

Aristotle calls the conditions responsible for the existence of a thing by a word which we translate as "causes," though the notion is wider than what we ordinarily mean by that English word. Understanding a thing means knowing its causes in this broad sense—and there are exactly four of them. For there are ultimately four questions we can ask about a thing. What is it made of? What kind of thing is it? How, by whom or by what, was it made? And what is it for?

The answer to the first question is the statement of the Material Cause, "that out of which a thing comes to be and which is present as a constituent in the product," as bronze is the matter of a bronze statue. Second, the Formal Cause, "the form or pattern, i.e. the formula of what it is to be the thing in question"; Aristotle gives as example the ratio 2:1 as the formula, or formal cause, of the octave. Third, the Efficient Cause, "that from which comes the immediate origin of the movement or rest; e.g. the man who gave advice is a cause, the father is cause of the child, and generally what makes of what is made and what causes change of what is changed." (This is most like what we ordinarily mean by "cause.")

Fourth and last, the Final Cause, "the end or that for the sake of which a thing is done, e.g. health is the cause of walking about. 'Why is he walking about,' we say. 'To be healthy,' and having said that, we think we have assigned the cause."[1]

The first book of the *Metaphysics* is the first history of philosophy. The scheme of organization that Aristotle employs is to show how his predecessors had, with more or less success, groped toward the solution of the problem of explanation which he had at last worked out in definitive form. The earliest thinkers, we are told, inquired only after the material causes of the world: "water," "the Boundless," "air" are answers to the question of what the world is made. Democritus made some attempts to discover efficient causes. Anaxagoras' Mind was supposed to be the final cause, but Aristotle agrees with Socrates that the use made of this notion was disappointingly meager. Socrates and Plato investigated formal causes. It remained for Aristotle, he himself assures us, to bring all these strands together.

This description of the evolution of philosophy serves better as an illustration of the Aristotelian conception of growth than as history. Philosophy had grown; in growth each stage is incomplete in itself but intelligible when, and only when, we see what it is pointing at. Only the mature organism is self-intelligible or, in Aristotle's vocabulary, actual. In the case of philosophy itself, actuality is conveniently Aristotelianism.

## Substance

Things are to be explained in terms of the four causes. But what are things? This may seem a surprising or oversimple or ineffably profound question. Aristotle speaks of the question, What is Reality? (or What is Substance?), as "the question that always has been and always will be worried about." His answer is neither simple nor dogmatic. Perhaps he had more than one answer.

If we asked the most general question of all, "What is there?" the Aristotelian reply would be "Everything." Shoes, rainbows, colors, sneezes, numbers, illusions, souls "are"—they exist. Aristotle makes a notable advance over Plato who supposed that since they all are beings they must have something in common— something, however, that comes in different concentrations: numbers most of it, souls next, and so on down the line. Aristotle teaches, to the contrary, that Socrates and the number seven both have full being, but in different ways. There are ten ways of being, ten "categories": the ways appropriate to substance, quantity, quality, relation, place, time, posture, condition, action, and being-acted-on. All except the first have dependent being. In the category of quantity, for instance, there is no number seven all by itself in splendid Platonic isolation; there are only seven Muses, seven Pleiades, and so on. But the fact that we can talk successfully about seven Pleiades is enough to warrant us in asserting that the number seven has being—the kind of being the number seven ought to have. Similarly there are red tomatoes, so Democritus was wrong in supposing that colors are somehow illusory. But if what he intended to deny was simply the view that reality contains colors alongside the atoms, that there could conceivably be colors without colored things (substances), then he was right. Aristotle puts this doctrine in technical grammatical form: all the terms that signify categories other than substance are "present in a subject" and "not as parts are present in a whole, but incapable of existence apart from the subject."[2] Substances are the subjects in which the things of other categories are present.

## The Individual Thing

Substance "in the truest and primary and most definite sense of the word" is the individual: the man Socrates, the horse Bucephalus. Aristotle's world is full of a number of things, and they are just the things that common sense calls things. It is characteristic of Aristotle that his philosophical conclusions tend to coincide with views commonly held by nonphilosophers. In this case Aristotle in effect noticed a complexity of language that Plato and others had overlooked. They had supposed that since yellow things all have something in common, namely a yellow color, and since 'real' is a noun modifier like 'yellow', therefore real things too must have some common quality—though so subtle that only a philosopher can discern it. But there would be no incentive to make this search if only it had been noted that the word 'real' behaves not so much like 'yellow' as like 'hard': stones, decisions, problems, and uppercuts may all be hard; yet it makes no sense to ask which is harder, a knockout blow or a calculus problem.

It is also characteristic of Aristotle that, having validated the common-sense view, he then proceeds to hedge it and qualify it in a Platonic way. After declaring that substance is the individual, he goes on.

> But in a secondary sense those things are called substances within which, as species, the primary substances are included. . . . For instance, the individual man is included in the species man, and the genus to which the species belongs is animal; these, therefore, the species man and the genus animal, are termed secondary substances.[3]

Plato has returned through the back door.

## Form and Matter

Every individual thing is a composite of form and matter, the Philosopher teaches. This is the ordinary distinction involved in such phrases as sonata form and formal dinner. The music of one sonata may be quite different from that of another, and a series of formal dinners may have different guest lists and menus. What makes a dinner a formal affair is not some added ingredient, as if some special dish had to be served. And sonata form is not something that could exist "pure": there cannot be a contentless sonata. But no more can there be a musical composition or a dinner that does not have some form or other. The distinction of form from matter is not one of part from part; while the two are distinguishable in any individual, they are not separable.

Aristotle's noting of this fact was another advance over Plato, the essence of whose philosophy was the "separation of the Ideas (Forms)"—he supposed that over and above all the chalk and plastic and shortbread triangles there is The Form Triangularity, the reality all by itself in itself. Yet Triangularity had to be also in the particulars—a requirement that led to the apparently insuperable difficulties that Plato himself called attention to in the dialogue *Parmenides*.

The form of a bronze sphere is simply its shape; indeed the Greek word for shape is sometimes used as a synonym for form. But the form of anything is what-it-is-to-be-that-sort-of-thing, its essence (which word is the one used by Roman writers to render the previous phrase), its *whatness* (as opposed to its *thisness*, which is its matter). What it is to be a knife is to be a cutting instrument; in this case the function, cutting, is the form. The function is of course closely connected to the shape but not identical to it. A rubber 'knife' is not really a knife, does not have the form of knife though it has the shape. As for the human being, what it is to be one is to have a vital capacity for rational activity. Consequently the human soul is the form of the individual. The form, formal cause, definition, and essence of a thing are the same.

But if the definition of a thing is always a statement of the form, what becomes of the matter? Is it indefinable, not to be talked about? In a way yes. If I talk about Socrates, I can say of him that he is a rational animal, talkative, bald, barefoot, virtuous, and so on. All these are remarks about forms of one sort or another (as Plato would heartily agree); they have to do with the *whatness* of Socrates. However fully I specify Socrates, it is never possible to tell just from my descriptions that I mean *this* particular individual and not some other just like him. In other words, you can never tell just from descriptions of Socrates whether Socrates is real or fictional. Can I reach the *thatness* of Socrates in language at all? In the end I must simply say "I'm talking about *that* fellow over in the corner" and point.

That is not to say, however, that there is anything mysterious or ineffable about Socrates. The form/matter distinction is relative to context. The form of Socrates is his soul, the matter is his body. The body, considered as a body, has a form— namely, its shape. That I can describe. The matter corresponding to that form is the flesh and bones. But they too have their forms. This is to say that when a context is specified there is a definite answer to the question what is form and what matter, but the distinction is never absolute. (Or hardly ever, as we shall see.) A board is a complex of form and matter, but it (the complex) is the matter of a fence.

## Change

Aristotle's distinction between substance and the nonsubstance categories enabled him to solve the philosophical puzzle about change that had beset the preceding two centuries. If things are made up of constituents which are the hot, the cold, the wet, the dry, is not change unintelligible? For if a wet blanket dries, what happens to the wet? It seems to disappear into nothing. If the green apple turns red, where did the red come from? Out of nothing? But such suppositions make reasoning about the world impossible.

Democritus, as we have seen, had a solution; though the price he paid—that of declaring the sensible qualities unreal—was high. At any rate, Aristotle found it sufficient to point out that we need not suppose that the wet becomes the dry or that the wet vanishes and the dry pops up. Rather, as we knew all the time, the blanket that was wet becomes a blanket that is dry. It is peculiar to substances that they admit contrary qualities, though not at the same time in the same manner. Through change, substance is conserved; that is enough. Red and green, wet and dry are real enough—that is to say, there are substances that really have these qualities from time to time.

## Potential and Actual

However, individual substances come into being and pass away, so it is not accurate to say that every substance is always conserved. Apples become horses and horses become glue. How can this kind of change—substantial change—be made intelligible?

What is conserved is the matter—or it would be better and closer to Aristotle to say the material. When an apple grows from a bud, that which takes on the form of the apple is earth, water, and air. We can say of the stuffs that contribute to the being of the apple that they were potentially an apple; that is, they had the capability, in suitable circumstances, of being incorporated into an apple. Now, similarly, the actual apple can nourish the horse. It does not become part of the horse the way a brick becomes part of a wall. The apple loses its form, its individuality, in becoming horse fodder; the brick in the wall keeps on being a brick. Both, however, illustrate how a substance may cease to be without vanishing into nothingness. Material or stuff in one case loses its form (as an apple) altogether to become the matter of a quite different form; in the other it (form and all) becomes the matter of a complex but individual thing, the wall.

Not just anything is potentially anything. Stones will not nourish horses, nor apples make a wall. Hence to say that the actual apple is potentially horseflesh is to give genuine information. But an apple is a potential pig or robin as well as horse, and a brick is a potential missile or (part of a) house. In general, substances have multiple potentialities. By and large also, the less articulated and organized something is, the more potentialities it has. Earth and water are potential apples, ceramics, bricks, mud pies, and so indefinitely (more strictly speaking, they are the potentialities of the next step in the process). Something definite and pure like a diamond has few, though concrete and no doubt important, potentialities. It is true that something so highly organized as an apple or a chicken may, by being eaten, become all sorts of things; but it must first be stripped of its form as apple or chicken. Thus, in a manner of speaking, matter and form are inversely related: the less definite the form of something is, the more it is the matter of diverse things. Correspondingly, the less actuality, the more potentiality.

One can look at Aristotle's distinction between potential and actual as the dynamic counterpart of the matter/form distinction. When we want to consider what a thing is here and now, statically, we talk about its matter and its form; whereas when we are interested in some process, we will speak instead of potential and actual.

## Prime Matter

The inverse relationship of matter to form suggests the notion of a scale or ladder with pure formless matter at the bottom and pure matterless form at the top. To a certain extent this is a valid conception in the Aristotelian world view. A series such as rock—mud—moss—apple—worm—horse—philosopher does exhibit a progression of form. But does it have a beginning and an end?

If it had a beginning, that would be something that was the matter of everything but itself without form. To say this is already to suggest the Boundless of Anaximander. However, as regards the elements of things, Aristotle adopted a modification of Empedocles' teaching. He held that the simplest bodies are earth, air, fire, and water; but he disagreed with Empedocles in allowing the transformation of each of these into the others. Fire, which is hot and dry, can become air, which is hot and moist; and that can go on to become water, which is cold and moist. Is there then something more basic that is conserved through these transmutations? Yes and no. Prime matter is conserved; but then, prime matter is only an abstraction.

By definition prime matter is that which is altogether potential, potentially everything—and not at all actual, not anything in particular. Prime matter, then, by definition does not exist; for to exist is to be actually something or other. So when fire becomes air, at every stage in the process something actually exists and is actually hot as well as actually of some degree of dampness.

The other end of the continuum has an occupant. There is something that is purely actual and not at all potential—form without matter. This, as we shall see, is God.

## Nature

Bricks become walls only when bricklayers lift and mortar them into position. Apples turn into horses only when the animals annihilate the apples considered as apples. On the other hand acorns become oaks, kittens become cats, boulders roll down mountainsides, and the stars revolve in their courses under their own power. These are the things they do and the changes they undergo when they are left to themselves. It is their *nature* to do so.

Aristotle defines nature as "a source or cause of being moved, or of remaining in the same condition, in the thing to which it belongs primarily and essentially, not accidentally." Every thing that has a nature is a substance, but not every substance has a nature. A table, for example, has not. If shoved out a window it will fall; but it falls because it is a heavy object (*i.e.* composed mostly of the heavy element earth), not because it is a table. If you chop it into pieces and plant the splinters, and if they take root they will develop into trees, not into tables. Moreover, heaviness belongs to the table *accidentally* not essentially. Accidents are the properties that things can have or not have while remaining the same substances. Some tables are wooden, some metal, some plastic; the material of which the table is composed is an accidental property, like its color. No doubt all tables are heavy enough to fall; nevertheless, heaviness is no part of the essence of table (which presumably is something like *piece of furniture having a flat surface elevated about waist high*). A weightless table might be convenient; in any case it would still be a table.

If the table is wooden, is the heaviness—the tendency to fall when unsupported—the nature of the tree from which the lumber was cut? No. Because although it is not a mere accident of trees that they are heavy, heaviness belongs primarily not to trees but to the heavy elements, earth and water. However, the tree has a nature, since there is an internal source of its motion—a word that as Aristotle uses it includes growth and qualitative change as well as change of place, 'loco' motion.

In general the distinction between substances that have natures and those that do not coincides with that between natural and artificial.

## Natural Science

Scientific knowledge is of the causes of substances. It means knowing the natures of substances, their patterns of development, and their powers—what they are capable of doing to other things and what can be done to them. (Knowledge of natureless substances presents no problem. Since they are all artifacts, they are made, hence understood, by human beings. Beehives and the like present minor exceptions.)

Natures are understood in terms of the four causes, which here in effect can be reduced to two: the matter and the essence. A natural motion is a transition from a state of being so-and-so potentially to being it actually: from kitten to cat, acorn to oak, boulder at top of cliff to boulder at bottom of cliff. Now the formal cause or essence, the what-it-is-to-be such-and-such, includes the nature. No definition or description of a cat could be complete if it did not mention the self-generated motions specific to cats; otherwise it would apply equally well to stuffed cats. But in the case of a nature, the final cause—that for the sake of which the thing exists—is simply its mature state, if it is a living being, or its state of natural rest (down for heavy things, up for light ones) if it is inorganic. The final cause, that is to say, is another aspect of its essence. Even the efficient cause reduces to the essence in natures, for (to use Aristotle's example) man begets man: the efficient cause is the same nature although it is not the same individual substance. Hence, as we should expect, natural science is knowledge of essences.

The final cause takes on central importance in Aristotle's philosophy. If you understand what a thing is for, or aiming at being, there is little more that you need to know about it and that little is easily discovered. Embryology, another science that Aristotle virtually founded, provides ample illustration. The structure of the embryo takes on meaning only once the connections of its parts with the organs of the mature animal are recognized. Natural motion is from potential to actual, but understanding must go the other way. "Nature belongs to the class of causes which act for the sake of something."[4]

But why not say that natural things just happen, by necessity, with no end in view? Why not say, in the fashion of Empedocles, that teeth develop in numerous random forms, of which only those organized in a way fit for tearing and chewing enable their possessors to survive and pass on the characteristic to their progeny? The Philosopher deemed such theories obviously false. Nature exhibits regular, not random, sequences. The more we study nature, the more we learn about her ends—for instance, that "leaves grow to provide shade for the fruit."

And yet, goal-directed as the Peripatetic philosophy is, the ends that play so important a role are not the conscious purposes of any personal being. When we, today, contemplate some kind of unlearned but complicated behavior with survival value—such as the nesting instinct of birds—we tend to suppose that only two ways of understanding it are possible: either (1) birds make nests because they are descended from creatures that by chance initiated this behavior pattern or (2) nesting behavior was conferred on birds by a personal power that was aware of its desirability for avian welfare. But Aristotle was neither a mechanist nor a supernaturalist. He held that the patterns of natural motion can be understood only in terms of their ends, yet those ends are not the purposes of any consciousness. Nature is a vast system of purposes with no purposers.

Aware of objections that might be brought against this paradoxical aspect of his system, Aristotle argued that deliberation is not a necessary component of a goal-directed sequence. "Art does not deliberate." If houses grew, they would grow in the same order in which they are built. Nature, he said, is like a physician healing himself: the motive force of the activity is in the thing moved. This is the only difference between nature and art.

# Potencies Active and Passive

A lump of sugar is capable of affecting your tongue in such a way as to produce a sweet taste; this is an active power of sugar. It is also capable of being dissolved in hot coffee; that is a passive potency. These are parts of the nature of sugar. But while a nature is a cause of motion, we must remember that this is said in the broad sense of the Aristotelian formal cause. Natures never *do* anything. They must, so to speak, be triggered by something external. It is the nature of a boulder to roll downhill, but something else must first remove the log wedged at its base.

Once the trigger is pulled, though, the sequence of actualizing the potency proceeds automatically and inevitably unless something else from outside interferes. However, this is true only of nonrational potencies. When the potency in question is under control of the rational soul of a human being, the case is otherwise. Rational potencies can produce contrary effects. If I were a physician I could use my knowledge and skill to cure you, or I could refrain from doing so because of legal risks, or I might even pervert my knowledge and skill in the direction of poisoning you. The matters that we deliberate about are precisely in the areas where rational potencies operate. This fact is of the greatest importance for ethics.

Was Aristotle a determinist? Did he believe that whatever happens happens of necessity, could not be otherwise? It is not easy to answer; perhaps the reason is that the Philosopher never put the question to himself in that way. As far as the realm of nonrational potencies is concerned, it seems that his views imply determinism even if he never says so. For he did deny that chance is another kind of cause in addition to the four. Chance he analyzed as the bringing about of something that ordinarily would be brought about purposively, but in circumstances such that the particular purpose was not intended at the time. For instance, I go to the market and meet someone there who owes me money, and I collect. I might have gone with the purpose of collecting but in fact I did not, I got paid "by chance." But of course everything that happened had its causes.

Where deliberation is involved, however, Aristotle was so far from postulating inevitability that he even argued, in a passage that has scandalized the logicians ever since, that some statements about the future cannot be either true or false. He pointed out that if someone says "There will be a sea battle tomorrow" and that statement is *now* true, then there *must* be a sea battle tomorrow; so it is no use for the admirals to deliberate about whether to fight or not. Likewise the futility of deliberation follows if the statement is now false. But, says Aristotle—always the foe of paradox—it is obvious that deliberation is not always futile. Therefore, although there must either be a sea battle tomorrow or not, neither the statement that there will be nor that there will not be is at present true. One of them will in due course *become* true.

Yet the actualization of a rational potency is not arbitrary or capricious. In at least one passage the Philosopher's doctrine looks deterministic. He there makes the point that unlike nonrational potencies, which must proceed to the act when the conditions are right, a rational potency requires the concurrence of desire or will. Here is a glass of wine. I do not automatically drink it; I do not automatically pour it down the sink: I deliberate. But, he goes on to say, if you have the desire and the potency, and the passive object is present, you *must* act. If I desire the wine and it is present, and my throat is not obstructed—and there are no inhibitory circumstances such as the presence of my teetotaling aunt—I must drink it.

But how can I be blamed for what I must do? The answer (in the *Ethics*) is that I should have trained myself earlier to have the right kinds of desires. However, it seems that the same kind of analysis and objection would have been applicable to what I did (or failed to do) when as a youth I was training myself (or being trained). Aristotle slides by this problem.

## The Priority of the Actual

The actual is prior to the potential in three ways. (1) In definition and knowledge: we can define a potential oak tree only by describing an actual oak and saying "This (acorn) is potentially that oak." And as already pointed out, we cannot understand the potential (the acorn) unless we first know what it is trying to become. (2) In time: man begets man, the actual oak produces the acorn, the hen comes before the egg. (3) In substantiality: for every substance is an actuality. There are no *mere* potencies. This is one reason why Aristotle rejected evolutionary theories of cosmic and organic development.

## Natural Kinds

At different times Aristotle seems to have had different opinions on what substance or the primary being of the world is, whether the individual thing or the essence. In the *Categories* substance is said to be both: "in the truest and primary and most definite sense of the word, it is . . . the individual man or horse. But in a secondary sense those things are called substances within which, as species, the primary substances are included; also those which, as genera, include the species. For instance, the individual man is included in the species man, and the genus to which the species belongs is animal; these, therefore—the species man and the genus animal—are termed secondary substances." In the philosophical dictionary comprising Book 5 of the *Metaphysics*, this view is repeated but without the qualifying adjectives primary and secondary; and necessary conditions of existence are added to the list. *Metaphysics* 7 and 8 are largely devoted to a tortuous discussion of the various candidates for the primacy in substances. Essence comes out ahead.

Aristotle's worries on this point perhaps stem from the tension between two views that are hard to reconcile and both of which he wanted to adopt. On the one hand his common-sensical temperament and lack of sympathy with Platonic otherworldliness led him to affirm the priority and fundamental status of material things. Over and over he tells us that in the end everything that is said is said of things. But on the other hand as a scientist he was committed to the view, which he also stated frequently and emphatically, that scientific theories take no notice of individuals; science consists of general truths. There is a science of man and of the stars, but there is no science of Socrates or of the Pleiades. Yet it would be absurd to suppose that the subject matter of science could be anything other than reality. Therefore man, star, animal, and so on—the species and genera, the formal causes and essences—have to be substance.

The issue here was given the name "problem of universals" by the philosophers of the middle ages. The question is what sort of status in reality species and genera, as distinguished from individuals, have. One extreme position is known as "realism"—an unfortunate because misleading label—which is the direct descendant of Platonism: universals are the fundamental reality of the world, individuals enjoying only a derivative and second-grade status through participation. Aristotle, though declaring reluctance to criticize "our friends" the Platonists, wrote at length against this doctrine. Most of the stock objections are found first in his writings. He complained that the Ideas merely reduplicate the particulars of the world without explaining anything. They are not causative; it is merely poetical to talk of them as "patterns," or to say that sensible things "participate" in them. If, however, you try to make literal sense of participation, you fall victim to the Third Man argument, *viz.*: If we ask for an explanation of why Socrates and Callias are both men, and answer that it is in virtue of their common participation in the Idea of Man, presumably we are being told that Socrates has something in common with the Idea of Man and so has Callias. But what we started out to explain was what Socrates had in common with Callias, and we are urged to assume the existence of the Idea of Man to account for it. But if we do, by the very same reasoning we are obliged to postulate a "Third Man"—something over and above both Socrates and the Idea of Man—to account for what Socrates and the Idea of Man have in common. Of course, then there must also be a fourth and a fifth and . . . Aristotle did not set out this argument, which he mentions by name as something already well known. It is found (using a different example) in the *Parmenides* of Plato.

The other extreme position on universals is Nominalism, according to which universals are merely names, linguistic entities. There is in nature no Man, there are only Socrates and Plato and Callias and . . .; for the sake of convenience only, so that we will not have to talk forever, we employ universal terms as abbreviations. If we did not have such words as 'man' and 'mortal', we could not say "All men are mortal" but only "Adam died and Eve died and Cain died and Abel died and . . ."—and we would never finish saying that, let alone anything else.

An objection to extreme nominalism is that the resemblance of Socrates to Callias is by no means a human convention, but as much a fact of nature as the existence of Socrates. And to revert to our example, how do we know what names to put in before the repetitions of the verb "died"? Why Adam and Eve and Cain and Abel and not Fido and Bucephalus and Glastonbury Abbey? Only because we know that Adam and company are human beings, the others are not. The word 'men' is not an abbreviation for an arbitrary string of names but a term signifying a class, membership in which can be gained only by possessing the proper credentials.

Yes, but the credentials have no reality over and above the members that display them. The universal is just the formal aspect of the individual thing. When a bronze sphere is made, the machinist creates neither matter nor form; he bestows form on this piece of matter, making an individual of it. But if he did not create the sphericity, where was it beforehand? The question makes no sense. It did not exist before; no more does it exist (on its own) now. What exists is the formed matter, the bronze sphere. But is there not a science of sphericity, namely spherical geometry? Yes, and it is uninterested in the bronzeness or woodenness or any other material constitution of spheres; it studies the form as abstracted. That is to say that it is indifferent to the science of spherical geometry—though perhaps not to some other science—what the objects it studies happen to be made of. To study an abstracted property is not to study a separated property. Aristotle was clear on this point; Plato was not. Plato, as we have noted, ran into difficulties because he could conceive of abstraction only on the model of physical separation. In consequence his Ideas were individuals, albeit ghostly ones. Just this individuality made them unsuitable for the tasks they were required to perform as objects of scientific knowledge. There is a science of circularity, but not of The Circle. This fact was obscured owing to the practice of letting a particular circle, drawn in sand, stand for circularity in geometrical demonstrations.

Nevertheless, one of the Platonic residues in Aristotle's philosophy is his taking for granted the impossibility of a form's changing. One consequence was denial of evolution, thus the end, with minor (Epicurean) exceptions, of that daring hypothesis of the earliest thinkers that the cosmos has a history of development. Aristotle, following the leads of Heraclitus and Plato, derailed Greek speculation, which had been on the right track. We must not, however, be severe in our judgment of him. The Milesians had taken over a belief in development from the creation mythologies. The presence of marine fossils on hilltops was as far as we know the one piece of direct evidence they had for cosmic change. This assumption and this one out-of-the-way fact could hardly prevail in the mind of a sober thinker against the overwhelming evidence of living things breeding true to type. Aristotle was wrong, but justified, in thinking that things had always been much the same.

## Aristotle's Theology

In Aristotle's world there is a god, or possibly 47 or 55 gods, in a straightforward sense not found in Plato. However, his god did not create the world, and indeed does not even take any notice of it or of us. God is a requirement of Aristotelian physical theory. One cannot pray to Aristotle's god, although it is perhaps possible to admire him, or it, or them.

The argument for the existence of a god is in brief outline this. Motion has to be eternal. This eternal motion requires an eternal cause. The cause cannot itself be in motion. It must therefore be an unmoved mover. Being eternal and unmoved it cannot be in any respect potential. Therefore, it is pure actuality. Therefore, it is without matter. Its actuality must be activity. The only possible activity for it is thought, and the only object of that thought is again thought. Therefore, God is a being who eternally thinks about thinking. He moves the world as final cause.

Aristotle has two arguments to prove the eternity of motion; one goes this way. Since some things are now in motion, there must always have existed a potentiality of motion. Suppose that among the things capable of moving some particular one was the first to move, that is, to actualize that potentiality. Since whatever is brought from potency to actuality must be brought by something already actual, contrary to supposition there must have been something actually moving previously. Therefore, there could have been no first motion; in other words, motion has existed from eternity. And it must keep on going forever because whatever destroyed the last thing capable of moving would itself be capable of moving, hence require something further to destroy it.

The other argument rests on the premise that time could not have a beginning, but time is essentially the measure of motion; therefore, motion must be likewise infinite.

Furthermore, eternal motion must be continuous. It is not enough, in Aristotle's opinion, that there should be merely an eternal series of overlapping motions, each motion itself having a beginning and an end. For in that case it would be at least *possible* that all the motions should stop at the same time. But there cannot be such a possibility. Therefore, something must exist eternally in a state of continuous motion. What could this be like? It would have to move either forever in the same straight line or forever in a circle. (All motions are compounds of straight and circular.) But it could not be in a straight line, for that would require infinite space, and the universe is not infinite in any spatial dimension. Therefore, it must be motion in a circle. This conclusion is confirmed by perception, which reveals that the heavens in fact do move eternally in circles.

Democritus supposed that motion, being eternal, did not require any explanation; that was a mistaken view, said Aristotle. The equality between the interior angles of a triangle and two right angles is an eternal relation; nevertheless, we are right in demanding an explanation of why it is eternally so. We know by perception that there is motion, and we can reason from this fact that there must eternally be motion. But why does there have to be any motion at all? Since motion is defined by Aristotle as the actualization of the movable, considered just as the movable, and since every body is movable, the question why there has to be motion is the same as the question why anything at all has to exist—why is there not just nothing? This is a question that has worried (some) philosophers through the ages and still does.

Aristotle's answer is, "Because there is an unmoved mover." Plato had argued that everything in motion is moved either by some other moving thing or by itself; as soul is the only self-moving thing, there must be a world soul. But Aristotle's analysis concludes that nothing can be essentially self-moving. The reason is that to move is to be active, to be moved is to be passive—and the same thing cannot be both agent and patient at the same time in the same respect. To be sure, every natural thing has an internal source of movement. It is necessary to distinguish, however, between that which does the moving and that which is moved. When you are rowing a boat, the boat is moved by the oars, the oars by your muscles, the muscles by—what? By your soul. The soul is the cause of the motion, but the soul is not itself in motion. (True, the soul is carried along down the stream with rower and boat, but this is accidental to the process, not essential.) The soul is an unmoved mover.

The heavenly bodies are the only eternal material things. Having matter, they have potentiality—but of one kind only, that of moving eternally in circles. This eternal actualization of potency must be eternally triggered by something actual; and to avoid endless regress, that actual thing must be purely actual, without matter. One might suppose that at this point Aristotle would declare with Plato that the heavens are moved by soul. And indeed he does. But he does not leave it at that. There must be something to provide a motive for the heavenly soul to move; and it is that, finally, which is the unmoved mover, or God. God is the final cause of heavenly motion: "The object of desire and the object of thought move in this way; they move without being moved." This is all we are told about God's modus operandi. It is literally true that "love makes the world go round."

The motions of the heavens are, however, more complicated than this account thus far makes them appear. Plato had proposed as a problem in his Academy to account for the motions of all the heavenly bodies, including especially the planets—the hard cases—on the hypothesis that they really followed circular paths. The brilliant mathematician Eudoxus, a close friend of Aristotle's, had solved this problem by postulating epicyclical motions for the planets. (An epicycle is the scalloped path traced by a point on a wheel rolling on the circumference of another wheel.) Aristotle accepted this mathematical analysis and gave it a physical interpretation. He held that the heavens consist of not less than 47 nor more than 55 transparent but solid spheres, some revolving around the earth at the center and the other smaller ones revolving between the larger spheres and keeping them apart, like ball bearings. The stars and planets are luminous spots on these spheres. Each sphere is a body with a soul that moves it. The outermost sphere, or first heaven, that of the so-called fixed stars, moves on account of love of God. Whether there are, in addition to the god moving the first heaven, also up to 54 other gods each motivating the motion of another sphere, is not certain. The account as we have it is obscure and probably contradictory. It seems likely that the Philosopher had different opinions on these matters at different times.

What is the pure actuality that is the unmoved mover? He is not in motion, but that does not mean he is not active. Aristotle distinguished between motion, which has a goal, and activity, which is its own goal. Focusing the eyes and learning how to ski are motions; seeing and skiing are activities. The description of God's activity is famous.

> On such a principle, then, the heavens and nature depend. It is a life such as ours is in its best moments. It is always at its best, though for us this is impossible. The first mover's activity is pleasure, even as we, too, most enjoy being awake, conscious, and thinking . . . Knowing, by its very nature, concerns what is inherently best; and knowing in the truest sense concerns what is best in the truest sense. . . . It is the activity of intellectual vision that is most pleasant and best. If God is always in that good state in which we sometimes are, this is wonderful; and if in a still better state, this is ground for still more wonder. Now, it is in this better state that God has being and life. For the actuality of thought is life, and God is that actuality; and God's self-dependent actuality is life most good and eternal. We say therefore that God is a living being, eternal, most good, so that life and duration continuous and eternal belong to God; for this is God.[5]

These are sublime words. Nevertheless, it is a puzzle what the being described in them has to do with the Aristotelian system. We are not told, and we can hardly guess, why love of this blessed being should inspire the stars to revolve in eternal tranquility. Worse still, the notion of a being who is purely actual, therefore not material at all, seems a Platonic intrusion that spoils what otherwise impresses us as the fundamental insight and principal virtue of the Aristotelian scheme of conceptualization—the insistence that every real thing is a complex of form and matter. Nor is our comprehension of the cosmos increased when we are assured that somewhere in the sky there exists an immaterial being eternally and solitarily enjoying himself.

# 17

# Aristotle on the Structure of Science

IT IS HARDLY AN exaggeration to credit Aristotle with inventing the notion of *a* science as we know it. To Plato and those who came before him there were the particular arts and crafts—shoemaking, shipbuilding, speechwriting, and the like—practical techniques accomplishing their results in a delimited field primarily by the application of rules shown by experience to work; and over against them science or wisdom or philosophy, a general theory of things in general. The philosopher grasps the whole entire. He knows the pattern of the world and this knowledge is relevant to all the techniques, for it makes their rules intelligible. If the pattern of the world is harmonious, then health is a harmony, and doctoring must aim at restoring the proper balance in the patient. So if he has a fever, chill him. Likewise a proper oration will consist of balanced phrases. We have seen how Plato took for granted that the philosopher would be competent to make final 'policy' decisions about every subject matter.

Since Aristotle viewed the world as an organic unity, we might have expected him to adopt and emphasize the Platonic conception of knowledge as a seamless web. But in fact he did not. Instead, he classified the sciences by subject matter—as sciences of number, figure, argument, motion, stars, living beings, human beings, souls, and so on—a classification that persists with little change to the present day. And while admitting that certain basic principles, those of metaphysics, are common to all the sciences, he insisted that each science has its own principles and methods of investigation as well as its peculiar subject matter. In the Aristotelian, though not Platonic, view there is no reason why there might not be an eminent biologist who knows next to nothing about planetary orbits. Aristotle was anything but a specialist, but he paved the way for specialization.

## Procedures in Science

In advancing a science, Aristotle says, we must go from what is better known to us to what is in its nature better known. He means that we have to start with what sense perception gives us—acquaintance with some set of particular things. Scientific knowledge, however, is of the causes and principles of these things: these are what are better known in nature. The Philosopher means by this curious phrase that simple awareness of the existence of particular things is only awareness of brute fact, not in itself intelligible. The brute facts become intelligible when we know their causes and principles, how they fit into the scheme of nature. To take his own illustration, we may be aware that among the heavenly bodies only the planets do not twinkle, but we have scientific knowledge of this fact when we realize that the cause of their not twinkling is their nearness to us.

Grasping the explanatory principle is the last step in doing science. There are no rules for obtaining it, other than that the scientist must be thoroughly familiar with the data, the things better known to us, and with the opinions of previous investigators. Intellectual insight or intuition may then yield the principle.

> Out of sense perception comes to be memory, and out of frequently repeated memories of the same thing develops experience. . . . From experience again—i.e. from the universal now stabilized in its entirety within the soul, the one beside the many which is a single identity within them all—originate the skill of the craftsman and the knowledge of the man of science, skill in the sphere of coming to be and science in the sphere of being. . . . These states of knowledge are neither innate . . . nor developed from other higher states of knowledge, but from sense perception. It is like a rout in battle stopped by first one man making a stand and then another, until the original formation has been restored. The soul is so constituted as to be capable of this process.[1]

What Aristotle is describing in this famous passage is the same, psychologically, as the Platonic grasping of an Idea. But in the last sentence he boldly declares the mind competent to work on the data of perception to yield new knowledge, in opposition to Plato who supposed the soul must have preexisted in order to have got it in some utterly mysterious manner.

## The Structure of Science

What is last in order of discovery, the principles, shall be first in order of exposition of the completed science. To systematize a body of knowledge is to set out the principles in explicit form and deduce the other statements of the science from them. Euclid, the great geometer, organized geometry in this way in the generation after Aristotle; but the scheme of this ideal structure was known earlier. It is called axiomatization; and to this day most philosophers of science regard it as the ideal. A particular science is thought to be mature or 'hard' to the extent to which its laws are derivable from a few principles of great generality, such as Newton's or Einstein's laws of motion in physics, or Maxwell's four equations in the theory of electromagnetism.

## Formal Logic

In the completed science, the statements that comprise the body of knowledge are explained by being inferred deductively from the axioms or principles. Logic is the systematic study of the principles of valid inference; that is, of the conditions under which, given that certain assertions are true, we may conclude that certain other assertions must be true also. Aristotle invented and brought to substantial completion one important branch of logic, the theory of the syllogism. A syllogism is an inference made up of three statements, each of the subject-predicate form; that is, of the form All (or No, or Some) As are Bs. Two statements in the syllogism, called premises, contain together three terms, one of which occurs in both of them; the conclusion joins the two other terms. Thus from the set of premises

> All planets are nontwinkling;
> All nontwinkling objects are near;

one can infer

> Therefore, All planets are near.

This is proper because the inference is of the *form* If All Ss are Ms and All Ms are Ps, then All Ss are Ps. This form of inference is self-evidently valid.

Whether or not the form/matter distinction was what suggested formal logic to Aristotle, it is clear that we have in the science a brilliant application of it. Aristotle worked out the complete theory of valid syllogistic inferences. Merely to have listed them would have been a tremendous accomplishment, but the Philosopher went much further. Throughout his exposition of the science he used symbols (letters, as above) to stand for the variable terms in the inference patterns. This is the earliest occurrence of a general symbolism. Furthermore, the exposition of the science itself constitutes an exemplar of the proper form of a science according to Aristotle; that is, it is put into a deductive system. The inference pattern quoted, and three others, are taken as axioms, and all the other valid forms are proved by being shown to be equivalent to one or another of these forms. There is no earlier known example of an axiomatized system. It is a happy illustration of Aristotelian "proper pride" when the author says at the end of his treatise on logic:

> Of this inquiry it was not the case that part of the work had been thoroughly done before, while part had not. Nothing existed at all. If, then, it seems to you after inspection that, such being the situation as it existed at the start, our investigation is in a satisfactory condition compared with the other inquiries that have been developed by tradition, there must remain for all of you, or for our students, the task of extending us your pardon for the shortcomings of the inquiry, and for the discoveries thereof your warm thanks.[2]

## Rhetoric and Poetics

From his dry style, his technical treatises, his intellectualizing God, and his invention of syllogistic reasoning, some people have formed a conception of Aristotle as coldly rational to the point of inhumanity and have contrasted him unfavorably to the passionate warmth of Plato. That this is unjust should be evident from a comparison of their lives but even more so from the content of their writings. If Plato was passionate, it was often in condemning the emotions. Aristotle writes calmly and unemotionally in approval and understanding of the emotions. Plato denounced oratory as cleverness in pandering to ignorant prejudice; Aristotle wrote a treatise on persuasive argumentation. Plato would have banished the theater from the ideal city and strictly censored poetry. Aristotle wrote the first and best work of literary criticism. It was Aristotle not Plato who wrote that "reason by itself produces nothing."

"All men by nature desire to know," the first sentence of the *Metaphysics*, shows how even the doing of science must have its basis in emotion. But there is more to life than doing science, and there are more arguments than strictly deductive ones in which all the sentences are necessary truths. To get on with life we must know how to reason from probabilities and how to urge what we advocate in a way calculated to influence other people.

> It is absurd to hold that a man ought to be ashamed of being unable to defend himself with his fists, but not of being unable to defend himself with speech and reason, when the use of rational speech is more distinctive of a human being than the use of his fists.[3]

In the *Poetics*, which we possess only in an incomplete version dealing solely with epic and tragic poetry, Aristotle defines tragedy as

> the imitation of an action that is serious and also, as having magnitude, complete in itself; in language with pleasurable accessories, each kind brought in separately in the parts of the work; in a dramatic, not in a narrative form; with incidents arousing pity and fear, wherewith to accomplish its catharsis of such emotions.[4]

"Catharsis" means cleansing or purification; what psychological theory the Philosopher had in mind in claiming that tragic representation effects a catharsis of pity and fear has been a subject of controversy. But at least part of his meaning must have been that a good cry in the theater is a kind of safety-valve release—a theory opposed to the view of Plato who deemed emoting, whether by actors or audience, unseemly and corrupting.

## Aristotle's Psychology

Nothing is more typical of the contrast between Plato and Aristotle than their treatments of the soul. To the Athenian nothing is more important than care of the soul, cleansing it from vice, so that the great drama of its successive bodily imprisonments and escapes may ultimately have a happy ending. Plato is offhanded about its nature and how it does what it does. When he considers such questions at all, as when in the *Republic* he divides it into three parts, his motive is something other than scientific curiosity and his result is likely to be hard to square with other views to which he is committed. On the other hand, the Stagirite is concerned wholly with the questions of how we are to conceive the soul (whether as substance, or attribute of the body, or what), what its functions are (in particular, what is sensation), and what is thinking. Although Aristotle has much to say about morals, the topic is not brought up at all in his treatise on the soul. The possibility of immortality is blandly dismissed in a single sentence; the arguments of the *Phaedo* are not even mentioned.

Aristotle rejects those theories of the soul (*psyche*, life principle) that make it some element or combination of elements, mainly on the ground that if it were a body it would have to have a natural motion, down or up, and a natural place—which is absurd. But he does not then proceed to declare that it is an immaterial thing. The matter/form conceptual scheme affords him the opportunity to think of the soul functionally. The official definition is this. Soul is "the first grade of actuality of a natural body having life potentially in it." "First [as distinguished from second] grade of actuality" refers to the difference between full capability of exercising a function and the actual exercise of it. A medical student is a potential physician; after earning an M.D. and securing a license, an actual physician. But there are two grades of this actuality: the first, as when the physician is sleeping or eating or playing golf; the second, when at that very moment doctoring someone. Aristotle calls the soul the first grade of actuality of the body because not all the vital functions are in exercise at every moment. The soul is the essence or *whatness* of the body, of which it is the formal efficient and final cause. (Our notion of personality approaches Aristotle's meaning.) Inasmuch as Aristotle allows essence to be substance or being, the soul is the substance of the body. He illustrates the relation of soul to body with an analogy: If the eye were a complete animal, sight would be its soul.

"From this it indubitably follows that the soul is inseparable from its body," Aristotle writes. But then as so often happens, Platonic afterthoughts induce him to add a qualification: ". . . or at any rate that certain parts of it are, if it has parts. . . . Yet some may be separable because they are not the actualities of any body at all." We shall see later what this concession comes to.

What is life, of which the soul is the principle? To be alive is to function in one or more of four ways. (1) To nourish the self, grow, and decay. (2) To move from place to place. (3) To perceive. (4) To think. Whatever is capable of doing any thing on this list is capable also of doing all the previous things on it. Plants nourish and reproduce themselves, as do all living things, "in order that, as far as their nature allows, they may partake in the eternal and divine. That is the goal toward which all things strive, that for the sake of which they do whatsoever their nature renders possible." This functioning is the nutritive soul. In addition, animals move around, and have sensation, which is indispensable to this ability: the sensitive soul. Man has thought, the rational soul, which "is capable of existence in isolation from all other psychic powers." However, these are not three souls; it is not to be supposed that a philosopher has reason plus the soul of a dog plus that of a stalk of celery. Rational nature feeds back and alters the character of sensation and nutrition.

## Sensation

"By a sense is meant what has the power of receiving into itself the sensible forms of things without the matter," as the wax receives the imprint of the seal. A sensible form is a form that can be perceived. Shapes are sensible forms, souls are not. The process of sensing is this. The sense organ consists of two or more of the four elements in a certain ratio, the combination being such as to be suitable matter for receiving a certain range of sensible forms. When I see a hippopotamus there is no hippopotamus in my eye. What is there is the matter of the eye, which has now taken on the sensible form of the hippopotamus and is thus qualitatively the same as the hippopotamus. I cannot see sounds or hear colors because the matter of the eye is such as to be the potentiality only of colors, and that of the ear only of sounds.

## Thinking

Thinking is different from perceiving, for there are no errors of perception strictly considered, but there are mistakes in thinking. Besides, all animals perceive but few think. And imagining is different from both. It is a sort of creative activity, since we can choose what to imagine, but we cannot choose what we are to perceive or think. Moreover, imagining does not produce emotional reaction. To see something frightening or to believe that something approaching is dangerous arouses fear; merely to imagine something frightful does not make us afraid. So the Philosopher assures us.

Yet imagination has its part in thinking; the other part is judgment. Even though it is impossible without sensation, imagination is not sensing; we do not imagine what we have never sensed. Imagination is "a movement resulting from an actual exercise of power of sense."

Mind is "the part of the soul with which the soul knows and thinks." Thinking, though it is not perceiving, is enough like it for us to conclude that mind is capable of being affected by forms. "Mind must be related to what is thinkable, as sense is to what is sensible." So mind can have no nature of its own. For unlike the sense organs—the matter of which restricts their potentialities to certain ranges of possible sensations—mind is not limited in its objects. Hence the surprising conclusion that mind "before it thinks is not actually any real thing. For this reason it cannot reasonably be regarded as blended with the body." It is "the place of forms."

This mind, however, is only "passive mind." In a celebrated and obscure passage we are told that although passive mind "is what it is by virtue of becoming all things," there is an active mind "which is what it is by virtue of making all things: this is a sort of positive state like light, for in a sense light makes potential colors into actual colors." This kind of mind

> is not at one time knowing and at another not. When mind is set free from its present conditions it appears as just what it is and nothing more: this alone is immortal and eternal (we do not, however, remember its former activity because, while mind in this sense is impassible, mind as passive is destructible), and without it nothing thinks.[5]

This is the immaterial immortal soul of Aristotle's philosophy. Like Parmenides', it is identical with what it thinks. Like Plato's, it rejoices in geometry and all necessary truth. Unlike Plato's, it is not a person. If you are immortal in the Aristotelian manner, you (*you*) will never know it.

# 18

## Aristotle's Ethics

THE READER OF PLATO'S *Republic, Phaedo,* and *Gorgias* may gain the impression that the human condition is desperate, that only the most revolutionary reforms can make it tolerable, and that in the meantime those who have a care for real goodness must withdraw from the center of activity and follow a way of living so unusual as to be called with justice "the practice of dying." Plato was not in so dark a mood all his 80 years, but at his most dramatic he was a pessimistic reformer. The Good shines on all reality, but most of the time we are in the deep shade.

In this respect too Aristotle offers a sharp contrast. He does not make nearly the fuss over morality that Plato does. Plato focuses his philosophy on the problems of ethics, of how to make the good life possible; that, ultimately, is the point of acquiring knowledge. And studies such as biology, which in Plato's opinion make little contribution to the good life, are not taken seriously. Aristotle on the other hand makes knowledge for its own sake the supreme good, the life of contemplation (in our terms, scientific investigation) the best life, and moral considerations subordinate. The best life cannot be lived if social arrangements do not make it possible, nor can a man live it if he is wicked. But the foundation of the good society and the abolition of vice were not at the head of Aristotle's priority list. They did not have to be, because he felt that some Greek city-states already provided decent conditions, and many more would if they were improved in certain unspectacular ways. People too, on the whole, are not utterly depraved. In ethics and politics as elsewhere, Aristotle's view was that the tendency of all natural substances to actualize their potentials is usually successful.

Plato's ethics consists of prescriptions for social arrangements and ways of life greatly at variance with the actualities of his day, but justified by their claim to flow from the superior knowledge of the philosopher. If you remove from Plato's works everything that bears on ethics and politics, hardly anything is left—the dialogues *Parmenides, Theaetetus, Sophist, Cratylus, Timaeus*—and even these would not escape abridgment. But Aristotle minus his three ethical treatises would still be Aristotle.

That is not to say that Aristotle's ethics is tacked on to the rest of his philosophy with no organic relation to it. The principal treatise, the *Nicomachean Ethics* (*i.e.* dedicated to his son Nicomachus), begins

> Every skill and every inquiry, and similarly, every action and choice of action, is thought to have some good as its object. This is why the good has rightly been defined as the object of all endeavor.

Thus the conception of progress toward an end, the central idea of Aristotle's whole philosophy, is the opening note. There is not, however, one single end of all endeavor, even of all human endeavor. Ends may be products of activities (as the shoe of shoemaking) or activities themselves (*e.g.* flute playing). The most general science of the good, we are told, is politics. If this sounds strange to our ears, we might paraphrase it as "principles of legislation." Aristotle's thought is that the constitution of a city is the sum of decisions about what sorts of things are to be allowed, encouraged, and discouraged. If we decide these questions in a nonarbitrary way we must appeal to political science, though not in the narrow sense: not merely the study of how states work but also of what is best for them.

Ethics, Aristotle insists, is a practical study. It aims ultimately at doing, not at knowing. Experience of life is required before the study can be pursued profitably. For this reason young people who do not yet know the way of the world ought not to engage in it. The indispensable foundation of moral goodness is the acquisition of right habits, so that doing the right thing *feels* good and is (as far as possible) effortless. And good habits are not learned by listening to lectures or reading books, or even by face-to-face discussions with philosophers—but by proper upbringing in youth.

## Criticism of Plato's Ethics

In showing that ethics is a practical study, Aristotle scrutinizes the Platonic Idea of the Good. There cannot be a common term corresponding to a single Idea of Good, Aristotle argues, because good is "predicable in all the categories"—that is to say, we speak not only of good things but of good qualities, quantities, relations, times, places, activities, and dispositions. Furthermore, even if there were an Idea of Good, something separate by itself, "it could not be an object of human action or aspiration." Objects of human aspiration are always particular things, or qualities, and so on—we do not seek a "good" apart from them. "Doctors practise on individuals, not on the species." And the good we aim at is always something good *for us*—something that satisfies some human interest or need. If we discovered The Good, and found with absolute accuracy what things participated in it and to what extent, the information would be filed away and forgotten unless it had some connection with our human interests. Therefore, ethics cannot be the study of The Good as such—there is no such thing—nor even of all the goods; it must investigate the good for human beings.

## The Human Good

Everyone agrees that the good is happiness, Aristotle says. The question is of what human happiness consists. Aristotle begins his investigation by asking what the unique function of man is, for the good of any thing is the efficient performance of its function. Unsurprisingly this function turns out to be reasoning. Human good then, which is happiness, is an activity, specifically "activity of soul in conformity with virtue."[1] Not holding with Plato that all human excellence boils down to one thing, Aristotle adds that "if there is more than one virtue, happiness will be activity in accordance with the best and most complete of them," and in a complete lifetime.

Aristotle claims that his definition of the human good agrees with common notions—significantly, this to him is a recommendation—and that it includes what is valid in rival conceptions, of which the two most widely held are happiness as identical with virtue and happiness as the life of pleasure. Happiness is not virtue, but a man who lacks virtue cannot be happy. Happiness is not pleasure, but the happy life is pleasant: the good man takes pleasure in virtuous activity.

Aristotle disagrees with the Platonic teaching that virtue is by itself sufficient for happiness—that, as put in the *Republic*, the just man is 729 times happier than the unjust even if he is wrongly condemned to die. No one, Aristotle remarks, would say something like that unless he were trying to maintain a thesis at all costs. To be happy one must enjoy reasonably good fortune—not be ignobly born or frightfully ugly or poverty-stricken or childless or friendless.

## Virtue

But what is human excellence or virtue? Obviously the virtue of the rational part of the soul is right theoretical reason. This is intellectual virtue. Moral virtue, however, pertains to the appetitive soul insofar as it is under rational control. It is a disposition of the soul to make right choices, in general, choices of a mean between the extremes of too much and too little. "The mean and the good is feeling at the right time, about the right things, in relation to the right people, and for the right reason."[2] For example, excessive fearfulness is the vice of cowardice; yet one who fears not at all, who takes no precautions in the face of danger, is not virtuous but rash. Courage is the mean between them. In matters of expenditure of money there are the spendthrift and the miser, between them the generous person. And so on. Some qualifications and explanations are added. Some actions, for instance adultery, are wrong in and of themselves; it is not a virtue to commit adultery with the right partner at the right time and place. And there are virtues, notably justice, that are not means at all. Where virtue is a mean between two vices, you cannot locate the mean by rote application of a rule. Even if we could give some sense to such an expression as "half-way between rashness and coward-ice," it would not follow that courage would be located there. Courage is in fact the opposite of cowardice and much 'farther' from it than from rashness, which is not its opposite.

Not only does the doctrine of the Mean not suffice to generate rules the observance of which will guarantee virtuous conduct: Aristotle held that there cannot even in principle be any such rules. In serious moral perplexity, the best we can do is try to act as "the man of practical reason would act." That is to say, we can form a conception of someone, such as Socrates, who is free of the partialities and weaknesses that vex us; ask ourselves what such a one would most likely choose to do; and then try to do it.

## Choice

Since virtue is a disposition to make a certain kind of choice, we must know what a choice is—that is to say, what actions are voluntary and what actions are not. Aristotle's discussion of this question is a model of judicious thoroughness. We act involuntarily when we are under compulsion or in ignorance of what we are doing. For these actions we are not praised or blamed, though we may be envied or pitied. But what constitutes compulsion? If the person compelled is moved from outside and contributes nothing to the act—pushed over a cliff, for example—that is involuntary. But what if he moves himself but under such coercion as might be exercised by a tyrant who had his family at his mercy? This kind of case, Aristotle says, is "more like" the voluntary, since the source of motion is internal to the agent; however, "no one would choose any such act of itself." Whether you are blamed for what you do in such a case depends on particulars. Here as elsewhere, Aristotle warns us, the nature of the subject does not permit the drawing of precise lines. One sort of attempted excuse for dereliction, however, is never to be tolerated—the line taken by one claiming to have been compelled by the temptation of pleasure. If we accepted that as an excuse, we would end by admitting that everything we did was involuntary. Besides, Aristotle shrewdly observes, "those who act under compulsion and involuntarily do so with pain."[3]

There are two kinds of ignorant action: acting *in* ignorance (*e.g.* when drunk) and acting *through* ignorance (*e.g.* "I didn't know it was loaded"). The former is not really involuntary, unless you were forced to get drunk. Consequently, acting in ignorance is blameworthy; indeed, Aristotle avers, the Athenians were right to impose double penalties on drunken criminals. But acting through ignorance is not blameworthy, although failure to acquire knowledge that you ought to have may itself be a moral dereliction.

"Being good or bad is something within our power." For being good consists in doing good things, and you *can* choose to do them. It is no excuse that you do not have the kind of character that is prone to make right choices: you make your own character through your own actions. We do not blame a man for being ugly; he was born that way and cannot help it. But we do blame him for being flabby; he could exercise and keep in condition. Aristotle holds that our characters are like our muscle tone, not like our facial features.

But can we choose to be bad—choose to do wrong in full knowledge that what we do is wrong? Aristotle says obviously we can, despite the contention of Socrates that all wrongdoing is involuntary, being due to ignorance. There is a distinction between having knowledge in the sense of having learned and not forgotten, and having knowledge as presently exercising it. People who do wrong and at the same time say they know what they are doing is wrong are "like actors speaking their parts"—the knowledge is not really present, whatever they may say. We should note, however, that Aristotle in taking this position hardly differs from Socrates except verbally. A perhaps more convincing analysis, which he also offers, relies on the difference between knowing some general proposition such as "Murder is wrong" and knowing that the proposition applies to the present case: "This is murder." You can know the former and fail to recognize the latter; that is, you may lack judgment. In any case, Aristotle finds it incredible that anyone should *really know* that what he or she is engaged in is wrong while doing it voluntarily.

## Pleasure and the Best Life

After a long discussion of friendship, Aristotle concludes his ethics with discussions of the place of pleasure in the good life and of what the best life is. Aristotle was no ascetic; he says plainly that people who talk down pleasure usually do so from a motive of trying to draw their listeners in the opposite direction because they think them too prone to give in to temptation. But, he goes on, when they are themselves found pursuing pleasure, as usually happens, the scandal negates their efforts. On the other hand, pleasure is not *the* good, even though Plato's arguments against hedonism are defective. If pleasure is not good because it is "unlimited," *i.e.* admits of degree, then neither is justice or health. As for the theory that pleasure is merely the replenishment of a lack—a transition from pain to a neutral feeling state—Aristotle points out that even if pleasure in fact always accompanied replenishment, that would not make it replenishment any more than pain is identical with undergoing surgery. To Plato's reproach that there are shameful pleasures, Aristotle replies that those so-called pleasures are not really pleasant, they only appear to be so to bad people. Thinking that this point may be unconvincing, he suggests alternatively that the proper way to look at the matter might be to admit that pleasure should be sought, but not at just any price—no more than health (always a good) should be purchased by betraying one's country.

Pleasure, though, is not *the* good. We would not want to be children all our lives, even if we were assured that our existence would consist of nothing but the pleasures that children enjoy. Nor (as just remarked) do we think it right to purchase pleasure at any price. Moreover there are things, such as vision, that would be valued even if they brought no pleasure. What then is the relation of pleasure to the good person? Aristotle's answer is that it "completes the activity, as an end which supervenes as the bloom of youth does on those in the flower of their age."[4] Aristotle's point seems to be that virtuous activity would still be good even if it brought no pleasure. But when it does, so much the better; that makes the activity "complete." For one who acts virtuously deserves to enjoy the activity.

Complete happiness must be the activity of contemplation. Indeed, if we try to imagine the life of the gods we quickly appreciate the absurdity of supposing their life to be mere fun, or even virtuous activities such as making contracts with one another and honoring their terms. There is but one way for a blessed being to be actively happy (so Aristotle tells us), and that is to engage in contemplation. To this extent then the contemplative life is divine. But—and here almost for the first time Aristotle takes issue with Greek received opinion, which held that human beings should "think mortal thoughts"—

> we should not follow popular advice and, being human, have only human ambitions, or being mortal, have only mortal thoughts. As far as is possible, we should become immortal and do everything toward living by the best that is in us. Even if it is small in bulk, in power and value it is far above everything.[5]

# 19

# Aristotle's Politics

IN HIS TREATISE ON government, as in his ethics, Aristotle stays close to the common sense of his time. Although he is not reluctant to pass judgments and make recommendations—and at the end indulges himself in sketching the outline of an ideal state—his book is primarily directed toward describing and understanding what government is and how it functions, and its spirit is close to that of political science as we understand the term today.

The researchers of the Lyceum collected descriptions of the political institutions in force in no fewer than 158 Greek city-states. All except the most important, that of Athens, have been lost. It may be somewhat hasty to assume, however, that Aristotle already had these studies before him when he composed his treatise or that if he did he was much influenced by them in his theorizing. For example, his method of classifying forms of government is a traditional one that must seem oversimple in the light of extensive data: his principle of division is the number of rulers—whether one (monarchy), a few (oligarchy), or many (democracy). Yet as he himself points out, the real difference between oligarchy and democracy is not whether rulers are few or many, but whether they are rich or poor. In fact the rich are few and the poor are many. But if it happened that in some city the rich were the majority and they alone exercised governmental power, it would be an oligarchy not a democracy.

Each of the three governmental types may be good or bad accordingly as it is constitutional or arbitrary. One-man rule bound by traditional and settled prescriptions is monarchy; he who seizes power and rules by decree is a tyrant. If the whole people make laws in observance of stated safeguards, that is a polity; in a democracy—which is bad—there are no checks on the power of the assembled people to make or repeal any laws they see fit, and whenever they please.

This insistence on constitutional safeguards as essential to the difference between acceptable and unacceptable governments is the most important of Aristotle's contributions to political theory. It was not original with him; Plato stated and subscribed to it in the *Statesman* and *Laws*. Indeed the recognition of legality as the hallmark of civilization was a main theme of Greek literature from the beginning, as seen in Aeschylus' *Oresteia* as well as in many of Heraclitus' utterances. Nevertheless, in Plato's *Republic* the difference between the philosopher king and the tyrant is not that the one respects a bill of rights while the other flouts it—both do exactly as they see fit—the difference is simply that the philosopher is virtuous and the tyrant is wicked. That this is an unsatisfactory and indeed disastrous way of trying to distinguish between good and bad governments is a lesson that must be learned over and over. Even Aristotle himself seems on the verge of forgetting it sometimes, as he deems it necessary to concede that if a city should contain a man really preeminent in virtue it would be absurd not to entrust the rule to him at discretion.

But cannot constitutions themselves be oppressive? Not constitutionality alone but concern for the general welfare is what makes a government good, Aristotle asserts. Thrasymachus enunciated the law that ruling cliques make laws in their own interest. Are then all governments partial and therefore bad? Aristotle, thinking of the legislation of Solon and other statesmen who had risen above their class viewpoints, believed that conscientious legislators could and would fashion codes embodying more than the selfish immediate interest of a particular group. They would not do this out of pure benevolence but from enlightened self-interest. For Aristotle had a grasp of the idea of the political bloc and its importance—that no government can be stable where any inherently powerful group is allowed no satisfaction of its demands.

Plato attempted to prevent internal strife by the drastic expedients of eliminating families and private property. Aristotle regarded proposals of this kind as impracticable and in any case undesirable. He accuses Plato of trying to make the state too unified. The city is not and should not be one big family; it is a different kind of organization altogether—an organization of organizations, each one with its own interest to be sure, but interests it is the duty of the statesman to harmonize or at least compromise.

## The State and the Political Animal

The state is "a community of families and aggregations of families in well-being, for the sake of a perfect and self-sufficing life, by which we mean a happy and honorable life."[1] The state is natural and necessary to the human being, who is "by nature a political animal," as the existence of language proves. That is, it is human nature to live in a community (*polis*). "He who is unable to live in society, or who has no need of it because he is sufficient to himself, must be either a beast or a god."

A political animal, however, is not necessarily a politician or even a citizen. The citizen is one who is qualified to vote in the assembly and sit on a jury. Slaves and resident aliens (such as Aristotle in Athens) are not citizens; neither are women, while underage males of citizen parentage are only potentially citizens. In a properly constituted state, men who work with their hands will not be admitted to citizenship. Aristotle, though he did not say so, was following the general rule of Greece that made citizenship coextensive with liability for military service. When in emergencies foreigners and slaves were drafted, they were customarily awarded some rights of citizenship, if they survived.

## Slavery

Aristotle has been much denounced for having defended slavery as according to nature. It might be said on his behalf that at least he faced the problem, as Plato did not. His view was that slavery is according to nature when, but only when, the slave is a natural slave. It turns out that only barbarians—either the northern, who are spirited like Greeks but not intelligent, or eastern and southern, who are intelligent but not spirited—are by nature slaves. For their own good these people should be under the direction of Greeks, who have both spirit and intelligence. Since natural slaves are incapable of happiness (which, it will be recalled, is activity of the soul in accordance with virtue), the state need not aim at making them happy.

Aristotle's defense of slavery is heavily qualified and somewhat shamefaced. The general form of the argument—"I am more intelligent or spirited than you; therefore, it is right for me to use you as my 'living tool'"—is hardly creditable to the inventor of logic. However, slavery as it existed in Aristotle's milieu was far more humane than the arrangements familiar to us from Roman and American history.

## The Best State

Plato was the greatest but not the only Greek inventor of a utopia. A variety of communistic schemes were proposed. Plato wished to abolish private property, at least among the ruling class; one Phaleas of Chalcedon proposed not to abolish property but to effect its equal distribution. Aristotle reviews and rejects them all, contending that common ownership increases occasions for quarrel, leads to carelessness, and removes the principal incentive to industry. Equalization of property would be difficult to enforce and would leave everyone dissatisfied. The advantages supposed to follow from greater equality are best brought about by reliance on private generosity, which is a virtue that would be eliminated under communism.

Aristotle's positive proposals for the best state are not startling. Instead of fastening on difficulties and making drastic proposals for their elimination, as Plato did, Aristotle is content to try to combine the best features of existing states. The best state should have a copious supply of pure water and the prevailing winds should be easterly. It should have access to the sea but not be itself a seaport. The population should be great enough for self-sufficiency and military security but not so great that the citizens cannot all know one another. Deformed children should be exposed (that is, abandoned to perish), but exposure should not be used merely to get rid of unwanted infants, as the practice was in Aristotle's time. Rather, population should be limited by abortion "before sense and life have begun." Women should marry at 18, men at 37, so that children will be healthy and the father not so young as to lack authority.

So far as possible the citizens should be of the middle class, neither very rich nor very poor, for such are the most industrious and the best upholders of order in a state. The constitution should be mixed oligarchical and democratic. Echoing Pericles' boast that all the Athenians were judges of policy even if not all could devise one, Aristotle held that approval of laws in the assembly, and the judicial function, should be reserved to the people as a whole—although executives should be chosen (not by lot) from a panel of especially qualified candidates. The advantages of having many judges is that it is more difficult, because expensive, to corrupt a multitude: the many are less apt to be overcome by emotion all at once; "and as a feast to which all the guests contribute is better than a banquet furnished by a single man, so a multitude is a better judge of many things than any individual."[2] Elimination of graft is the most important measure to take, for knowledge that officials are corrupt is what leads to contempt for government and to revolution.

Like Plato, Aristotle lays great stress on the importance of education.

> That education should be regulated by law and should be an affair of state is not to be denied, but what should be the character of this public education, and how young persons should be educated, are questions which remain to be considered. As things are, there is disagreement about the subjects. For mankind is by no means agreed about the things to be taught, whether we look at virtue or the best life. Neither is it clear whether education is more concerned with intellectual or with moral virtue. The existing practice is perplexing; no one knows on what principle we should proceed—should the useful in life, or should virtue, or should the higher knowledge, be the aim of our training; all three opinions have been entertained.

Aristotle believes there is a place for all of them, though least for the first, for "to be always seeking after the useful does not become free and exalted souls."[3] The curriculum should include reading, writing, gymnastics, drawing, and music. Free children should learn to perform on musical instruments "for intellectual enjoyment in leisure," and they cannot be good critics of music if they do not know how to play. But they should not be taught difficult instruments like the flute or the harp, nor strive for a professional level of skill. After a discussion of which musical styles are most appropriate, Aristotle's *Politics* ends abruptly—whether because he wrote no more or because the remainder has been lost, we do not know.

## Aristotle's Supposed Indifference to Empire

Aristotle has been reproached and even ridiculed because in writing of politics he ignored the most stupendous political development of his time, the establishment of the Macedonian Empire, which made the city-state politically irrelevant. How, we are asked, could a man who grew up at the Macedonian court and who in middle age was Alexander's tutor be so oblivious to what went on around him?

The charge misfires. In the first place, it is not even historically true that Alexander eliminated the Greek city-state. He was looked upon by himself and others as the leader of a federation. Greek cities were jealous of their freedom of action in external as well as internal affairs; therefore, to have any part of their policies dictated from outside was felt as grievous injury. This had indeed been what substance there was to complaints against Athenian imperialism. Many Greeks resented Alexander as applying improper pressures. But that was far from eliminating the city-state, especially its local autonomy, which in fact persisted well into Roman times.

More importantly, Aristotle in his *Politics* was discussing the requirements for the fulfillment of human nature. He simply agreed with unanimous Greek opinion that this fulfillment could take place only where meaningful participation in political decision processes was possible, and that meant the city-state. There were vast empires, notably the Iranian, in Aristotle's time and before; but Iranians were not citizens, only subjects. Aristotle was well aware that out of all the people there have been and will be, very few could vote in assemblies or sit on juries. Only those who do are fully free and capable of realizing their human potential. If Aristotle had been told that from his time forward the decisions made by city-state assemblies would cease to make any difference—that only the decrees of emperors would be significant—this to him would have meant the end of politics as a rational pursuit, and a great leap backwards. As we shall see, that indeed was just what his immediate philosophical successors felt.

# III

# Greek Philosophy
# After Aristotle

Equestrian statue of Marcus Aurelius, *c.* A.D. *165. Bronze. Capitoline Hill, Rome.*

# 20

## The Hellenistic Era

ALEXANDER THE GREAT HAS been praised for his one-world view. He is supposed to have aimed at breaking down Greek exclusiveness and prejudice against barbarians. He arranged a mass wedding between officers of his army and Iranian ladies, himself setting the example by marrying two princesses at once. He appointed barbarians to important posts; he trained Iranian soldiers in Macedonian tactics; and he wore Iranian royal dress and instituted Oriental court etiquette, including ceremonial prostrations before his imperial presence. But some unkind chroniclers say nothing of any contemplated fusion of east and west; they ascribe his orientalizing to vanity and a desire to free himself from the constraints to which a merely Macedonian king was subject by tradition. In his last years Alexander began putting old and loyal followers to death, including Callicrates, Aristotle's nephew, who objected to paying him divine honors.

But it matters little what Alexander's intentions were, since before he could carry them out he died suddenly without making provision for an orderly succession. He left an infant son; another was born after his death. In a few years both sons, their mothers, and most of their relatives had been murdered by each other's supporters. Alexander's generals divided his empire between themselves and immediately began to fight one another. Things got more or less sorted out at the beginning of the third century B.C.: Ptolemy had Egypt and most of the eastern Mediterranean coast including Palestine; Seleucus had the rest of Alexander's conquests in Iran, Armenia, and India; while Greece was disputed between Cassander and Lysimachus. These kingdoms, together with Rome and Carthage in the western Mediterranean, constituted the great powers of the time. While Rome was busy fighting Carthage, the kings in the east were free to intrigue and fight one another, their usually rebellious subjects, and Celtic invaders. Carthaginian power came to an end in 201 B.C., after which Roman influence was decisively asserted in the eastern Mediterranean. Half a century later Carthage was utterly destroyed. In the same year (146 B.C.) the same fate befell Corinth, at that time leader of an anti-Roman coalition, and all Greece became a Roman province. The Seleucid Empire succumbed in 65 B.C., and on the death of Cleopatra in 30 B.C. Egypt was annexed, making the Mediterranean a wholly Roman lake.

This period of nearly three centuries is called the era of the Hellenistic (*i.e.*, Greek*ish*) kingdoms. But what is thought of as Hellenistic culture—barbarism with a Greek veneer—did not come to an end in 30 B.C., for Rome was, or became, Hellenistic.

300–201 B.C., the first of the three Hellenistic centuries, is of prime interest to science and philosophy. In science it was a period of culmination; in philosophy, a period of alteration in function and decline of vitality. Both developments are connected to the drastically altered political circumstances. The fine arts in this period achieved perfection of technique and an extravagant virtuosity of which the statuary group *Laocoon* is a typical example.

## Hellenistic Politics

Nobody could have burned with patriotic fervor for the Seleucid Empire, and nobody was expected to. The sole civic duty of the ordinary subject was to pay heavy taxes to support the bureaucracy and the army, consisting mainly of Greek mercenaries, of which there was always a plentiful supply due to the impoverishment of Greece. Greek culture hardly spread from the garrisons to the natives; but the contrary process of infection of Greeks by Oriental superstitions was common. One king, Antiochus IV (175–164 B.C.), did make a vigorous effort to Hellenize his subjects. The scheme came to grief in the heroic resistance of the Jews when commanded to eat pork.

While the Seleucid Empire contributed little but superstition to the ancient world, Alexandria, the new capital city of Hellenistic Egypt, in some respects surpassed even Athens as the intellectual center of the world. The difference between Egypt and Seleucia seems to have been almost entirely due to personal differences in the dynasties. The Seleucid kings cared little for culture whereas the Ptolemies had a passion for literature, philosophy, and science. In Alexandria we encounter for the first time large-scale government subsidies for the sciences and the birth of grantsmanship.

## The Museum

The first Ptolemy was from boyhood a close associate of Alexander. Possibly he shared in the tutorial sessions Aristotle held for the crown prince; at any rate, his patronage of learning would have gladdened the Philosopher had he lived to see it. Members of the Lyceum had leading roles in founding the Museum and Library of Alexandria.

The Museum—the corporation dedicated to the cult of the Muses, the nine goddesses of the arts and sciences—was a research and graduate-teaching institution. It was like the Lyceum and Academy, except that it had more money. Ominously, in the end disastrously, the funds and the control that went with them came from the royal treasury. From the beginning, in consequence, research into political science leading to conclusions unwelcome to the Pharaoh was forbidden. Pharaoh also appointed the faculty. For the first century this was the most brilliant assemblage of scientific talent in the world. Then the Ptolemies, becoming more and more Egyptianized and under priestly influence, grew indifferent or even hostile to science. That was the end, in effect, of the Museum.

In its great period the Museum numbered among its staff Euclid the geometer; Hipparchus, who made an accurate positional catalogue of the stars; Herophilus the anatomist, who practiced vivisection on condemned criminals supplied by Ptolemy; the engineer Ctesibius, who invented the pipe organ; and Hero, who invented the steam turbine (but apparently never put it to any use). Archimedes of Syracuse, who had no successor of comparable genius in theoretical physics until Galileo 18 centuries later, was as it were a corresponding member.

## The Library

The Library, separate from the Museum though in close cooperation, was a more enduring institution. No one knows just when it went out of existence; it was still a major target for Christian trashing seven centuries after its foundation. At its height it contained nearly half a million volumes, that is papyrus rolls. Its only rival was the royal library of Pergamum, a small state in northern Asia Minor which managed to keep its independence until near the end of the second century B.C. The kings of Pergamum were almost more cultivated than the Ptolemies. The Pergamene collection, however, was absorbed into the Alexandrian Library about 33 B.C. when Mark Antony confiscated it and presented it to Cleopatra.

Great scholars and literary men were appointed to the office of Librarian. Most notable was Eratosthenes (*ca* 276–*ca* 194 B.C.), who rivaled Aristotle in the scope of his learning. By observing differences in the lengths of shadows cast at noon on the same day in northern and southern Egypt he measured the arc on the earth's surface of a degree of longitude, from which he was able to calculate the size of the earth's circumference with an error of one-fifth of one percent.

The Library attracted so many visiting scholars that feeding and housing them became an important industry. Copying services were provided so that the Library was in effect a publishing house as well. In this way the diffusion of learning was greatly aided. Nevertheless, it remains a puzzle why printing was not invented; there is nothing in the printing process that should have been beyond Alexandrian ingenuity. Perhaps the scarcity of papyrus, made laboriously in small sheets, was the factor that made printing unfeasible. But there were not even woodcuts for illustrations. Furthermore, the pages of a book continued to be pasted together into a continuous roll that had to be clumsily wound and unwound by hand on two sticks, causing great loss of time to the reader and wear to the roll—no one thought even of a simple reading frame of two wheels provided with hand cranks! An accumulation of obstacles such as these intensified the state of war that exists by nature between librarians and readers. The acquisition of learning was difficult and rare, and the learned were often vain and pedantic.

## Hellenistic Greece

Conditions on the Greek mainland were in many ways more miserable than in the empires. On the whole, the kings of Macedon were powerful enough to bully the Greek cities but lacked resources to impose peace and order on them. The situation was worsened by continual bloody struggles between rival claimants to the Macedonian throne. The Greeks thus lost the advantages of city-state sovereignty without the compensation of the internal peace enjoyed for tolerable stretches of time by the slaves of Seleucus and Ptolemy. Moreover, at a time when overpopulation was acute, the Greek economy declined sharply. One reason was the blow to commerce occasioned by the rise of piracy in the eastern Mediterranean. The fleets of Athens and of Tyre in Phoenicia had kept piracy in check before Alexander; but the Macedonians, a land power, had destroyed the fleets and never replaced them. The island of Rhodes, which retained independence into the Roman era, was the greatest naval and commercial power of the time, but she was unable to cope alone with the pirates. Nor was it entirely in her interest to do so, as long as she could keep them from her own ships and leave them free to harass her competitors.

Life was uncertain; there was nothing new in that. The novel terror was the sense of helplessness. When the city-state was the political unit there were things you could do when menaced: you could campaign for your political party or stir up a revolution. If the enemy was a foreign city bigger than yours, you could negotiate for an alliance with someone still bigger, or you could repair the city walls, or if all else failed you could die heroically. It was different when your city was in the middle—between two mercenary armies in the service of remote personages who cared nothing for you and whom you could in no way influence— and you knew that whichever army won would plunder your city because that was the only way the soldiers could be paid. Praying to the gods of the city would not help; they were as powerless as you. No wonder that Fate was the leading notion and Luck the most popular goddess of the age.

## The Ethical-Political Problem

For the Greeks the central question of ethics always was that of the nature of the good life and how to lead it. Aristotle, Plato, and their predecessors were agreed that the answer could be given only in a political context. Politics and ethics were not really separate, for "man is a political animal." But what happens when the community is effectively annihilated, when the city is no longer a possible focus for loyalty and aspiration? Ethics must be divorced from politics, a theory of the good life must be worked out that can dispense with political attachment— or else provide another kind of community worthier of dedication.

## Cynicism

The Stoic school was not founded until the end of the fourth century, but its members traced their philosophical lineage through the Cynics back to Socrates. Antisthenes (*ca* 445–*ca* 365 B.C.), of Socrates' circle, taught a philosophy stressing the master's moral earnestness and self-sufficiency even more than Plato did. Socrates held that nothing could compare in importance for a man's happiness with the cultivation of his soul, which is the practice of virtue. But virtue, he held also, is knowledge. We have seen how for Plato this led to an intellectualistic world view. Antisthenes interpreted Socrates in a simpler way. According to him, virtue is all-important, and virtue can be taught straightforwardly. Mathematics and astronomy have nothing to do with it. You learn just to do those things that you ought to do, avoid doing those things you ought not to do, and you shun temptation. You simplify your life as far as possible. For it is attachment—to city, possessions, family—that distracts from the cultivation of the soul.

Antisthenes' father was an Athenian citizen but his mother was not; so Antisthenes taught in a gymnasium called the Cynosarges, which was set aside for persons of ambiguous lineage. Accordingly, it is said, the name "Cynic" applied to his school came from this place-name. Another explanation has it that the word, which means "canine," was first applied abusively by opponents. Whether Antisthenes was doglike in his behavior we do not know, but much has come down to us concerning the Cynic way of life. Virtue, the Cynics held, consists in living "according to nature"—what nowadays is called being "sincere," being a "real person." Everything conventional and artificial is false, a hindrance, and must be thrown off: conventional dress, conventional food and drink. The Cynics wore a kind of poncho, usually very dirty, and carried a leather pouch to hold food and other indispensable possessions—whatever those were.

The most famous of the Cynics was Diogenes (*d ca* 320 B.C.). He came to Athens early in the fourth century, having been, with his father, condemned to leave his home town of Sinope on the Black Sea: "And I condemn you to stay here," he retorted to his judges when sentence was passed. The Cynics set out deliberately to attract attention by shocking the middle classes. This was harder to do then than now, for the Greeks were sophisticated and tolerant. However, Diogenes managed. He masturbated publicly, remarking to the spectators that he wished he could assuage his hunger for food by rubbing his belly. When Plato's Academy, laboring to define Man, produced the formula "featherless biped," Diogenes plucked a chicken and threw it into the lecture hall. It was he who went around with a lantern at midday, saying that he was looking for an honest man. (The point of this story is somewhat elusive.) Asked why the passersby were giving so much more spare change to a blind beggar than to him, he replied that they could easily conceive of themselves going blind but not becoming philosophers. Diogenes was living in Corinth when Alexander the Great made his triumphal entry into that city. Seeking out the aged celebrity, who did not even rise from the ground where he lay sunning himself, Alexander in the fashion prescribed for royalty said "Ask me a favor and it shall be granted." "Stand out of the sun," the Cynic responded.

The most notable disciple of Diogenes was Crates of Thebes (365–285 B.C.), esteemed the Socrates of his time. His body was misshapen, but the anecdotes told of him stress his cheerful nature and lovable qualities, in contrast to the sarcasm of Diogenes. Hipparchia, a beautiful and wealthy Athenian girl, fell in love with him and insisted on their marrying, although that meant giving up the life of high society. It was a happy and enduring marriage, which began with consummation in public, in accordance with the Cynic principle that no natural function is intrinsically shameful—only 'convention' makes it so.

Cynicism was a way of life, but not a philosophy in the full sense, since Cynics did not concern themselves with the detailed elaboration of a world view. Nor was it a religion. It is hard to say whether we should call it a quasi or even antiphilosophy. It would be a misunderstanding, however, to think of the Cynics as merely a sect of nonconformists. Some individuals no doubt were crackpots; any Movement rejecting established values was bound to attract them, just as the emphasis on sincerity made infiltration by frauds inevitable. Nevertheless, the aims of men like Diogenes and Crates were legitimate and important. The offense for which Diogenes and his father were banished from Sinope was defacement of the coinage; the old man had been master of the mint. Diogenes said he was out to deface the coinage of the whole world. He meant that he would make people aware that what was artificial, "coined," was dispensable and usually rotten. He was—to praise him very faintly—at least sincere.

The Cynic attitude toward life is recurrent and is found in numerous and various cultures, the necessary conditions being tolerance and a certain weariness. There could be no Cynic movement either in the Soviet Union or on the American frontier. Cynicism persisted in the ancient world until it became absorbed into Christian asceticism, for which it furnished the model.

# 21

# Stoicism

BEGIN THE MORNING BY saying to yourself, I shall meet with the busybody, the ungrateful, arrogant, deceitful, envious, unsocial. All these things happen to them by reason of their ignorance of what is good and evil. But I who have seen the nature of the good that it is beautiful, and of the bad that it is ugly, and the nature of him who does wrong, that it is akin to me, not only of the same blood or seed, but that it participates in the same intelligence and the same portion of the divinity, I can neither be injured by any of them, for no one can fix on me what is ugly, nor can I be angry with my kinsman, nor hate him. For we are made for co-operation, like feet, like hands, like eyelids, like the rows of the upper and lower teeth. To act against one another then is contrary to nature; and it is acting against one another to be vexed and to turn away.[1]

This passage, one of the noblest in all literature, was written in his private note-book by the Roman emperor Marcus Aurelius Antoninus (A.D. 121–180).

Of things some are in our power, and others are not. In our power are opinion, movement toward a thing, desire, aversion, and in a word, whatever are our own acts; not in our power are the body, property, reputation, offices, and in a word, whatever are not our own acts. And the things in our power are by nature free, not subject to restraint nor hindrance; but the things not in our power are weak, slavish, subject to restraint, in the power of others. Remember then that if you think the things which are by nature slavish to be free, and the things which are in the power of others to be your own, you will blame both gods and men; but if you think that only which is your own to be your own, and if you think that what is another's, as it really is, belongs to another, no man will ever compel you, no man will hinder you, you will never blame any man, you will accuse no man, you will do nothing involuntarily, no man will harm you, you will have no enemy for you will not suffer any harm.[2]

This is from a report of the teaching of Epictetus (ca A.D. 55–ca 135), who after being a slave for much of his life became a teacher of philosophy in a village in (what is now) Yugoslavia.

Stoicism was the dominant philosophy of Greece and Rome for 500 years. Chrysippus (ca 280–ca 207 B.C.) alone, who was called the second founder of the school, wrote more than 700 volumes. Yet the emperor's memorandum book, the summaries of the ex-slave's lectures, and some essays by Seneca (ca 4 B.C.–A.D. 65) are the only complete works that remain from the vast literature of Stoicism.

The considerable fragments from other works, however, and accounts of Stoic teaching, show that the loss was not a catastrophe. The Stoic school produced no geniuses to rank with Plato and Aristotle; Epictetus and Marcus, the last of its eminent representatives, were also its greatest. From their writings we can reconstruct the essence of Stoicism—we could make a fair show, in fact, if we had only the two passages quoted above.

It is an arresting fact that of the two greatest Stoics, one was an emperor the other a slave. It would be a mistake to infer from that, however, that Stoicism had universal appeal. It was an attempt to make the essential Cynic message—that we should live according to nature—acceptable to people who had no desire for a life of physical discomfort and at the same time to provide some systematic philosophical answer to the inevitable question "Yes, but what *is* nature?" Cynicism, being not only antisensual but anti-intellectual, was too extreme to attract many adherents.

## Zeno of Citium

The founder of Stoicism was not a Greek; he was a Phoenician merchant from the island of Cyprus. He came to Athens to trade, as the more probable story has it, or because he was shipwrecked, according to the more dramatic account. Passing the time in a bookstore reading about Socrates, he asked the proprietor whether there were any men like him still in Athens. "Follow that man," was the answer, as Crates happened to be passing in the street.

Zeno (*ca* 335–263 B.C.) became a disciple of Crates—not going so far, however, as to rid himself of his possessions, which included slaves. He must have studied other philosophies, especially Aristotelianism (of which Stoicism is in many respects a simplified version) and the doctrines of Heraclitus. At length he began teaching in a structure known as the Painted Porch, *stoa poikile*. His fate was the opposite of Socrates': his teaching was popular; he was the friend and confidant of leading personages; official honors were paid him in his lifetime; and when he died, he was given a state funeral.

## The Stoic Worldview

To the Cynics what was natural was simply whatever was not conventional. They took for granted that living according to nature was a good thing. Argument to them was just another set of conventions; that was part of the message Diogenes conveyed when he got up and walked out of a lecture in which an Eleatic philosopher was discoursing on the impossibility of motion.

Zeno, convinced that the Cynics were right in principle, perceived nevertheless the crudeness and naivety of this conception. Aristotle was right after all to insist that man is a political animal—at least it is natural for human beings to live together, to make and make use of artifacts, to have laws and courts. What was conventional might still be natural also in an important sense. The making of the relevant distinctions could not be entrusted to instinct but required reasoning.

Hence the Stoic division of philosophy into three parts: logic, physics, and ethics. Ethics, the science of how to live well, is the goal. But to know how to live well you must first know what the world is like so that you can make your plans realistically; hence you must study natural science, physics. But again, neither physics nor ethics can be pursued profitably without previous mastery of the art of reasoning. Thus, in point of time, logic comes first in the curriculum. The Stoics compared ethics to the yolk of the egg, physics to the white, logic to the shell. Again, logic to the orchard fence, physics to the trees, ethics to the fruit.

## Stoic Logic and Linguistics

The logicians of the Porch made contributions second in importance only to those of Aristotle himself. They developed the fundamentals of the propositional calculus; that is, arguments in which validity depends on the relations between propositions rather than (as in the syllogism) between classes of things. For example, dilemmas, such as

> If you enter public life, you must be either honest or
> dishonest;
> If you are honest, men will hate you;
> If you are dishonest, the gods will hate you;
> Therefore, if you enter public life, either men or
> gods will hate you.

However, their logical discoveries were almost entirely forgotten until the present century.

Grammar is a Stoic invention. Even Aristotle had explicitly recognized only nouns and verbs. The Stoics analyzed the forms of the Greek language so thoroughly and satisfactorily that the names of parts of speech, cases, and tenses used ever since are nothing but Latin translations of their technical terminology.

## Stoic Physics

Unlike their elegant logic and elevated ethics, the Stoic conception of nature was a mixture of Olympian, Orphic, Heraclitean, Platonic, Aristotelian, and—ominously—Chaldean notions. The Stoics were materialists, holding that everything real is a material thing. Some of the earlier members of the school held that this applies even to numbers and virtue. Platonic Ideas and Aristotelian Forms were explicitly rejected. However, the kind of distinction Aristotle intended by the oppositions matter/form and potency/activity reemerge in Stoicism as the active and passive aspects of the material world. That which is active is Fire, God, Zeus, Logos, World-Soul: all these terms are treated as synonyms. The universe as in Plato's *Timaeus* is a living creature, a great all-inclusive animal.

The cosmic world-animal is eternal; however, it exists through finite periods separated by holocausts: everything burns up and then a new period starts. One period is exactly like another down to the tiniest detail: I (or someone just like me) have written this book infinite times in the past; you (or someone of the same name) will read it infinite times in the future. This curious notion of the eternal return is recurrent in diverse philosophies. Its origin is obscure; its justification seems to lie in the argument that if the stuff of the world is finite but lasts an infinitely long time, all the possible arrangements of it must be gone through, after which there is nothing to do but to start over again in the same way.

The Porch was likewise deterministic. Everything happens as it must happen, as it is fated. Because there is no such thing as chance, divination—fortune-telling, omen reading—is possible and (some held) actually exists as a science.

Fate, however, is not blind. God, the World-Soul, directs everything for the best. Wisdom indeed consists in perceiving the perfection of the natural plan, the way in which everything that exists cooperates with everything else to produce the best possible effect.

## Stoic Ethics

The human being is part of nature, a microcosm, like the great world, in being a body with a soul-aspect. The movements of the body, like all motions, are according to fate. The real human nature, however—the soul, the 'ruling faculty'—may take different attitudes to these motions. It may be reasonable: having learned physics, the chief lesson of which is that all is for the best, it will acquiesce joyfully in whatever happens. It will be in harmony with the macrocosm. To be reasonable is to be happy. The Stoics agreed with Aristotle that happiness is activity of soul in accordance with virtue. Such happiness is in our power. The sage achieves the condition of 'apathy'—'nonsuffering,' not listlessness. The sage is active, or at any rate tries to act. He cannot be made unhappy by those things which are not in his power, that is all external circumstances. These he accepts, as we still say, "stoically." Things not in one's power—wealth, health, free birth, good looks, good fortune—are "things indifferent," to be taken as they come. "Seek not that the things which happen should happen as you wish," Epictetus counsels, "but wish the things which happen to be as they are, and you will have a tranquil flow of life."[3]

*ataraxia*

This is a philosophy that has given consolation and strength to many in many ages. The common meaning of the phrase "taking things philosophically" refers precisely to the Stoic ideal. Yet this doubtless admirable attitude to life leads to a problem that arises in any ethic taking virtue or the good will itself as primary, not what the good will accomplishes or tries to bring about. Since all wills by definition try to do something, the good will can evidently be distinguished from the bad will only by some difference in what it tries to bring about. But in the theory's own terms, there is nothing any will could possibly bring about but (a) changes in externals or (b) changes in the characters of other wills. Now if I try to change external things—if for instance I try to bring peace on earth or put an end to disease, injustice, and poverty—I am only trying to change "things indifferent," things having nothing to do with what is really morally good. They therefore cannot serve to distinguish of themselves my will from a bad will, one that can only will to produce some other set of indifferents—say pestilence, famine, and tyranny. It is no answer to say that the good will is the one that "follows nature"; for whatever we mean by nature, experience teaches that she produces health and disease alike. Hence the good will must be distinguished by its aim to produce virtue in other wills. To say this, however, is only to move the problem back a step. My good will aims to make your will good; I know I have succeeded when you start willing to make somebody else's will good. . . . But we cannot go on this way; somewhere or other we have to come to some other kind of distinction. However, the theory is set up in such a way as not to allow the drawing of any other distinction.

Some later Stoics tried to escape from this impasse by dividing "things indifferent" into two classes, "those to be preferred" and "those to be rejected." The first class included health, wealth, and the other things that ordinary people and Aristotle speak of as the goods of life.

Even if the Stoics dealt satisfactorily with the problem of what virtue aimed at, they were still faced with another vexation: how, within Stoic principles, to make a real nonarbitrary distinction between things in our power and things not in our power. If the motions of my muscles including those of my tongue are fated, it seems implausible to maintain that the will behind my muscular and vocal exertions is in my power. If I am not free in what I *do*, at least sometimes, what help is it—indeed what sense does it make to say—that I am free in what I *will* to do? Thus Stoicism, fundamentally dependent on the distinction between things in our power and things not, has trouble keeping the more important side of it from evaporating. However, we must remember that the Stoics were the first to raise this Problem of the Freedom of the Will in substantially the form in which it has been discussed for more than two thousand years. Since in these millennia it has still not been solved to everybody's satisfaction but remains perhaps the most voluminously debated of all philosophical problems, we are hardly in a position to reproach the Stoics for failing to lay it to rest.

## Later Stoicism

Zeno's successor as head of the Porch was a certain Cleanthes (301?–232? B.C.). His *Hymn to Zeus*, which has been preserved, displays grandeur in its pantheistic sentiment. Cleanthes is less honorably remembered for having proposed a prosecution of the astronomer Aristarchus of Samos because he put forward the hypothesis that the earth revolves around the sun.

Stoicism, a religious philosophy, was in continual danger of becoming frankly a religion. Cleanthes almost took it over the brink; he was a religious zealot, short on intellectual stature. It was the next head of the school, Chrysippus, the "second founder," who pulled it back. His 700 volumes, of which none remain, are said to have been obscure as well as heavily padded with quotations. Epictetus bases on the difficulty of his style a remark that has made expositors and commentators wince through the ages: "When a man is proud because he can understand and explain the writings of Chrysippus, say to yourself, 'If Chrysippus had not written obscurely, this man would have had nothing to be proud of.'"[4]

Chrysippus turned the Porch in the direction of technical studies such as logic and grammar. Later Stoics, notably Panaetius (*ca* 180–109 B.C.) and Posidonius (*ca* 135–*ca* 51 B.C.), cultivated the natural sciences. When in the second century B.C. it became the fashion for upper-class Romans to acquire a veneer of Greek culture, Stoicism was the philosophy with the most appeal. Seneca, one of only three Romans writing in Latin who have some claim to be considered of importance in philosophy, was a Stoic. Under Roman influence there occurred in the Porch a revival of emphasis on ethics. Epictetus complained that although it is more important to refrain from lying than to prove that we ought not to lie, the logicians had brought things to a pass where "we lie, but the demonstration that we ought not to lie we have ready to hand." The later Stoics, Epictetus and Marcus, were, however, by no means mere antiquarians. In their hands and in those of the Roman jurists, Stoicism became the philosophical groundwork of the Roman doctrine of "natural law," a code applicable to all human beings regardless of their local legislation. It was fitted for this purpose because of its conception of a universal community to which we all belong on an equal footing simply by virtue of being human. Zeno, when asked what his city was, replied that he was "a citizen of the cosmos": *cosmopolites*. The Stoics, moreover, conceived of a "law of nature" that was both a description of how things are fated to move harmoniously together and a prescription for virtuous activity "according to nature." The history of these conceptions is continuous to this day. Whenever anything is denounced as "against nature," we are hearing an echo from the Porch.

# 22

# Epicurus

AT NEARLY THE SAME time as Zeno founded his school in the Painted Porch, Epicurus (341–270 B.C.) bought a garden or orchard in an Athenian suburb and there set up a philosophic community. Its aim was achievement of "ataraxy," "un-stirred-up-ness," a condition of the soul not very different from Stoic "apathy" or un-passion. Moderation of desires was recommended in the Garden as in the Porch as the principal technique for achieving happy tranquillity. The agreement of the schools, however, did not go beyond this joint pursuit of self-sufficiency. Instead of a world in which everything happens according to a cosmic plan, Epicurus revived the Democritean concourse of atoms as basis for all things and rejected every kind of purposive explanation. Instead of virtue as sole good, Epicurus proclaimed pleasure, to be pursued by a policy of cautious avoidance of commitments and risks.

## Life of Epicurus

Epicurus was born the son of Neocles, an Athenian schoolteacher in Samos, where he grew up. In the convulsions of 323 B.C. attendant on the death of Alexander, the Athenians were expelled from the island. Neocles and his family happened to be visiting Athens at the time. Unable to return to Samos and having lost all their property, they moved from place to place in Ionia. Epicurus' mother was obliged by circumstances to make a living as a sort of witch doctoress, making hexes and casting spells for small sums; young Epicurus had to assist in her performances. To his disgust at these rites has been attributed the hatred of superstition that is a leading motive of his philosophy.

During his travels Epicurus managed to acquire a higher education, particularly from one Nausiphanes, who in Teos expounded the philosophy of Democritus—almost forgotten elsewhere. Some time in his twenties Epicurus set up as a philosopher in his own right, first at Mytilene and afterwards at Lampsacus. In 307 B.C. he and his disciples made the move to the center of things.

The group included three of Epicurus' own brothers. This astonishing and unparalleled fact puts in vivid light the outstanding personal characteristic of Epicurus: by all accounts he was one of the most lovable human beings who ever lived. Not only did he attract followers, he held them, and in difficult circumstances. The Garden was not just a school but a commune with residents of both sexes, free and slave. It is hard to believe that none ever quarreled or defected, but so we are assured.

Head of Epicurus, *third century* B.C. *Marble.*
*The Metropolitan Museum of Art, Rogers Fund, 1911.*

Epicurus inspired devotion by being himself a devoted friend. His will, which has been preserved, makes detailed provisions for those in his circle and for the upbringing and education of their children as well. A letter from him to a child happens to have survived.

> We have arrived at Lampsacus safe and sound, Pythocles and Hermarchus and Ctesippus and I, and there we found Themista and our other friends all well. I hope you too are well and your mamma, and that you are always obedient to papa and Matro, as you used to be. Let me tell you that the reason that I and all of the rest of us love you is that you are always obedient to them.

As George Sarton remarks in his history of science, "this document is unique in ancient literature."

Epicurus died in his seventy-first year of kidney stones, the pains of which are said to be the most excruciating of any disease. At the end he wrote this.

> On this blissful day, which is also the last of my life, I write this to you. My continual sufferings from strangury and dysentery are so great that nothing could augment them; but over against them all I set gladness of mind at the remembrance of our past conversations. But I would have you, as becomes your lifelong attitude to me and to philosophy, watch over the children of Metrodorus.

Epicurus did not deliver formal lectures in the manner customary for philosophers of his time. He was, however, the most voluminous of all the ancient writers, his works filling more than 300 rolls. Chrysippus the Stoic surpassed the number—out of envy of Epicurus, we are told—but only by incorporating long quotations, a practice which Epicurus entirely eschewed. Indeed Epicurus carried pride of originality to an extreme point. He claimed that he had learned nothing from his teachers and referred to Nausiphanes, Democritus, and Leucippus in insulting and contemptuous terms. This is puzzling, for his debt to them is impossible to overlook and the sentiments are the only unamiable ones ascribed to the Master.

## Epicurus against Religion

None of Epicurus' 300 rolls survive. We have only three letters which briefly summarize his teachings on physics, meteorology, and ethics. However, Epicurus' philosophy was expounded at length and accurately in the great Latin epic poem *On the Nature of Things* by Titus Lucretius Carus, who lived in Rome from about 99–55 B.C., but of whom nothing is known. (Worse than nothing: Eusebius, a Christian bishop, wrote that Lucretius, driven mad by a love potion, wrote his poem in intervals of sanity before ending his life. This story—obviously nothing but malicious gossip—continues to be repeated in the histories, including, alas, this one.) No other philosophy has been presented so elegantly.

Democritus' motive for doing philosophy seems to have been the "desire to know" that Aristotle ascribes to all human beings. The reviver of atomism, however, had a different aim. "Do not think that knowledge about the things above the earth," he wrote, "whether treated as part of a philosophical system or by itself, has any purpose other than peace of mind and confidence. This is also true of the other studies." You may wonder why atomic physics should be thought conducive to peace of mind. The answer for Epicurus was that only thus could fear of the gods be banished—fear of their capricious and malicious action, in this life and the next. If superstitious terror was not the only cause of human misery, it was the chief one, and in any case the one we can do most about. Near the beginning of his poem, Lucretius depicted the enemy and the Master's victory.

> When human life lay grovelling in all men's sight, crushed to the earth under the dead weight of religion whose grim features glowered menacingly upon mortals from the four quarters of the sky, a man of Greece was first to raise mortal eyes in defiance, first to stand erect and brave the challenge. Fables of the gods did not crush him, nor the lightning flash and the growling menace of the sky. Rather, they quickened his manhood, so that he, first of all men, longed to smash the constraining locks of nature's doors. The vital vigor of his mind prevailed. He ventured far out beyond the flaming ramparts of the world and voyaged in mind throughout infinity. Returning victorious, he proclaimed to us what can be and what cannot: how a limit is fixed to the power of everything and an immovable frontier post. Therefore religion in its turn lies crushed beneath his feet, and we by his triumph are lifted level with the skies.[1]

Never has a victory been celebrated more prematurely. Yet these lines express the breathtaking sense of liberation felt by Lucretius and many others upon learning that their secret doubts are shared. Even in ancient times critics made fun of Epicurus for exaggerating the terrors of religion. Lucretius replied by relating in pathetic verses the story of how King Agamemnon was induced to make a sacrifice of his own daughter. This gruesome legend, so familiar in the ancient world, is made a symbol for all priestly atrocities, and leads up to a cry heard through the ages.

*Tantum relligio potuit suadere malorum!*

So much evil has religion succeeded in instigating!

This is not the first occurrence of the moral argument against religion—Xenophanes has priority—but it is the classic formulation.

Epicurus was not an atheist; he admitted and even insisted on the existence of gods. They are material beings, immortal because the atoms of their substance is continually replenished, who live the blessed life in the calm regions between the dense whirls of the innumerable worlds—an existence eternally free from all pain. It is a consequence of their carefree life that they do not trouble themselves about us, nor even know about us. As far as we are or ought to be concerned, they simply constitute models of the ideal life toward which we should aspire. The Master was a frequent visitor to temples, where he would sit for hours in contemplation.

## Perception and Knowledge

Epicurean belief in the existence of gods was not arbitrary but followed from a theory of knowledge that went even beyond Stoicism in the exclusive emphasis it laid on sense perceptions as the basis of all knowledge. All sensations are true, even "visions seen by madmen or in dreams . . . for they stir the mind, and that which is not real does not do so."[2] People see and hear the gods—in dreams and visions—therefore the gods exist. For seeing in a dream is a kind of perception, and like all seeing is explained by Epicurus in the Democritean manner as the impingement on the soul atoms of filmy images that continually peel off the surfaces of objects and fly through the air into our eyes. To be sure, some images get distorted in transit, and some even originate out of fragments in the air, hence represent no objects. Apparently this was not supposed to be the case with the gods, because so many people so often see the gods. Most beliefs about the gods though, such as that they menace us, are false opinions not dictated by the sensations. The thought behind Epicurus' view is that if we would but confine ourselves to what we directly apprehend, we would never make any mistakes. Error arises only when we go beyond the perceived to make inferences that anticipate other perceptions or substitute for them. This is a common and plausible theory, but it is hard to defend on Epicurean principles. And of course it is in direct opposition to Democritus' disparagement of sense perception in favor of a separate faculty of pure reason.

## Epicurean Atomism: The Swerve

Not all inferences are under Epicurean suspicion, however, for the assertion that there are atoms and void is inference not sensation. The arguments presented are on the whole factual and convincing. Something can be material without being visible, as the existence of wind shows. Apparently solid bodies, such as porous rocks, really contain void spaces, for water passes through them. The wearing down of finger-rings and stone stairways shows that matter must be composed of exceedingly fine particles—but not infinitely divisible, for destruction is easier than construction. If there were no limit, everything would by now be utterly pulverized.

Epicurean atoms differ from Democritean atoms in two ways only: (1) besides the inherent properties of size, shape, and solidity, they have weight; and (2) they sometimes swerve.

(1) Democritus' atoms had always been in motion and always would be, and the direction of their motion was entirely determined by their previous history of collisions. Thus on the average at any given time as many atoms are moving in one direction as in any other. Ascribing weight to the atoms meant for Epicurus that the atoms have a preferred direction of motion, which is downward. Not downward toward the bottom of the universe—there is none, the universe is infinite—but in the head-to-foot direction. An atom moving through the void and encountering no other atom will move in that direction, and at a maximum velocity that is the same for all atoms.

(2) It follows that if at any time all the atoms move only under the influence of their weights, no atom will ever hit another, since they will all move in the same direction at the same speed, maintaining the same relative positions forever. Think of cars on a highway, all traveling at exactly the speed limit. Epicurus seems to have held that this condition did in fact obtain once upon a time. How then could the world of atomic collisions and aggregations get started? The Swerve provides the answer.

Lucretius writes

> When the atoms are travelling straight down through empty space by their own weight, at quite indeterminate times and places they swerve ever so little from their course . . . but only a very little . . . For we see plainly and palpably that weights, when they come tumbling down, have no power of their own to move aslant, so far as meets the eye. But who can possibly perceive that they do not diverge in the very least from a vertical course?[3]

Lucretius' embarrassed tone here is understandable, for even in his day the Swerve was an object of merriment to the opponents of the Garden. Rightly so, for it was in flat contradiction of the principle so emphatically insisted upon—that nothing can come from nothing. The idea was that if all the atoms are moving at enormous velocity, a little swerve by one nudging the next and that one another, and so on, would in the end produce all sorts of collisions: one car on the highway swerves out of its lane ever so slightly, and then . . . But the cars on the highway, if not moving relatively to one another, are yet moving very fast relative to the road itself. If we can imagine the highway and the whole earth removed without altering the cars, we comprehend that there would be no difference between the condition of all cars moving very fast at the same rate and none of the cars moving at all. But to get from the state of no cars moving at all to one of infinite furious collisions would require more than a "very little" swerve of one or two vehicles. Whether he appreciated this point or not, Epicurus with his swerve was in fact claiming that motion had a beginning, and at the same time he was refusing to provide a cause for it.

Why did he thus violate his own first principle? In order to make the ethics reasonable, as Lucretius tells us in the continuation of the passage just quoted.

> If all movement is always interconnected, the new arising from the old in a determinate order—if the atoms never swerve so as to originate some new movement that

will snap the bonds of fate, the everlasting sequence of cause and effect—what is the source of the free will possessed by living things throughout the earth? Why, I repeat, is the source of that will-power snatched from the fates, whereby we follow the path along which we are severally led by pleasure, swerving from our course at no set time or place but at the bidding of our own hearts? There is no doubt that on these occasions the will of the individual originates the movements that trickle through his limbs . . . So also in the atoms you must recognize the same possibility: besides weight and impact there must be a third cause of movement, the source of this inborn power of ours, since we see that nothing can come out of nothing. For the weight of an atom prevents its movements from being completely determined by the impact of other atoms. But the fact that the mind itself has no internal necessity to determine its every act and compel it to suffer in helpless passivity—this is due to the slight swerve of the atoms at no determinate time or place.

Not all *our* motions are determined; our acts of free will are not. But we are made of atoms. Therefore, there must be indeterminacy in the atoms themselves.

This argument has been found compelling in our own day by some who, feeling with Epicurus that "it would be better to accept the myths about the gods than to be a slave to the determinism of the physicists,"[4] hail the so-called Indeterminacy Principle of Werner Heisenberg (1901–1976) as refuting determinism and there-fore making a place for free will. Unfortunately, this Epicurean move does not work. Granted that we know we have free will, we are unable to connect this fact with uncaused motions. Whatever we may mean by "I do such-and-such of my own free will," we certainly do not mean "I did such-and-such quite unpredictably, as a result of an internal motion that had no cause at all." Fate and determinism may be depressing, being at the mercy of cruel and capricious gods may be worse—but worst of all must be the prospect that whatever sets us in motion is infected with the Swerve so that we can have no reason to suppose that in the next hour we will not jump over a cliff or take an axe to our dearest friend. Blacking out is not freedom.

## The Soul

Epicurus distinguished three souls: breath, heat, and a "nameless element," as he called it. All are composed of fine atoms; the "nameless" is the finest. It is what has (or is) consciousness—which like color, taste, and odor is property of arrange-ments of atoms, not of atoms individually. When the proper kinds of atoms are enclosed in the body, the happenings that we call sensations, thinking, and the like can occur. At death they are dispersed and consciousness ceases, as the whiteness of sea foam vanishes when the atoms rearrange themselves more compactly.

## Natural Philosophy

Epicurus gave the standard Ionian whirlpool account of the development of this world. The earth is a flat disc. This was of course an out-of-date and, one may even say, ignorant view to take in the third century B.C. But Epicurus was not interested in science for its own sake and did not pretend to be. Thus he advocated explana-tions according to a principle of "multiple causation": the same phenomenon may have many different kinds of causes; there is no use trying to find out what *the* cause is, even if there should be only one; and in any case it does not matter, as long as you exclude supernatural causes. Thus on the phases of the moon he offers all the explanations hitherto expounded, except, as it happens, the right one.

> The wanings of the moon and its subsequent waxings might be due to the revolution of its own body, or equally well to successive conformations of the atmosphere, or again to the interposition of other bodies; they may be accounted for in all the ways in which phenomena on earth invite us to such explanations of these phases; provided only one does not become enamored of the method of the single cause and groundlessly put the others out of court, without having considered what it is possible for a man to observe and what is not, and desiring therefore to observe what is impossible.[5]

This may seem like a lazy philosophy. In Epicurus' defense, we may stress the universal failure of the ancients to develop sound methods for testing hypotheses. In such a situation it was indeed more sensible to list alternatives in the explanation. Contrast the page after page of dogmatic nonsense in Plato's *Timaeus*. Nor was it arbitrary for Epicurus to exclude the supernatural; that was ruled out by the first principles of atomism, for which he did argue competently.

## Ethics

The opening of the Letter to Menoeceus, on Ethics, is as noble as one will find in classical literature.

> Let no one when young delay to study philosophy, nor when he is old grow weary of his study. For no one can come too early or too late to secure the health of his soul. And the man who says that the age for philosophy has either not yet come or has gone by is like the man who says that the age for happiness is not yet come to him, or has passed away. Wherefore both when young and old a man must study philosophy, that as he grows old he may be young in blessings through the grateful recollection of what has been, and that in youth he may be old as well, since he will know no fear of what is to come. We must then meditate on the things that make our happiness, seeing that when that is with us we have all, but when it is absent we do all to win it.

Pleasure was held to be the sole good; hence the misunderstandings, often willful, of the Epicureans as mere voluptuaries, inherent in the common modern meaning of the word. But it was not the cultivation of transient and exciting sensations that Epicurus proposed as the life goal; it was rather "ataraxia," the absence of pain, especially of anxieties. Prudence was the chief virtue, "more precious than philosophy itself." Epicurus might have said that the whole aim of philosophy was to make a background for prudence by eliminating anxieties— about the wrath of the gods and the terrors of the afterlife—from the world view.

This much accomplished, the rest consists in living so as to avoid the pains and anxieties of this life. "Live unknown" was the Epicurean motto—excellent advice no doubt, especially in so turbulent a period. One ought to abstain not only from politics and other ways of perhaps fatally attracting attention, but from sex also: "Sexual intercourse never did anyone any good, and a man is lucky if it has not harmed him." It is better not to marry and have children, for families are constant sources of anxiety. You should not overeat or drink much, for fear of indigestion and hangover. Epicurus deemed a little bread and cheese to constitute a banquet. The genuine Epicurean life is, in R. D. Hicks's phrase, one of "plain living and moderately high thinking." Not plain to the point of Cynicism, however: "There is also a limit in simple living. He who fails to heed this limit falls into an error as great as that of the man who gives way to extravagance."[6]

*Whose* pleasure constitutes the Good? Your own. The theory of Epicureanism is a frankly egoistic hedonism. Even friendship, the most positive of pleasures, is recommended on the ground of the usefulness of friends to oneself. Lucretius may sound heartless to some ears when he sings at the beginning of the second book of his poem

> Out on the mighty main, when hurricanes heave up the billows,
> Sweet is the sight from shore of the deep distress of another;
> Though 'tis no joy and delight that any should thus be afflicted,
> Yet 'tis a comfort to see what mishaps you yourself have eluded.[7]

However, the ancients were not much given to sentimental cant. Lucretius goes on to deplore the unnecessary troubles that other people get into on account of their "blindness." We should remember that he assumed the burden of composing his poem to help cure this blindness. And Epicurus, with amiable inconsistency, said that "on occasion the wise man will even die for a friend."

## The Cyrenaic School

It is uncertain how long the Garden continued as a school, but it did survive for several centuries, well into the Christian era. Its most distinguished alumnus was, of course, the poet Lucretius. Julius Caesar was rumored to be a closet Epicurean.

Epicurus himself was not, even indirectly, in the Socratic succession. But Aristippus of Cyrene (*ca* 435–366 B.C.), a member of the Socratic circle, founded a school of hedonism in his home city in North Africa. His right to claim Socratic inspiration may seem slight—though after all Socrates was no ascetic, as the *Symposium* testifies—and Plato even pictures him espousing (or at least seriously considering), in the *Protagoras*, the hedonist principle that things are good just to the extent that they are pleasurable or pleasure-producing.

At any rate, Aristippus taught a hedonism that had a more sensual cast than Epicurus'. The school moved to Alexandria and persisted for some time, including among its leaders an atheist and a woman. Perhaps the most interesting figure associated with it was one Hegesias, called the Death-Persuader. He held that since pleasure is the good, no life is good on balance, for pain always predominates in the long run. Therefore the rational hedonist will kill himself. Hegesias expounded this thesis with such eloquence that the authorities found it necessary to suppress his lectures after many of his auditors had committed suicide. Hegesias himself, we are told, lived to be a very old man.

# 23

## Greek Skeptical Philosophies

Cynic, stoic, epicurean, skeptic: these names of Hellenistic philosophies have dropped their capital letters to become common words in all the languages of Europe. The last of them is the commonest and most indispensable. Its modern everyday usage, however, has little overlap with what it means in philosophy, ancient or modern.

We call one a skeptic who is less gullible than most of us, who demands to be shown evidence before accepting statements that others take on trust. It is common to be skeptical about particular subjects or areas of alleged knowledge—flying saucers, religion, sociology, psychoanalysis, military prognostication—while believing what everybody else believes about most other things. Indeed, to be skeptical about (say) the scientific status of sociology seems to require of the skeptic a confidence that there is some other science, say physics, with whose impeccable credentials an unfavorable contrast can be drawn. To be a religious skeptic is to hold that the evidence for the truth of such dogmas as infant damnation or papal infallibility is inferior in credibility to the evidence for (say) the Nazi holocaust and the mathematical competence of Isaac Newton. Common skepticism may be called retail or Missourian.

On the other hand, philosophical Skepticism is wholesale. Not this or that area or bit of knowledge is questioned, but knowledge as such is declared to be an ideal impossible of attainment. At any rate, the philosophical Skeptic rejects the claims of non-Skeptical philosophers, called "dogmatists," to have attained certain knowledge about anything.

As retail skeptics are not (usually) wholesale Skeptics, so conversely philosophical Skeptics may be as gullible as anyone else in ordinary affairs. Thus in the course of making the point that different animals presumably perceive the world differently, Sextus Empiricus—the physician and Skeptic from whom most of our knowledge of Greek Skepticism comes—wrote

> Some animals originate without sexual intercourse . . . Some come from fire, as the little animals which appear in the chimneys, others from fermented wine, as the stinging ants, others from the earth, others from the mud, like the frogs, others from slime, as the worms, others from donkeys, as the beetles, others from cabbage, as caterpillars, others from fruit, as the gall insect from the wild figs, others from putrified animals, as bees from bulls, and wasps from horses.[1]

Philosophical Skepticism is, however, a development from common retail skepticism. Since it presupposes the existence of philosophical theories of knowledge to be Skeptical about, it is a particularly sophisticated point of view which of necessity was late in appearing on the scene.

## The Growth of Skepticism

Socrates was in the habit of saying "*Skepteon*": "[We] ought to investigate [this]." The word Skepticism derives from that usage. A willingness to investigate, to question, to demand evidence—what we call a skeptical turn of mind—is of course the very foundation of the scientific and philosophical world view. Dialectic by its nature requires at least Missourian skepticism. The Greeks as a people were well endowed with this attribute. "Eyes are better witnesses than ears," said Heraclitus. "So the priests told me, but I do not believe it," is a remark that Herodotus (*ca* 484–between 430 and 420 B.C.) frequently makes in his History. We have seen how the philosophers unanimously rejected popular religion.

Even eyes are not unimpeachable witnesses, Parmenides emphasized. That things are often not what they seem is a commonplace doubtless as old as thought itself. It remained for the philosophers, however, to give reasons for casting doubt wholesale on the veracity of the senses. Apparently, for good or ill, it was Democritus who first began to worry about the perceptual situation. The tomato is out there: when we say we see the tomato, what is really happening is that certain material bodies are being thrown off the tomato and received in our eyes. These bodies, which are what we are in direct contact with, are not the tomato. That fruit suddenly becomes problematic: do we really know what it is like? How? "We really know nothing about anything, but each man's opinion is the flow toward him."[2]

Democritus was not a complete Skeptic because, like Parmenides, he believed in a "finer instrument"—a pure reason that, independent of sense imagery, could tell us the truth. His fellow townsman Protagoras rejected this consolation. The view attributed to him that every person's opinion is true, is really Skepticism phrased more cheerfully than usual. For to say that no one can be mistaken about anything is to say that no ground exists for criticizing claims to knowledge; but if there is no criterion for distinguishing the true from the false, then there is no knowledge in the usual sense of the word.

## Socrates and Plato

Socrates and Plato, setting themselves resolutely against Protagorean Skepticism, developed a non-Skeptical theory of knowledge having the Ideas as objects. They were, however, willing to concede much to the Skeptics: in effect, all so-called knowledge of the whole sensible world. In casting doubt on the ability of our senses to give us accurate reports of the world, Plato, especially in the *Theaetetus*, repeated and elaborated the arguments already developed by Democritus and Protagoras. He went beyond Democritus in denying the possibility of an exact science of physics, saying it was at best "a likely story."

In the *Apology*, Socrates concluded that he was wiser than his fellows only in that he knew he knew nothing, while they did not know even that much. This seems a thoroughly Skeptical pronouncement. However, Socrates was doubtful not about the possibility of knowledge but about its existence at that particular time and place. Plato cast aspersions on sense knowledge in order to provide a contrast for the superior certainty of knowledge of the Ideas. In spite of elements of Skepticism in their philosophies, Socrates and Plato were far from making a system out of doubt.

## Academic Skepticism

Yet it was in the Academy founded by Plato that Skepticism in the full philosophical sense made its appearance in Athens. Arcesilaus (*ca* 315–241 B.C.), head of the Academy at the time when Zeno was founding the Stoa, and Carneades (214–129 B.C.), head during the period of Chrysippus, combatted the Stoic doctrine concerning knowledge. Zeno and Chrysippus held that the ultimate test of knowledge is the sense of certainty that you experience when you are affected by a "compelling appearance." They admitted that in perception, at least of sights and sounds, we are not in direct contact with the object perceived. Furthermore, when an object is distant or otherwise obscured, we are often wrong in our judgments. Nevertheless, there are certain circumstances—such as noon-day sun, close-up view—when our apprehension cannot be mistaken. Similarly in ethics and all other subjects of investigation, although there are hard cases, there are also occasions where our assent is compelled; in these, at least, we have a grasp of the truth.

This Stoic theory of knowledge, even though it had linkages with the views of Plato himself, was the target of attack from the Academy. Any theory is easy to criticize that makes some state of mind in the perceiver the criterion of truth in what is perceived. It is a common lesson of experience that feeling sure is no guarantee that things are so. But if subjective certainty cannot testify to objective fact, what can? Arcesilaus and Carneades replied that nothing can—there is ultimately no way of knowing that we have grasped the truth of things. But although nothing is certain, some things are more probable than others: "Probability is the guide of life."

In 155 B.C. Athens sent three philosophers as special ambassadors to Rome. In the intervals between negotiations they gave public lectures—the first introduction the Romans had to philosophy. Carneades, one of the envoys, created a sensation. On successive days he delivered two lectures on justice. In the first he eulogized it and exhorted to its practice. Next day he pointed out the impracticability of a just policy: how in particular the Romans, if they decided to practice justice, would have to give up all their conquests and return to living in huts. This balancing of one argument against another, a basic Skeptical tactic, smacked of sophisticated degeneracy to the upright Romans. Shortly afterwards they enacted a law against philosophers.

## Pyrrhonism

The Skeptical, or to be more exact the Probabilistic, period in the Academy—the "New Academy" as it is called—lasted until the first century B.C., when the headship passed to a certain Antiochus who in effect converted the school to Stoicism. Skepticism, however, did not die; it moved to Alexandria where under the name "Pyrrhonism" it flourished, especially among the local physicians, for two or three centuries.

Pyrrho of Elis (*ca* 360–270 B.C.) accompanied the army of Alexander the Great to India. There he is said to have made the acquaintance of the "Gymnosophists," *i.e.* "naked sophists." This is the first known contact between Greek and Indian philosophies. Disappointingly, we do not know what the Gymnosophists taught Pyrrho or whether he accepted what they taught. It is tempting to speculate that the gist of their teaching was that everything is illusion.

Upon his return to Elis, Pyrrho taught suspense of judgment, nonaffirmation, and "no thing is any more this than that." There is no real nature of things, he declared; everything is custom and convention. Typically, but in this case surprisingly, the philosophy was recommended as leading to ataraxy, the imperturbability that was the goal of the Epicureans also. Pyrrho held that if you were a dogmatic philosopher—that is, if you believed in a reality that was the object of certain and absolute knowledge—you would be afflicted with two kinds of cares. First, tension would be generated by the contrast between the Truth, known to you, and the conventional untruths, such as those about the gods, to which you would have to pay at least lip service if you were to avoid being endlessly harassed. Second, you would be bound to entertain doubts about the real validity of the system to which you subscribed. To neither of these anxieties would the Skeptic be liable. If there is no Truth to know, there is no occasion for worrying about whether you have attained it. And if there is no reality beyond convention, there can be no objection to behaving in an entirely conventional way. Thus Skepticism in philosophy was the ally of conservatism in morals and politics. *disagree?*

Pyrrho is said by one account to have lived a thoroughly conventional life, and to have been so popular among his fellow townsmen that they made him high priest and in his honor exempted all philosophers from taxation. The implausibility of this last detail makes it possible to give hearing to a more sensational tradition according to which "he led a life consistent with his Skepticism, going out of his way for nothing, taking no precaution, but facing all risks as they came, whether carts, precipices, dogs or what not, and generally, leaving nothing to the judgment of the senses. But he was kept out of harm's way by his friends who used to follow close after him."[3] When his aged teacher in philosophy fell into a bog and called to him for help, Pyrrho did nothing, on the ground that he had no reason to suppose that being saved would benefit him. The public condemned Pyrrho's heartlessness; his teacher, however, after being rescued by some unphilosophical person, commended his pupil for his Skeptical consistency.

There was no direct line of succession from Pyrrho to the Pyrrhonists, who adopted him as a patron, so to speak. Probably the doctors of Alexandria, like others elsewhere, were sympathetic to Skeptical teachings as a consequence of their traditional hostility to all-embracing theories that were supposed to have as consequences certain prescriptions for the treatment of the sick. But like logic among the Stoics, what was in origin an auxiliary and defensive study came to be pursued for its own sake in the course of time.

Sextus Empiricus, of whom nothing is known except that he was a physician living in Alexandria about the turn of the third century A.D., wrote voluminous polemics against the various species of "dogmatists" vexing the intellectual scene in his day. His works happen to have been preserved, so that we are better informed about the Pyrrhonists than about any other of the later Hellenistic schools.

"The fundamental principle of the Skeptical system is especially this," Sextus wrote, "namely, to oppose every argument by one of equal weight, for it seems to us that in this way we finally reach the position where we have no dogmas." To the criticism that Skepticism refutes itself—inasmuch as the Skeptic in declaring that he knows nothing is claiming to know something: to wit, that he knows nothing (a piece of cleverness going back to Plato)—the reply was made that the Skeptical principles apply to themselves "just as cathartic medicines not only purge the body of humors, but carry off themselves as well."

When the claim to knowledge is given up, we are left with appearances. Feelings are exempt from Skeptical doubts. If you feel warm you cannot think that you do not.

> It appears to us that honey is sweet. This we concede, for we experience sweetness through sensation. We doubt, however, whether it is sweet by reason of its essence, which is not a question of the appearance, but of that which is asserted of the appearance.[4]

Aenesidemus, the leading Pyrrhonist of the first century B.C., compiled a digest of ten Skeptical considerations supporting the conclusion that we have no certain knowledge of how things really are. Men, beasts, insects, birds, mites are so different that it is implausible to suppose their perceptions of things are not equally various. But why should ours be more valid than the bird's or the flea's? Even among human beings there is great diversity to be found, and no way of preferring one to the other: you are hot when I am cold, you find oysters tasty but they disgust me. In the same person the same thing may be both pleasant and unpleasant: Camembert is pleasant to taste but unpleasant to smell. How I perceive the world depends on my personal condition: on whether I am sane or insane, well or ill, awake or asleep (dreaming counts as perception). It depends further on my location: perspective, illumination, and medium all enter. The tower looks round at a distance, square close up. The oar looks straight when out of water, bent when in it. "The egg in the bird is soft, but in the air hard." The context of perception varies the impression: the jaundiced person sees everything as yellow. The quantity and constitution of the object vary the perception: horn is black, horn filings are white; wine in small quantities makes us cheerful, in large draughts puts us to sleep. And nothing is perceived by itself, but only in relation to a certain perceiver in a certain condition, through a certain medium; it is not possible to separate these and get at the object as it is all by itself. Further, our reactions depend on objectively irrelevant considerations such as rarity: the sun is far more astonishing than a comet, but because we see it every day we react in the opposite order. In the end, all is custom; in philosophies as in myths, there is no agreement to be found.

These considerations, as it is easy to see, are of various weights. After Aenesidemus, Agrippa set out five considerations against the possibility of logical proof. The existence of controversy about the nature of reality shows that no statement about it is universally accepted. Therefore, it is always in order to call for a proof of a dogmatic statement. But it does no good to base the proof of the statement on other statements equally in need of proof. To try to avoid it by basing proof on perception gets us into the difficulties already noted based on the relativity of perception. There is then nothing left to do but base the proof on assumptions, which is useless—one might as well assume the conclusion at the beginning—or else you go in a circle by putting your conclusion among your premises.

Later Skeptics reduced the contentions to two summary heads: nothing is self-evident and nothing can be proved.

## Influence of Skepticism

The Skeptics were quiet people. We may hope that this formidable argumentative array had the desired effect of permitting the Skeptical doctors to go their rounds in peace and ataraxy. But we do not know; the history of ancient Skepticism after Sextus Empiricus, if there was any, is lost. Skepticism like Cynicism is perhaps better described as an antiphilosophy than as a philosophy. The existence of Skeptical arguments is generally thought to be a good thing for philosophy in that it requires the dogmatists to pursue rigor in their formulations to escape Skeptical refutation.

Skepticism provided the defenders of Christianity with some of their more effective apologetic tactics, at least in the beginning, for the arguments could be used to counter the pretensions of the pagan philosophers to a superior knowledge. But the subsequent history of Skepticism belongs mostly to modern philosophy.

# 24

---

# Plotinus and Neoplatonism

WE HAVE SEEN HOW after Aristotle there was a tendency for philosophers to withdraw from the world into themselves or a small group of the like-minded. After five hundred years this culminated in a philosophy of almost complete withdrawal from the familiar public world into a communion with the supernatural. Not inappropriately the core of this movement was an adaptation from Plato, the most other-worldly of the great Greeks.

Neoplatonism made its appearance in the lectures of Ammonius Saccas of Alexandria in the first part of the third century A.D. Ammonius wrote nothing, and little is known of him beyond the fact that he was at one time a Christian but abandoned that religion. Of his many pupils two attained great eminence: one was Origen (ca 185–ca 254), intellectual defender of Christianity against pagan attack; the other was Plotinus, whose writings gave definitive form to the last of the pagan systems.

## Life of Plotinus

Plotinus (205–270), believed to have been an Egyptian, did not begin the study of philosophy until he was 27. After eleven years in the school of Ammonius, in order to get an opportunity to study the philosophies of Iran and India he joined the expedition of the emperor Gordian against the Parthians. But Gordian was murdered soon after setting out. Plotinus escaped from the demoralized army. Instead of returning to Alexandria he went to Rome where, for the rest of his life, through a low ebb of Roman fortunes, he taught philosophy in tranquillity and popularity.

His disciple Porphyry wrote his biography, or rather an account of his final six years. This document begins

> Plotinus, the philosopher of our times, seemed ashamed of being in the body. As a result of this state of mind he could never bear to talk about his race or his parents or his native country. And he objected so strongly to sitting to a painter or sculptor that he said to Amelius, who was urging him to allow a portrait of himself to be made, "Why, really, is it not enough to have to carry the image in which nature has encased us, without your requesting me to agree to leave behind me a longer-lasting image of the image, as if it was something genuinely worth looking at?"[1]

He did not, however, try to live in solitude. He was on terms of personal intimacy with the Emperor Gallienus, a cultivated and innovative but unfortunate ruler whom he almost persuaded to decree the founding of a city near Rome to be run according to the constitution of Plato's *Laws*. His house was full of orphaned children whose parents had named him guardian because of his kindness and honesty. He was gifted with extraordinary powers of concentration, so that his business did not keep him from writing voluminously during the last 15 years of his life. The mass of separate essays was rearranged after his death by Porphyry, somewhat arbitrarily, into six groups of nine each called Enneads (*ennea* = nine).

Porphyry testifies of his master.

> When he was speaking his intellect visibly lit up his face: there was always a charm about his appearance, but at these times he was still more attractive to look at: he sweated gently, and kindliness shone out from him, and in answering questions he made clear both his benevolence to the questioner and his intellectual power. Once I went on asking him for three days about the soul's connection with the body, and he kept on explaining to me.[2]

Four times in his last six years, Porphyry tells us, Plotinus achieved mystical union with "the First and Transcendent God, Who has neither shape nor any intelligible form, but is throned above intellect and all the intelligible."

## The One

Plato taught in the *Republic* that the Good is not Being but something higher in dignity even than Being; that it is to the intelligible world what the sun is to the visible world, the source of intelligibility and reality as the sun is the source of visibility and organic life. Plotinus' conception of reality is a working out of these images.

The intelligible world is made up of the One and of two other essential principles which flow from it, first Mind and then Soul. When Mind is said to flow or emanate from the One and Soul from Mind, these words are not to be understood as signifying processes in time. It is not as if at some time there had been only the One, then later Mind came into being. The relation of Mind to the One is timeless, like the relation of the theorems of geometry to the axioms from which they are deduced or as the Aristotelian world is to Aristotle's god. The One causes, produces, creates Mind and Mind causes Soul—but these productions are not happenings.

The One is called also the Good and even God, but nothing positive can be said about it that is literally true. It can only be described negatively: it is not in space, not in time, not visible, not this and not that. "We must think and speak of it as one and the same nature, not applying any predicates to it, but explaining it to ourselves as best we can."[3] It is simple and self-sufficing; it is in nothing else and nothing is above it. If we can imagine ourselves disembodied and looking into a completely dark and empty space in which there shines one point source of light, we may be able to conceive something analogous to the complete simplicity and indescribability of the One. It has no form, not even intelligible form. It is "beyond being" inasmuch as it is not an Idea or Form nor any particular definable thing. It is infinite, but in power not extent (it has no extent). It is not thought, for there is no distinction, no otherness in it. It has no function, no activity. But it has life—all life—in itself.

Perhaps the least misleading thing to be said about the One is that it is absolute unity. Plotinus holds that to be is to be a unity, citing as examples a ship, an army, a house. All unities must derive from absolute unity; that is why the One is the source of all being.

## Mind and the Ideas

The earliest philosophers had tried to derive the many from the one; that is, they had tried to make intelligible how the diversity of the world could be traced back to some unified original principle. They had usually conceived of the unity as breaking up or separating—which seemed to imply that it had not really been a unity in the first place, but merely a mixture. Plotinus could avoid some of the difficulties of such accounts because his One, not being spatial, did not have to furnish the materials for the diverse world. Indeed his One is not at all affected by the circumstance that the many are derived from it. Nevertheless, there was for Plotinus as for others a problem of how and why the many come from the One. His answer is that all things produce when they are in their perfection. They produce something akin to themselves: fire heats and snow cools. The One cannot produce another One, but it can and does "overflow" to produce something akin to itself—the Mind which contemplates it.

Mind tries to contemplate the One. But what happens is that it thinks, instead, the Ideas. To think the Ideas, the intelligible objects, is to *be* those objects. Thus in Neoplatonism the Ideas become God's thoughts—for Mind is God also. That does not mean, however, that they are in any sense subjective. Why, however, does Mind think the many Ideas? The answer seems to be this: thought necessitates a many—to think always of the absolutely simple would be the same as not to think at all. But the many that the Mind thinks are no separate independent individuals.

> Mind as a whole is all the Ideas and each individual Idea is an individual Mind, as a whole science is all its theorems and each theorem is a part of the whole science.[4]

This is Platonic, or at least compatible with Plato's views: for him such Ideas as Beauty and Justice were not separate entities so much as aspects of the Good. To return to the analogy of the point source of light in empty space, if there is to be anything besides the light—if there is to be a multiplicity furnishing objects for thought and if this multiplicity is at the same time to be dependent on the light— it must be a breaking-up or complication of the light rays. Let us suppose then that various lenses, perhaps of different colored glasses, are set about the light source. We should now have a multiplicity dependent on unity. In this respect the relation of the lenses (or rather of the light shining through them and being diffracted) to the point source would be somewhat like that of Mind to the One.

The Ideas that constitute Mind are not abstract and lifeless exemplars of the things in the sensible world. To the contrary, all that is here below is in the heaven of Mind also, but alive and intelligent. There "everything is filled full of life, boiling with life."

Plotinus has a further argument to show that the objects of thought must have life and intelligence. The Mind that contemplates these objects, it is conceded, is alive and intelligent. If then what it contemplates does not have these properties, the objects must be distinct and separate from Mind. But in that case what is in the Mind cannot be the realities, but only some substitutes that falsify their exemplars. Therefore, either the Ideas have life and intelligence, or Mind is totally deceived. The thought behind this argument is fundamental to all Idealist philosophy. It is that the relational statement "*A* knows *B*" requires an underlying identity of *A* and *B*; if they were entirely distinct the sort of fusion involved in knowing could not take place. This thought in its turn is implicit in such expressions as "comprehend," "understand" ( = "stand under"), "grasp," which are used to name the relation. The hand grasping the handle cannot be of a nature entirely different from that of the handle. For Plotinus the relation is simple and direct: "Mind makes being exist by thinking it."

## Soul

The emanation or overflow of Mind is Soul, of which our own souls are parts. In Mind there is already multiplicity, in the sense that the Ideas which are Mind's thoughts are different. Mind, however, thinks them all at once, not one after the other. On the other hand, Soul, as we know from our experience, cannot attend to everything at once; it can think only discursively. This is true even when the soul contemplates the eternal truths, of geometry for instance; the lower activity of Soul, which is sense perception, is yet more time bound. It is thus at the level of this emanation that time enters. Time is an image of eternity: time is to Soul as eternity is to the One.

Soul is the link between the intelligible world, from which it proceeds, and the sensible world which it creates. It faces, so to speak, both ways, as again we know from our own experience. Soul in its union with Mind is not divided—there are no sharp lines in Plotinus' system. Here in the sensible world it is divided, "but undivided as well: for the divided part of it is divided without division." Plotinus means that in being associated with different bodies, Soul is divided; but Soul, which is essentially not spatial at all, is not in its essence thereby divided. This is an important point, for it makes possible the ultimate reunion of the individual's soul with the One.

## Nature and Matter

Nevertheless, there is a hierarchy of souls, or of grades of Soul. The lower souls create living beings. Like Plato's cosmic Craftsman, they make objects as copies of the Ideas. Yet because Soul itself does not possess Form itself, but only derivatives, the copies it makes contain a contribution of its own—so that the product is imperfect, a sort of "sediment of the prior realities."

The mode of creation by the lower Soul, also called Nature, is this. The Soul contemplates, as well as it can, the Ideas in Mind, as the geometer contemplates his figures; thereupon it makes what it sees. All action is from contemplation; however, the kind of action that we call creation is the least noble.

> Everywhere we shall find that making and action are either a weakening or a consequence of contemplation. . . . For who, when he is able to contemplate that which is truly real, deliberately goes after its image? Dull children, too, are evidence of this, who are incapable of learning and contemplative studies and turn to crafts and manual work.[5]

It would not be accurate to say that Soul creates bodies out of matter, for matter has no prior being, nor indeed any being at all. Matter is nonbeing, absolute formlessness—the end of the line, the darkness into which the One shines. It is the evil principle. Soul imposes form on the formless.

There has to be formlessness, evil, both because the emanations of the One must come to an end and because without the formless on which to impose form there could be no visible universe. From Plotinus' shame of his body and the extreme otherworldliness of his philosophy, one might suppose that he despised the material world as hopeless, fit only to be fled from. Not so. The visible world has being, though diluted. Its being is of the Ideas; the sight of its harmony not only reminds us of the higher world but is delightful in itself.

> Will anyone be so sluggish in mind and so immovable that, when he sees all the beauties of the world of sense, all its good proportion and the mighty excellence of its order, and the splendor of form which the stars, for all their remoteness, make manifest, he will not be seized with reverence and think, "What wonders, and from what a source?" If he does not, he neither understands the world of sense nor sees that higher world.[6]

## Hope

This passage is one of many echoes in Plotinus' writings of the description in Plato's *Symposium* of the soul's ascent—beginning with love of physical beauty, through appreciation of abstract beauty, and culminating with the vision of Beauty itself. This is the key to salvation. It is a pity that the soul has given of itself to a body; but the situation is remediable. The soul of the individual may return to the One via the path of dialectic combined with a regimen of physical austerity to strengthen resistance to the solicitations of the bodily passions. The human intellect by its essence rightfully belongs on a higher plane, which it can regain. Reunion with the One is not an absorption that annihilates individuality: "The intellects There do not cease to be because they are not corporeally divided, but each remains distinct in otherness, having the same essential being."

The experience of union with the One, the mystical illumination, is indescribable not only because of its rapturous quality but for the same kind of reason that the One Itself is above description: the lack of any differentiation to which we might apply words. Nevertheless, like most mystics Plotinus struggles to provide symbols of a certain adequacy. In the union the soul, he tells us, sees "that Light by which it is enlightened; for we do not see the sun by another light than his own."

> This is the life of gods and divine and blessed men, deliverance from the things of this world, a life which takes no delight in the things of this world, a flight of the alone to the Alone.[7]

## Career of Neoplatonism

Neoplatonism (the term is a modern label) is properly named. In its main outlines it is either genuinely Platonic or arguably a legitimate development of Platonism. This applies even to certain somewhat embarrassing features, such as Plotinus' taking over Plato's belief that the stars are live and particularly virtuous animals.

But Plotinus also incorporated into his philosophy, as was inevitable, not only features and doctrines from Aristotle and the Stoics but some of the superstitions that abounded in his time, giving them a philosophical justification. He believed in demons as well as in angels. Fortune-telling works, for everything is linked to everything else in the great world-animal. Likewise, magic works though prayer does not. "When a man prays to anything, some influence comes from it upon him or upon another: the sun, or another star, does not hear his prayer."

These superstitious elements, which on the whole were minor in Plotinus' philosophy, were elaborated and added to by his successors in Rome, Alexandria, and elsewhere. Neo-Pythagoreanism, frankly a system of magic, merged with it in some grotesque conflations. But no matter what we may think of the difficult and astounding metaphysics of Neoplatonism, the purer sort of it is fundamentally a rational worldview. It was introduced into Plato's Academy near the beginning of the fifth century, eight hundred years after the foundation of that school. It continued to be taught until 529, when the Emperor Justinian forced the institution to close.

# IV

## Philosophy in the Christian Era

*Francesco Traini*, St. Thomas Aquinas, *fourteenth century. Fresco.*
*Church of Santa Caterina, Pisa.*

# 25

# The Christian Revolution

ROME'S POSITIVE CONTRIBUTION TO philosophy was comparable to that, say, of the island of Rhodes. The Roman people were unexcelled until recent times in the building of roads, bridges, and aqueducts, and in massive concrete architecture—in all of which they masterfully exploited the arch, which however was not a Roman invention. This is nearly a complete list of native Roman contributions to world culture. By themselves the Romans produced almost no science, and almost no significant art or literature.

If we tend to think of ancient Rome differently, it is invariably because we do not separate out the Greek contribution. The Romans wrote histories and poems—but after Greek models. There was a Roman theater, for comedies at any rate, but the plays were adaptations from the Greek. Roman architects with aspirations to elegance copied the Greek orders. Roman philosophers for the most part contented themselves with uncritical expositions of the tenets of the Greek schools.

Some nations that borrow alien cultures make them their own and go ahead to contribute of themselves. Not so Rome with the civilization of Greece. The Greek veneer was thin. The theater was the ordinary entertainment of all classes in Athens; in Rome it played to a comparatively small audience of highbrows. Roman popular amusement continued to consist of public execution of criminals, combats to the death between men, combats to the death between beasts, and combats to the death between men and beasts. The efforts of Lucretius, Cicero, and Seneca to initiate philosophizing in the Latin language founded no tradition.

It is necessary to mention Rome in this history, however, because the Roman Empire was the medium within which Christianity germinated, with the most profound consequences for philosophy.

## Roman Imperialism

In the days of Alexander the Great, Rome was an insignificant town. If Alexander had lived longer he no doubt would have annexed her in a minor campaign preliminary to an attack on Carthage, the most formidable of the powers in the western regions. As things turned out, however, the kingdoms into which Alexander's empire splintered occupied themselves with fighting each other and the Celts, so that in the third and second centuries B.C. they were unable to play any effective part in the struggle that ended with the annihilation of Carthage in

146 B.C. In the same year Roman troops dealt in a similar manner with the great Greek city of Corinth. Less than a century afterwards the whole Mediterranean basin was under Roman dominion.

In the first flush of empire this vast area was divided up into provinces administered—or rather plundered—by Roman senators who in this way amassed enormous fortunes. The common people of Rome shared the wealth to the extent of being not only exempted from taxation but even provided with free food, principally grain imported from Egypt. Wealthy politicians courted their support by paying the expenses for great slaughter shows. This was the policy of "bread and circuses" that kept the populace contented for more than two hundred years.

Rome, become capital of the western world, attracted so many ambitious men from everywhere that the descendants of the original Romans were swamped. Romans, whether old or new, gradually lost their preferred status. Roman citizenship was extended ever more widely, a process that culminated early in the third century A.D. in its grant to all free inhabitants of the Empire by decree of the Emperor Caracalla, himself born in France of an African father. In effect, however, what this meant was not that everybody had the Roman franchise but that nobody did. There was no more voting, not even rigged voting. The Emperor was an absolute despot except that his Imperial guards could, and usually did, murder him when for some reason they became dissatisfied.

Thus the later Roman Empire was not Roman in any important sense; it was just the political organization that the Mediterranean basin happened to have. Effective rule was exercised by the imperial bureaucracy. Despite numerous border wars and internal tumults, the world for the first two centuries of the Christian era was more peaceable than it ever was before or afterwards. Yet so far was the period from being a golden era of plenty and progress that general misery increased and led to breakdown in the next century. The causes were complicated and obscure; but for whatever reasons, just as the zest went out of Greek life after Alexander, so it was drained from the whole Mediterranean world after Augustus. For the vast majority the rudimentary security afforded within the Empire meant in practice no hope of escape from a life of drudgery on the subsistence level, for productivity was low and any surplus went to landlords and tax collectors.

## The Religious Situation

The hopelessness of this world could be redeemed only by hope of another world to come. An upsurge of religious fervor was inevitable. The only question was which religion would take the lead, for there were many candidates.

The official Roman religion was out of the running. Traditionally the Romans had worshiped Jupiter and Mars, both primarily war gods, and Quirinus, the deified founder of the city, called Romulus while on earth. As with the Greeks, there was no afterlife of any consequence. This was hardly a religion at all in the sense with which we are familiar. It was a creed of patriotism, which no doubt played its part in the Roman expansion, but became irrelevant thereafter. After Rome became an empire the emperors decreed that they themselves should be worshiped. But burning a pinch of incense in front of the Emperor's statue was no more than a salute to the flag.

Real religious fervor was centered in a variety of otherworldly salvation cults imported from the East. These superstitions were brought into the Mediterranean world from the old Iranian Empire and adjacent territories, mainly by Alexander's soldiers. They poured into Rome in the persons of the slaves who constituted the most valuable booty of the conquests. Roman governors in the provinces were tolerant of whatever religious practices their subjects chose to indulge in. In the homeland during the earliest days of empire there was resistance to the importation of foreign religions as there was to philosophy; but later complete freedom for religions was granted as long as the official cult of the Emperor was not interfered with. Most of the cults were content with the policy of peaceful coexistence, living in terms of more or less friendly rivalry—like Masons, Elks, and Odd Fellows among us. Nor was there anything to prevent individuals from belonging to more than one cult at the same time. The two notable exceptions to this *détente* were the Jews and the Christians.

The earliest and for a long time most important exotic cult in Rome was an Egyptian import, the worship of Isis and her family. Isis, originally a cow goddess, was in the Egyptian manner both sister and wife of Osiris, the god of civilization, to whom she bore a son Horus, represented in art as a baby at her breast. Osiris was murdered, but Horus became Osiris again. Isis was served by priests who shaved their heads and took vows of celibacy. Her worshippers burned candles before the shrines in which she was depicted holding the infant Horus. As with all Egyptian sects, immortality was promised to the believer.

A later arrival in Rome that came close to becoming the universal religion was Mithraism. It was a version of the traditional Iranian belief that the world is the eternal battleground between the forces of good and evil. Mithra was god of light, the good god. He slew a sacred bull, from whose blood came life and salvation. To be washed in the blood of this bull was to obtain eternal life. The Mithraist had to go through an initiation in which a bloodbath literally took place: the priest on a raised platform cut the throat of a bull; the devotees underneath let the blood run over them. Even though one bull might suffice for several initiates—and later be eaten by the priests and congregation—the expense was considerable. This put Mithraism at a disadvantage in comparison to Christianity, which required only water for baptism.

## The Jews

These were times when distinctions were blurred. National exclusiveness was lessened; there was a sense of Roman identity though it may have been no more than equal slavery to the universal bureaucratic despotism. In philosophy the tendency was for the schools to amalgamate: Platonists, Aristotelians, and Stoics saw each other's virtues and devoted their ingenuities to reconciling their teachings into a philosophical conglomerate hoped to be composed of the best elements from each. In religion the cult of Isis, itself a radical fusion of many distinct Egyptian cults with Greek elements thrown in for good measure, joined hands with Roman worship of Jupiter (already for centuries identified with the Greek Zeus) and with the Iranian sun god. In architecture a temple or palace was more likely than not to combine in one facade the three Greek orders with Iranian or Egyptian or old Roman elements.

There were two notable resistances to these tendencies toward amiable and formless synthesis. In philosophy the Epicureans preserved the teachings of the Master uncompromised. In nationalism and religion the Jews held aloof.

The Jewish people, not numerous or powerful, inhabited the seacoast of the eastern Mediterranean south of Phoenicia. Since routes for trade and invasion between Egypt and the Mesopotamian countries passed through their land, the Jews were continually being caught up in other people's wars. Early in their history, the written records of which extend back to the second millennium B.C., these people began to develop a religion different from that of their neighbors and kinsmen. Of the many gods worshipped in this part of the world the chief was the war god Baal, represented by idols of various forms and worshipped with burnt offerings including babies. The Jews in contrast honored only one god, Yahweh, who abominated idols and human sacrifices, requiring instead circumcision and the observance of an elaborate moral and dietary code. Religious differences from their neighbors made the Jews a tightly knit nation; reciprocally, national solidarity accentuated religious differences.

The greatest crisis came in the sixth century B.C. Nebuchadnezzar, king of Babylon, carried off almost the entire population as slaves to his capital city. There they languished for 70 years—almost three generations—until released when Cyrus the Iranian brought Babylon low.

> By the rivers of Babylon, there we sat down, yea, we wept,
>     when we remembered Zion.
> We hanged our harps upon the willows in the midst thereof.
> For there they that carried us away captive required of us a
>     song: and they that wasted us required of us mirth,
>     saying, Sing us one of the songs of Zion.
> How shall we sing the Lord's song in a strange land?
> If I forget thee, O Jerusalem, let my right hand forget her
>     cunning.
> If I do not remember thee, let my tongue cleave to the roof
>     of my mouth; if I prefer not Jerusalem above my chief
>     joy.
> Remember, O Lord, the children of Edom in the day of Jeru-
>     salem; who said, Rase, it, rase it, even to the found-
>     ation thereof.
> O daughter of Babylon, who art to be destroyed; happy shall
>     be he, that rewardeth thee as thou hast served us.
> Happy shall he be, that taketh and dasheth thy little ones
>     against the stones.[1]

Though the Jews did not forget Jerusalem, in Babylon they became forever independent of it, a nation liberated from geography. In this great sophisticated metropolis, the Jewish traditions and religion were gathered together and written down; the Jews became the first People of the Book. When after the Iranian conquest they were free to leave Babylon, many chose to remain; of those who departed, only a fraction returned to Palestine. The rest settled then and thereafter all over the accessible parts of the world. These Jews of the Dispersion, as they were known, became more numerous than the inhabitants of Palestine. In the cities of the Iranian Empire, later of the Hellenistic kingdoms, later still of the Roman Empire, they formed in each city a group—living usually by trade and thus in daily intercourse with non-Jewish people, yet preserving their distinctive worship and customs and their ties with other Jews in other lands.

## The Jewish Worldview

As we have seen, the more philosophical among the religious Greeks, the Platonists and Stoics, moved in their religious thought toward a conception of a single god. So pronounced was this tendency that Philo of Alexandria, a Jewish writer of the first century A.D., accused Plato of having plagiarized from Moses. Nevertheless, there were vast differences. The god of the Greek philosophers was the world soul, not separate from the cosmos and not the creator of it, although perhaps its arranger. Yahweh on the other hand was entirely distinct from the earth and stars, which he had fashioned out of nothing by pure magic, the exercise of will without any physical intermediary. Yahweh's world moreover, although excellent in its order, was not conceived by the Jews as providing data from which the intellect might infer the character of its creator.

Nevertheless, knowledge of Yahweh and of his intentions was held to exist insofar as he had seen fit to reveal himself through the prophets. In summary, this knowledge was as follows.

Yahweh was creator of the world, the only true god. But he was also especially the god of the Jews, who were more important than other peoples and the direct objects of Yahweh's concern. If so, though, why did they suffer as they did? The reason was that they were not obedient, as they should have been, to the Lord's commandments. Yahweh demanded righteousness, but they were unrighteous. Their falling away from proper worship was being properly punished. In the end they would see the light, resume the right relationship to the Lord, and then they would regain the status due the chosen people: mastery of Palestine and leadership of the world. Yahweh would send his Anointed One—'Messiah' in Hebrew, 'Christos' in Greek—to lead them to victory.

## Jesus

Within this general framework, Jewish thought was complex and varied. Some Jews held that Yahweh's favor could be regained only by the strictest observance of the dietary laws and other rituals, while to others the important thing was the perfection of social justice. There were differences of opinion as to the permissible extent of Hellenization and on such a fundamental question as immortality, which was not a traditional Jewish belief but had nevertheless become widespread in Hellenistic times.

About 26 A.D. a young Rabbi, Jesus of Nazareth (*ca* 6 B.C.–*ca* A.D. 30), rose to prominence through his preaching. He took an extreme antiformalist position— deliberately and ostentatiously violating the prohibition of work on the Sabbath; associating with prostitutes, tax collectors, and other low types; and in general shocking the respectable Jews of the Roman province of Judea. This He did to give point to His message, which was an exhortation to moral reform. Outward conformity to the details of the Law was nothing, He taught; inner righteousness was everything. The two essential commandments, He reminded His fellow religionists, were to love God and one's neighbor. One who was "born again"— having got rid of hostility, hypocrisy, and self-deceit and become again as a little child—would have attained thereby the "kingdom of heaven": the condition of inner bliss which was salvation. Jesus emphasized that the "kingdom of heaven" was not reserved for Jews alone but was open to all human beings.

These teachings attracted a multitude of followers to the Rabbi when he preached in the town of Capernaum and other places around the Sea of Galilee. His followers attributed magical powers to Him, and it began to be said of Him that He was the Messiah come to deliver the Jews from the yoke of Rome. Naturally enough, Jesus' scorn of the ritual laws and His frequent and eloquent denunciation of religious dignitaries made many dangerous enemies.

In the spring of 29, Jesus, accompanied by twelve disciples and numerous enthusiastic followers, came to Jerusalem to preach. He had not been there long, however, before His outraged and powerful enemies, the chief priests of the capital city, denounced Him to the Roman governor as a subversive person. Apparently His references to the "kingdom of heaven" were taken as hinting at a revived Jewish sovereignty, even though He explicitly stated that His kingdom was "not of this world." At any rate the claim that He was the Messiah was made either by Him or by His followers. He was convicted of blasphemy and crucified. The authorities dealt with the case quickly and forcibly so that there could be no public disturbance by His followers. Even some of His closest disciples denied that they had ever had anything to do with Him.

However, the story was soon told and believed by many that Jesus, taken dead from the cross on Friday afternoon and entombed, had on Sunday come back to life and emerged from the sepulcher; had met and spoken to a number of His followers, exhibiting the wounds in His hands and feet where he had been nailed to the cross; and had ascended into the sky. This was taken as confirmation that He was indeed not a mere man but the Son of God, who would return in glory— within the lifetime of many who were already grown men—to judge humanity and grant eternal life to those, and those alone, who had faith in Him.

## The Spread of Christianity

Those who had faith, the Christians, were inspired to expend great energy in making converts. At first they preached only to the Jews; but as these people formed communities in touch with one another all over the world, the message quickly spread to all the great cities and to Rome itself. Then the great decision was made to extend baptism—the prescribed initiation into the sect—to the uncircumcised, that is, non-Jews. Circumcision, a painful operation when performed on an adult, would have greatly restricted the number of converts if it had been retained as a requirement.

## Paul of Tarsus

The greatest of the early teachers and missionaries, and the man who in effect gave Christianity the form it was to have as a world religion, was Paul of Tarsus (*d.* A.D. 64? or 67?). He was a Jew with a Hellenistic education, fluent and eloquent in the Greek language, and as a Roman citizen a member of a privileged class exempt from many common harassments. By a catastrophic personal experience, Paul was changed instantly from being a persecutor of Christians into becoming their recognized leader. The development of doctrine in his thought was away from Jewish ritualism and particularism in the direction of accommodation to a pattern more typical of the religions of the time. The figure of a dying and resurrected god was to be found in many cults: of Adonis in Syria, Dionysus in Greece, Osiris in Egypt. The origin is the same for all: the god's death is a sacrifice for the good of mankind, a symbol of planting; his resurrection is the new growth. The worshipper had to go through a ceremony symbolic of his own spiritual death and rebirth. Paul interpreted the history of Jesus in this sense, thereby striking a sympathetic chord in non-Jewish religious consciousness and preparing the way for conversion. But Paul's greatest gift to the church was administrative. It was he who made the sectaries of Jesus the Messiah into The Church, a tightly knit international organization the like of which had been hitherto unknown in the world, something that as a whole could not be destroyed no matter what disasters might befall this or that cell.

## Persecutions

Stephen, an early convert among the Jews of Jerusalem, was stoned to death for blasphemy, thus becoming the first Christian martyr. Orthodox Jews every-where tried to check the spread of the new sect; Paul himself was a professional Christian-hunter before his miraculous conversion.

Every ancient nation, including the Roman, enforced respect for its gods within its own territory with legal penalties for blasphemy and sacrilege. However, as a matter of courtesy it was expected that the gods of foreigners would not be insulted. The Romans did not interfere with the religions of the peoples they conquered, nor would the notion ever have occurred to them of imposing their own gods on foreigners. As we have noted, it was the other way around: the foreigners imposed their gods on the Romans. The Emperor Tiberius put an end to all prosecutions for offenses against religion with the remark that "injured gods ought to be able to look after themselves."

The Jews, however, presented a problem to the Romans. Alone among the subject peoples, they would not willingly pay the moderate price for toleration which consisted in acquiescing in the formality of emperor worship and in refrain-ing from giving offense to devotees of other religions. They claimed that their God was the only God, that all the others were impostors; consequently, they refused to take part in paying divine honors to the Emperor. Cities where Jews were numerous, especially Alexandria, were often scenes of bloody riots between Jews and gentiles. The Romans tried to conciliate the Jews, even going so far as to grant them a unique exemption from emperor worship. But sometimes in exas-peration they took to forceful methods. In A.D. 70 Titus, son of the Emperor Vespasian, completed the suppression of a rebellion by taking Jerusalem and destroying it utterly, including the great Temple.

The Romans extended to the earliest Christians the distrust commonly felt toward the Jewish nation. But it was more intense, for two reasons. The Jews were conceded to be following their traditional observances, for which no one could be blamed; but the Christians were innovators. Moreover, the Jews did not try to make converts, while the Christians actively proselytized. In doing so they ridi-culed the gentile gods, for which reason they were commonly called atheists.

The first reference to Christians in non-Christian literature is the Roman histo-rian Tacitus' account of how the Emperor Nero, in 64, blamed the great fire of Rome on them in an attempt to turn suspicion of arson away from himself.

To get rid of the report, Nero fastened the guilt and inflicted the most exquisite tortures on a class hated for their abominations, called Christians by the populace. Christus, from whom the name had its origin, suffered the extreme penalty during the reign of Tiberius at the hands of one of our procurators, Pontius Pilatus, and a most michievous superstition, thus checked for the moment, again broke out not only in Judea, the first source of the evil, but even in Rome, where all things hideous and shameful from every part of the world find their center and become popular. Accordingly, an arrest was first made of all who pleaded guilty; then, upon their information, an immense multitude was convicted, not so much of the crime of firing the city, as of hatred against mankind. Mockery of every sort was added to their deaths. Covered with the skins of beasts, they were torn by dogs and perished, or were nailed to crosses, or were doomed to the flames and burnt, to serve as a nightly illumination, when daylight had expired. Nero offered his gardens for the spectacle. . . . Even for criminals who deserved extreme and exemplary punishment, there arose a feeling of compassion; for it was not, as it seemed, for the public good, but to glut one man's cruelty, that they were being destroyed.[2]

For two and a half centuries the Christians were persecuted from time to time. The continuity and severity of these episodes have been much exaggerated. Only the persecutions of Decius in the middle of the third century and of Diocletian at the beginning of the fourth could be said to have been severe. When a person was accused of being a Christian, and consequently of being disloyal to the Emperor, every means—even torture sometimes—was employed to prompt the accused to establish innocence by consenting to burn a pinch of incense before the Emperor's statue. Only those were martyred who insisted on it. According to the largest estimate, the total number put to death amounted to about two thousand.

## The Triumph of Christianity

Christianity was a revolt against the Roman Empire and Hellenistic civilization. To become a Christian was to declare no confidence in the authorities and institutions of this world, to abandon all hope of worldly improvement, and to stake everything on the direct intervention of God.

To a degree, adherence to any of the salvation religions from the east was likewise a rejection of this-worldly Hellenistic values. But only to a lesser degree. Devotees of Isis or Mithra could hedge their bets, keep a foot in each world. With Christians, commitment and rejection alike were total. This fact was a source of strength for Christianity in its competition with the rival mysteries, for it meant that more than the others it would attract the vigorous, the adventuresome, the fanatical. Christianity was in other ways also more definite than its rivals. Whereas they offered a somehow blissful future in a nebulous hereafter, the Christian message was of the literal coming in a blaze of glory of God Himself in human form to stand on the earth, or not far above it, and award the faithful eternal life in their bodies here on the earth—but bodies made perfect, the earth become Eden again. As the years and centuries went by, this event kept being postponed and the outlines of what it would be like grew hazier; however, by that time the rival religions were extinct.

Yet the abhorrence of most people for this essentially non-Hellenistic religion was so great that by the beginning of the fourth century only five or at most ten percent of the population were Christian. However, the Christians were concentrated in the cities and in the army, and they were organized. Diocletian, the great

Emperor who at the end of the disastrous third century effected a reorganization and centralization of imperial power that staved off collapse for two hundred years, was persuaded reluctantly that all his efforts would be for nothing if the Christians were left free with their empire inside the Empire. So he and his successor Galerius tried to smash them. The persecution was more vigorous than any preceding one. But by that time it was far too late. Galerius admitted defeat and granted toleration.

Less than a quarter of a century later, in the year 325, Constantine the Great extended the toleration by removing all civil disabilities from Christians. Shortly afterwards he made Christianity the official religion of the Roman Empire. Probably he hoped thereby to make available for imperial defense the energetic talents that had proved to be concentrated within the Christian fold. Constantine himself received baptism on his deathbed. (It was the prudent custom to postpone baptism—which washed away all previously committed sins—to the last possible moment.)

## Orthodoxy and Heresy

In the time of Jesus and Paul, Christianity was a simple creed, like Judaism, that anyone could understand. But when it was taken up by Greeks schooled in subtle distinctions and metaphysical notions, it began to get complicated. Since salvation depended on having the right beliefs, questions about the exact nature of God, Christ, and the relation between Them assumed positions of consummate importance. Furthermore, the tight organization of the Church demanded that such questions be answered definitively. There thus arose for the first time in the world the conception of heresy—a Greek word meaning 'choice' or 'opinion' but applied pejoratively by orthodox ( = 'right-belief') Christians to opinions at variance with the Truth.

Jesus, it was agreed, was the God-Man; but what was a God-Man? The followers of Nestorius held that Jesus was really of two natures, human and divine, in two persons: the human person was born of Mary and died on the cross, but the divine person was eternal. The Monophysites (One-nature-ites) to the contrary said that Jesus had only the divine nature, in one person. A consequence of this would have been that He had not really died on the cross. Both these views were heretical. Orthodoxy consisted in holding that Jesus combined two natures, one divine the other human, but in only one person.

The problems presented by the concept of one God were even more difficult. The Scriptures seemed to make it clear that there was exactly one God, but were also interpreted as attributing divinity to the Father, to His Son Jesus Christ, and to the Holy Spirit. If They were conceived as mere manifestations or aspects of one person, as the Sabellians taught, difficulties arose as to the meaning and significance of the divine entrance into the world, the Incarnation. If the Person were made too distinct, though, the result would have been to give up the unity of God.

These were not issues merely debated by a few theologians in their seminaries. The world was distracted by riots and massacres over these issues—events of the largest scale. Constantine made Christianity the established religion at a time when a conflict approaching the dimensions of a civil war was taking place over the question of the Son's relationship to the Father. Athanasius, Bishop of Alexandria, headed the party which held that the Trinity consisted of three Persons in one Substance—the Son was "consubstantial" (*homoousios* in Greek) with the Father and just as eternal. His rival Arius, taking the scriptural phrase "only begotten Son" literally, taught that the Son was created by the Father and was "of similar substance" (*homoiousios*).

One of Constantine's first acts as Emperor was to try to cure this dissension. The custom had grown of settling controversies within the Church by calling councils of bishops (who at the time were elected by popular vote). Constantine summoned a general council to meet at Nicaea, a town near his new capital city of Constantinople. Though unbaptized, he presided in person. Arius and Athanasius were both heard; the vote went in favor of Athanasius, whose position thereby became orthodoxy. This council drew up a creed defining the essentials of the faith. On the Father-Son question the formula was "Jesus Christ, only begotten Son of God, born of the Father before all the ages." Nevertheless, the Arian heresy raged for another half century—being supported by most of the emperors, including Constantine—until Theodosius the Great (Emperor 378–395).

## Gnosticism and Manichaeism

As early as the second century several heresies arose that have been lumped together under the label of Gnosticism, from a Greek word for knowledge. The common bond of these sects was the claim to a special esoteric knowledge of the supernatural that was not to be divulged to the rabble. Gnostics followed or rather exaggerated Neoplatonism in identifying the soul and everything spiritual with good, and identifying the body and matter with evil. Some went so far as to reveal that Yahweh—whose real name according to them was Ialdabaoth—who created the material world, was really the devil disguised as God; the serpent in the Garden of Eden was a messenger from the true God trying to warn Adam and Eve—who, having souls, were not wholly bad—against the impostor. The Gnostics recommended extreme ascetic practices, including abstention from all sexual activity, in order to free the soul from bodily trammels and indeed to eliminate bodies altogether.

In the second century an Iranian named Mani founded a new religion from Gnostic-Christian elements combined with the fundamental dualism of light/dark, good/bad, which for ages had been the basis of the Iranian worldview. Mani, like Jesus, was crucified, but he was not resurrected. Nevertheless, his teachings spread rapidly throughout the Mediterranean world as well as to China in the east. The first great Christian philosopher, St. Augustine (354–430; see Chapter 26), was for 13 years a Manichaean.

## Early Christianity and Philosophy

Jesus was not a philosopher, nor were His disciples, nor was St. Paul—who warned the faithful to "beware lest any man spoil you through philosophy and vain deceit." Christianity was a worldview and a way of life based on revealed truth. Believers did not worry about whether it was reasonable or not, if indeed the question occurred to them.

But when Christians attempted to convert more educated people, it became necessary to argue. However, not all persuasion is based on rational argument; indeed, some of the apologists (as those who tried to justify Christianity to the pagans are known) frankly exhorted their hearers to abandon the entire Greek heritage as heathenish. Most notable of these was Tertullian (*ca* 160–230), famous for his scornful question "What has Jerusalem to do with Athens?" and his defiant paradox "I believe because it is absurd." Subtler apologists appropriated the weapons of the Epicureans against pagan religion and the arguments of Skepticism against philosophy—leaving the field clear, they hoped, for faith.

However, the success of the new religion in attracting Hellenistic converts necessarily led to the Hellenizing of the creed to a certain extent. The process is apparent very early, in the fourth Gospel, attributed to St. John, the first sentence of which is "In the beginning was the *logos*, and the *logos* was with God, and the *logos* was God." The influence of Greek philosophy is apparent throughout this Gospel, the most popular of the four in the formative years. The greatest apologist of the third century, Origen, had been a classmate of Plotinus in the Neoplatonic school of Ammonius Saccas in Alexandria. The Nicene Creed strives to define the Holy Trinity in terms of the Aristotelian category of Substance. Theology is in fact not only a Greek word but an enterprise wholly Greek in origin.

# 26

## St. Augustine

HE WAS A BRAVE man, they say, who first ate an oyster. It took extraordinary qualities, too, to be the first to write an autobiography. The honor for this innovation belongs, it seems, to Aurelius Augustinus (354–430). The story of his life, the *Confessions*, is as long as Plato's *Republic*. As its title suggests, it was written as a record of the grievous sins committed by the author and forgiven by God.

> I will now call to mind my past foulness, and the carnal corruptions of my soul: not because I love them, but that I may love Thee, O my God. For love of Thy love I do it; reviewing my most wicked ways in the very bitterness of my remembrance, that Thou mayest grow sweet unto me; (Thou sweetness never failing, Thou blissful and assured sweetness); and gathering me again out of that my dissipation, wherein I was torn piecemeal, while turned from Thee, the One Good, I lost myself among a multiplicity of things. For I even burnt in my youth heretofore, to be satiated in things below; and I dared to grow wild again, with these various and shadowy loves: my beauty consumed away, and I stank in Thine eyes.[1]

The Saint's account goes on and on like this. In intervals we learn that he was born in 354 in Tagaste, a small town of what is now Tunisia. His father, whom he detested, was a pagan; his mother, upon whom he doted (and vice versa), was the Christian saint Monica. Augustine was a bright boy, and his despised father, though poor, saw to it that he got the best education available in that part of the world. This required that at the age of 17 he should go to Carthage, which since its rebuilding under Augustus had again become the greatest city of North Africa. There Augustine fell in love, or, as he put it

> To Carthage I came, where there sang all around me in my ears a caldron of unholy loves ... I defiled the spring of friendship with the filth of concupiscence, and I beclouded its brightness with the hell of lustfulness.[2]

His girl friend, whose name Augustine does not record, stayed by him for twelve years, until he sent her away in preparation for marriage to a lady of whom his mother approved. The marriage was delayed and Augustine took up with another girl. In the end there was no marriage; he became a priest and took the vow of celibacy.

While in Carthage as a student, and later as a teacher of rhetoric, Augustine disappointed his mother yet more grievously by becoming a Manichaean. The explanation the Manichaeans offered for why there is evil in the world seemed the most reasonable of those he had heard. However, he discovered that their teachings about astronomy, which members of the sect were expected to accept as solemn revelations, were demonstrably in error; even the greatest Manichaean intellectuals turned out to be men of no profound learning. So when he went to Rome in 383, he soon found himelf attracted to the tenets of Skepticism.

The odyssey was nearly over. After a year in Rome he accepted an invitation to teach rhetoric in Milan, at that time capital of the western Roman Empire, whose bishop was the great St.Ambrose (339–397). Ambrose befriended Augustine; his mother St. Monica came over from Africa; in three years his conversion to Catholic Christianity was accomplished. St. Ambrose himself baptized him on Easter Sunday 387 and composed a thanksgiving hymn in honor of the occasion. Four years later Augustine abandoned the teaching of rhetoric, entered the priesthood, and returned to his home town to establish a monastery. With some reluctance he was induced to become bishop of the nearby city of Hippo in 395. He retained this office for the remaining 35 years of his life, dying at age 86 in the midst of a siege by the Vandals.

St. Ambrose knew the value of Augustine when he rejoiced so greatly at his conversion. Augustine wrote, or rather dictated, more than ten times as many pages as Aristotle did. And this vast literary output was only part of his astounding activity as administrator, teacher, propagandist, and defender of orthodoxy against all manner of heretics. More than any other single man after St. Paul, Augustine defined Catholic Christianity for a thousand years. Not until St. Thomas Aquinas in the thirteenth century, did another teacher of such authority arise.

## Was Augustine a Philosopher?

No one today is a Heraclitean, Parmenidean, or Empedoclean in any but a metaphorical sense. If there are Platonists, Epicureans, and Aristotelians around they are learned persons, few if any of whom would subscribe to the doctrines associated with the label without modification.

In contrast there are at this time millions who accept the worldview of St. Augustine. To hear it expounded one need only turn on the radio or TV to the gospel channel or attend a storefront church service. Sermons can be and no doubt are plagiarized directly from his writings. Few politicians can afford to be deemed hostile to his teachings.

Nor is that the limit of his influence. Puritanism and the division of people into good guys and bad guys, while not unknown in pagan Greece, were never prominent in Greek or Hellenistic thought. As leading principles of a world outlook they were importations from Judaism. Despite their emphasis in early Christian thought, they were not especially prominent in the fourth century. Origen had taught that the punishments of hell-fire were only corrective and temporary; even

Satan would go to heaven in the end. The Nicene Creed made no mention of hell. In Augustine's time Pelagius, a cheerful monk from Wales, was persuading Christians that good behavior was a guarantee of heaven after death and—in agreement with Origen—that hell would be closed down after it had done its work of convincing sinners of the error of their ways. Augustine set himself firmly and successfully against this trend. He vindicated the eternity of hell and the justice of everlasting punishment for the souls of babies who had died before being baptized.

So Augustine had a definite worldview, and one of the most influential in history. But was he a philosopher? If we go by the definition adopted in this book, a worldview is not enough; to be philosophical it must be defended by an appeal to reason, as distinguished from authority or tradition. Augustine's thought does not in general meet this requirement. His great work *The City of God* is, to be sure, a reasoned defense of Christianity against pagan attacks. However, the objections considered are mostly to the effect that Christianity is pernicious, not that it is false. Thus he does not find it necessary to present a rational vindication of Christian *belief*, much less of belief in a god. Similarly in his defenses of Catholicism against heretics he deems it sufficient to argue that his position is the only one compatible with the texts that Catholics and heretics alike acknowledge as divinely inspired.

Augustine may indeed be said to have been nonphilosophical on principle. "Except ye believe, ye shall not understand"—a mistranslation, as it happens, of *Isaiah* 7, 9—was a text on which the Saint leaned heavily. He held that ever since Adam's fall human nature has been so corrupt that by itself it is capable of nothing good; in particular, the reasoning faculty is not to be trusted on its own. Reason is reliable only if the reasoner is a recipient of divine grace. But you could not have divine grace and not believe. Therefore, the questioning of the fundamentals of Christian belief is proof of the questioner's depravity and consequent worthlessness of his or her reasoning powers. It would be both useless and pointless to argue.

It seems appropriate to call Augustine's view an "insulated theory"—one which implies that nonacceptance of itself must be due to defective character, rational incompetence, or prejudicial motivation on the part of the objector. Insulated theories are very common in religion, but they also crop up in purportedly scientific contexts, for examples Marxism and psychoanalysis.

## The Primacy of the Will

If Augustine were reproached for having made his fundamental appeal to authority rather than to human reason, he probably would have replied that making such an appeal implies a wrong conception of human nature. One who appeals to reason is assuming that the human mind is of such a character that good reasons are inherently compelling to it. This Augustine questions. There is not for him any natural harmony between the intellect and its object. The necessity of calling rationality into question follows from the principle at the base of his view of human nature and indeed of God: the principle of the primacy of will.

The meaning of this principle can best be grasped by contrast with an axiom of Greek thought: the primacy of the intellect. The definition of Man as Rational Animal implied that knowledge, or at any rate belief, is the determinant of human action. We aim at goals that we know, or think we know, to be good; what we do is what we know, or think we know, to be effective for attaining those goals. Socrates drew the conclusion that virtue is knowledge—for the only way we can go wrong is by being mistaken either about the desirability of the goals or the effectiveness of the means, and both these mistakes are intellectual errors. Socrates' rigor in drawing the consequences of this conception of action led to paradoxes that Aristotle and the Stoics tried to soften. Yet in the end they did not reject the basic view as stated in Plato's *Protagoras* that "To pursue what one believes to be evil rather than what is good is not in human nature; and when a man is compelled to choose one of two evils, no one will choose the greater when he may have the less."[3]

Augustine made a radical break with this tradition. St. Paul had written "For the good that I would I do not: but the evil which I would not, that I do."[4] Augustine made no attempt to explain away this evident fact of experience. He drew the conclusion that the will, not the intellect, is human essence. Belief does not determine the will; on the contrary the will determines belief. The phrase "will to believe," made famous in our century by William James, comes from the Saint's writings.

But if the will determines the belief, what determines the will? The answer is: nothing does; the will is free. There are good wills and there are bad wills. Good wills are wills that will the good, which in the intellectual sphere is truth. But nothing can make a will good except God's grace. Grace does not compel the will to be good, it supernaturally removes the disabilities of sin which we inherited from Adam. Therefore, there can be no natural way to break into the circle of truth. Philosophy, if it is supposed to be a body of truth built up on natural reason and experience, is impossible. Philosophy must be redefined more narrowly as the enterprise of making a coherent worldview starting from premises divinely revealed. Philosophy is the handmaiden of theology.

We may be inclined to ask why a man who assigned such a subordinate place to reason should have troubled himself to write ten times as much as did Aristotle. In the main, the answer is that Augustine's writings are controversial pieces specifically addressed to refutation of various heresies. This work the bishop regarded as his duty. Concern for souls, his own as well as those of others, demanded authoritative answers to the doubts and authoritative corrections of the errors into which the faithful might be seduced. Augustine's autobiography shows that he had an inquiring mind that could not rest until its perplexities had been stilled. He was at the opposite pole from the type of simple believer who does not see inconsistencies and does not care about them when they are pointed out. Augustine reproved the frivolous man who, when asked what God was doing before the Creation, replied "He was preparing hell for pryers into mysteries." The subordination of intellect to will did not mean for the Saint a lazy acquiescence in whatever beliefs were most pleasant. The will to believe was also the will to inquire.

## God

In God as in man Augustine put will above intellect. God is a great spirit, an immaterial substance. He has the three attributes of infinite power, wisdom, and goodness—but the latter two depend on the first. God knows all things, and indeed the Saint accepts the reality of Platonic or Neoplatonic Ideas as being "contained in the divine intelligence." This guarantees their eternity and immutability, but makes knowledge, like everything else, dependent on the being and power of God. If He ceased to exist, not only would the created world vanish (for He sustains it in existence), but even the eternal exemplars would dissolve: the number seven would go, along with the seven Pleiades. However, this Neoplatonic element in Augustine's thought did not lead him in the direction of pantheism. God is utterly distinct from His creation.

God's goodness is yet more obviously an adjunct of His power. The fate decreed for humanity in the Augustinian system is not what some would regard as exemplifying the highest degree of benevolence, since, for example, the souls of millions are doomed to burn eternally. This feature does not temper the Saint's fervent rhetoric of worshipful praise in the slightest. The reason is that he makes God the source not only of instances of valuable things but of value itself: as triangles are triangular because the Platonic Idea of Triangle is in the divine intellect, so good things are good because they are willed by God—notwithstanding Plato's objections in the *Euthyphro* to this line of thought. This is not to say that Augustine could maintain disinterested serenity in the face of evil. To the contrary, the problem of evil was the greatest of the perplexities with which he struggled.

## Creation

God created the world, not out of nothing, but out of formless matter, "almost nothing," simultaneously with the beginning of time.

> For where there is no form, no order, nothing whatever comes or passes away; and where this does not occur, there are certainly no days, no alteration of temporal durations.[5]

He did it, as described in *Genesis*, by willing it. And indeed Augustine does not recognize any causation except will.

> The cause of all things, which makes but is not made, is God; but all other causes both make and are made. Such as all created spirits, and especially the rational. Material causes, which may rather be said to be made than to make, are not to be reckoned among efficient causes, because they can only do what the wills of spirits do by them.[6]

By "material causes" the Saint here means bodies acting by impact. Like Plato, Augustine thinks of matter as essentially inert cloddish stuff that can shove other pieces of matter but has no inherent motion or power. When it moves it must be started by immaterial power. However, Augustine's doctrine must be distinguished from Plato's. Plato held that Mind ruled all things for the best. His was a typically Greek notion of action proceeding with a certain necessity from knowledge of the good. When Augustine teaches to the contrary the causation of all things by spirit, he means a will that is purely and simply will: it may be informed or ignorant, good or bad. There is no guarantee that spirits will produce what they ought to, and in fact few of them do—except God; and the goodness of God's actions, as we have noted, is more laid down by definition than inferred from experience.

## Humanity

God created Adam and Eve: the infinite will created a pair of finite willful creatures in His image. Adam and Eve were finite in that they did not know everything and they had but limited power—no power at all to create by direct act of will as God could. But in a way their wills were no more limited than God's: though there are many things people cannot accomplish, there are none they cannot will (or at any rate wish).

Yet human virtue consists in the will being in harmony with the divine will. Adam and Eve, alas, were not thus disposed; almost immediately after their creation they rebelled; that is, they turned their wills from their proper object, God. For this sin they were justly punished by being cast out of Eden. Moreover, their sinfulness infected all their progeny, so that every human will is corrupt and unable to refrain from sin without the gift of divine grace.

God knew from eternity that Adam would sin. He knew of all the sins Adam's descendants would commit. All men and women, being sinful, deserve hell; and all would spend eternity in its flames had God not sent His Son, uniquely without sin, Who by the example of His perfect life could inspire some to turn their wills back to God. That is, to some who were baptized in the name of Jesus, thus being purged of original sin, God would grant the grace not to relapse. These, the elect—through this exercise of divine mercy—would be granted the gift of heaven. Those to whom grace was not granted, the reprobate, would go to hell. God did not grant His grace to the good ones and withhold it from the bad; rather it was the granting of grace that made some good. It was the withholding of grace that left the others in their inherited state of corruption. What then was the basis of this predestination of some to eternal bliss, others to eternal torment? There was none. It was an entirely arbitrary act of God's will.

Evidently there are a number of problems with this system. It may seem monstrously unjust of God to damn His creatures for something they cannot help—and not even to maintain impartiality in doing it. The Saint replies that free will is the greatest of God's gifts (excepting grace), for without it we would be mere zombies of no intrinsic worth at all. The fact that God knows what we are going to do with our free wills does not warrant the conclusion that God is responsible for our misdeeds: for what He knows is what we will do *of free choice*. Our wills, to be sure, are corrupt, for we have inherited the sins of our first parents. Nevertheless, the corruption does not destroy freedom. Our punishment is therefore just. Nor ought we to complain that some of our fellows, by divine grace, are allowed to escape: that is mercy, another good thing.

To the objection that a good God ought to have created nothing at all rather than bring into being souls doomed to eternal torment, Augustine replies in a Neoplatonic way that evil is only nonbeing; there must be a hierarchy of gradations of being between God and nothingness. The more there is in between the better. Even an evil soul is better than a soulless beast or a stone, for what is positive in it is good; all being is good. Everything, even evil, has its place in the harmonious totality. No one would choose to make a meal of Cayenne pepper, but pepper makes its indispensable contribution to the casserole. Furthermore, God shows His power in making good come from evil; to make good come only from good would be too easy.

## Philosophy of History

After the *Confessions*, the work of Augustine most read today is *The City of God*. This enormous book started out to be a defense of Christianity against pagans who claimed that the collapse of the Roman Empire, so awfully manifested in the capture and looting of the very city of Rome by the Goths in 410, was due to the abandonment of the old gods who had made Rome great. Augustine, after easily disposing of such misguided reproaches, proceeds to develop a philosophy or theology of history on a grand scale.

Before Christian times the most widely accepted speculation on cosmic history was the cyclical theory of the Stoics, according to which there are infinite world periods exactly alike and separated by conflagrations. Plato and Empedocles also had affirmed world cycles. Even the thought of the Epicureans was essentially cyclical, inasmuch as they supposed that there are an infinite number of atomic whirls—of which our world is but one—that go through similar processes of development and eventual decay.

To these Augustine opposed a conception new in the Hellenistic world: history is a straight line with a beginning, middle, and end. There can be only one world, for Christ died but once. The beginning is the creation; before that there was nothing but the "nearly nothing," undifferentiated and hence unmoving; even time did not exist. The middle of the world is the incarnation of God in Jesus Christ. The end will be the Last Judgment—the destruction of this world. Heaven and hell will go on forever, but nothing new will happen ever again.

In this world the drama of salvation is being worked out. Here there are only free wills, making their choices of good or evil for which they are to be eternally rewarded or punished. There are "those who wish to live after the flesh, and those who wish to live after the spirit." They are the citizens of the (metaphorical) two cities: the one the City of God, Jerusalem; the other the City of the Earth, Babylon. The Saint sees all history as the interaction, the warfare, between these two cities. In the end the City of God will triumph. In the meantime the Devil has his sway, but that is no reason why the people of the City of God should not strive to thwart him by reforming the institutions of government in accordance with Christian precepts. Augustine advanced the view, soon to become universally held in the West, that the Church is by its nature superior to the State and should therefore rule in all disputed cases. It should also be able to call on the power of the State when needed. Augustine in his capacity as Bishop of Hippo did in fact require the local authorities to aid him in the suppression of heresy. Charlemagne (742–814; see Chapter 27), four hundred years later, based his conception of a Holy Roman Empire on his understanding of the Augustinian political theory.

"The drama of salvation" is a natural phrase to use in describing Augustine's view of history. And indeed some essential ingredients of drama, or rather of melodrama—the good guys and the bad guys—are there. Augustine remained a

Manichee in temperament to the end of his days. Officially, Ambrose converted Augustine to Catholicism; it would be at least a half truth to say instead that Augustine converted the Church to Manichaeism.

Yet in many respects the metaphor of a drama is hardly appropriate. God is the only spectator. He knows the whole script before the curtain goes up. On the other hand, the actors do not know the script; they improvise it ad lib as they go along. In the last scene the sole spectator steps onto the stage to award prizes to the heroes and chastisements to the villains. But it was He, the Spectator, who did all the casting in the first place.

# 27

# The Dark Ages

SEVEN CENTURIES SEPARATE AUGUSTINE and Anselm (1033–1109; see Chapter 28)—a period of almost complete collapse of civilized conditions in Western Europe during which there arose only one philosopher of major stature, John Scotus Erigena (*ca* 810–*ca* 877). However, in the Eastern Empire, which included the Greek homeland, a relatively high level of culture was maintained for a thousand years after Augustine without the emergence of even one first-rate philosopher. This is not surprising; the Greek intellect had turned from philosophy to theology.

## The Division of the Empire

If the pony express were the fastest means of communication, it would be inconvenient to have the capital of the United States located in Portland, Oregon. The city of Rome was in somewhat that position with respect to the Empire. Wealth, population, and defense problems tended to concentrate at the eastern end of the Mediterranean basin. As the city of Rome ceased to have more than sentimental primacy, the emperors moved the seat of administration to the more central position of Milan—Denver as it were. Constantine went all the way: he made his capital in the equivalent of Washington, D.C.—the ancient Greek city of Byzantium, *alias* Constantinople (now Istanbul), on the straits between the Mediterranean and the Black Sea. The emperors found it necessary also to decentralize the government, appointing vice-emperors to rule large regions despite the temptation to rebellion this practice inevitably created. At length, when Theodosius died in 395, the Roman lands were formally divided between his two sons into a Western Empire with its capital at Ravenna and an Eastern Empire ruled from Constantinople.

## Philosophy in the Byzantine Empire

The extent of the Byzantine Empire continually fluctuated, but originally it comprised roughly the old Hellenistic kingdoms of Macedon, Syria, and Egypt. It therefore included the two great centers of learning, Athens and Alexandria. The tradition of learning in the capital of Egypt was strong; even among its Christians were to be found cultivated men such as Clement and Origen. St. Cyril, Bishop at the end of the fourth century, put an end to that. Under his leadership the Christian mob instituted a reign of terror against Jews and pagans. Temples were torn down and libraries burnt. It happened that at this time the school of Neoplatonism was presided over by the most eminent female philosopher of antiquity, Hypatia. She is said to have been graceful, modest, and beautiful. The historian Gibbon describes her fate.

> On a fatal day, in the holy season of Lent, Hypatia was torn from her chariot, stripped naked, dragged to the church, and inhumanly butchered by the hands of Peter the Reader and a troop of savage and merciless fanatics: her flesh was scraped from her bones with sharp oyster shells, and her quivering limbs were delivered to the flames.[1]

This event in 415 may be taken as marking the effective end of philosophy in Alexandria, although there is some reason to suspect the presence there of a Neoplatonist underground as late as 500.

The end of the schools of Athens was less violent. Despite official discouragement, the Academy was still functioning in the early sixth century; it might almost have been said to be flourishing. The dean of its distinguished faculty was Simplicius, the great commentator on Aristotle, to whose careful scholarship we owe thanks for much of what we know of the early history of philosophy. The schools were closed by edict of the Emperor Justinian the Great in 529. Legal forms were observed: it was held that the schools had no standing in law, being chartered as corporations dedicated to the service of the Muses, who were nonexistent. The professors fled to the court of the Shah of Iran. Fourteen years later the Shah made a clause in a treaty with Justinian requiring the Emperor to grant the philosophers safe conduct to return to Athens. Simplicius and others did so, but the schools did not reopen.

Justinian founded a sort of university in his capital, but it produced no original thinkers. The Byzantine intellect concerned itself almost exclusively with theological dispute of the subtlest sort, conducted according to the patterns for rational discourse that had been worked out in Athens, but dealing with a curious subject matter and deriving its premises from revelation. Plato was venerated as having anticipated Christianity in some respects. Aristotle continued to be read and copied by a few antiquarians. But the year 529 marked the end of philosophizing in the nation where it had begun eleven centuries earlier.

## Philosophy in the West

It would hardly be fair to speak of a decline in philosophy in the Western Empire, for as we have seen Greek philosophy and science never really took root in Rome. Greek books were in general not translated into Latin, as the few learned persons interested in the matters of which they treated could read the originals. In consequence, when the Empire was split and knowledge of the Greek language became rare in the West—after the translation of the Holy Scriptures by St. Jerome [*ca* 374–419 (or 420)], it was no longer deemed necessary to keep up instruction in it—hardly any scientific or philosophical works were available in Latin. There existed, curiously, a translation of Plato's fantastic *Timaeus* and some of the logical works of Aristotle, with an introduction to the *Categories* by the Neoplatonist Porphyry. These, together with some dialogues by Cicero and the essays of Seneca, were what the West was cut adrift with. Lucretius was not read, unless surreptitiously; his poem survived to modern times in a single manuscript copy.

It is usual to think of the Dark Ages as the period when the Church, especially the monasteries, managed to keep the lamp of knowledge flickering through the long night of German barbarism. There is some truth in this picture, but not much. The Teutonic takeover of the Empire was on the whole gradual and even peaceful: largely a matter of Germans, long employed as hireling troops in the so-called Roman armies, rising to be officers and at length to policy positions in the imperial administration. The process culminated in the seizure of the imperial throne itself by Odovakar in 476, an event taken as the Fall of the Roman Empire but not regarded at the time as extraordinarily noteworthy. Some Teutonic bands were destructive and "barbarous"; the Vandals did not get their reputation for nothing. Nevertheless, the great disorganization and depopulation of western Europe occurred not in the fifth century, the time of the so-called barbarian invasions, but in the sixth. Plague was a principal cause.

The invaders, moreover, were Christians (though often heretical) and respected Church property. It was no illiterate beer-swilling blond beast but Pope St. Gregory the Great (*ca* 540–604) who at the end of the sixth century commanded the destruction of the greatest public library remaining in Rome. Gregory believed that the triumph of the Church could never be complete and secure until all relics of paganism had been cut away. And that meant everything connected with Greece: the whole heritage of inquiry. Gregory grudgingly countenanced literacy in the Latin tongue because it was indispensable to the ritual and administration of the church; but he did his best to stamp out all remnants of elegance and of love of literature as such. He succeeded.

## Monasteries

In Christianity as in other religions certain of the faithful felt that the cultivation of holiness required a life apart from the world. In Egypt especially there were many hermits, seeking to cultivate the spirit by mortifying the flesh, often in ingenious ways. St. Simeon Stylites is said to have existed for 30 years atop a pillar from which he never descended. The genius of Christianity for communal forms of organization discouraged the solitary life, however, even for exclusively religious purposes. Devotees tended to live in communities. But as long as each dweller in a religious colony was able to pursue his devotions as he saw fit, idleness, dissension, anarchy, and the scandalization of the secular populace were inevitable.

The sixth century saw the solution of these problems through the rise of monasteries, wherein the religious life was organized and disciplined. St. Benedict (*ca* 480–*ca* 547) founded at Monte Cassino the abbey whose rules were held as a model to subsequent monkish orders. The most important rule required the monks to do useful work. One kind of approved work was the production of books.

The library of Monte Cassino became justly celebrated. Nevertheless, monkish industry in bookmaking was a principal cause of destruction of ancient learning. Most of the books produced were lives of saints and other devotional works. Since trade with Egypt had ceased, and in consequence papyrus was unobtainable, writing had to be done on parchment—sheepskin—which was expensive. It was less costly to obtain old books, scrape the ink off the pages, and recycle them. So the principal role of monasteries in preserving ancient learning, at first, was this: they collected more old books than they needed and kept them in relatively safe places. Subsequently, when the value of these texts came again to be appreciated, they were to be found in the storerooms.

## Cassiodorus and Boethius

A large share of the credit for the preservation of learning must go to two men who, though of exemplary piety, did not achieve sainthood. Both, as it happened, were high officials in the administration of the Gothic king Dietrich or Theodoric, who in 489 defeated Odovakar and made himself Emperor of the West. Cassiodorus (*ca* 480–575) retired from the imperial civil service at the age of 50. A wealthy man, he founded a monastery on his private estate. Under his direction the monks read and copied the Latin classics.

Boethius (*ca* 475–525) was for a time Theodoric's prime minister, but having fallen under suspicion of treason he was imprisoned and put to death. While in prison he wrote *The Consolation of Philosophy*, a work which has had the distinction of being translated into Anglo-Saxon by King Alfred the Great and into English both by Chaucer and by Queen Elizabeth I. A dialogue in mixed prose and verse, this charming and noble work is essentially Stoic and Neoplatonic in its outlook. "Philosophy," a beautiful lady, convinces Boethius that all that exists is good, reality being a hierarchy of goods with God at the apex.

Boethius had planned to translate all the works of Plato and Aristotle into Latin and to write commentaries on them. But at his untimely death he had completed the translation only of the logical works, together with a commentary not directly on them but on Porphyry the Neoplatonist's commentary. This was an enormously influential work in that it set the main problem of pure philosophy for the middle ages, the Problem of Universals.

## The Moslem Conquests

Toward the end of the sixth century it might have looked as if the worst was over for Christendom. The upsets incident to the Teutonic takeover were quietening, and the Catholic Church—described by Thomas Hobbes as "the ghost of the deceased Roman Empire, sitting crowned upon the grave thereof"—was proceeding efficiently and successfully with the work of Christianizing even the most ferocious barbarians, such as the Saxon conquerors of England. The armies of Justinian the Great (483–565) had reimposed 'Roman' rule in Italy and North Africa. Recovery seemed possible or even probable.

Then, in the first half of the seventh century, a new prophet arose in Arabia. With astounding suddenness the Bedouin followers of the new religion of Islam ("Surrender") founded by Mohammed seized the Syrian and Egyptian provinces of the Byzantine Empire. These conquests were not regarded as disasters nor resisted fanatically by the local populations, who favored heresies persecuted by the imperial authorities and furthermore found Moslem taxation less ruinous than Christian. All of North Africa, at the time probably more populous than Europe, was under Moslem rule by the end of the century. The armies of the Caliph crossed the Straits of Gibraltar in 711; in a few years all Spain had fallen except for the northeast corner. Then they poured across the Pyrenees into France, advancing to the Loire Valley. There, near Tours, in 732, 100 years after the death of the Prophet, Charles Martel ("The Hammer") and his Frankish army saved what was left of Christendom. At about the same time the Byzantines at the opposite end of the Mediterranean fought off an attack by the revived and Moslemized Iranian Empire. These victories were won because the Franks and the Greeks possessed a new weapon, the eighth-century equivalent of the tank: the heavily armed and armored cavalryman riding an armored horse. The key to this terrifying combination was the invention of the stirrup. (This obvious—to hindsight—device was unknown to the horsemen of ancient times. They had to expend so much energy and skill in simply staying on their mounts that they had little left for fighting, and carrying anything heavy was out of the question.) Huge specially bred and fed horses were used to carry the enormous weights. All these—the horses, their fodder, the armor—were expensive. Charles Martel found it necessary to impose taxes on Church lands to raise the money to pay for them. As a result Charles found himself excommunicated and damned by the Church he had saved.

After Tours, Christendom was no longer in danger of extinction. More than half of it, however, was gone forever; and it took seven hundred years to drive the Moslems back past Gibraltar. For centuries "free" Europe was a sort of colonial dependency of Islam. The Moslem countries looked on Europe mainly as a source of slaves, who were to be bought from Jews and Vikings.

## The Papacy

One result of the Moslem conquests was the rise of the Bishop of Rome, the Pope, to supremacy in the Church. Other bishops, indeed even parish priests, were originally called Popes—*Papa* in Latin, from the Greek word for "Daddy"—and although the Bishop of Rome was always the most important clergyman in Western Europe, he had his equals in the great sees of Constantinople, Antioch, and Alexandria. The Moslem conquest eliminated two of these rivals, while at Constantinople both clerical and lay officials had their hands full just surviving. The Bishop of Rome thus succeeded to supreme power, not only in the Church but as temporal ruler of central Italy and, at least sometimes, as a super-ruler of all Christian Europe. The Popes had Mohammed to thank for freeing them from lay control, which as the historian Hugh Trevor-Roper has remarked is "the only thing which keeps the clergy within the bounds of sense."

However, papal power did not grow merely by default; as in any fluid situation, authority was acquired by its aggressive assertion. Since at this time popes, like all bishops, were elected by the faithful of the diocese (or at any rate their appointment had to be popularly ratified), it is possible to regard the spread of papal power as a sort of second Roman conquest.

The greatest of the popes in the critical period, the man who can be said to have created the papacy, was St. Gregory, Pope from 590 to 604. In the generation before the Moslem conquests, this energetic man arrogated to himself authority over all the bishops of the West and even some of the East. He simply told the other bishops what to do, and so great was the force of his character that they did it. He was equally imperious to the Gothic kings with whom he had to deal, though he adopted an humbler tone toward the Emperor in Constantinople. The organization of the Church and its rituals, even its music, were put by him into forms which have lasted to this day. It was he who sent the mission that converted the Anglo-Saxons to Christianity. Gregory, as we have already seen, was uncompromising in his hostility to all things smacking of paganism, including ancient learning. His anti-intellectual policy was continued by the popes of the succeeding four centuries.

After the fact came the justification. The scriptural argument for papal supremacy was based on *Matthew* 16, the dramatic chapter in which Peter, after some coaxing, is first to proclaim Jesus to be the Messiah.

> 13   When Jesus came into the coasts of Caesarea Philippi, he asked his disciples, saying, Whom do men say that I the Son of man am?
>
> 14   And they said, Some say that thou art John the Baptist: some, Elias; and others, Jeremias, or one of the prophets.
>
> 15   He saith unto them, But whom say ye that I am?
>
> 16   And Simon Peter answered and said, Thou art the Christ, the Son of the living God.
>
> 17   And Jesus answered and said unto him, Blessed art thou, Simon Bar-jona: for flesh and blood hath not revealed it unto thee, but my Father which is in heaven.
>
> 18   And I say also unto thee, That thou art Peter, and upon this rock [*petra* in Greek] I will build my church; and the gates of hell shall not prevail against it.
>
> 19   And I will give unto thee the keys of the kingdom of heaven: and whatsoever thou shalt bind on earth shall be bound in heaven: and whatsoever thou shalt loose on earth shall be loosed in heaven.
>
> 20   Then charged he his disciples that they should tell no man that he was Jesus the Christ.

There is no mention in the Scriptures of any visit by Peter to Rome—not even in St. Paul's long Letter to the Romans, which concludes with greetings to 27 Christians of Rome by name. Nevertheless the tradition was fostered that St. Peter went to Rome, founded the Church there, suffered death by crucifixion (upside down), and was buried under the site of the present Basilica of St. Peter—where indeed his bones are said to have been discovered within the present century. He was thus the first Bishop of Rome, the first Pope, and the authority conferred upon him by Jesus descended to his successors.

The second prop of papal authority, this one for his sovereign temporal power, was the Donation of Constantine. This document purported to be the deed of gift uttered by Constantine the Great when he removed his capital to Constantinople, bequeathing the city of Rome and all of his Western dominions to Pope Sylvester and his successors out of gratitude for his miraculous cure from leprosy. During the Renaissance, Lorenzo Valla proved this document to be an eighth-century forgery; the reigning Pope showed historic aplomb in appointing Valla to be his personal secretary. In earlier times, however, the more brutal and anarchic actual conditions were, the greater was the passion for legalism—so that the Donation had been of the greatest importance. In a way, something like it had an existence in fact. Pepin, King of the Franks (714?–768), who at that time had some claim to sovereignty in Italy, had formally resigned it to the Pope in return for a declaration of the legitimacy of his royal title.

## The Holy Roman Empire

Charles the Great or Charlemagne (*ca* 688–741), son of Pepin and grandson of Charles Martel, subjugated nearly all of Western Christendom on the European continent. In defeating the Saxon tribes of northern Germany he accomplished a feat that not even the Roman armies at the height of their power had been able to do. He then gave the Saxons the choice between being baptized and being massacred. They chose the former.

Charlemagne shared the medieval respect for legalism, and like the popes would not be content with merely de facto power. Now in legal theory the Roman Empire had never come to an end. No one in the West any longer claimed the title of Emperor, but that meant that de jure imperial authority reverted to the Emperor in Constantinople. Happily for Charlemagne, at the beginning of the ninth century the imperial throne was occupied by a woman, the Emperor (so she styled herself—not Empress) Irene. Holding that since it was absurd in law as in grammar for a female to be an Emperor, the throne was vacant, and Charlemagne induced the Pope to crown him. He bestowed upon himself a title, however, with an addition intended to be significant: *Holy* Roman Emperor. Christendom, in his intention, was to be a unity in which Church and State were to lend mutual support to each other; St. Augustine's City of God was to encompass all Europe.

Pious he was, but piety to Charlemagne was far from meaning submission to priests. On the contrary, he considered himself more competent than they to advance the Christian cause. In the intellectual sphere his direction of affairs was noteworthy. He castigated the clergy for their hostility toward learning. He set up schools and procured teachers such as the celebrated Alcuin from such far-off places as York in England. With a great part of Europe more or less unified and peaceful under a patron of learning, there occurred a flowering of the arts known as the Carolingian Renaissance.

Its span was brief. Charlemagne's son, Louis the Pious, let himself be dominated by priests—hence his designation. In the next generation France broke free of the Empire. Thereafter until 1808 there was in theory a Holy Roman Emperor. He was in practice a German prince, usually a Hapsburg, with enough power to work mischief in Germany and Italy, but not enough to impose unity and peace.

## The British Isles

From the seventh century on into the ninth England, settled down after the Saxon invasions and not yet ravished by the Dane, was relatively peaceful and prosperous. Learning flourished there as nowhere else in Europe. The Venerable Bede (673–735), a monk of Jarrow in Yorkshire, was the most celebrated scholar of the age. His 40 books were mainly on theology and history, but he wrote also a book *On the Nature of Things* in which he expounded as much of science as had survived in the western world. He knew Greek and Hebrew. Alcuin (735–804; his name in English was Ealhwine), whom Charlemagne brought to France to enlighten his court, was educated in the monasteries around York which in effect formed a university. Indeed the Carolingian Renaissance was in large part an exportation from England to the continent.

Ireland had an older tradition, for it had been converted to Christianity in the fifth century and after that time had not succumbed to heathen invaders. Little can now be learned about the great period of Irish monasteries, since they were utterly destroyed by the Vikings in the tenth century. Yet the level of culture in Ireland in the ninth century must have been high, for it produced the greatest (and only) philosopher of the age.

## John Scotus Erigena

John Scotus Erigena was born about 810 and died after 877. His name means "John the Scot Born in Ireland." But we must remember that "at this time the Scots were known as the Irish and the Irish were called Scotsmen," as the authors of *1066 and All That* summarize the situation. About 845 he arrived at the court of Charles the Bald, grandson of Charlemagne and King of France. This monarch had received as a gift from the Eastern Emperor a book that no one in his kingdom could read, for it was written in Greek. John made his reputation by translating it; it became a medieval best seller.

The work in question was *On the Divine Names*, supposed to have been written by St. Dionysius the Areopagite, an Athenian converted to Christianity by St. Paul. It could not have been written by that man—being in fact a piece of Neoplatonic theosophy—but because of its ascription to St. Paul's disciple, it had to be regarded as orthodox Christianity. This circumstance introduced grave complications into medieval theology.

John was profoundly influenced by the writer (referred to now as "Pseudo-Dionysius") he had translated, whose conception of God was subtle and far removed from common picture thinking. God is indescribable, he held. Words such as good, wise, even real, as we use and understand them, mislead when we try to apply them to God. If by wise we mean possessing the qualities that count as wisdom among men, then God is not wise; He is not the possessor of a set of complex and painfully acquired properties such that the upshots of His ruminations are expedient. Nevertheless, it would be shocking to say "God is not wise," since that would be misunderstood as asserting that He is foolish; we should say instead that God is super-wise. What is super-wisdom? We don't know. And so for the other attributes: God is super-good, super-powerful, and super-real.

The relation of God to the world is set out in John's most famous book, *On the Divisions of Nature*. There are four divisions, based on the two distinctions creative/uncreative and created/uncreated. That which creates and is not created is, obviously, God. That which creates and is created is the assemblage of (Neo)Platonic Ideas. Those things which are created but do not create are the sensible things of our everyday world. The last division, that which neither creates nor is created, is God again, but now considered as goal of return rather than source of being.

This scheme is an elegant presentation of the Neoplatonic doctrines of emanation and of the soul's return to its source. As such it denies any absolute distinction between creator and creature, hence it is heretical. Worse still, the return of creatures to God in the fourth division was held by John to be all-encompassing, so that his doctrine was incompatible with the eternity of hell. John, in his simple Irish (or Scotch) way, supposed that he was giving a philosophical exposition of what reason shows to be necessarily entailed by the conception of an all-powerful God Who is the source of all being—as faith teaches He is. "Authority is the source of knowledge," he declared, "but our own reason remains the norm by which all authority must be judged." As far as we know, John did not get into serious trouble in his lifetime. In the eleventh century, however, his doctrines were declared heretical and his books were burnt.

## The Darkest Dark Ages

The Greeks and Phoenicians had been great sailors, but their conquerors the Romans were not. Seamanship and naval architecture went into a thousand years of decline after the defeat of Carthage. Then suddenly there appeared, in the time of Charlemagne, the long ship of the Norsemen—the fastest, most maneuverable, most seaworthy craft ever built of wood. The heathens of Denmark and the Scandinavian peninsula found it easy and exciting to make their living by sea raids on coastal towns, especially in England and Ireland, where undefended monasteries and churches were full of treasure. In the century of John Scotus and the next, the Vikings pillaged everywhere in Europe—not only the Atlantic seacoasts but throughout the Mediterranean as far as Constantinople itself, which they besieged; up the Seine to Paris and on other rivers to other cities; and at last, overland (though still fighting as ship's companies) into the hearts of Britain in the west and Russia in the east. It was the fury of the Norseman—looting everything lootable and transporting such of the population as escaped massacre to be sold as slaves to the Arabs—that brought Europe to the lowest depth it had known in historical times.

# 28

# Early Scholastic Philosophy

BY THE YEAR 1000 the worst was over. Many of the Viking sea raiders had settled down in the ravaged territories of England, Ireland, Normandy, Sicily, and Russia—as well as in Iceland and Greenland, which were not ravaged only because no one had been there to be ravaged. They sent back to Scandinavia for their wives and kinfolk, let themselves be converted to Christianity, and earned honest livings. In Norway itself King Olaf Trygvesson, successor to Haakon the Bad, was knocking Christianity into Viking skulls. Eventually his subjects threw him into the sea; but his cousin Olaf Haraldson finished the business and thereby achieved sainthood, a remarkable honor for a medieval Norwegian.

The city of Rome was by no means exempt from the degradation and depravity of the tenth century. Popes were still popularly elected, that is to say appointed by the local power elite, with often strange and deplorable results. The churchly structure tended to rely for economic support on simony, as ecclesiastical graft is called.

This distressing situation was corrected. Widespread disgust with the papacy found an effective center of reform in the new and strictly ruled abbey of Cluny in France, and support from those German princes who styled themselves Holy Roman Emperors. There was an increase in the power of the Empire at this time, both relatively because of disasters on the periphery of Europe and absolutely in consequence of a rise in the population of Germany, which occurred when the invention of the iron plough suddenly increased agricultural productivity. The emperors were able to dictate the selection of popes. Later in the eleventh century the College of Cardinals was created and the election of popes regularized. Within the Church simony was greatly reduced. By forbidding the marriage of priests the popes strengthened the churchly class by unifying it, making it more economical to support, and heightening the awe in which lay people held it as a class set apart.

In 999 a monk named Gerbert assumed the papacy and ruled for four years as Pope Sylvester II. Gerbert was the most learned man of his time, suspected of being a magician because he knew mathematics beyond elementary arithmetic. He was influential in introducing the so-called Arabic numerals into Christendom. His election marked the reversal of the anti-intellectual policy of the Church. From Sylvester II until the Galileo case, the Catholic Church on the whole encouraged and patronized learning and science as long as they presented no direct threat to dogma and power.

## Scholastic Philosophy

From the fall of Rome to the time of the Renaissance, schooling, such as it was, was a monopoly of the Church and largely restricted to clergymen. The philosophy developed and taught in association with the schools of the Catholic Church is referred to as "scholastic." This philosophy, which is still actively taught today, is not a single definite body of doctrine. Much variety, even irreconcilable opposition, exists among the teachings of such men as Thomas Aquinas, Duns Scotus (1266?–1308) and William of Ockham (*ca* 1285–*ca* 1349). Nevertheless, these teachings have enough in common besides their origin to justify a common name.

The nature of scholastic philosophy flows mainly from the circumstance that every scholastic philosopher was a theologian first, a philosopher second. Christian theology takes as its first principles revealed truth: the statements of the Bible and such others, for example the pronouncements of popes, as are deemed authoritative. The aim of theology is to elucidate these truths, to explore their implications and their relations to each other—in a word to systematize them. To reject a revealed truth is not theologically possible. However, the theologian may find that the meaning of some revelation is rather different from what was previously supposed to be its intent. Thus it is revealed in Scripture, hence certainly true, that God made the first man out of dust. But the theologian may determine that making from dust, in this passage, really amounts to "allowing organic evolution to proceed," rather than anything literally like what happens when sculptors model clay figures. The theologian deals with sacred documents somewhat as the lawyer or judge deals with the constitution and statutes.

Thus there are limitations on what the theologian can do when he turns to philosophy. No speculation is allowable that casts doubt on the truth of revelation. Philosophy may be permitted to show only that reason confirms the revealed truths, or leads up to them, or is incapable of aspiring to approach them.

With the required conclusions given in advance—like answers in the back of the book (however, the back of the book was to be read before attempting the problems)—it was not to be expected that philosophy would be bold and original. While in every age there is some range of orthodoxy from which the philosopher deviates at his own peril, in the middle ages this range was more confined than ever before. As time went on, penalties for error grew more severe. What drew a mild rebuke in the eleventh century might get the author roasted in the fifteenth.

"Philosophy is the handmaiden of theology." This famous summation was the utterance of Peter Damian (1007–1072), Cardinal and Saint, who had a Tertullianist contempt for the servant girl. God's power, he held, was not to be limited by Aristotle's law of noncontradiction: God could make the past not to have been or make a statement and its negation both true, should He see fit. Other scholastic philosophers were not so extreme; but until William of Ockham none rejected the picture of Theology as Queen of the Sciences, with Philosophy at her beck and call.

Scholastic philosophy was largely concerned with three interrelated subjects: the faith-reason controversy, natural theology, and the problem of universals.

We have seen how St. Augustine held that faith is prior to reason even to the extent that there is no reason to trust the reasoning of a man without faith. John Scotus, on the other hand, asserted that "although authority is the source of knowledge, our own reason remains the norm by which all authority must be judged."[1] Common opinion agreed with Thomas Aquinas that some truths can be known by the unaided reason, some only by faith, and some—notably the existence of God—can be known both ways; but in any case faith could never be contrary to *true* reason.

Natural theology (the term is not medieval) is the enterprise of demonstrating truths of religion by premises established without appeal to revelation. The various proofs offered of the existence of God are the best known efforts of this discipline. Although they occupy comparatively little space in the writings of the schoolmen, they are of particular interest just because they are, somewhat paradoxically, the least trammeled of medieval philosophical speculations. Since everyone held that God certainly did exist, it was possible to consider the arguments calmly and without rancor. One's orthodoxy did not fall under suspicion just because one rejected the validity of a certain argument for the existence of God, or even denied the possibility of such argumentation. (However, this is no longer the case since the Vatican Council in 1870 decreed it to be an article of faith that God can be known "with certainty with the natural light of human reason.")

## The Problem of Universals

Of purely philosophical problems, almost the only one debated—but that very fiercely—during the middle ages was the problem of Universals. This was bequeathed to the West in the version of Porphyry in his *Introduction to Aristotle's Logic*, as translated by Boethius.

> Whether genera and species are subsistent entities or whether they consist in concepts alone; if subsisting, whether they are material or immaterial and, further, whether they are separate from sensible objects or not.

Otherwise put, the question was: What do universal names name? Do "mammal" and "cat" name entities that have their own reality over and above Garfield, Mehitabel, and all the other particular, individual cats? Or do "mammal" and "cat" name "concepts alone," the ideas in our minds, having no counterparts outside them? If what are named by "cat" and "mammal" have their own reality, are the objects material (*n.b.*: no one took this position) or immaterial? Assuming that there is some objective reality, cathood, of which "cat" is the name, is cathood separate from Garfield, Mehitabel, et cetera, or not?

The doctrine that genera and species are subsistent, immaterial, separate entities is of course the essence of Platonism; that they consist in concepts alone is, roughly, Aristotelianism. However, since the schoolmen had no Plato except *Timaeus*, and until the thirteenth century none of Aristotle's criticisms of Platonism, they had to go through the moves on both sides all over again. Or rather, they worked out with great subtlety a spectrum of positions on which Platonism and Aristotelianism occupy only two points.

Those who took the Platonist side called themselves Realists, by which misleading label they signified belief in the reality of universals outside the mind. The anti-Realists, holding universal terms to be mere names, *nomina*, were referred to as Nominalists. Both positions, in their extremest forms, came upon the scene toward the end of the eleventh century. The subsequent history of the problem was mostly one of projected compromises.

John Scotus Erigena, in the ninth century, may be said to have been (by anticipation) an extreme Realist, inasmuch as that position is integral to Neoplatonism which holds the Platonic Ideas to occupy an intermediate place between God and the sensible world. The Realists of the eleventh century, however, seem to have based their doctrine not on Pseudo-Dionysius so much as on their interpretation of Aristotle's logic. The terms that appear in the syllogism are universal; what knowledge we gain by syllogizing, therefore, is of universals; and if universals do not name real things, we have no knowledge. That is to say, the things in the real world must be capable of being related as the terms in the syllogism are if there is to be any correspondence between our reasoning and what we reason about. This is at bottom the same thought that made Aristotle reluctant to abandon Platonism altogether and led him to declare essences to be substances.

The extremest Nominalism was taught by Roscelin (*ca* 1045–1120), of whom little is known. He held that outside the mind nothing exists except individual things; universals are mere "vocal winds" (*flatus vocis*).

It may not be clear on its face why the problem of universals should have inspired so much intellectual effort and aroused so much emotion as it did throughout the middle ages. But to read Plato may provide a short answer to the question: the ability to get excited about the problem of universals is a test of philosophical capability and temperament. This dry-seeming question impinges on some sensitive spots. Platonic Realists are apt to think of the universal terms as denominating the rational structure of the world, the *Logos*. If nothing is real but the individuals, if kinds and connections are only human inventions, if as the arch-Nominalist David Hume (1711–1776; see Chapter 39) was to declare "things are entirely loose and separate," then reasoning must be ultimately a delusion. Nominalists on the other hand like to think of themselves as tough-minded devotees of the facts who look down on the so-called Realists as fuzzy-minded believers in occult entities, in confusion spawned by mistaken views about language.

Among the schoolmen religious motives and considerations operated in the controversy as well. For example Odo of Tournai (*d.* 1113), a Realist, held that humanity is one and the same in all human beings. When a baby is born a new substance does not come into being; all that happens is that the one substance, humanity, has a new property. On this basis Odo could explain away the apparent injustice of saddling the sin of Adam onto each newborn babe, as the dogma of Original Sin demanded.

> In Adam's fall
> We sinned all[2]

is paradoxical; "Through Adam, Humanity was infected with sin" sounds all right.

Nominalism was in some respects theologically risky. We do not have the writings of Roscelin because they were condemned as heretical. Their author had to retract and abjure them on account of the consequence that if only individuals are real, then there are three Gods—the Father, the Son, and the Holy Ghost. "Trinity" would be only a "wind."

Yet Realism too had its dangers. If there is only one substance, Humanity, in all individual men and women, it is hard to see why there is not just one substance,

Animality, in men, giraffes, flies, etcetera—indeed there seems to be no stopping short of collapse into one substance of all things. But that would be Pantheism, another heresy.

Perhaps the most important theological implication of the problem of universals lay in the question whether intellect or will is primary in God. God, it was agreed, creates everything in a supremely good way. But in what does the goodness of creation consist? The Platonic, intellectualist, Realist answer was that the Divine intellect, being aware of the objective good (the universal "goodness"), directs creation accordingly. The Voluntarists, on the other hand, felt that to look at the matter this way was to detract from Divine power: if God *had* to follow a pre-existing pattern of goodness, He was not after all free and all-powerful. These men therefore held that the Divine Will is primary, that is, not subject to the Divine intellect; God is not trammeled by an eternal self-subsistent Logos. But to deny the reality of these intelligible objects was to be a Nominalist. Extreme Voluntarists had to hold that God's creation was entirely arbitrary, as is the goodness of things: if God commanded lying and murder, lying and murder would be good. There were various intermediate positions between these extremes, some of which we shall note later.

## St. Anselm

The greatest of the early schoolmen was Anselm (1033–1109). Born in Aosta in northwestern Italy, he spent much of his life in the Norman French monastery of Bec. From 1089 until his death he was Archbishop of Canterbury. Such an international career was not unusual in the middle ages, when nation-states had not yet been invented and Christendom was in practice as in theory a unity, at least for the learned who spoke Latin.

Anselm was a follower of St. Augustine. As such, he held that reason without faith is worthless. But he taught also that with faith, reason is unlimited. Those who are blessed with faith can demonstrate by pure reason the soundness of all the articles of faith—not just the existence of God but even what are ordinarily thought to be mysteries, such as the Incarnation and the Trinity. These demonstrations, however, would be intelligible and convincing only to the other faithful ones inside the circle.

To understand the things of the world, Anselm said, we must first have experience of the world. If we could not see or hear or touch objects, we should never come to understand them. Likewise, he went on, in the religious realm faith provides the data for understanding. So it is not possible to understand the doctrines of true religion yet not believe them; in his famous phrase, "I believe in order that I may understand."

## The Ontological Argument

"The heavens declare the glory of God," sang the Psalmist, "and the firmament sheweth his handywork."[3] This is the gist of the argument that God must exist because the universe in its harmonious complexity could not have come about otherwise than as the product of an intelligent designer. This line of thought is certainly natural, and if it is not as old as belief in gods, it must be at any rate as old as doubts about them. Significantly we find also in the Psalms[4] a denunciation of the "fool" who "hath said in his heart, There is no God."

Plato and Aristotle accepted this argument from Design and produced versions also of the Causal argument, reasoning that there must be some ultimate explanation of motion—the world process—and that the only possibility is something of the nature of soul. The ancients did not produce other ways besides these two for rationally establishing the existence of God. But Anselm did.

Anselm prayed that it might be given him to understand that which he believed, that God exists. The prayer was granted. Anselm reasoned: The fool who says there is no God understands what he means by the word 'God', namely "a being than which nothing greater can be conceived." God, thus defined, then exists in the fool's understanding. Now to exist in the understanding is not the same as to exist in reality—the picture the artist is going to paint exists in his mind but not yet on canvas. However, could it be the case that God existed in the understanding alone? No, said Anselm. For suppose He did: then it would be possible to conceive of another being, just like the one who existed in the understanding alone, with the one difference that this other being existed also in reality. But then this other being would be conceived as being greater than the one conceived as existing in the mind only; for it is greater to exist in reality than not to. Therefore, the being conceived as existing in the mind alone could not be the being than whom a greater was not conceivable. Therefore, the being than whom a greater cannot be conceived must exist in reality as well as in the mind.

Indeed, Anselm continued, He cannot even be conceived not to exist. For it is possible to conceive of a being which cannot be conceived not to exist: and this is greater than one which can be conceived not to exist.

Anselm is said to have remained on his knees throughout the time he wrote down this proof. Seven centuries afterwards Kant gave it the name "Ontological Argument"—argument from the nature of being—a label of questionable appropriateness which nevertheless has become standard.

This argument has an importance in philosophy that goes beyond its immediate purpose of providing rational foundation for religion. For here the most extreme possible claim is made for reason—that what must be thought of as existing must exist: from what is found to be in the mind we can read off what has to be outside the mind also. A conclusion as radical as this—inspiring to some, dismaying to others, exciting to all—was bound to be the subject of a controversy that continues to this day.

Anselm was challenged almost immediately. A monk named Gaunilo published a reply saucily entitled "On Behalf of the Fool." Gaunilo made two points. First, God does not exist in our understanding in the manner required for the proof. We can form a conception of a man unknown to us because we know some men and can form, from that acquaintance, a notion that any other man must conform to: he must have two legs, walk upright, be minimally reasonable, and so on. With God, however, since we have no experience of Him at all, we are at a loss to give any content to the notion. God is above our conceptions; hence the description "being than which a greater cannot be *conceived*" is faulty if it implies that we can form a conception of the divine being. But if this point is waived, Gaunilo continued, and we can form a conception of God as necessarily existing because perfect, we can likewise form the conception of any perfect thing—say, a perfect island—and argue in the same manner that it must exist for otherwise it would not be what we conceived it to be: the island than which a greater could not be conceived. As it is absurd to think of defining islands into existence, so is it also with the enterprise of establishing God's existence by definition.

Anselm issued a rebuttal to these able objections. On the first point he appealed—perhaps not quite fairly—to Gaunilo's faith as a Christian to admit that God does indeed exist in the mind, that we have a conception of Him, however incomplete it must be granted to be. To the second point Anselm argued with great subtlety to show that his reasoning applied to God and God alone. From the mere conception "greatest conceivable being" it follows that if such a being did exist, His nonexistence would be impossible—a being, that is to say, that had the property of necessarily existing would be greater than an otherwise similar one the existence of which was mere matter of fact that might have been otherwise. But we cannot even conceive of an island, or any other such limited being, as having the property of necessary existence. Hence the argument applies to God and God alone.

## Abelard

In Anselm's time higher education was for the most part not organized into institutions. A teacher would set himself up much as a doctor or lawyer does today; the greater his reputation the more pupils he would attract. Naturally, teachers tended to cluster in the centers of population, the greatest of which was Paris.

At the close of the eleventh century one of the most eminent Parisian teachers was William of Champeaux, whose position on universals was extreme Realism. To his school one day came an intelligent, articulate young cleric of noble birth named Peter Abelard (1079–?1144), formerly a student of Roscelin the Nominalist. In the formal disputations which were the accepted medium of philosophical instruction, Abelard proved himself such a master of dialectic that he accomplished an unheard-of feat: he made his teacher change his mind. But not only did poor William suffer the humiliation of publicly abandoning extreme Realism, he lost his pupils too. Abelard set up his own school in the town of Melun, whereupon most of William's students migrated thither.

Such was the beginning of Abelard's immensely influential career as a teacher. His acute mind, both vigorous and subtle, raised philosophical discourse to a higher level. Thus with respect to universals, Abelard rejected both Nominalism and Realism. Realism cannot be right; there is no cathood separated from the particular cats that happen to exist. On the other hand, contrary to Roscelin's Nominalism 'cat' is more than vocal wind. It is a noise, no doubt, but not just a noise: it is a meaningful noise. The problem of universals, then, is just the problem of explaining how noises (and gestures and marks) have meaning.

Abelard freed himself from the assumption common to both Realists and Nominalists before him that meaning must consist in the naming, labeling, of some particular or group of particulars, whether sensible or intelligible. What happens when we consider various small furry creatures, according to Abelard, is this: we pay attention to the respects in which they are similar, while neglecting their particular differences. Thus by abstraction we form the conception that is the meaning of the word 'cat'. This word—the universal, the vehicle of meaning—signifies something real; namely, the really existing similarities of Mehitabel and

Garfield. Also it signifies that which is in our understanding—the concept we have of cats—but it is not a label for any particular thing or things, whether physical or spiritual. Universals exist before particulars, as models in the mind of God; they exist in the particular things, though not as parts of them; and in their linguistic aspect, as conceptions formed by abstraction, they can be said to exist after things also. Abelard's solution to the problem is thus essentially the same as Aristotle's. But he worked it out independently, the relevant writings of Aristotle not yet being available in Europe.

Abelard was no religious skeptic. However, even more thoroughly and straight-forwardly than Anselm, he sought to minimize the appeal to authority in theology and to find rational foundations for Christian belief. In keeping with this constructive purpose of rationalizing and systematizing Christian knowledge, he wrote his famous book *Yes and No*. This contained 158 propositions concerning which conflicting opinions were collected from eminent authorities, including the Fathers of the Church. Abelard's discussions are judicious, aimed at reconciling the contrary opinions where possible. It is not surprising, however, that the book scandalized some of the faithful.

Abelard wrote also on ethics, developing the theory that morality lies not in action but in intention. No action can be described that is in all circumstances wrong. Killing, by a soldier in a just war or by the public executioner, may be allowable or even obligatory. Nor is there any kind of action that is always right: donations to charity made to impress influential persons may be sinful. Nevertheless, rights and wrongs are not arbitrary inventions of men, nor even of God.

## Abelard and Heloise

When in 1113 Abelard moved his school from Melun to Paris he was in his thirties, already recognized as the most formidable dialectician of his generation; moreover, he was a surpassingly strong and handsome man. A neighbor of his—one Fulbert, an official of the cathedral—had living with him under his guardianship a niece from the country, Heloise, in her teens, beautiful and intelligent. Education for girls, especially higher education, was not usual; but Fulbert, seeing no reason why his niece's brains should go to waste, arranged for Peter Abelard to tutor her privately. Abelard later described these lessons.

> I cannot cease to be astonished at the simplicity of Fulbert; I was as much surprised as if he had placed a lamb in the power of a hungry wolf. Heloise and I, under pretext of study, gave ourselves up wholly to love, and the solitude that love seeks our studies procured for us. Books were open before us, but we spoke oftener of love than philosophy, and kisses came more readily from our lips than words.

When at length Heloise bore Abelard a son, Fulbert demanded that Abelard marry her. Abelard was willing, and did so; but he insisted, with Heloise agreeing, that the marriage be kept secret—for he was in holy orders and his career would have been wrecked were it known that he was not celibate. When Fulbert went ahead anyway and publicized the marriage, both Abelard and his wife issued denials. Fulbert, by this time in a frenzy of rage, hired thugs who waylaid Abelard and castrated him.

After this catastrophe Abelard retired to the monastery of St. Denis outside Paris. Heloise entered a convent. Not until twelve years had passed did they begin that exchange of poignant letters that make these two the best remembered human beings of the twelfth century. Abelard at length founded a monastery and school of his own—he continued to attract multitudes of students. Heloise rose to be abbess of her nunnery and was held in honor by the Pope himself.

Abelard died in 1142, Heloise 22 years later. She was buried at his side.

## St. Bernard

Abelard's last years were made bitter by persecution at the hands of St. Bernard of Clairvaux (1091–1153). This countryman of Abelard's was like him in his energy, his disputatious nature, and his surpassing ability to attract disciples. In all other respects they were exact opposites. Bernard's aim was to purge the Church of all its corruptions. Early in life he became a Benedictine monk; however, as the rules of that order were insufficiently strict he founded his own brotherhood, the Cistercians or Trappists—to this day the most austere of all the orders.

Cistercian abbeys and monastic buildings were severely plain in their architecture and almost without ornament, in contrast to the luxuriant decorations of the Romanesque and Gothic churches being built at the same time. Bernard desired to purge church doctrine of superfluous ornamentation also—emphatically including the subtleties of philosophical theology. In opposition to the intellectualism of Anselm and Abelard, Bernard wrote "I believe though I do not understand; I hold by faith what I cannot grasp with the mind."

Bernard was merciless toward Abelard. Twice, in 1121 and again 20 years later, Bernard persuaded councils of the Church to condemn Abelard's doctrine of the Trinity as heretical. At the latter of these sessions Abelard, still not without powerful friends, was persuaded to attempt to defend himself; but he was worn out and his rhetorical powers failed him. He died in the following year.

# 29

# The Aristotelian Revival

## Moslem Philosophy

PHILOSOPHY EXISTED IN THE Moslem world for just three centuries. It began about 800 with the translation of Greek works into Arabic. It ended about 1100, strangled by muftis, mullahs, imams, and ayatollahs.

Moslem philosophy consisted principally of attempts to reconcile Aristotle with the teachings of the Koran. The Arabs came first into contact with Greek philosophy when they conquered Syria and Iran at the beginning of their breakout from the Arabian peninsula in the seventh century. Two hundred years earlier Syria had been infected by the Nestorian heresy, according to which Christ had two distinct personalities, human and divine, rather than two natures in one person. The Nestorians were much given to philosophy, and to that end translated many Greek works into the Syriac language. When the Byzantine emperors persecuted them, they emigrated to Iran and there enlightened their hosts. Thus by the time the Moslems took over that part of the world, Aristotelian texts existed in Greek, Syriac, and Farsi. They were then translated into Arabic from all three sources, but chiefly from Syriac.

The situation was complicated by the fact that some of the *Enneads* of Plotinus were translated under the title "Aristotle's Theology." As the Moslem philosophers never became aware of this error, their "Aristotle" was in important respects a Neoplatonist—emanations and all—a curious hybrid who nevertheless was to them the acme of Greek wisdom.

## Al-Farabi

Al-Farabi (*d.* 950), who worked in Baghdad in the first half of the tenth century, set the pattern for succeeding Moslem Aristotelians. He conceived of philosophy not as a rival to religion but as an assistant. Thus the Aristotelian logic was looked at as an aid in the development of the intelligence that is Allah's greatest gift to humanity.

Following Aristotle, Al-Farabi showed that God's existence can be proved in two ways. There must be a prime mover to account for the existence of motion in matter, which in its own nature is inert and motionless. Second, the things of which we are aware exist only contingently; that is, they would not exist unless other things, from which they derive their being, had existed beforehand. These, the causes, are in turn the contingent effects of prior causes. But somewhere, Al-Farabi insisted, there must be something that exists not contingently but necessarily—that exists because it must exist, no matter what else exists. Otherwise there would be no ultimate support for anything, and everything would collapse like a series of coathangers, each hanging on another but nowhere hanging on a peg. This Necessary Being is God.

Al-Farabi's picture of the world was derived from Neoplatonism: a series of emanations from the One or Allah, through Mind and the World Soul, down through the heavenly spheres and man. This scheme was congenial to Moslem mysticism, with which Al-Farabi was in sympathy. However, the world of the Greek philosophers had existed from eternity; the Koran, following *Genesis*, proclaimed the creation of the visible world by Allah out of nothing. Here was a conflict that persisted through three centuries and was an important cause of the ultimate extinction of philosophy in Islam.

## Avicenna

Avicenna (as his name, Ibn Sina, was Latinized; 980–1037), an Iranian, was an infant prodigy and a universal genius. He memorized Aristotle's *Metaphysics* by reading it forty times, but did not understand it. Then he came upon Al-Farabi's commentary, whereupon suddenly all became clear. In his active life as doctor and high government official, he found time to write some 160 books on a wide range of topics.

Avicenna's philosophy is an elaboration and systematization of Al-Farabi's Neoplatonic Aristotelianism. The elaboration can be seen in the circumstance that Avicenna deduces the existence of no fewer than ten Intelligences between the One and the visible world. The tenth and lowest of these is the Giver of Forms, which (or rather, who) like the Craftsman of Plato's *Timaeus* created individuals by impressing the Forms upon prime matter, that which is purely potential. This Intelligence is also the human active intellect.

The systematization leads Avicenna into determinism, even fatalism. Like Al-Farabi he proves God's existence by the argument that there must be a necessary being on which contingent beings depend. But although things other than God are not necessary beings, they nevertheless follow from their causes by necessity: given the cause, the effect must be so and not otherwise. Consequently, what Allah the First Cause has willed to be must be. But since Allah is absolutely good, the world that flows from Him must be the best possible—which is as much as to say that there could not be any other world than this one. There seems thus to be no freedom anywhere, not even in God.

The difficulty here is one that faces any theologian who wants to hold that (a) there is only one God, (b) He is all-powerful—so He could create any world He chose to, (c) He is all-knowing—so He would know which world was the best, and (d) He is perfectly good—so He would create the best world He could. These postulates are evidently reasonable requirements for an exalted conception of God. It follows from them that this is the best of all possible worlds, and the one and only one that could exist given God's nature as described in (a) to (d). Here is a double difficulty for theology, for it turns out that in worshipping God one seems to be worshipping Necessity—a paradoxical and disturbing thought. Even more distressingly, the conclusion creates the Problem of Evil. It seems obvious that this is *not* the best of all possible worlds. If, then, the theory of God leads to the conclusion that this is the best of all possible worlds, there must be something wrong with the theory. These are the two most serious problems besetting any rational theology.

Two points from Avicenna's psychology may be noted. First, the "man in space"—his thought experiment to show that we have, or at least could have, an idea of being that is not an idea of any material thing and not derived from experience. Imagine a man created, floating in space, without eyes or ears, and with his limbs so disposed that they could not touch one another. Such an unfortunate, Avicenna maintained, would have no data from which he could form the notion of a material thing. Nevertheless, he would be aware of his own existence, which is the same as to say that he would have a notion of being. In this argument of Avicenna's we have perhaps the first appearance of the (alleged) conception of a pure consciousness—not the consciousness *of* anything, but just consciousness—as constituting the core or inmost essence of the self, a conception destined for a central role in the disputes of modern philosophy.

Second, Avicenna found it necessary to distinguish in human thinking two intellects: one passive and personal, the other an active intellect which is a unity, identical with the Tenth Intelligence that imposes forms on prime matter. His reasoning was this. Aristotle had supposed that our minds are capable of forming abstractions: we look at many perceptible triangles of all shapes, colors, and sizes, and then by intuition form the conception "triangle" apart from the particular variations. In this act the mind becomes identical with what it knows, that is to say it becomes the intelligible form. Before the act the mind was potentially the form "triangle"; after the act, it is actually this form.

However, Avicenna pointed out, the process thus described violates the fundamental Aristotelian principle that nothing can be brought from potency to actuality save by something already actual: what is potentially afire must be ignited by an actual fire. Hence if my mind is brought into the state of actualizing the form "triangle," there must be a cause that is already in the actual state. This is the active intellect. Since the function of the active intellect is to give form to what is potentially formed, Avicenna felt himself justified in identifying it with the Tenth Intelligence.

This is Avicenna's solution to the problem of abstraction which Plato has solved by postulating the preexistence of the soul in direct communion with the Ideas. Aristotle seems not to have concerned himself overmuch with this problem. Nevertheless, it is evident (from *On the Soul*, Book III, Chapter 5) that the Philosopher was aware of the difficulty to which Avicenna called attention, and his own solution may have been like Avicenna's. It is hard to be certain, though, because the passage is brief and obscure. Avicenna is clear; yet the vision of the Tenth Intelligence's inspiring babies to form the notion of cathood smacks more of Plotinus than of Aristotle.

## Averroes

The position of philosophy in the Moslem world was precarious. It was tolerated chiefly because it could not be easily disentangled from the Greek scientific writings—mathematical, astronomical, biological, and above all medical—which nobody wanted to lose.

Of the foes of philosophy, the most effective was an Iranian ex-philosopher, Algazel (Al-Ghazali, 1058–1111), who wrote an influential book called *The Destruction of the Philosophers*. In this he showed how philosophers contradicted not only the plain teaching of the Koran but also one another and even themselves—so that no trust was to be put in them.

The reply, *The Destruction of the Destruction*, was written in the succeeding century by Averroes (Ibn Rushd, 1126–1198) of Cordova in Spain. He developed the standard line taken by philosophers in placating the orthodox, that the truths of the Koran were to be understood not literally but metaphorically. The unlearned, to whom they were addressed, were incapable of apprehending the literal truth; therefore, they had to be spoken to in parables. Philosophers, however, can grasp the exact meaning. There is thus a *double truth*—allegorical in religion, literal in philosophy.

Like his predecessors, Averroes was principally a commentator on Aristotle. He composed three sets of commentaries: the greater, the lesser, and the summaries. These were more accurate than what had gone before, as well as more detailed. Averroes purged Aristotelian interpretation of many of the Neoplatonic elements that had previously confused it. The emanation theory was dropped. Allah was the First Cause, but not in time. The particular substances that make up the world were drawn from prime matter by Allah's final causality.

Averroes taught that Aristotle's doctrine of the soul entailed the immortality of the active intellect which, however, is the theorizing intelligence, the same in all rational animals—what we do geometry by, not what we remember our experiences by. There is thus no immortality for the individual, the person.

Averroes was a physician and astronomer as well as philosopher. He held high posts in the government of Cordova. However, his enemies triumphed in the end. He died an exile in Morocco, while in Spain his books were being burned and intellectual Islam was congealing into superstitious stagnation from which it has yet to emerge.

## The Recovery of Aristotle in Europe

In the twelfth and early thirteenth centuries, the works of Aristotle were made available to Europe. There were two principal centers of translation: Toledo in Christian Spain, where a corps of translators under the direction of the Archbishop labored at rendering into Latin the learning possessed by the Moors and Jews; and Sicily, recently recaptured from the Moslems, and the favorite residence of the Holy Roman Emperor Frederick II—learned, skeptical, and an admirer of Arabian philosophy. At Frederick's court the commentaries of Averroes were translated only a few years after the death of The Commentator, as he was justly called.

It is not surprising that Aristotle's *Metaphysics*, for example—a work obscure enough in the original—should have become gibberish in the process of translation from Greek to Syriac to Arabic to Latin. But some versions made directly from Greek into Latin were produced soon afterward. As one consequence of the Crusades—especially of the Fourth, which ignored the Holy Land to capture and loot Constantinople (1204)—Greek manuscripts, together with men who could read them, were becoming known again in the West.

Europe's rapid recovery from the chaos and misery of the tenth century made possible the Crusades. They in turn, being wars of aggression fought on foreign soil, created a boom at home. The popes demanded and got internal peace in Christendom while the infidel was being smitten. Over most of Europe the twelfth and thirteenth centuries were a time when trade flourished, travel was commonplace and unhindered, and the great Gothic churches were rising. They were being decorated with paintings of sacred scenes in which the backgrounds often and significantly depicted nature—this sensible, material world closely observed. The land could support more lawyers and doctors. Universities came into being for the training of these professional men. The clergy also pursued their studies in the faculties of theology of these new schools.

Learning was no longer the monopoly of priests. Bologna and Salerno, the first universities in the modern sense, originated when groups of students banded together to hire teachers. The students used the power of the purse to enforce strict standards on the professors. Less unnatural modes of organization prevailed at the University of Naples, founded by the Emperor Frederick II; Paris, which developed from the school attached to the cathedral; and Oxford, a corporation of scholars. These institutions quickly grew to enormous size: the University of Paris is said to have had an enrollment as great as 20,000 in the thirteenth century.

Thus Aristotle was available and an audience for him existed. His impact was enormous. The scholars of the time were well aware how great the loss of ancient learning had been. Now here it was, recovered all at once—or at any rate its climactic works. Try to imagine what it would be like for us if the works of Newton, Darwin, and Wittgenstein were suddenly published after having been unavailable for a thousand years.

There was powerful opposition to the assimilation of Aristotle into Christendom as earlier there had been into Islam, and for the same reasons. The Philosopher, after all, was a pagan, who contradicted two central Christian doctrines: he taught the eternity of the world and he denied the immortality of the soul. Thus Christian theologians were presented again with the problem that had exercised the Moslem world for the previous three centuries. In Islam, religious fanaticism suppressed Aristotelianism; in Christendom, after two centuries of relatively genteel and academic dispute, the supporters of Aristotle won general acceptance. However, the Philosopher's Christian advocates were more prone to compromise than Avicenna and Averroes had been.

## Franciscans and Dominicans

All the most important philosophers of the later middle ages were professors, mainly of theology; all were associated at some time or other with the University of Paris; and all were members of one or the other of two religious orders founded at the beginning of the thirteenth century.

St. Francis of Assisi (Francesco Bernardone, 1181–1226) was a young nobleman who after undergoing a religious conversion abandoned the life of pleasure to minister to the unfortunate, lepers especially. Like the Cynics of Greece he lived by begging, having got rid of all his possessions. Cheerful and joyful, he attracted a multitude of followers to his enterprise, which grew to be no less than the cure of the luxuries and corruptions of the Church. The Pope of the time, Innocent III, was young, vigorous, and fond of power. He dealt most adroitly with the problem posed by this dangerous holy man: how to utilize his energy and popularity in the service of the Church without carrying out the reforms demanded. While Francis was away from Italy preaching to Moslems in Egypt—without being harmed, even though a Crusade was in progress—Innocent reconstituted the Franciscan Order into a properly authoritarian and hierarchical organization, with the vow of poverty greatly de-emphasized. St. Francis himself resigned from the Order when he learned what had happened. The claim that Jesus had lived in poverty was declared heretical, and St. Francis' closest followers were persecuted for teaching it. The Franciscans became principally an order of teachers and missionaries.

St. Dominic (Domingo de Guzman, 1170–1221), a Spaniard, was a different sort of man, on whose organizational and preaching talents Innocent could rely completely. Dominic was given the mission of stamping out the Albigensian Heresy. This movement had gained control of the region around Albi and Toulouse in the south of France, at the time perhaps the most prosperous and cultivated region of Europe. The Albigensians were said to be infected with Manichaean notions—the Iranian light-darkness dualism—which had arrived from the Near East via Bulgaria. They aggravated their doctrinal errors by denouncing worldliness of the Church, exhorting the clergy to virtuous austerity, and rejecting the authority of Rome. St. Dominic tried valiantly to argue these people into repenting of their ways, but eventually he lost hope for them. In his farewell sermon he said

> For many years I have exhorted you in vain, with gentleness, preaching, praying, and weeping. But according to the proverb of my country, "where blessing can accomplish nothing, blows may avail." We shall rouse against you princes and prelates, who alas! will arm nations and kingdoms against this land . . . and thus blows will avail where blessings and gentleness have been powerless.

The prophecy came true. Innocent III preached a Crusade against the Albigensians. Anyone who joined the holy army received absolution automatically—that is, he was assured of going straight to heaven if he was killed. Furthermore, Southern France was very rich; according to the custom of the time, to the victor belonged the spoils. In addition to these powerful incentives, there was the fact that the King of France was annoyed by the Count of Toulouse's insubordination. The Crusade (1208–1213) was a great success, despite the tenacity with which the Albigensians defended their country. It was necessary to massacre most of them. The survivors were scrutinized carefully for signs of heresy and imprisoned for life or burnt at the stake if they could not prove their innocence. Their possessions were forfeited to the King and the Pope.

These methods of extirpating heresy were so successful and profitable that they were continued elsewhere in Europe after the Albigensians had been dealt with. St. Dominic founded the Order of Preachers—the Dominicans—in 1215; almost at once the brotherhood was entrusted with conduct of the Inquisition, as it was called. The activities of this organization and of the Spanish Inquisition—similar in methods and aims but under direct control of the King of Spain—continued down to the nineteenth century. When the supply of heretics was in danger of being exhausted, the Inquisition turned its attention to the suppression of witchcraft. Estimates of the number of human beings found guilty and burnt alive range from several hundred thousand to two million.

## St. Bonaventura

On the whole the Dominicans were enthusiastic to assimilate Aristotle to Christian philosophy, the Franciscans less so. The philosophical tradition of the Franciscan brotherhood was Augustinian, hence at bottom Platonic, although few of the dialogues of Plato were available in the thirteenth century.

The most eminent Franciscan of the thirteenth century was St. Bonaventura (John of Fidanza, 1221–1274), almost the exact contemporary of his countryman St. Thomas Aquinas, the great Dominican. He was a student of Alexander of Hales, an Englishman who became the first Franciscan professor of theology at Paris. Bonaventura in turn was appointed professor in 1256, but relinquished the chair a year later to become Minister General of his order.

Bonaventura was hostile to Aristotelianism because he found in it no place for mystical communion with divinity, nor for Christ. The Saint held that in any case no non-Christian philosophy could be adequate, not even as philosophy. He argued that if we are to study man and the world to any purpose we must study actual men and the world as it actually is. But men have a supernatural origin and destiny; the world is God's creation. The Aristotelian "natural man" and "natural world" are mere abstractions. Hence there cannot be any sharp line drawn between philosophy and theology.

Reason unaided by faith establishes that God exists, is one, and is all-powerful. This Bonaventura admitted and insisted upon. However, the philosopher if he stops there cannot know—because reason cannot show it—that God is three persons in one Substance or that God saves man and resurrects him. Therefore, the philosopher does not know God as He is. That is to say, the philosopher has a wrong notion of God; hence his philosophy—considered purely as philosophy—is mistaken.

Bonaventura deployed several arguments to show the existence of God: the "footprints of God" to be found in nature, the necessity of a first cause, and the Anselmian proof. He reasoned also that since our wills are oriented toward the good, the supreme Good (which is God) must exist. Moreover, the very existence of the notion of imperfection requires the existence of perfection, God, as the standard by which we judge of what fails to be perfect. This last argument is reminiscent of Plato's contention in the *Phaedo* that there must be an Idea of Equality with which we are acquainted if we are to account for our judgments of the inequalities of things in the world.

As against Aristotle, who purported to prove that the world must be eternal, Bonaventura had an argument to show that the world had to have a beginning in time. If it did not, he reasoned, then it must be the case that already before today an infinite number of days have elapsed. It follows that the world has passed through an infinite series. But this is absurd, for an infinite series by definition is one that cannot be passed through. Furthermore, if the world were infinitely old, it would be infinity years old, and also infinity months old. From this it would follow that infinity = 12 times infinity—which is also absurd, so the Saint held.

About the nature of the world that God created, however, Bonaventura was not so anti-Aristotelian. He followed the Philosopher in holding that every individual thing is a composite of matter-potency and form-actuality. Even angels, since they possess the possibility of becoming other than what they are already, have matter—though, to be sure, a spiritual matter. The principle of individuation Bonaventura found neither in matter nor in form, but in both together.

Every human soul is created by God out of nothing. On this point, one of the few where Bonaventura disagreed with Augustine, the Franciscan's teaching has been accepted as orthodox by the Catholic Church. (This makes difficulties for the doctrine of our inheritance of original sin from our first parents.) The soul is the form of the body. The Averroist doctrine of one active intellect for all humanity Bonaventura denounced as contrary both to reason and to experience: to reason, because intellect is a perfection of individuals, who differ as rational beings, not just as animals; and to experience, for different persons think different thoughts, even abstract ones.

The intellect was created "naked." There are no innate ideas, not even of first principles, not even of God. Our ideas come from two sources: sense experience and reflection on the nature of ourselves. The latter is the source of our idea of God. Indeed, the trinity of memory, intelligence, and will that we find in our minds furnishes an analogy to help us understand the three-in-one nature of God—although it does not afford a proof of that article of faith.

Despite the fact that the soul is the form of the body, its immortality can be proved, Bonaventura held, from the existence in all men of a desire for perfect happiness, which is unending life or at least involves it. Since God exists and is good (as can also be proved), this desire could not have been implanted in us unless it were possible for it to be fulfilled.

The highest good, however, is remote from the experience of most people—being that mystical ecstasy of which a foretaste has been attained in this life by only a favored few, such as Plotinus and Saints Bernard, Francis, and Bonaventura.

## Medieval Aristotelianism and Natural Science

One would have expected the recovery of Aristotle's scientific writings to be followed by a spurt of advance in science. In fact, however, the Aristotelian revival did not accelerate scientific progress and may even have retarded it. Those who contributed to science in the middle ages were generally the ones least in awe of Aristotle.

There were two main reasons for this state of affairs. In the first place, uncritical adulation of the Philosopher by his partisans did not spur them to original investigations. In some circles Aristotle came to be paid the reverence otherwise shown for Holy Writ. As far as natural science was concerned, his works were supposed to be both infallible and complete. The second reason was the paradox that Aristotelian rationalism, when developed in combination with Christian theology of the intellectualistic sort, resulted in a worldview so complete as to render further scientific studies uninteresting and seemingly useless. Aristotle said that explanation had to be teleological: the final cause had to be ascertained—along with the material, formal, and efficient—if the thing was to be understood. This demand did not render empirical investigations superfluous for the ancient Peripatetics; quite the contrary. The final cause of a thing, the actualization of its nature, could be determined only by a study of its normal development. In Christianized Aristotelianism, however, the final cause of everything was the same: the fulfillment of God's purpose. But what was God's purpose? Those who held that in God the intellect is primary were led to conclude that they could tell what God's purpose is, both in general and in particular cases. God wills the good. The good is something objective, like the multiplication table, accessible to the rational but finite human intellect. Now since we know (they reasoned) both by reason and by scripture that God's general purpose is the glorification of Himself and the salvation of the elect, to understand a thing is to understand how it contributes to these ends. Here natural science, as we understand the term—and for that matter as Aristotle understood it—went out the window. Knowledge of pelicans does not arise from careful observation of their habits but from noting that the female pelican feeds her chicks on her own blood, thereby signifying forth Our Saviour's sacrifice. Comets and plagues do not belong within the provinces of astronomy and public health but of divine admonition and penology. In general, everything in the world, at least everything interesting and puzzling, was to be understood by interpreting it as symbolic of something else. Creation was a language that the wise and pious might read.

On the other hand, if God's purposes were inscrutable, not to be fathomed by the human intellect, the world would have to be understood in some other way if it was to be understood at all. This is what the Augustinian tradition held. Good is not something God recognizes, it is just whatever God by fiat makes it. God is an entirely free agent. The ultimate reason why God has created what He has created is known and knowable only to God. It follows that human beings cannot hope to understand the world, if understanding means possessing final-cause explanations. We can, however, make progress in understanding the divine modus operandi, *how* things work as opposed to why (in an ultimate sense of "why") they are as they are. We can do natural science. If knowledge of "second causes" is not the highest conceivable knowledge, at least it is the highest we can attain, and it is worth the effort. We do not know, and will never know, what end God had in mind in creating the pelican. We can, however, observe the pelican—perhaps closely enough to discover that she does not, after all, feed her young on her blood but on regurgitated fish.

The positions sketched above are two extreme poles never taken by actual scholastics. No one of importance in the middle ages rejected Aristotle utterly, and no one accepted every word.

## Two English Franciscan Men of Science

Robert Grosseteste (*ca* 1169–1253), a Franciscan, was one of the first men recognizable as a scientist in the modern sense. He was a man of astounding learning—he knew Greek, Hebrew, medicine, mathematics, and music, as well as the usual disciplines of the time—who occupied high positions in the learned world and in the Church: he was Chancellor of Oxford University after 1221 and Bishop of Lincoln after 1235. He was indeed so powerful in the English church that he successfully resisted the Pope in the matter of certain ecclesiastical appointments.

Grosseteste himself translated Aristotle's *Ethics* from the Greek and commented on him: he wished to reconcile the Philosopher with Augustine. Nevertheless, Aristotle did not overawe Grosseteste, any more than the Pope did. The Bishop was capable of thinking for himself and preferred to do so. In keeping with Augustinian Neoplatonism, he found great significance in light, which he held to be the "first form of corporeity"—that is to say, the basis of three-dimensionality (for light, beginning from a point, extends infinitely in three dimensions), hence of the physical world. Light for him, however, was not of merely mystical or metaphysical import. He proceeded to study its manifestations in an empirical and quantitative manner. The outcome of his research was an essentially correct theory of the rainbow.

Grosseteste's most famous pupil, Roger Bacon (1214–1294), was even more self-reliant and insubordinate. Since he did not have the Bishop's influence, he got into serious trouble with his ecclesiastical superiors. St. Bonaventura, as General of his order, forbade him to publish his writings. In 1278, when he was in his middle sixties, his books were condemned and he was imprisoned for 14 years.

Hostility to Bacon was occasioned more by the offense he gave personally to dignitaries than by his doctrines. In anatomizing the sources of human stupidity he enumerated uncritical veneration of authority, persistence in habitual ways, acquiescence in the prejudices of the mob, and—most insidious—the pretentiousness that seeks to mask ignorance and incompetence by seeming profundity. However, Bacon did not question the fundamental doctrines of Christianity. Indeed, he combined Averroes and Augustine to hold that the active intellect is one, and identical with, the Holy Spirit—so that all knowledge of necessary truths is, directly, divine illumination.

This was not, however, a theory of innate knowledge. Bacon meant only that the first principles of reasoning, the ability to reason, are received directly from God. The actual reasoning, which is fallible, is ours. Nor is the armchair enough. Bacon was the first thinker to have a clear grasp of the essentials of scientific procedure: a hypothesis, preferably expressed in quantitative terms; deduction from that hypothesis; and experimental verification of the deduced consequences. It was in this last particular that his originality consisted. The ancient philosophers were fertile enough in hypotheses and deductions. But having come up with an account satisfying to the intellect, they were usually content to leave the matter at that stage. Bacon to the contrary wrote

> If a man who has never seen fire should prove by adequate reason that fire burns and injures things and destroys them, his mind would not be satisfied thereby, nor would he avoid fire, until he placed his hand or some combustible substance in the fire, so that he might prove by experience that which reasoning taught. But, when he has had actual experience of combustion, his mind is made certain and rests in the full light of truth. Therefore, reasoning does not suffice, but experience does.[1]

Bacon had a grasp, too, of the possibilities for practical application of science in technology. In the middle of the thirteenth century he wrote

> Machines for navigation can be made without rowers so that the largest ships will be moved by a single man in charge . . . cars can be made so that without animals they will move with unbelievable rapidity . . . flying-machines can be constructed so that a man sits in the midst of the machine revolving some engine by which artificial wings are made to beat the air like a flying bird . . . machines can be made for walking in the sea and rivers, even to the bottom without danger.[2]

# 30

# St. Thomas Aquinas

THE DOMINICANS WERE THE revisionist party within the medieval Church in comparison to the Franciscans who stood for the Augustinian theology of the founders and indeed strove—some of them—to recapture the original revolutionary fervor. But the pro-Aristotelian Dominicans won the power struggle, so that revisionism became the new orthodoxy. Their principal theoretician was Thomas Aquinas (1225–1274).

Thomas was born in Roccasecca, near Naples, the son of the Count of Aquino. At the age of six he went to study at the abbey of Monte Cassino, where he remained for nine years, and then went to the University of Naples. This institution, the foundation of the Emperor Frederick II, was a cosmopolitan hotbed of advanced thought. Under the Emperor's personal patronage, the Aristotelian texts with their Arabian commentaries formed the core of the curriculum. Thomas' teacher was an Irishman named Peter, whose zeal for the Philosopher was unhindered by religious scruples. Thomas, however, absorbed all that Peter had to teach while still standing firm in his faith. In the thirteenth century every idealistic young intellectual entered one or the other of the two new mendicant orders. In 1244, at age 19, Thomas chose to become a Dominican. Naturally, there was opposition from his prominent family. When he stopped at home on his way to the University of Paris they detained him forcibly for a year, during which time his brothers subjected him to various unseemly pressures and temptations. At length, however, they were obliged to admit that they could not shake his constancy, and to let him go on his way. Thomas' life after that was entirely placid.

In Paris, Thomas became a disciple of the Dominican professor of theology St. Albert the Great (1206–1280), the first philosopher of note to come out of Germany and, indeed, even to go back into it. ("The Great" was not a title attesting to Albert's preeminence, not originally at any rate; it was a translation of his German name, Albrecht Gross.) Albert was, exceptionally, a man whose enthusiasm for Aristotle had the effect of inspiring him to advance scientific investigation. He pursued botany and zoology by observational and even experimental methods. It was he who contributed to chemistry the fundamental concept of chemical affinity. His theology was so excellent that he achieved sainthood and the honorific appellation "Universal Doctor."

Thomas Aquinas was a big man—in middle age indeed fat. (There have been only two fat philosophers: the other was David Hume.) In Albert's classes, moreover, he habitually sat listening without entering much into discussions. His class-mates sneered at him as "the dumb ox." The professor, who knew more about his intellectual capacity, retorted "the bellows of this dumb ox will awaken all Chris-tendom." When in 1248 Albert returned to his native Cologne to set up a Domin-ican house of studies, Thomas went along and stayed for four years. Returning to Paris, he took the Master of Arts degree in 1256 and was appointed to a profes-sorship of theology in 1259. Immediately, however, he was summoned to the court of the Pope, where he taught until 1268. He managed to return to his Paris chair from 1268 till 1272, when he was commissioned to set up a Dominican house at his alma mater, the University of Naples. In 1274, while on his way to a great Church Council at Lyons, he died, being only 49 years old.

St. Thomas Aquinas' *Summa Theologiae* is longer than the entire extant works of Aristotle. It is, however, only one of some 60 books that he dictated—some-times to four secretaries at once—all in the last 20 years of his life, while at the same time energetically carrying out his professorial and administrative duties. These works include the *Summa contra Gentiles* (*i.e.* "Summary of Arguments against Paganism"), written before the *Summa Theologiae* and shorter, but covering much the same ground; extensive commentaries on Aristotle's *Metaphysics, Ethics, Politics, Physics, On the Soul, Meteorology, On Interpretation,* and *On Generation and Corruption* (Thomas knew little Greek, but his friend and colleague William of Moerbeke provided him with very literal Latin translations); commentaries on various Christian books; and treatises *On Princely Rule, On the Eternity of the World, On the Unity of the Intellect Against the Averroists, On Evil, On Being and Essence, On Spiritual Creatures,* and *On the Virtues.*

## Faith and Reason

Throughout the thirteenth century the University of Paris was distracted by the subversive doctrines of Averroists, as the followers of Aristotle were called who interpreted the Philosopher in the manner recommended by the Commentator. These men were ensconced principally in the Faculty of Arts; that is, they were professors of philosophy and not of theology. Nevertheless, it was required of them that they should be good Christians. When denounced for propounding scandalous doctrines, their standard defense was to protest that they were merely teaching the history of philosophy—they were not affirming anything other than that the Philosopher had in fact taught the propositions in question. Some, how-ever, employed an outrageous stratagem: double truth. Averroes had indeed said that what was false in philosophy might be true in religion, but he meant only that a statement in a sacred book might be false if interpreted literally though true in a symbolic sense. The Latin Averroists (*i.e.* the Averroists of the Latin Quarter in Paris, the neighborhood of the University where Latin was the language of teach-ing, and even ordinary conversation among the faculty and students from all over Europe), however, went so far as to claim that philosophy and theology were entirely autonomous disciplines, each self-sufficient. Thus for instance on the question of the world's eternity, the philosophical truth, guaranteed by the proofs in Aristotle's *Physics*, is that the world has always existed; while in theology, the truth revealed in *Genesis* is that it was created out of nothing some few thousand years ago. Which is *the* truth? The Averroists refused to admit that the question made sense. There were only truths relative to the two closed systems.

This curiously neo-Protagorean thesis was condemned repeatedly by the Church authorities. Official prohibitions of the teaching of Aristotle's *Physics* and *Metaphysics*, the root of the evil as it was thought, were issued more than once, but without much effect. It was necessary to baptize Aristotle.

St. Thomas' solution to the problem was diplomatic. Philosophy, he declared in opposition to St. Bonaventura, is an autonomous discipline, as the Averroists maintained. What is proved by sound philosophical argumentation is true, absolutely, not to be overruled even by religious revelation. On the other hand, revealed truth is proof against philosophical undermining. There are truths (such as the trinitarian nature of God, the creation of the world) that cannot be either proved or disproved by unaided reason. In the middle there are a certain number of truths that have been revealed in the Holy Scriptures but are also capable of being proved by reason—chief among these the existence of God. At no point is there conflict, nor can there be. Reason and revelation are both from God.

Reason tells us about the natural world, revelation adds on the knowledge of the supernatural world. But what is reason, and what is revelation? Revelation is ultimately what the Church, through popes and councils, says it is. Reason is, roughly, Aristotle. They do not conflict. But what is to be done when they *seem* to?

Aquinas offers an example of his mediating procedure in his treatment of the question of the world's beginning. The conflict is on its face irreconcilable. Aristotle says, and proves, that the world is eternal. *Genesis* is revelation, and cannot be rejected. However, it can be interpreted. To affirm that the world is God's creation does not entail its having had a beginning in time. The requirement is only that the world should be dependent on God for its being; and one eternal object can be dependent on another in this respect. "Creation from eternity" is then not a contradictory notion. And, the Saint admits, the argument is strong that the effect of an eternal cause must itself be eternal: how could the cause be in existence, with nothing hindering it from producing its effect, yet not produce?

Aquinas came to the conclusion, however, that there was nothing impossible in the supposition of God's willing that nonbeing should be followed, in time, by being. On the other hand, the argument of Bonaventura for the necessity of a beginning was fallacious. In the case of an infinite series without a first member—for example an infinite number of years previous to this one—our existing at a certain place in the series does not imply that the whole series has been passed through: "passing through" implies not only ending at the end but beginning at the beginning; and the type of series in question is precisely that which has no beginning. This kind of series can be added on to at its "finite end."

The arguments of Aristotle and others to show that the world must be eternal—ten are brought out and scrutinized in the *Summa*—are likewise rejected as nondemonstrative. The Saint indeed claims, in a dubious interpretation of the relevant passages of Aristotle's *Physics*, that the Philosopher never intended to assert any more than the probability of the world's eternity. In any case, according to Aquinas, it is possible to give a direct proof of the impossibility of proving either the eternity or newness of the world. The world depends on the will of God, and nothing necessitates His will; therefore, eternity cannot be proved. On the other hand, a demonstrative proof of the finite age of the world would have to proceed from the essence of bodies—that is, it would have to be a necessary truth about the sun, or a stone, that it could not have existed from eternity. But since essences have no reference to time, such inferences are impossible.

Therefore, as far as reason takes us, we cannot tell whether the world is eternal or not. Therefore, we are to accept revelation, which unequivocally tells us that the world did have a beginning.

Aquinas' treatment of the question of the eternity of the world can be taken as an example not only of how he mediated between theology and philosophy in hard cases but also as an illustration of his critical power. With uncanny acumen he spotted the fallacy in Bonaventura's argument about infinity. What is more, in his direct proof of the impossibility of settling the eternity question by argumentation from necessary premises, he comes close to enunciating a general principle to the effect that matters of fact are incapable of being established by reasoning *a priori*—that is, from principles not based ultimately on inductions from observation of what the facts are. Whatever may be thought of the truth, plausibility, or desirability of such a principle, at any rate it has been considered the mark of the tough-minded in every age, and indeed as the shibboleth of the "empiricists."

## God

But if what there is in the world can be settled only by looking, equally what there must be above the world has to be determined by reason and faith. The things in the sensible world are all of them contingent, dependent; they would not be what they are, or indeed be at all, if something else had not been what it was. Now what the dependent being is dependent on may itself be dependent on something else, and so on—but not ad infinitum. In the end not every coathanger can hang on another coathanger; there must be a peg somewhere. The world peg is necessary being: something which could not fail to exist no matter what might be otherwise. Necessary being is not apparent to the senses but human reason is capable of proving its existence, beginning with knowledge derived from the senses and proceeding according to first principles. Or rather, His existence: necessary being is God.

Thomas rejected, vehemently, the argument of St. Anselm. It is not easy to see why, for Thomas admitted, indeed insisted, that God's essence entails His existence. The professor's reasons for rejecting the Archbishop's proof were two. The first depends on a dubious application of Aristotle's distinction between what is better known by nature and what is better known to us. Aquinas admits that the equivalence of God's essence to His existence is evident in itself, but on account of the weakness of our intellects we are unable to grasp this truth in the requisite manner. Therefore, other proofs—from the effects of God in the world—are needful for us. (This is a strange objection that seems to amount to saying that we cannot really understand the ontological argument, although a superior intellect would—and would perceive its cogency.)

The second objection follows.

> Granted that everyone understands that by this name *God* is signified something than which nothing greater can be thought, nevertheless, it does not therefore follow that he understands that what the name signifies exists actually, but only that it exists mentally. Nor can it be argued that it actually exists, unless it be admitted that there actually exists something than which nothing greater can be thought; and this precisely is not admitted by those who hold that God does not exist.[1]

In other words: Granted that the meaning of the name "God" is "Being than which nothing greater can be thought" and granting further that by definition "God" signifies "Being which, among other attributes, has that of existence," we still cannot conclude "God therefore exists." All we are entitled to infer is the triviality, "If anything corresponding to the definition of 'God' exists, then that thing exists." We cannot get rid of this *if* without begging the question, that is, assuming what we purport to prove. (This is in substance identical to one of the refutations of the argument advanced by Kant.)

St. Thomas held that there are five valid demonstrations of God's existence. None of these celebrated Five Ways is original with the Saint, but his statement of them is usually considered definitive. Four of them will be reproduced here, not only on account of their intrinsic historical importance but also as illustrating Aquinas' method of procedure in the *Summa*: statement of question; statement of objection (*i.e.* opinions opposed to his own); followed by *"On the contrary"*, introducing an authoritative judgment on his side; then the author's *"I answer that"*, introducing the body of the article; after this the conclusion, consisting of answers one by one to the objections raised at the beginning.

*Summa Theologiae*, Part I, Question 2

Third Article

WHETHER GOD EXISTS

*We proceed thus to the Third Article:*—
*Objection 1.* It seems that God does not exist; because if one of two contraries be infinite, the other would be altogether destroyed. But the name *God* means that He is infinite goodness. If, therefore, God existed, there would be no evil discoverable; but there is evil in the world. Therefore God does not exist.

*Objection 2.* Further, it is superfluous to suppose that what can be accounted for by a few principles has been produced by many. But it seems that everything we see in the world can be accounted for by other principles, supposing God did not exist. For all natural things can be reduced to one principle, which is nature; and all voluntary things can be reduced to one principle, which is human reason, or will. Therefore there is no need to suppose God's existence.

*On the contrary,* it is said in the person of God: *I am Who am* (*Exod.* iii. 14).

*I answer that,* The existence of God can be proved in five ways.

The first and more manifest way is the argument from motion. It is certain, and evident to our senses, that in the world some things are in motion. Now whatever is moved is moved by another, for nothing can be moved except it is in potentiality to that towards which it is moved; whereas a thing moves inasmuch as it is in act. For motion is nothing else than the reduction of something from potentiality to actuality. Thus that which is actually hot, as fire, makes wood, which is potentially hot, to be actually hot, and thereby moves and changes it. Now it is not possible that the same thing should be at once in actuality and potentiality in the same respect, but only in different respects. For what is actually hot cannot simultaneously be potentially hot; but it is simultaneously potentially cold. It is therefore impossible that in the same respect and in the same way a thing should be both mover and moved, *i.e.*, that it should move itself. Therefore, whatever is moved must be moved by another. If that by which it is moved be itself moved, then this also must needs be moved by another, and that by another again. But this cannot go on to infinity, because then there would be no first mover, and, consequently, no other mover, seeing that subsequent movers move only inasmuch as they are moved by the first mover; as the staff moves only because it is moved by the hand. Therefore it is necessary to arrive at a first mover, moved by no other; and this everyone understands to be God.

The second way is from the nature of efficient cause . . .

The third way is taken from possibility and necessity, and runs thus. We find in nature things that are possible to be and not to be, since they are found to be generated, and to be corrupted, and consequently, it is possible for them to be and not to be. But it is impossible for these always to exist, for that which can not-be at some time is not. Therefore, if everything can not-be, then at one time there was nothing in existence, because that which does not exist begins to exist only through something already existing. Therefore, if at one time nothing was in existence, it would have been impossible for anything to have begun to exist; and thus even now nothing would be in existence—which is absurd. Therefore, not all beings are merely possible, but there must exist something the existence of which is necessary. But every necessary thing either has its necessity caused by another, or not. Now it is impossible to go on to infinity in necessary things which have their necessity caused by another, as has been already proved. . . . Therefore we cannot but admit the existence of some being having of itself its own necessity, and not receiving it from another, but rather causing in others their necessity. This all men speak of as God.

The fourth way is taken from the gradation to be found in things. Among beings there are some more and some less good, true, noble, and the like. But *more* and *less* are predicated of different things according as they resemble in their different ways something which is the maximum, as a thing is said to be hotter according as it more nearly resembles that which is hottest; so that there is something which is truest, something best, something noblest, and, consequently, something which is most being, for those things that are greatest in truth are greatest in being, as it is written in *Metaphysics* ii. Now the maximum in any genus is the cause of all in that genus, as fire, which is the maximum of heat, is the cause of all hot things, as is said in the same book. Therefore there must also be something which is to all beings the cause of their being, goodness, and every other perfection; and this we call God.

The fifth way is taken from the governance of the world. We see that things which lack knowledge, such as natural bodies, act for an end, and this is evident from their acting always, or nearly always, in the same way, so as to obtain the best result. Hence it is plain that they achieve their end, not fortuitously, but designedly. Now whatever lacks knowledge cannot move towards an end, unless it be directed by some being endowed with knowledge and intelligence; as the arrow is directed by the archer. Therefore some intelligent being exists by whom all natural things are directed to their end; and this being we call God.

*Reply Objection 1.* As Augustine says: *Since God is the highest good, He would not allow any evil to exist in His works, unless His omnipotence and goodness were such as to bring good even out of evil.* This is part of the infinite goodness of God, that He should allow evil to exist, and out of it produce good.

*Reply Objection 2.* Since nature works for a determinate end under the direction of a higher agent, whatever is done by nature must be traced back to God as to its first cause. So likewise whatever is done voluntarily must be traced back to some higher cause other than human reason and will, since these can change and fail; for all things that are changeable and capable of defect must be traced back to an immovable and self-necessary first principle, as has been shown.

In Aristotelian terms, all these are arguments *a posteriori*: from what is more evident to us to what is more evident in itself. They all have factual premises: that there is motion; that there are at least two things one of which is the cause of the other; that there is at least one thing that comes into being and passes out of being; that there are at least two things one of which is better than the other in some specifiable respect; and that there is at least one nonintelligent thing that acts for an end. Aquinas claims certainty for his proofs because each of these premises is known with certainty, by observation, to be true.

The Saint like the Philosopher means by "necessary being" something that cannot not exist, *i.e.* something that is eternal. He does not mean that the non-existence of a necessary being is inconceivable; though we must qualify this to the extent that if we did really comprehend the divine essence we would find His nonexistence inconceivable. Consequently, Atheism is not, as it was to Anselm, a logically contradictory position; it is merely incompatible with the most obvious facts.

We can argue from the world to God, but not vice versa. If the world is, God must be; but from the mere knowledge that God existed, it would not be possible to infer that He had created anything. Creation was a free act of God; He was not necessitated to create anything at all, much less this particular world. On this point Thomas disagrees with the Neoplatonists.

Today, when alleged demonstrations of God's existence are out of fashion—at any rate among philosophers—some people suppose they are defending Thomas when they advance the notion that in these Ways the Saint intended only to confirm the faithful in their faith. But it does little credit to Aquinas to suppose that he conceived these arguments to be anything less than what he said they were—to wit, proofs.

## Our Knowledge of God

We know by reason and revelation that God exists; but what can the word 'God' signify to us? This poses a difficult problem for Thomas, for he holds with the Philosopher that there can be nothing in the intellect that is not first in the senses. What we can meaningfully talk about, then, must be limited to conceptions that have their bases in our sense experience. The primary objects of the human intellect are essences of particular, material, individual things. At first sight it seems, then, that we can have no conceptions of purely spiritual beings such as angels and God.

The Saint's solution is subtle. Although in the human condition the intellect has to start, in knowing, from corporeal being, yet the primary object of the intellect is being as such. Mental imagery is not indispensable for knowing—indeed, mental images are not even intelligible by themselves: they enter into the intellectual process only as raw materials for the operations of the active intellect. By this faculty we can form a conception, though not a pictorial one, of spirit and even of God. Talk of God, therefore, is not meaningless verbiage.

That is not to say, however, that grave difficulties do not remain for us when we attempt to understand God. The Saint admits and insists that we do not have an adequate notion of Him. But we are not cut off altogether. As with John Scotus Erigena, we can approach God by the negative way: we can say that God is not this or that, because He exceeds the limitations inherent in the term applied. Thus God is not corporeal, because corporeality necessarily implies limitations—of spatial position, for instance, and potentiality. Nor is God complex, for any complex whole is dependent on its parts; but God, as a unity, cannot be thus limited. Yet God must not be supposed to lack any of the perfections that corporeal and complex entities may have.

However, the Saint teaches, there is available to us an affirmative conception of God. When we apply words like powerful, glorious, wise, and good to God, we must not suppose they mean the same as when we apply them to human beings. A man is glorious, let us say, who has won a great victory against heavy odds; but

God could never be in the position of having to do that. A good woman is cheerful in adversity; but God is never in adversity. Indeed, most of our laudatory adjectives signify dispositions; but God, being pure actuality, has no dispositions. Yet these words when applied to God are not merely equivocal—as 'fast' has one meaning when applied to dyes, another to fetters, and a third when describing racehorses. The words are applicable to God by analogy. As God (an infinite immaterial being) is to us, so God's wisdom, power, and so on, are to our wisdom, and so forth. Certainly we cannot form any exact conception of what they are; but we have enough notion to appreciate their appropriateness.

## Angels

The world that God created is a hierarchy of levels of being, from the disorganized and homogeneous—the four elements and unstructured mixtures such as mud—up through crystals, plants, lower animals, higher animals, and finally man among material beings. Man is the unique material being with an immaterial soul. But reason tells us there cannot be a gap between man and God; revelation confirms the existence of finite but immaterial and immortal intelligences, the angels, at this level.

St. Thomas Aquinas enjoys the official title Angelic Doctor, not as a compliment to his disposition but in recognition of his preeminence in the sacred science of angelology. The *Summa* contains 358 articles concerning angels.

Aquinas disagreed with Bonaventura about how angels are differentiated from one another. The Franciscan held that even though angels have no material bodies, there are species of angels containing pluralities of individual angels within them. He deemed it absurd to suppose that angels should differ from each other only according to species—that is, as dogs differ from cats, not as Mehitabel differs from Garfield. However, the Angelic Doctor accepted this consequence of the Aristotelian metaphysics. Since matter is the principle of individuation within a species, it follows that there can be but one angel per species. The number of species, however, is very great. Following Pseudo-Dionysius, they are grouped into three hierarchies of three choirs each: seraphim, cherubim, thrones; dominions, virtues, powers; principalities, archangels, and (plain) angels.

Angels can make themselves apparent to us—'angel' means messenger—by assuming quasi-bodies of thick air. Although they are not spatial, they exclude one another: there cannot be two angels in the same place. The question how many angels can dance on the point of a needle was not discussed in the middle ages. Nevertheless, the answer is one only—leaving aside the question whether an angel can be said to dance. Angels can, however, move, both continuously and discontinuously; that is, an angel can move from heaven to earth without traversing the intervening space. The velocity of an angel depends upon his will.

## Nature

Thomas discusses angels and human souls at length, as well as the questions concerning the beginning and end of the world. The rest of creation he leaves to the Philosopher for description and explanation. Thomas, unlike his teacher Albert the Great, had no interest in natural science—or perhaps he had no time for it.

But why should there be a world at all? And how can there be evil in a world that is the creation of a supremely good God?

To the first of these questions there is, in a sense, no answer possible. From the fact that God is the necessary being we must not infer, Thomas warns us, that what God does is of necessity. God in no way does anything because He has to. We can reason from the world to God but not from God to the world. If He had created nothing at all He would still have been the all-knowing, all-powerful, perfectly good being. His creation of the world was a perfectly free act.

Here it is natural to ask: Granted that God did not have to create a world at all; nevertheless, once He decided to do so, must not His creation be the best of all possible worlds? Thomas replies that this line of thought depends on a presupposition: God plus one kind of world would be better than God plus some other kind, so that just one particular world would be maximally good. This presupposition is false, according to the Saint. The goodnesses of the Creator and His creation cannot be added together this way. There cannot be any world required by divine goodness. This is not the best of all possible worlds if that is taken to mean that it would have been logically impossible to create a better one. God could have done so, Thomas declares, by making a bigger one, for instance—if your notion of "better" entails goods as being addable in such a simple way that twice as much is twice as good.

Nevertheless, the Saint admits, the question of evil is serious and difficult. One short answer we have seen already in his reply to the first objection to the thesis of God's existence: it is "part of the infinite goodness of God, that He should allow evil to exist, and out of it produce good." Thomas wrote several treatises dealing with the problem at greater length. They are fundamentally Augustinian in their conception of evil as privation rather than positive existence, therefore not something that God created. The Saint furthermore distinguishes between three kinds of evil: natural, moral, and punitive. Natural evil, such as the pains that signal danger, and disease, death, and decay are in a sense willed by God—for the order of nature requires them. Thus they are not really evil. Moral evil, the evil perpetrated by wicked men, is really evil—although Aquinas in a surprisingly Socratic way refuses to admit the possibility of even the most depraved person's willing evil as such. However, moral evil is due to human freedom, which is such a great good that it immeasurably recompenses. God, when He created Adam and Eve, foresaw this evil and permitted it, though He did not will it. As for punitive evil, it is really a good—including the eternal punishment of hellfire, which is one of the things that occasions the rejoicing of the blessed in heaven.

## The Human Creature

Perhaps the most difficult problem for anyone engaged in Christianizing Aristotle concerns the soul. For the Philosopher's functional conception of the soul seems to make immortality out of the question. While he allowed the possibility of the intellect's survival, he explicitly excluded memory, hence personality.

The doctrine of soul as form of body is furthermore so closely bound up with the central Aristotelian conception of things as unions of form and matter that it could be rejected only at peril of being left with an incoherent mishmash instead of an articulated philosophy. St. Thomas did not take this way. On the contrary, he restored a purer Aristotelianism by opposing an earlier compromise solution according to which the individual human being is a compound of matter and a "form of bodiness" fulfilling at least verbally the requirement for form while allowing the soul to be something else—a Platonic immaterial individual, loosely and temporarily united to the body. Thomas rejected also the doctrine of the active intellect, here in company with Bonaventura and contrary to the Arabians.

The way Thomas managed to preserve the immortality of the soul while remaining an Aristotelian was this. He declared the soul to be the form of the body, the *substantial* form—by which he meant the form that makes of the body a substance. The substantial form, he declared, is capable of existing in separation from matter. It is doubtful whether this expedient could be justified from the standpoint of Aristotelian interpretation. The Philosopher's doctrine of substance is notoriously obscure. There are passages in which he speaks of forms as substances (beings) and of immaterial substances; and some forms are separable from matter, since perception requires the sensible form to be taken into the mind of the perceiver. To combine these diverse leads, however, and fashion a form separable in fact from what it is the form of was hardly in the Stagirite spirit. Yet it is probably impossible to maintain personal immortality without becoming a Platonist, at least on this point.

Thomas devised a kind of argument for the soul's immortality from some of Aristotle's own views heavily dosed with Platonism. He repeated Aristotle's argument that the soul cannot be a body since it must be capable of knowing all bodies, and that involves receiving their forms. But then he went ahead to add, Platonically, that if the soul is not a body it must be a spirit—therefore incorruptible, therefore immortal. He accepted also the argument which concludes immortality from the principle that no natural desire can be without its object, combined with the (alleged) fact that all human beings naturally desire to live forever.

The soul after death cannot have sensations, however, since these depend on the body. Happily it does not follow that we are faced with an eternity of total insensibility. In our mortal existence the soul is subject to the limitation that it can be acquainted only with "phantasms"—not tomatoes themselves but the mental images of tomatoes. In an unexplained manner, death will free us from this kind of bondage: we will be able to acquire a direct knowledge even of spirits, bypassing the meandering mechanisms of the sense organs.

The Saint's doctrine on this point is related to some important teachings about knowledge. Thomas distinguished between the "phantasm" or image in the mind, which is particular and definite—the mental picture I have of Socrates—and, on the other hand, my general idea or concept of man, which is not pictorial; it is not even a fuzzy picture. The concept is the work of the intellect, which abstracts from my sensations, and the images resulting therefrom, the "intelligible species." Furthermore, the abstract concept is not the object of human knowledge but the means thereto. These are important points, historically at least, since a principal difference between scholastic and so-called modern philosophy consists in the latter's tendency to deny the validity of these distinctions, with consequent refusal to admit the existence of abstract ideas.

## Ethics

Every human being has a supernatural end, to spend eternity in heaven. Perfect happiness is to be enjoyed only in the life to come. Conceding this much to the demands of theology, St. Thomas proceeds to discuss the natural human end, happiness in this life, in complete agreement with the precepts of the great pagan philosopher. After centuries of dormancy the intellectual virtues again came in for a share of attention and commendation in the Thomistic ethics, though the moral virtues were paid greater notice and the theological or monkish virtues, of which Aristotle had never heard, were superadded.

As one would expect, Thomas had difficulty reconciling priestly poverty and celibacy with the doctrine of the Mean.

Thomistic ethics, however, lays stress on the Stoic and Roman inheritance of Natural Law. Our moral obligations are founded on the law of reason. From understanding human nature—our function and our end—we can derive precepts of obligatory behavior: we must be honest, keep our promises, refrain from adultery and sexual perversion (because these frustrate the natural ends of generation and family life), and so on. The Natural Law is entirely unchangeable—although this dictum turns out not to be quite so absolute as it may sound. Theft is against natural law, thus always wrong. But then, the Book of Exodus tells us that when the Jews fled from Egypt they took with them property belonging to the Egyptians, by the direct and express command of God. The Saint resolves this difficulty by asserting that since God is the ultimate owner of all property, He was disposing of His goods as He saw fit, so that there was really no theft in it.

The natural law—that is, our reason—tells us what we should do and avoid. And we can do what we ought; we have free choice, as the Philosopher teaches. So when we are not compelled by another, our free choice is the cause of our own movement. But can a Christian hold this? Is not God the first cause of everything? Yes, the Saint replies, but that does not cancel our freedom.

> Just as by moving natural causes He does not prevent their actions from being natural, so by moving voluntary causes He does not deprive their actions of being voluntary.[2]

This doctrine, however, becomes heavily qualified if not reversed when Thomas turns to the consideration of divine grace. Here all becomes sombre and Augustinian. Without God's favor we cannot avoid sin and consequent damnation; nor can we do anything, on our own, to obtain or even merit grace. Nor can we know for sure whether we have been granted it. If we complain that we are being dealt with severely in being punished for what we can in no way help, the Saint replies that receiving grace is nothing but turning to God—and "Man's turning to God is by free choice. But," he continues, "free choice can be turned to God only when God turns it."[3]

## Politics

Contrary to earlier Christian theorists who held that the State is one of the punishments incurred by the original sin of Adam and Eve, Thomas assented to the view of Aristotle that man is by nature a political animal. The State exists not merely to provide for the common defense against enemies without and criminals within, but to coordinate, facilitate, and direct for the common good—to promote the general welfare.

To this end princes have their authority from God. It is not entirely clear whether Thomas held that secular sovereigns derive their authority directly from God—so that they are answerable to no mortals at all—or whether the political authority resides in the people, who then delegate it to the prince. The latter, somewhat daring, interpretation is favored by the fact that Thomas held it justifiable to depose tyrants (though not to assassinate them). The main point of substance perhaps is that in either case, according to Aquinas, secular power does not depend on spiritual power—kings are not to be regarded as vassals of the Pope, even though some popes had made this claim; indeed in the case of King John of England the subordination had been conceded and ritually solemnized.

However, Thomas did not teach separation of church and state. Although the church should refrain from interfering with the State's autonomy in its own sphere, still the Church is the higher power, being spiritual, and kings must be subject to priests because the supernatural end takes precedence over the natural end. The State exists to facilitate salvation. In particular, it is the duty of the State to put heretics to death.

The laws of the State exist to give effect to the Natural Law. Consequently any statute that disagrees with natural law is not a law but a perversion of law. No one is bound in conscience to obey the law of the state when it is thus unjust; and priests must be ultimate judges of whether the law is in accordance with natural law.

As a matter of practice, monarchy is the best form of government, though it should not be absolute but "mixed," as Aristotle taught.

## The Triumph of Thomism

In his lifetime Thomas did not secure total victory for Aristotle. Bonaventura, with whom Thomas was personally on good terms and with whom he carried on a more or less continual debate for many years, spoke with equal or perhaps superior authority. Less than three years after the Saint's death the Bishop of Paris issued an attack against 219 propositions, threatening excommunication and other penalties against anyone who continued to teach the offending doctrines in the University. Most of the offensive propositions were held by the unreconstructed Aristotelians, or Averroists; it is hard to discern more than a few peculiar to Thomas, and two of those have to do with his angelology.

> God cannot produce many individuals within one species apart from matter.

> Because Intelligences have no matter, God cannot make several of the same species.

Of philosophical theses, the only one of St. Thomas' that was declared to be an "obvious and detestable error, an empty and insanely false assertion" was the argument he had urged in rebuttal of Bonaventura's proof of the world's beginning.

> Time is infinite both ways, for although it is impossible to pass through infinites of which some portion has to be passed through, still it is not impossible to pass through infinites of which no portion has to be passed through.[4]

Nevertheless, the effect was, as it was intended to be, the discouragement of the friends of Aristotle.

However, the Dominicans were powerful in Paris and even more at the Papal court. Thomas was elevated to sainthood in 1323, 98 years after his birth and 49 years after his death. In 1567 he was declared a Doctor of the Church, ranking equally with the four great Church Fathers: Augustine, Ambrose, Jerome, and Gregory. In 1879, Pope Leo XIII in his encyclical "On the Restoration of Christian

Philosophy" confirmed the preeminence of Thomas among philosophers. In 1918 the Vatican directed the education of all priests in philosophy and theology to be conducted on Thomistic principles. Catholic writers point out that in spite of all this, disagreement with St. Thomas is not in itself heretical, sinful, or even forbidden. Nevertheless, the Saint's position is a special one.

Looking at his work not from the standpoint only of the Church but of the history of philosophy, if we ask what Thomas' accomplishment was, the answer is that he staved off for four centuries a crisis in which the best minds of Europe—well-informed of advances in thought—would find it no longer possible to believe what the Church insisted they should believe. In the thirteenth century, Aristotle and his Arabian commentators represented the spearhead of intellectual progress. Avant-garde professors, intoxicated from reading the latest translations from the Arabic, were saying things like these.

> Being according to the Faith is not worth bothering about, nor does it matter when something is said to be heretical because it is contrary to the Faith.

> Creation is not possible, although the opposite has to be held according to the Faith.

> Knowing theology does not mean an increase of knowledge.

> There are fables and lies in the Christian religion, as in other religions.

> A human being who is well regulated in his intellect and in his feelings, as he may well be through the intellectual virtues and the other moral virtues of which the Philosopher speaks in the *Ethics*, is adequately disposed for eternal happiness.

> Simple fornication, as between a man and a woman who are not married, is not a sin.

> The separated soul does not in any way suffer from fire.

> The Christian religion hinders learning.[5]

Thomas showed that it was possible to be the intellectual superior of people who talked like this and yet not to affirm these conclusions. The Augustinian dualism—become so tense as to break out into the explosive doctrine of double truth—he replaced by Aristotelian hierarchy. The legitimate demand of the medieval enthusiasts for Aristotle—that this world, this life, should be taken seriously—could be thus satisfied without denying the claims of religion.

Thomas' Aristotelianism can be overemphasized. He was after all a theologian first and foremost, and on most points Aristotelianism is not so much incompatible or hard to reconcile with Christian theology as simply irrelevant to it. Thomistic theology, even where the Philosopher has some bearing on it, is mostly Augustinian, the great exception being the doctrine of the soul's nature.

It comes to this. St. Thomas showed that Aristotle's philosophy can accommodate the Christian God without being mutilated beyond recognition. From the other side, nothing prevents Christians from agreeing that their God saw fit to create an Aristotelian world—hierarchical, teleological, matter-form, potency-act. The magnitude of this achievement has to be measured against the antecedently great unlikelihood of anyone's being able to bring it off; for the Stagirite, unlike Plato, was not discernibly a Christian before his time.

# 31

# The Later Scholastics

IN THE CENTURY AFTER the death of Thomas Aquinas the dominant philosophical figures, among those who did not follow the Saint in every respect, were again two British Franciscans: Duns Scotus and William of Ockham. In the Augustinian tradition of their order they emphasized the distinction and separation of reason from revelation, thereby also the separateness of philosophy and theology. In Ockham this distinction became almost absolute.

## Duns Scotus

Scotland, at any rate the lowlands thereof, came upon the philosophical scene with Duns Scotus (1265?–1308), the Subtle Doctor. He was educated at Oxford University, having entered the Franciscan Order when barely into his teens. In the first years of the fourteenth century he lectured in the University of Paris, from which he was expelled by royal edict for having taken the side of the Pope in a quarrel with the King of France. He died in Cologne—after burial, a gruesome tradition tells us.

Between the Subtle and the Angelic Doctors important differences exist with respect to (1) the proper object of the human intellect, (2) the status of individuals and our knowledge of them, (3) the will in relation to the intellect, and (4) the possibility of philosophical theology.

1. Following Aristotle, Aquinas taught that the human intellect by its nature is fitted to know primarily the essences of bodies. On this view it is difficult to explain how we can have knowledge of God. As we have seen, Thomas' position in the end was almost agnostic: we know that God exists, but as to His attributes we can only make shift to comprehend them by analogies that are at best suggestive, never capable of conceptualization. Even God's being, His mode of existence, is known only by analogy (whatever this may mean) to our knowledge of the beings of tomatoes, souls, and truths.

Duns declared that, on the contrary, the primary object of the human intellect is being as such—being, existence, whether of material or of immaterial things. Moreover, he declared, the concept of being is univocal: when we say that a tomato exists and that God exists, we are using the word 'exists' in the same sense. The knowledge of existence that we have we derive by abstraction from our knowledge of creatures—that is the only possibility. And if this concept did not apply to God, we should have to face the consequence that we had no knowledge of God's existence at all; the word 'analogy' would not save us.

The same applies, according to Duns, to the other attributes of God, for instance wisdom. God is not wise in the way men are wise, just as the way a bird flies is not the same as how an angel does; nevertheless, the word 'fly' is not used in different senses of birds and of angels. Just so, the wisdom of Solomon and of God fall under the same concept, though they are not otherwise comparable.

Duns was obliged to allow, however, that though the being of immaterial things is as proper to the human intellect as that of material things, yet in our earthly state—as a consequence of Adam's sin—the intellect is moved to knowledge only by sensible things.

2.   Aristotle famously pronounced that the world is made of individual things. But notoriously also he failed to carry through this insight, in fact equating substance with essence and Platonically degrading the individual to the status of mere exemplar of the species, which is the object of scientific knowledge.

On this question Duns can be said to have been in a way more Aristotelian than the Philosopher. He held knowledge to be of essences, but he equated essence with existence and dared to assert that there are essences of individuals. There is not only the essence of man, there is also Socrates-*ness*, and knowledge thereof. To know Socrates is to know his essence, and that is not the same thing as knowing only those respects in which he is the same as Plato. The species is a unity, but the individual is a more perfect unity. "Thisness" signifies a mode of being that is "the ultimate reality of the form."

The doctrine of Thisness required revision of the Aristotelian matter-form scheme. Duns held that in no sense is a mere potency anything real; therefore matter as such, if it is real—and it is—has its own existence and is intelligible. The matter-form combination is of entities, not of "principles." The union of the two, nevertheless, is a substantial unity if they are "naturally determined" to one another—as the body and soul of a human being are.

3.   Against the Aristotelian and Thomistic view that the intellect determines the will—that ultimately we can do nothing other than what our intellectual nature rightly or wrongly certifies to us as choiceworthy—Duns reasserted the voluntarism of Sts. Paul and Augustine. The intellect presents us with the object of our action; however, this presentation is not the cause but only the necessary condition of the act of will. So far from intellect commanding will, the opposite is often the case: we can, for example, remember or concentrate attention by efforts of will. Furthermore, will is essentially nobler than intellect. The reason for this is that we cannot speak of anyone who is not free as being truly rational. But knowledge—the product of purely intellectual activity—is not itself free, for it is determined by the object known. Consequently, the human perfections, freedom and rationality, pertain to will not intellect. This is not to say that intellect has no worth or is dispensable, so that a person need not think beforehand in order to act rightly. Duns' point was that the will, like an old-fashioned king, can take advice or reject it. Aristotle and Thomas had made the will into a constitutional monarch bound to follow the counsel of his prime minister.

4.   Duns agreed with Aquinas that it is possible for the human reason unaided by revelation to prove the existence of God. He elaborated the argument from contingency to necessary being. He emphasized, however, the impossibility of establishing rationally what the characters of the creation would have to be—for God, as absolutely free agent, was not constrained even by reason to create things in one way rather than another. In particular, Duns denied the possibility of

proving the immortality of the soul. We know by revelation that we are destined for eternal life, but there is nothing about the soul as such that requires or guarantees its continued existence after the death of the body.

## William of Ockham

William of Ockham, born some time between 1280 and 1290, studied and lectured at Oxford from 1310 until 1324. When the Chancellor of the University complained to the Pope that William had asserted 51 erroneous propositions, William was obliged to proceed to the Papal court at Avignon to defend himself. (This was during the period 1309–1377 known as the "Babylonish Captivity," when the Popes resided in southern France and were especially subservient to the King of France.) The case dragged on and was not yet settled when late in 1327 Michael of Cesena, General of the Franciscan Order to which William belonged, appeared also in Avignon to answer a charge of heresy. Michael took St. Francis' emphasis on holy poverty seriously enough to refuse to allow Franciscans to own any property. The Papacy, however, had declared it heretical to teach that Christ and His disciples had owned no worldly possessions. In the spring of 1328 William and Michael escaped from Avignon and fled to Munich, to the court of Ludwig, Holy Roman Emperor, who was also embroiled in a quarrel with the Pope. Excommunicated at once, William nevertheless lived under Imperial protection for 21 years, dying in 1349, presumably of the Black Death which raged in Europe at that time.

Ockham earned his keep and safety by polemical writings against three Popes, whom he did not hesitate to accuse of heresy. He upheld the position that a General Council of the Church had an authority superior to that of the Pope. This Conciliar Movement, as it is called, gained momentum through the fourteenth century—especially during the scandalous Great Schism (1378–1417) when there were two and sometimes even three Popes, all reciprocally excommunicated.

Ockham was a pupil of Duns Scotus. On many topics he agreed with the Subtle Doctor: on the equation of existence and essence, on the univocal character of the concept of being with the consequent denial of the Thomistic doctrine of analogical predication, and on the impossibility of a proof of immortality. In other respects Ockham's philosophy was a continuation, perhaps to extremes, of trends initiated by Duns.

Thus Ockham criticized destructively all the Five Ways for proving the existence of God propounded by St. Thomas. All versions of the First Cause argument are flawed, according to William, because of the impossibility of proving the impossibility of infinite regress in the sense demanded by the Ways. It is not impossible that the series parents-grandparents-great-grandparents . . . should be infinite, having no first member. So much had been admitted by Thomas; but Ockham went further to deny the necessity of there being a permanent cause of the series as a whole—a reason, that is, why this particular series and not some other should exist. It would have been better, Ockham asserted, to emphasize the necessity not of a precedent cause of being but of a conserver of being. That is to say, if something exists, there must be something else to conserve it in existence; and that conserver must itself be conserved. And this series of conservers cannot be infinite: there must be something that conserves without itself having to be

246 / CHAPTER 31 The Later Scholastics

conserved. There must therefore be a First Conserver. Unfortunately, as far as the argument goes, there might be more than one—so we cannot prove by this argument that God is one.

The argument from the design found in nature, Thomas' fifth Way, is logically deficient: it begs the question. Its major premise is that things lacking knowledge and volition nevertheless act for an end. But we cannot know this to be true unless we know beforehand that God moves them toward the end—and that is what we have to prove.

In any case, Ockham averred, even granting that we could demonstrate the existence of a Supreme Being, we could not go on to prove that the Being would have to be infinite. Here also we come up against a logical point: if there is a valid deductive argument with the conclusion "God is infinite," it must contain a premise known to be true which states that something, X, is infinite—and to avoid question begging, X cannot be identical to God by definition. But, Ockham points out, there is not and cannot be any such known truth.

The consequence is that philosophy and theology are entirely separate. Contrary to St. Thomas, there is no region of overlap containing truths knowable both by reason and by revelation. Religion has no rational foundation but rests entirely on revelation.

Likewise, Ockham makes absolute the contrast between God and His creation. God is a perfectly free and independent being, not limited in His creation by antecedently existing ideas in His mind. Nothing is prior to God. Everything in the created world is contingent, dependent. In consequence, there can be no *a priori* knowledge of the world; there is nothing that would not have been otherwise had God chosen to make it so. Therefore, nothing but experience can reveal the nature of the world to us.

William carried this Voluntarism to the extreme of declaring even the moral law to be contingent. There is no essentially immutable natural law. "By the very fact that God wills something, it is right for it to be done." Why, for instance, is adultery wrong? Because God has commanded us to abstain from it. But why did He see fit to issue this commandment? That is an improper question in Ockham's opinion. There is no reason to be sought beyond the Divine will. Then God, had He chosen, could have made adultery a virtue? Ockham does not shrink from admitting that He could have. However, in other writings William developed an ethical theory according to which virtue consists in acting in accordance with "right reason" from the motive of desire to act in accordance with right reason. It is difficult to reconcile these two ethical theories—one absolutely authoritarian, the other absolutely rationalistic.

The achievement for which William of Ockham has been best remembered is his solution of the problem of universals. In Ockham's treatment this problem, hitherto often conceived as one of metaphysics—of what does reality consist? individuals alone, or also species and abstractions?—is reduced to a problem about the uses of language, of the terms of discourse. Hence Ockham's position on universals is called Terminism.

The solution depends on two linguistic distinctions. The first is between the *signification* and *supposition* of a term. Signification is the relation of a sign to the thing signified: as of the string of marks T O M A T O, a conventional sign, to a concept summoned to mind when the marks are read by English-speaking persons. The concept is the same as that summoned to the mind of an Italian by the

*Artist's impression of William of Ockham. Sketch labeled* Frater Occham
iste. *Page from Gonville and Caius MS 464/571, f. 69 + 1r. With
permission of the Master and Fellows of Gonville and Caius
College, Cambridge.*

marks P O M I D O R O. This concept is a natural sign for certain edible objects.
(This notion is found in the work of Peter of Spain, a native of Lisbon, who became
the only logician Pope, John XXI.)

Terms have signification all by themselves. But they have *supposition,* that is
they *stand for* whatever they stand for, only in sentences. In "This tomato is juicy,"
the supposition of the term 'tomato' is an individual object. In "The tomato is a
berry," the supposition of the same term is all the tomatoes there are.

The second distinction is between terms of *first* and *second intention.* A term of
first intention is one the supposition of which is something other than a sign. A
term of second intention has as supposition one or more signs. Thus in the sentence "English conjunctions are mostly short," the term 'conjunctions' is of second
intention because it stands for the set of words (signs) containing 'and', 'but', 'or',
and so on.

Now we note that the *term* 'universal' is in all its occurrences a term of second
intention, for its supposition is always *other terms* not things. If we are asked to

produce a collection of universals, we shall not collect objects from the world, we shall compile a list: man, elephant, redness, beauty . . . all of which are signs. If someone objects that it is not the words that are the universals but what the words signify, the concepts, Ockham will reply that those concepts are still signs— natural signs—of individual things. A universal, that is to say, is a term of (usually) first intention, such as 'whale' or 'tomato'. Its signification is individual things; and so also, ordinarily, is its supposition.

We can now return our attention to the question whether universals exist. It makes sense to say that tomatoes exist, because the universal term 'tomato' is a term of first intention whose supposition in the sentence is individuals. But the sentence "Universals exist" makes no sense, for 'universal' is a term of second intention without individual supposition. Or rather, if the sentence does make sense it does so only trivially: it informs us that there are in fact words, signs— such as tomato, whale, man. Only individual things exist.

To the Platonic rebuttal that after all there is a real similarity between one tomato and another—that is, they share a real common essence, the universal tomato*hood*—Ockham would reply that from their likeness it does not follow that there is something they share. They agree not *in* something but *by* something, namely themselves. If they had a common essence, the consequence would have to be that when one tomato was eaten the other would be affected, inasmuch as its essence would be altered—which is absurd.

The upshot of Terminism is that we can explain how we intelligibly use words of general signification without, for purposes of our explanation, having to postulate the existence of anything beyond singular individual entities. This argument against Realism illustrates the famous principle known as "Ockham's Razor," usually stated as "Entities are not to be multiplied beyond necessity." This principle was not original with Ockham—it goes back at least to Aristotle's complaint that Plato's Ideas merely duplicated the world without explaining it—nor did Ockham state it in the words just quoted. He said, rather, "It is vain to do with more what can be done with fewer." However, Ockham made such copious and elegant use of the Razor in his philosophy that he deserved the honor of having it named after him. In science the Razor is sometimes called the Principle of Parsimony, expressed in the form that if two theories both explain the known facts the simpler is to be preferred—the simpler being the one requiring the postulation of fewer unobservables.

## Ockhamism and Ockhamites

Ockham's vigorous and rigorous thought was immediately influential. Ockhamites, or Moderns, as they proudly called themselves, were soon to be found in all the universities of Europe, often occupying professorial chairs.

William does not appear to have been inclined to religious skepticism. His denial of philosophical foundations for religion was intended to free theology from rationalist shackles. And although he expressly asserted that God could produce in us immediate and intuitive knowledge of a nonexistent object, he was not a skeptic about the validity of human knowledge.

Some Ockhamites, however, tended to draw skeptical inferences. John of Mirecourt, in the middle years of the fourteenth century, declared that no proposition can be certain unless it is analytic, that is unless its denial would be a contradiction in terms. Drawing on the Ockhamist doctrine of the contingency of the world, he concluded that all statements asserting existence are subject to error, with the one exception of the assertion of one's own existence. The principle of causality is not analytic, he pointed out; it could never amount to contradiction to say of something that it did not have the cause that things of that sort usually have, or even that it had no cause at all.

Nicholas of Autrecourt, at about the same time, allowed certainty to judgments of immediate perception—"this is green" as opposed to "this is grass"—but in agreement with John's observations on causality he denied the possibility of inferring with certainty the existence of one thing from that of another. Such inference would have to be based on the causal principle. But inferences from causes to effects or from effects to causes do not rest on necessary truths of reason; they are merely habits of expectation based on our experiences of regular sequence. Nor can we infer with certainty the existence of substances, nor of souls. In 1347 Nicholas was obliged to burn his writings and recant, and he was deprived of his teaching position in the University of Paris.

# Notes

## Chapter 1 *What Went Before*

[1]H. Frankfort and others, *Before Philosophy* (Penguin Books, 1949), p. 184.

[2]Same, p. 197.

[3]Same, p. 196.

[4]Same, p. 193.

[5]*Theogony*, lines 116–138. Translation by author.

[6]Same, lines 27 *f.*

## Chapter 2 *The Milesians*

[1]Aristotle, *Metaphysics*, 983b22.

[2]*Greek Science*, I (Penguin Books, 1944), p. 32.

[3]Aristotle, *Physics*, 204b27.

[4]Diels/Kranz, *Die Fragmente der Vorsokratiker*, 6th ed., 12 A 23.

[5]Same, 12 A 10.

[6]Same, 12 A 30.

[7]Same.

## Chapter 3 *Pythagoras and Xenophanes*

[1]This and subsequent quotations in this chapter are from the fragments of Xenophanes, Diels/Kranz, 21 B. Translations by author.

## Chapter 4 *Heraclitus*

[1]This and subsequent quotations in this chapter are from the fragments of Heraclitus, Diels/Kranz, 22 B. Translations by author.

## Chapter 5 *The Eleatics*

[1]This and subsequent quotations in this chapter, unless otherwise noted, are from the fragments of Parmenides, Diels/Kranz, 28 B. Translations by author.

[2]Plato, *Parmenides*, 128 C–D.

## Chapter 6 *Empedocles*

[1]This and subsequent quotations in this chapter, unless otherwise noted, are from the fragments of Empedocles, Diels/Kranz, 31 B. Translations by author.

[2]*On Ancient Medicine*, Chapter 1. Corpus Hippocraticum, trans. Jones, Loeb Classical Library.

## Chapter 7 *Anaxagoras*

[1]This and subsequent quotations in this chapter, unless otherwise noted, are from the fragments of Anaxagoras, Diels/Kranz, 59 B. Translations by author.

[2]*Metaphysics* A, 984b15.

[3]Plato, *Phaedo*, p. 98.

[4]*Metaphysics* A, 985a18.

[5]R. G. Bury, *History of Greece*, Modern Library ed., p. 332.

## Chapter 8 *Leucippus and Democritus*

[1]By John Burnet, *Early Greek Philosophy.*

[2]This and subsequent quotations in this chapter, unless otherwise noted, are from the fragments of Democritus, Diels/Kranz, 68 B. Translations by author.

[3]*On the Heavens*, Book III, Chapter 4, 303a29.

## Chapter 9   *Intellectual Life in Athens*

[1]Thucydides, Book II, pp. 37–41, Crawley translation.

[2]Plato, *Protagoras*, 318e.

## Chapter 10   *Socrates*

[1]This and subsequent quotations from *The Clouds* of Aristophanes are from the translation by H. J. and P. E. Easterling (Cambridge, England: W. Heffer & Sons, 1961).

[2]*Phaedo*, 96.

[3]*Apology*, 29, trans. Hugh Tredennick, in *The Last Days of Socrates* (Penguin Books, 1954).

[4]Jowett translation.

[5]*Phaedo*, 115, Tredennick translation (see 3).

[6]A. E. Taylor, *Socrates*.

[7]*Phaedo*, 116–118. Jowett translation.

## Chapter 11   *The Life of Plato*

[1]Seventh Letter, 326B.

[2]*Republic*, 501.

## Chapter 12   *The Theory of Ideas*

[1]*Republic* V, 473D.

[2]*Republic* VII, 518C, F. M. Cornford translation (Oxford University Press, 1945).

[3]Seventh Letter, 341C, Morrow translation.

[4]*Republic* V, 478–479, Cornford translation (see 2).

## Chapter 13   *Plato's Politics*

[1]*Republic*, 424D. Cornford translation.

## Chapter 14   *Plato on the Human Good*

[1]*Phaedo*, 66B. Jowett translation.

[2]*Republic* IX, 571D. Cornford translation.

## Chapter 15   *Life of Aristotle*

[1]*Nicomachean Ethics*, Book IV, Chapter 3; trans. Ross (Oxford: Clarendon Press).

## Chapter 16   *Aristotle's Philosophy of Nature*

[1]*Physics*, Book II, Chapter 3. This and subsequent quotations from Aristotle, unless otherwise noted, are from the Oxford Aristotle translations edited by Sir David Ross.

[2]*Categories*, Chapter 2.

[3]Same, Chapter 5.

[4]*Physics*, Book II, Chapter 8.

[5]*Metaphysics*, Book XII, Chapter 7.

## Chapter 17 *Aristotle on the Structure of Science*

[1]*Posterior Analytics*, Book II, Chapter 19.
[2]*Sophistical Refutations*, Chapter 34.
[3]*Rhetoric*, Book I, Chapter 1.
[4]*Poetics*, Chapter 6.
[5]*On the Soul*, Book III, Chapter 5.

## Chapter 18 *Aristotle's Ethics*

[1]*Nicomachean Ethics*, Book I, Chapter 7, 1098a17.
[2]Same, Book II, Chapter 6, 1106b20.
[3]Same, Book III, Chapter 1, 1111a19.
[4]Same, Book X, Chapter 4, 1174b32.
[5]Same, Book X, Chapter 7, 1177b31.

## Chapter 19 *Aristotle's Politics*

[1]*Politics*, Book III, Chapter 9.
[2]Same, Book III, Chapter 11.
[3]Same, Book VIII, Chapter 2.

## Chapter 21 *Stoicism*

[1]Marcus Aurelius, *Meditations* II, 1.
[2]*The Manual of Epictetus*, 1.
[3]Same, 8.
[4]Same, 49.

## Chapter 22 *Epicurus*

[1]Lucretius, Book I. Trans. Latham, slightly modified (Penguin Books, 1951.)
[2]Diogenes Laertius, *Life of Epicurus*.
[3]Lucretius, Book II. Latham translation.
[4]Epicurus, *Letter to Menoeceus*.
[5]Epicurus, *Letter to Pythocles*.
[6]*Vatican Sayings*, p. 63.
[7]*Lucretius on the Nature of Things*, trans. W. Hannaford Brown (Rutgers University Press, 1950).

## Chapter 23 *Greek Skeptical Philosophies*

[1]*Outlines of Pyrrhonism*, Ch. 14.
[2]Democritus, Fragment 7.
[3]Diogenes Laertius, *Life of Pyrrho*.
[4]*Outlines of Pyrrhonism*, Ch. 10.

## Chapter 24 *Plotinus and Neo-Platonism*

[1]*Plotinus*, trans. A. H. Armstrong, slightly modified (Collier Books, 1962), page 45.
[2]Same, p. 47.
[3]*Enneads* 2, 9, 1; trans. Armstrong, p. 49.

[4]*Enneads* V, 9, 8; trans. Armstrong, p. 71.
[5]*Enneads* III, 8, 4; trans. Armstrong, p. 95.
[6]*Enneads* II, 9, 16; trans. Armstrong, p. 134.
[7]*Enneads* VI, 9, 11; trans. Armstrong, p. 148.

## Chapter 25 *The Christian Revolution*

[1]Psalm 137.
[2]*Annals* XV, 44; Church and Brodribb translation.

## Chapter 26 *St. Augustine*

[1]*Confessions*, Book II, Chapter 1.
[2]Same, Book III, Chapter 1.
[3]358D.
[4]*Romans* 7, 19.
[5]*Confessions*, Book XII, Chapter 9.
[6]*City of God*, Book V, Chapter 9.

## Chapter 27 *The Dark Ages*

[1]Gibbon, *Decline and Fall of the Roman Empire*, Chapter 47.

## Chapter 28 *Early Scholastic Philosophy*

[1]Quoted in Anne Fremantle, *The Age of Belief* (Mentor Books), p. 80.
[2]*New England Primer.*
[3]Psalm 19.
[4]Psalm 14.

## Chapter 29 *The Aristotelian Revival*

[1]*Opus Maius*, Part VI; trans. Robert Burke (University of Pennsylvania Press, 1928).
[2]Quoted in Singer *et al.*, *A History of Technology*, 3 (Oxford University Press, 1957), p. 719.

## Chapter 30 *St. Thomas Aquinas*

[1]*Summa Theologiae*, Part I, Qu. 2, Art. 1, Reply Obj. 2.
[2]Same, Part I, Qu. 83, Art. 1, Reply Obj. 3.
[3]Same, Qu. 109, Art. 6, Reply Obj. 1.
[4]Condemnation of 1277, quoted in Katz and Weingartner, *Philosophy in the West* (Harcourt Brace and World, 1965), pages 532–542.
[5]Same.

# Index

This index covers both volumes of *A New History of Philosophy*. Pages 1–249 are in Volume I; pages 250–485 are in Volume II. Page numbers in **boldface** refer to the more central discussions.

## A

Abailard. *See* Abelard, Peter
Abdera, 53
Abelard, Peter (1079?–1144), **217–19**
abortion, Aristotle on, 144
Absolute (in Hegel), 404–07
abstraction
  Abelard on, 217–18
  Aristotle on, 132
  Avicenna on, 222
  Berkeley on, 343
  Locke on, 318–19
  Plato on, 126–27
  Russell on, 463
  Thomas Aquinas on, 239
absurd. *See* Existentialism
academic freedom, 298
Academy, Platonic, 84–85, 179
  and Aristotle, 111, 113
  closing of, 203
  and skepticism ("New Academy"), 170
  *See also* Plato
acquaintance/description, 462–63
Acragas, 38
activity/passivity, Aristotle on, 125–26
Aenesidemus (1st c. B.C.), 172
Aeschylus (525–456 B.C.), 58–59
affection (Empedocles), 40–43
Agrigento. *See* Acragas
Agrippa (1st c. B.C. or A.D.), 172
Albert the Great, St. (1206–80), 230–31
Albigensians, 225
Alcibiades (*ca* 450–404 B.C.), 70, 80
Alcuin (735–804), 208
Alexander III (the Great) (356–323 B.C.),
  112–14, 149
  and Diogenes, 153
Alexander VI, Pope (1431–1503), 255
Alexander of Hales (*d.* 1245), 226
Alexandria, 150–51
Al-Farabi (*d.* 950), 220–21
Algazel (1058–1111), 223
Al-Ghazali. *See* Algazel
alienation, 415–16
Ambrose, St. (340?–397), 195
Ameinias (6th c. B.C.), 29
"America, or The Muses Refuge: A Prophecy"
  (Berkeley), 335–36
Ammonius Saccas (3d c. A.D.), 174, 193
*Analysis of Sensations* (Mach), 411
analytic philosophy, 470–485 *passim*
analytic propositions, 326, 331

Anaxagoras (*ca* 500–428 B.C.), **44–47**, 48,
  52–54, 57
  Socrates on, 77–78
Anaximander (610–*ca* 547 B.C.), **11–14**, 15–17,
  21–23, 31–32, 40, 42, 48, 52, 54, 57, 375
Anaximenes (6th c. B.C.), 12, **14–15**, 16, 23, 27,
  32, 40–41, 52
  and experimentalism, 48–50
  as first Positivist, 408
Andronicus (1st c. B.C.), 115
angels
  Bonaventura on, 226
  Thomas Aquinas on, 237
anguish. *See* Existentialism
animism, 57, 266, 408
  in Berkeley, 346
  in Xenophanes, 22
Anselm, St. (1033–1109), **215–17**
*Antichrist, The* (Nietzsche), 444
*Anti-Dühring* (Engels), 420
antinomies (Kantian), **387–89**
Antiochus IV Epiphanes (*ca* 215–163 B.C.), 150
Antiphon (*ca* 479–411 B.C.), 69
Antisthenes (*ca* 455–*ca* 365 B.C.), 83, **152**
apathy, 157
*Apology* (Plato), 75–77
*a posteriori* knowledge, 327
*a priori* knowledge, 326, 331
Aquinas. *See* Thomas Aquinas, St.
Arcesilaus (*ca* 315–241 B.C.), 170
Archelaus (5th c. B.C.), 74
Archilochus (8th?–7th? c. B.C.), 26
Archimedes (*ca* 287–212 B.C.), 150, 265
Archytas (5th–4th c. B.C.), 85
*Areopagitica* (Milton), 299
Aristarchus (3d c. B.C.), 158, 260–61
Aristippus (*ca* 435–366 B.C.), 83, 167
Aristophanes (*ca* 450–*ca* 388 B.C.), **72–74**
Aristotle (384–322 B.C.), **111–145**
  on Anaxagoras, 47
  on atomism, 55, 58
  Bacon on, 265–66
  on beginning of philosophy, 10, 18, 49
  on education, 145
  ethics, **137–141**
  and Existentialism, 466
  on knowledge, 34
  logic, 132–33
  on motion, 128–30
  and Nietzsche, 443
  on Plato, 111
  on Platonic ideas, 77
  political philosophy, **142–45**

soul
Anaximenes on, 15
Aristotle on, 134–36
Bonaventura on, 227
as cause of motion, 128–30
Empedocles on, 38–39, 42–43
Epicurus on, 165
Heraclitus on, 27–28
Homer's conception of, 79
La Mettrie on, 374
Leibniz on, 330–32
Neoplatonism, 177
Plato on, 96–97, 106–08
Pythagorean views of, 18–19, 96–97
Socrates on, 79–80
in Thales' thought, 10
Thomas Aquinas on, 238–39
transmigration of, 18–19, 38–39, 42–43
*See also* consciousness; immortality; mind
sovereignty
Hobbes, 294–95
Locke, 322
Rousseau, 378
Thomas Aquinas, 240–41
space
Hegel on, 405
Kant on, 383–84
Leibniz on, 332
Parmenides on, 33–34
Zeno on, 35–36
Sparta, 101. *See also* Peloponnesian War
Speusippus (*d.* 339 B.C.), 111, 113
Spinoza, Baruch (later Benedict) (1632–77), 297–309, 325–26, 367, 403, 464
sport, 19, 22
Stagira, 111
Stalin, Joseph (Iosif Vissarionovich Dzhugashvili, 1879–1953), 422
state, the
Nietzsche on, 443
Thomas Aquinas on, 240–41
state of nature. *See* nature, state of
Stephen, St. (1st c.), 189
Stephen, Sir Leslie (1832–1904), 285
Stoicism, **154–59**
in Academy, 170
and Spinoza, 300
substance, 34, 214–15
Aristotle on, **119–130**
Berkeley on, 337–47 *passim*
in Christian theology, 191–93
Descartes, 281, 302
Hume, 360–62
Kant, 385–87
Leibniz, 329–32
Locke, 319–20
Odo, 214
Russell, 461–63
Spinoza, 302–05
Wittgenstein, 474
substantial forms, 239

substratum. *See* substance
Sulla (138–78 B.C.), 115
*Summa Theologiae* (Thomas Aquinas), **231–242**
Superman, 443
swerve, atomic, 163–65
syllogism, 132–33
Mill on, 434
Sylvester II, Pope. *See* Gerbert
symbolism, logical, 133
sympathy, 367, 440
*Symposium* (Plato), 95, 178
synthetic *a priori* judgments, 382–99 *passim*
Syracuse, 70, 84
*System of Nature, The* (d'Holbach), **375–76**
*System of Positive Politics* (Comte), 410

T

Tacitus (*ca* 55–*ca* 120), 189–90
tar-water, 336, 348
taste (sense of), Democritus on, 59
tautology, 474
teleology. *See* explanation, human action as model for
terminism. *See* universals
Tertullian (*ca* 160–230), 193
Thales of Miletus (625?–547? B.C.), 3, **9–10**, 32
*Theaetetus* (Plato), 105, 272
*Theodicy* (Leibniz), 325
Theodosius (the Great) (*d.* 395), 192
*Theogony* (Hesiod), 6–8, 31
*Theologico-Political Treatise* (Spinoza), 298, **299–300**
theology, 193, 203, 212, 222, 242, 352
natural, 212–13, **363–66**
William of Ockham on, 246
*See also* God, existence of; religion
*Theory and Practice of Bolshevism, The* (Russell), 458
theory of knowledge, 32–34
Locke on, 320–21
*See also* idea(s); mind; perception; skepticism; soul; thought; *and under names of individual philosophers*
thinking. *See* thought
"Third Man," 127
Thirty Tyrants, 83
thisness, 244
Thomas Aquinas, St. (1225–1274), (*portrait* 180), 212, 213, **230–242**, 254
ethics, 239–40
political philosophy, 240–41
Thomism. *See* Thomas Aquinas, St.
thought
Aristotle on, 135–36
*See also* consciousness; Descartes, René; mind
thought and reality, 30–34, 80
Thrasymachus (5th c. B.C.), 70–71, 92, 94
*Three Dialogues between Hylas and Philonous* (Berkeley), **338–47**
*Three Impostors, On the,* 255